Techno-Nationalism

How It's Reshaping Trade, Geopolitics and Society

Alex Capri

WILEY

This edition first published 2025

Registered Offices
John Wiley & Sons, Inc., 111 River Street, Hoboken, NJ 07030, USA
John Wiley & Sons Singapore Pte. Ltd, 134 Jurong Gateway Road, #04-307H, Singapore 600134

For details of our global editorial offices, customer services, and more information about Wiley products visit us at www.wiley.com.

Wiley also publishes its books in a variety of electronic formats and by print-on-demand. Some content that appears in standard print versions of this book may not be available in other formats.

Library of Congress Cataloging-in-Publication Data is Available:

ISBN 9781119766063 (Cloth)
ISBN 9781119766179 (epub)
ISBN 9781119766162 (epdf)

Cover Design: Wiley
Cover Image: © Evgenii_Bobrov/Getty Images

Set in 11/14pt, Murray by Straive, Chennai, India
Printed and bound by CPI Group (UK) Ltd, Croydon, CR0 4YY

C9781119766063_090824

For Dad and Mom, now and forevermore.
And for Zee, Nic and Mandy, whose trust
and unwavering love and support eclipse all else.

Contents

List of Illustrations & Diagrams   *xvii*

List of Images   *xix*

Part I   The Elements of Techno-Nationalism   **1**

Introduction: My China Lessons   3

Three Important Lessons   5
The Origins of This Book   9

Chapter 1   Techno-Nationalism   11

The Power of the State   14
The Great Reorganisation   17
The Great Bifurcation   19
Paradoxes and Contradictions   21
A Steady Shift Towards Decoupling   22
States and Firms in a Grey Zone   24
The Big Questions   27
Overview of Sections and Chapters   29

Chapter 2   The Technology Feedback Loop   31

Early International Talent Wars   32
Early British Export Controls   33
History's Technology Feedback Loop   34
The Dutch Seafaring Technologies   39
Techno-Nationalism and the Four Industrial
        Revolutions   41

	Physics and Chemistry Wars	42
	Computers, Atomic Bombs and a Space Race	44
	The Manhattan Project	46
	The Third Industrial Revolution (3IR)	47
	China's 4IR Feedback Loop	49
Chapter 3	**Paradigm Shift and Paradox**	**51**
	Paradigm Shift Becomes Policy	52
	CEOs versus Techno-Nationalists	56
	The Wicked Paradox	59
Chapter 4	**The In-China-for-China Grey Zone**	**63**
	Welcome to the Grey Zone	63
	The Traditional 'In-China-for-China' Model	67
	China's Tech Subsidies: From TVs to EVs	67
	China's Anti-Espionage Laws	70
Chapter 5	**De-Risking and Decoupling**	**75**
	Stratified Global Value Chains	77
	States versus Firms	79
	The Ukraine War, De-Risking and Decoupling	80
	Decoupling from Russia	81
	De-risking and Decoupling from China	82
	China's De-Americanisation Long Game	84
Chapter 6	**Export Controls**	**85**
	Export Controls in the Modern Era	87
	Blacklisted Entities	90
	Extraterritoriality	91
	Workarounds, Loopholes and Backdoors	94
	High Approval Rates, Long Grace Periods and Binge-Buying	95
	Cloud Access, Third-Party Backdoors and Black Markets	97
	A Revamped, Multilateral Export Control Regime	99

Chapter 7	Semiconductor Ground Zero	103
	Chip-Centric Geopolitics	104
	What are Semiconductors?	105
	Semiconductor Global Value Chains	107
	Moore's Law	108
	Chip-Manufacturing Choke Points	111
	Packaging	117
	Rationalised Supply Chains	118
Chapter 8	China's Semiconductor Problem	121
	Trailing-Edge Chips	123
	Leading-Edge Chips	125
	China's False-Positive Chip Test	127
	The Road Behind and Ahead	129
Chapter 9	Re-shoring Chip Manufacturing to America	133
	The CHIPS and Science Act	134
	CHIPS and the Trailing-Edge Revolution	138
	Challenges, Scepticism and Assumptions	140
Part II	**Undercurrents and Power-Multipliers**	**145**
Chapter 10	The War Against Huawei	147
	The Three Points of Reference	150
	The Supermicro Antecedent	150
	America's Historic Telecoms-Espionage Monopoly	151
	Senate Investigations into U.S. Telecoms and Spy Agencies	152
	China's Brand of Economic-Techno-Nationalism	154
	State-Backed Cheap Credit for Emerging Markets	156
	Huawei and China's Digital Belt and Road Initiative	157
	How the Neoliberal Model Backfired with Huawei	159
	Huawei and the Quest for Chip Self-Sufficiency	160

Chapter 11 Tradecraft, Stealth and Technology   **165**

The Distractions of the U.S. War on Terror   166

The Technology that found Bin Laden   168

The Technology that Killed Bin Laden   170

Chinese Tradecraft and Helicopter Stealth
  Technology   171

Operation 'Byzantine Hades'   172

Fifth-Generation Fighter Jets   174

Skunkworks Legacy Feedback Loop Meets
  China Tradecraft   176

A New 'Stealth' Innovation Race Driven by AI   178

The Rise of the Drones   179

Chapter 12 Data, Biotech and Geopolitics   **181**

The Elements of Data Geopolitics   183

What is Data and Why is it Important?   185

Techno-Authoritarianism and Surveillance
  Capitalism   185

Genetic Data and National Security   186

The Biosecurity–Genome Technology
  Feedback Loop   187

Pharmacogenomics and Techno-Nationalism   188

Data Capitalism in the Digital Commons   190

User-Generated Content   190

Original Data Suppliers   191

The Human Genome and Data Capitalism   192

American Sci-Tech Data Hegemony   193

Data Intermediaries   194

The Different Regulatory Landscapes Around
  the World   195

Data Geopolitics, Soft Power and Information
  Wars   196

The Cambridge Analytica Milestone   196

How Data Analytics Shape the Geopolitical
  Landscape   197

Russian Influence Campaigns in Social Media   198

The Spread of Information Wars   199

Social Media Influencers and Bloggers   200
Platform Diplomacy   201
Intelligence Agencies Relying on Private
   Companies   202
Government Demands for Data Access   203

Chapter 13 The AI Arms Race   205
AI Designs a Breakthrough Drug   207
AI and the Weapons of War   208
AI and Cyberwarfare   210
AI Superpowers: The U.S. versus China   212
AI Misinformation, Deepfakes and Narrative
   Wars   215
AI and Chip Wars   216

Chapter 14 Quantum Technologies   219
What is Quantum Computing and Why
   does it Matter?   221
Quantum Supremacy and Limitations   223
Quantum Technologies and Techno-Nationalism   225
Potential Sectors and Practical Applications
   of Quantum Computing   226
Reinventing Public Key Cryptography   228
Patent Filings as a Benchmark   230
Quantum Key Distribution (QKD)   230
The Race Between Companies   231
Techno-Nationalism and the Future of
   Quantum Technologies   232
Export Controls and Ring-fencing of Strategic
   Ecosystems   233
Techno-Diplomacy and Quantum Technology   234
Quantum Ethics, Standards and Rules   234

Chapter 15 Hypersonic Speed   237
China's Hypersonic Technology Snapshot   238
'Carrier Killer' Missiles   240
The Role of AI   242
The DARPA Answer   244

Chapter 16 **The Great Undersea Cable Decoupling** — 247

Geopolitics, Data and Undersea Cables — 248

The Technology and Competitors — 252

Techno-Diplomacy and Undersea Cables — 253

The SEA-ME-WE-6 — 254

States and Firms in the Grey Zone — 255

Cable Sabotage and Warfare — 256

Chapter 17 **Space-Based Internet** — 259

Trends in Satellite Technology and Space-Geopolitics — 260

Low Earth Orbit Satellites — 261

A Revolution in Smallsat Technology and Manufacturing — 262

SpaceX and the Rocket Revolution — 263

The Militarisation of Space-Based Internet — 264

The Grey Zone: Blurring the Line between Defence and Commerce — 265

Export Controls, Sanctions and Bifurcated Global Value Chains — 266

Starlink Internet and the Russia–Ukraine War — 267

Lethal Eyes, Ears and the Drone Revolution — 269

Open-Sourced War in the Digital Global Commons — 269

The Grey Zone: State versus Firms — 270

The Rise of Space Monopolies — 272

A Multilateral Rules Framework for Space? — 272

Chapter 18 **The Twenty-First-Century Space Race** — 275

The Commercialisation of Space — 277

The New Space Markets — 278

Emerging Space Industries — 279

Space Robots — 281

The Rise and Rise of SpaceX — 282

Semiconductors and the Twenty-First-Century Space Race — 286

Neolibs versus Techno-Nationalists 288
Tech Start-Ups 290
The Militarisation of Space 292
The Bifurcation of Space Research 294
De-Risking Aerospace Global Supply Chains 295
Re-Shoring 297
Space Blocs 298

Chapter 19 Drones, Robots and Autonomous Weapons 301
The Rise of the Machines 302
Inflection Points 303
The Russia–Ukraine War 304
Turkish and Iranian Drones 304
Kamikaze in a Backpack 306
The Shift to Lethal Autonomous Weapons 307
The Ethical Dilemma of Lethal Autonomous
    Systems 311

Part III **Climate, Cleantech and Agritech** **313**

Chapter 20 Climate Change and Geopolitics 315
The Geopolitics of Energy Infrastructure 317
The Cleantech Arena 318
Climate Competition in Emerging Markets 318
China's Infrastructure-For-Resources Deals 320
Values-Driven Infrastructure Projects 321
Multilateral Infrastructure Alliances 322
The Digital Infrastructure Nexus 324
China's Island-Building Diplomacy 326

Chapter 21 The Geopolitics of Electric Vehicles 329
The Core Areas of EV Techno-Nationalism 330
Twenty-First-Century Electrification of the
    Automotive Industry 331
New Regulations and Funding 332
The EV Ecosystem and Composition of EVs 333

The Simplicity of Electric Motors   334

China: EV Techno-Nationalist Ground-Zero   335

China's Dominance of Rare Earth Materials   336

Accelerated Decoupling in Rare Earths Supply
        Chains   337

The Re-shoring and Ring-fencing of Rare Earths   338

China's Dominance of Lithium-ion Batteries
        and Related Supply Chains   339

Critical Components and Minerals   340

The Geographic Ring-fencing of Li-ion Battery
        Production   340

A Story of China's EV Battery Techno-Nationalism   341

Forced Reliance on Chinese Suppliers   342

America and Europe's EV Subsidies, Initiatives
        and Techno-Nationalist Road Map   343

U.S. EV Techno-Diplomacy   343

Emerging EV Fragmentation and Clusters   344

Chapter 22   Semiconductors and Electric Vehicle Wars   347

The Blurring of Automotive and Technology
        Companies   348

The Challenges of 'Dual-use' EV Technologies   349

Cross-Border Microchip Innovation   350

Foreign Venture Capital in a Geopolitical
        Context   351

An EV Software and Hardware Open Platform   352

Silicon Carbide and Gallium Nitrogen Chips   353

Connected Cars and National Security Risks   354

Subsidies for the EV–Semiconductor Nexus   355

The Road Ahead   356

Chapter 23   Food Security and Techno-Nationalism   357

Food Protectionism on the Rise   358

The 'Friend-shoring' of Food Supply Chains   359

Technology and Food Security   360

Precision Agriculture   362

Vertical Farming   363

Laboratory-grown Protein   364

Agritech and Industrial Espionage   364
Water Scarcity and Technology   366
The Geopolitics of Water Scarcity   366

**Part IV   Innovation, Academia, Alliances and
              Diplomacy   369**

Chapter 24 Techno-Nationalism on Campus   371
            The Changing Academic Landscape   373
            Academic Ring-Fencing   374
            Middle-Country Universities   375
            Student Nationalities   376
            China's Thousand Talents Programme and
                Academic Espionage   377
            Rule Frameworks and Research Security   379
            Screening the Sources of Funding   380
            The Military and Academia   382

Chapter 25 Chip Schools   385
            Purdue's Silicon Moment   386
            The Rise of the National Chip Hubs   388
            Chip School West: Arizona State University 389
            Academic Cross Border Friend-Shoring   391
            Taiwan's Global Talent Development
                Strategy   393
            A Worldwide Shortage of Talent   394

Chapter 26 The Innovation Horse Race   397
            Government Activism: Why it Matters   399
            Public–Private Partnerships   400
            R&D and the Paradigm Shift   402
            Milestones of Chinese Techno-Nationalism 404
            A Brief Reflection on the Benefits of Industrial
                Policy   405
            Japan   406
            Taiwan   407
            Germany   408
            The Origins of America's Chip Policies   410

Chapter 27 India Rising?   413

India's Fertile Economy and Technology
    Landscape   415
Accelerated Decoupling from China   416
India's Digital Landscape   417
Software and Engineering Research &
    Development (ER&D)   419
The Pain-of-Doing-Business in India   420
Smartphones and Geopolitical Influence   422
Building World-class Clusters with Local
    Manufacturers   423
Printed Circuit Board Assembly and
    Semiconductors   424

Chapter 28 Fragmented Finance   427

Central Bank-backed Digital Currencies   427
Ideology and Digital Currency: A Clash of
    Civilisations   430
Digital Dystopia   431
New Accounting Standards Aimed at Chinese
    Companies   433
The U.S. Outbound Investment Transparency
    Act   434
International Banks Caught between Beijing
    and Washington   435
China Punishes HSBC   436
Techno-Nationalism and FinTech Decoupling   438
Sovereign Wealth Funds and Geopolitics   439

Chapter 29 Techno-Diplomacy and the Road Ahead   441

From FTAs to Mini-Lateral Arrangements   443
The Chip 4 Alliance (Fact or Fiction)   445
The Indo-Pacific Economic Framework   447
The AUKUS Trilateral Security Agreement   448
The Quadrilateral Security Dialogue (QUAD)   450
Bilateral Techno-Diplomacy   451

AI Ethics and The Promise of Open-Sourced
          Platforms   452
The Great Reorganisation will Go On   455

Notes   *457*

Acknowledgements   *505*

Index   *509*

List of Illustrations & Diagrams

LIST OF FIGURES

Figure 1.1	Foundational and Strategic Technologies of the Twenty-first Century.	13
Figure 2.1	Richard Arkwright's Coveted Spinning Frame.	35
Figure 2.2	Alexander Hamilton's Report of Manufacturers Presented to the U.S. House of Representatives in 1791.	35
Figure 2.3	Portrait of Samuel Slater, Father of the American Manufacturing System.	36
Figure 2.4	Portrait of Alexander Hamilton, America's First Secretary of the Treasury.	36
Figure 2.5	Illustration, The Techno-nationalist Feedback Loop.	37
Figure 2.6	Cornelius Corneliszoon's 1593 Wind-powered Sawmill.	39
Figure 2.7	ENIAC, the first digital computer, developed for the U.S. Army at the University of Pennsylvania, during the Second World War.	44
Figure 2.8	The Manhattan's Project's Atomic Bomb, at Los Alamos, in 1945.	44
Figure 5.1	Made-In-China 2025 List of Priority Technologies.	83
Figure 7.1	Apple's Chips Stacked with Billions of Transistors.	108

Figure 7.2   Semiconductors: The Foundational
Technologies.   112

Figure 7.3   The Chip Manufacturing Process.   112

Figure 7.4   ASML DUV Photolithography Machine.   113

Figure 7.5   ASML EUV Photolithography Machine.   113

Figure 9.1   Partial List of New Chip Fabs in the U.S
(Announced and In Progress, 2024).   136

Figure 10.1   Backside of the Huawei Mate 60 Smartphone,
Showing Camera Lens.   161

Figure 10.2   The Kirin 9000 7-nanometre Chip, Designed
by HiSilicon and Fabricated by Semiconductor
Manufacturing International Corporation
(SMIC) for the Huawei Mate 60 Smartphone.   161

Figure 11.1   US Military Bell Invictus Helicopter with the
latest Stealth Technology.   171

Figure 11.2   Frontal View of a US Airforce F-35 Stealth
Fighter.   174

Figure 13.1   Countries Ranked by their Artificial
Intelligence (AI) Capacity.   212

Figure 13.2   The IBM Blue Gene Supercomputer.   214

Figure 14.1   How Quantum Computing Works.   222

Figure 14.2   Quantum Computing versus Classical
Computing.   223

Figure 14.3   Practical Applications of Error-Free Quantum
Computing.   226

Figure 15.1   China's Dong Feng 27 Hypersonic Missile.   240

Figure 15.2   Artist Rendition of Northrop Grumman's
Scramjet Hypersonic Engine.   244

Figure 16.1   Undersea Cable Networks.   249

Figure 17.1   Low Earth Orbit (LEO) Satellite Constellation.   261

Figure 17.2   LEO CubeSats and SmallSats: Compact and
Inexpensive.   262

Figure 18.1   The SpaceX Falcon 9 Heavy Rocket.   282

Figure 18.2   Payload for the NASA-SpaceX Psyche 16
Asteroid Mining Mission.   283

Figure 18.3   A SpaceX Rocket First Stage Landing Upright
after Returning to Earth.   284

Figure 18.4   Payload of Starlink LEO Satellites on Top of
a SpaceX Falcon 9 Rocket.   285

Figure 18.5 The Secretive X37-B Autonomous Robotic
Orbital Space Plane: Reusable for Military and
Intelligence-related Missions.   292

Figure 19.1 The Turkish Aerospace Industries Anka-3
Combat Drone.   305

Figure 19.2 Iranian Shahed 136 Drones, and Arash-2 Long
Distance Drone.   306

Figure 19.3 Drone Swarms (Artist Rendition).   308

Figure 19.4 The US Airforce MQ-9 Reaper Killer Drone
made by General Atomics.   309

Figure 19.5 Dorothy Engelhardt, Director, Unmanned
Systems, Deputy Assistant Secretary of the
Navy (Ships), Christens the Orca XLUUV Test
nAsset System during a Ceremony April 28,
2022, in Huntington Beach, California.   310

Figure 20.1 Floating Chinese-built Solar Farm in
a Hydro-power Reservoir.   319

Figure 21.1 Electric Car and Lithium Batteries.   339

Figure 23.1 Editing the DNA of Plants for Hardier, Climate
Change Resistant Food.   360

Figure 27.1 Map of India's Traditional Technology Hubs.   419

Figure 29.1 Digital Democracies Equal Approximately
50% of Global GDP (PPP Basis).   452

LIST OF IMAGES

Image 28.1 Photograph of Meng Wanzhou, the CFO of
Huawei who was placed under house arrest in
Canada, for three years, for the alleged
involvement in U.S. Export Controls Violations. 437

PART I

The Elements of Techno-Nationalism

Introduction:
My China Lessons

Since the opening of China to foreign commerce in the late 1970s, Beijing's central planners have presided over the largest and most rapid transfer of wealth in human history. It was primarily Western companies that made this possible, as a decades-long torrent of money and technology flowed into China's state-centric economic system.

The numbers are staggering. If we count official foreign direct investment (FDI) figures along with estimates of unofficial capital flows via offshore financial centres—such as Hong Kong, the Cayman Islands and the British Virgin Islands—at least US$6 trillion flowed into China over a 30-year time frame.[1,2]

That is a conservative estimate. If we factor in forced technology transfer and stolen intellectual property just from American private and public entities, the number comes to at least US$10 trillion, or more than half the value of China's entire gross domestic product (GDP) in 2023.

The U.S. Trade Representative (USTR) has estimated that China's forced technology-transfer practices cost the U.S. economy hundreds of billions of dollars more per year, while agencies such as the National Bureau of Economic Research claim that China's ongoing cyberattacks on U.S. companies drain off billions more.

These vast transfers of wealth were feasible because of the spread of powerful and affordable new technologies, combined with the Chinese Communist Party's (CCP) iron-willed and methodical pursuit of its modernisation goals.

I would come to learn all these things first hand, as my professional career landed me right in the middle of this historical inflection point. I arrived in Hong Kong in 2003 as an American expat, two years after China's accession to the World Trade Organization (WTO). I would eventually become a partner at KPMG, the global accounting and consultancy firm, and would take over as the regional head of its Asia Trade and Customs Practice.

In my work, I provided multinational companies with advice on their global operations, which often meant that, for economic and practical reasons, their supply chains would pass through China. There were foreign trade zones to manage and a host of cross-border transactions to monitor. There were customs duties, indirect taxes and trade agreements to optimise.

After China's successful accession to the WTO, companies ramped up their investments and began directing higher-valued activities into China. By 2017, according to PWC, the global consultancy, about 80% of the corporate R&D money spent in China came from foreign multinationals, most of them American and European.

During my tenure in Hong Kong, global trade hit a historic high. Except for the year following the global financial crisis, in 2009, seven out of my first eight years on the job yielded double-digit growth rates in the value of world trade. And between the U.S. and China, the annual value of bilateral trade in goods and services had crossed the US$ half-trillion threshold.

By the mid-2000s, incredibly, Walmart, the world's largest retailer, was importing so much from China that it accounted for more than 11% of China's annual exports, according to the Brookings Institution.[3]

Meanwhile, as foreign money and technology continued to pour into China, so did international talent. The professional services industry, composed of management consultants, accountants, tax planners, head-hunters, academics and lawyers, quickly soaked up the economic opportunities. Large consulting firms such as Accenture, KPMG, PWC and McKinsey became fixtures in China's business landscape.

Scholars have yet to fully gauge the magnitude of influence that consultancies had in accelerating the growth of China. In just over four decades, firms like mine served up a menu of mostly neoliberal economic advice to thousands of companies—and to Chinese government entities—as foreign money saturated Beijing's centrally planned land-scape, funding greenfield sites, joint ventures and technology transfers. This transformed China into the world's largest manufacturing and sup-plier base and made it the world's top exporter.

I did not fully understand it at the time, but in my position, I was simultaneously enabling history's most remarkable period of trade and globalisation and, unwittingly, contributing to the eventual upending of the Western-led rules-based order.

THREE IMPORTANT LESSONS

Soon after settling into life in Hong Kong, my worldview became conflicted. I arrived as a true internationalist: As the son of a U.S. dip-lomat, I had grown up in eight countries on three continents, studied international relations in college and my first job had been with U.S. Customs at one of the world's busiest trading ports—Los Angeles.

From my desk in LA, as a trade specialist, I watched the phenomenon of globalisation unfold, from the late 1980s until the late 1990s, when I left the government for the enterprising world of consulting.

From Hong Kong, I began to witness, close up, the incongruities (incompatibilities, actually) between China Inc.'s nonmarket economy and Western laissez-faire capitalism.

Over time, three lessons emerged from what I will call 'my China classroom'.

The first lesson was that most foreign business executives naively construed geopolitics and business as separate issues. Most Western CEOs had no understanding (and still do not) of the resoluteness of China's five-year plans and the CCP's longstanding quest to achieve Chinese self sufficiency.

The truth was, Beijing had been pre-emptively decoupling from its chief benefactors, playing the 'long game', as Rush Doshi would call it, by shrewdly calculating what it could extract from others and how to prevent them from taking from the Middle Kingdom.

My second lesson taught me how deeply nationalism had permeated the business landscape. Most of my Chinese colleagues and friends (regardless of whether they had been educated in the West) quietly harboured a deep-rooted sense of national pride and grievance.

I learned about the 'Century of Humiliation' narrative, which posits that for eight centuries, from the Han dynasty to the early modern period in the nineteenth century, China had been the world's largest, wealthiest and most sophisticated world power. It was the European colonial empires and China's next-door neighbour and long-time tormentor, Imperial Japan, that brought its global prominence to an end.

The Century of Humiliation, from 1849 until 1949, as it is widely taught to school children, ushered in a series of catastrophises, including the Opium Wars with Britain and the ravages of the Sino-Japanese Wars. Seven decades after the ascension of Mao and the CCP in 1949, these themes continue to influence China's policymaking.

Other similarly influential views had seeped into the national narrative. Not surprisingly, one was the unapologetic call for 'China's Return to Greatness', with the underlying theme that China was reclaiming its rightful place again at the top of the world order.

Parallel to this were increasing references to the 'decline of America and the West'. When the global financial crisis hit in 2007–2008, it emboldened China's technocrats even further. With the meltdown of financial markets and the symbolic collapse of Lehman Brothers, the 158-year-old Wall Street investment bank, the Western economic model came under further disregard.

These themes are harnessed by the modern-day communist party to stoke righteous indignation and invigorate nationalist policies. This has been a decades-long campaign, starting in the classroom and buttressed by a barrage of carefully crafted and censored narratives across the Internet, on millions of blogs, and on influencer platforms. Present day Western business executives are shocked to learn that China's 'Millennial' generation (born 1981–1994) and 'Generation Z' (1995–2010) are far more nationalistic than their parents.

Foreigners who have not worked and lived in China simply do not understand the extent to which nationalism fuels the 'return-to-greatness narrative' and, in turn, how it is driving modern policies around economic nationalism and China's quest towards self-reliance.

Here, intellectually, is where I committed a common mistake made by Westerners. I tried to dismiss these narratives as sentimentalist and assumed they would fade away as China integrated with the West.

How could they not? To experience China as a foreigner in the early 2000s was to be an ambassador for all the good things that free trade and cross-border exchange could offer. Surely a rising tide would lift all ships, as John F. Kennedy had said.

I did not fully realise it at the time, but to witness the beginnings of great power competition during my early years in China changed me from an avowed internationalist to a practical realist. Meanwhile, the paradox of the Free World's economic entanglement with China would grow more complicated and more challenging with the passage of time.

I can trace my realisation of this paradox to a single defining moment, late one night in Shanghai, in 2004, when I strolled down an almost empty Nanjing Road West, under razor-edged high rise buildings and towering electric billboards. The immense scale of it was exhilarating, but I knew I was living dangerously; there was something vaguely dystopic and foreboding about that moment.

What happened next? I pushed these thoughts out of my mind, and, myopically, turned my attention back to my work.

Consider that at the time, America was still hanging on to the last vestiges of its so-called 'unipolar' moment. We were a little over a decade removed from the Cold War triumph over the former Soviet Union, which had collapsed in 1991. The Cold War had been the central fixture of international relations for more than 40 years, and we had won.

Before I moved to China, during a decade-long career at U.S. Customs, I had administered and enforced American antidumping and countervailing duty laws, import quotas and other laws designed to pommel Japan into geopolitical submission. Recall that Japan, in the 1980s and 1990s, was perceived as a threat to American economic hegemony. The lesson here was that by the late 1990s Washington had won that geopolitical competition as well, and Japan was already slipping into its so-called 'lost decades.' Would not China fall in line too?

My worldview, at the time, had been sustained by a steady diet of neoliberalism. In the mid 1990s I took a sabbatical from Customs to attend the London School of Economics. There, I was influenced by the writings of Francis Fukuyama, who wrote about the triumphs of liberal democracy and free markets and the inevitable retreat of authoritarianism. I was drawn to Kenichi Ohmae's book, *The Borderless World* which inspired me to become an international trade consultant and was a big reason I eventually ended up in China.

Ohmae, who had been a partner at McKinsey, the elite consultancy, sold me and countless others on the promises of global trade and the unlimited potential of unrestrained ideas, goods and people crossing borders. And what better place to be during the heady years of globalisation than in Hong Kong, right on the doorstep of China's growing economic juggernaut?

The third and most consequential lesson was about the pivotal role that technology would play in the coming great power rivalry between Washington and Beijing.

China's elite had gone all-in on leveraging technology for the Middle Kingdom's return to greatness, thanks to China's second greatest gift (after epic inflows of foreign investment) which was the Fourth Industrial Revolution (4IR). A treasure trove of new, accessible technologies had become the new game-changer. From Beijing's perspective, the great geopolitical power shift would rely upon continual access to leading-edge technology.

I find it more than coincidental that the week after I arrived in Hong Kong, China launched its first astronaut, Yang Liwei, into Earth's orbit. The Shenzhou 5 mission blasted off from Jiuquan Satellite Launch Centre in Inner Mongolia on October 15, 2003. Since then, this date marks an important milestone for me regarding the twenty-first-century technology race.

At that time, China might as well have been 100 years behind the U.S. in the Space Race. When Shenzhou 5 occurred, it had been almost 40 years since 12 separate American astronauts had walked on the Moon during NASA's Apollo missions, which ended in 1972.

Yet, in less than two decades since Shenzhou 5, China has all but closed the technology gap between itself and the U.S.

Such were my early China lessons.

I needed to explore these themes further. Clearly, technology-facilitated China's ambitious five-year plans, as did free markets and foreign businesses. Here, the themes of nationalism and technology stuck with me.

Thus began my motivation for writing this book.

THE ORIGINS OF THIS BOOK

In 2015, I joined the faculty of the National University of Singapore (NUS) as a visiting senior fellow. I was to draw upon my earlier career and focus my research and teaching on global supply chains and trade, with an emphasis on Asia.

Two themes would consistently emerge in my work: geopolitics and technology. Current events made these topics impossible to ignore. The technology revolution was not just fundamentally innovating and transforming global value chains and commerce, it was also at the centre of a great power competition that was spilling over into the business landscape.

In 2016, Donald Trump was elected the forty-fifth U.S. president, and my work on what I began to categorise as 'techno-nationalism', took on a new sense of purpose. U.S. tariff hikes on Chinese goods, for example, the weaponisation of semiconductor supply chains and Washington's all-out campaign to stop Huawei—the Chinese telecommunications equipment manufacturer—and other Chinese tech firms from capturing foreign market share became the focus of my research.

I designed a series of MBA courses at the NUS Business School that dealt with the challenges of sanctions, export controls and other technology-transfer restrictions in supply chains. In my curriculum, I pushed my students to navigate around these obstacles and figure out how to mitigate risks and spot new opportunities in this shifting landscape.

The same year that Trump was elected, I began co-teaching a course, Trade Policy and Global Value Chains, with Professor Razeen Sally at the Lee Kuan Yew (LKY) School of Public Policy at NUS.

Professor Sally and I had been discussing trade and political economy for a long time, going all the way back to our time together, in 1995, at the London School of Economics.

The world had changed significantly by the time we started teaching our course at NUS. Each year, as U.S.–China geopolitical tensions continued to escalate, we welcomed into our programme another cohort of diplomats, lawyers, journalists and others from around the world. It became clear that geopolitics was reshaping the international trade landscape, more than anything else, and it seemed that this was the topic everyone needed to discuss.

In 2019, three years into Prof Sally's and my course at the NUS LKY School, I became a research fellow at the Singapore-based Hinrich Foundation, a trade-focused think tank.

The first Hinrich Foundation paper I authored was entitled 'Semiconductors at the Heart of the U.S.–China Tech War'.[4] It was initially published in January 2020, about a year ahead of what would soon become a full-blown American tech war. I chose to employ the term 'techno-nationalism' in that report, a powerful juxtaposition of words that the academic and statesman Robert Reich had used, more than 35 years earlier.

What started as an analysis of the global semiconductor sector quickly morphed into a string of dozens of other research publications, all of which highlighted 'twenty-first-century techno-nationalism' across a range of industries and dimensions.

Meanwhile, to satisfy the growing demand for public discourse, I was publishing articles related to techno-nationalism in Forbes, Nikkei Asia, the Diplomat and other media platforms. The demand for public discussion grew by the day. With the Trump sanctions and other China-related actions, I began fielding regular requests from global media.

Such are the origins of this book.

Chapter 1

Techno-Nationalism

This book is about how governments pursue technology as a power multiplier and how tech-competition between nations is reshaping global affairs in the twenty-first century.

Call it 'techno-nationalism;' a mindset that equates the technological prowess of a state's chosen actors with the strength of its national security, its economic prosperity and its social stability. Techno-nationalism seeks to attain competitive advantage for its stakeholders, on a local and global scale, and to leverage this advantage for geopolitical gain.

This is not a new phenomenon. As long as there have been nation-states, especially with the evolution of modern states in seventeenth- and eighteenth-century Europe, governments have sought to harness the power of technology to advance their interests.

It was the French writer, Antoine de Saint-Exupéry, who famously wrote: 'Every *nation is selfish, and every nation considers its selfishness sacred*'.

The twentieth century saw firsthand the effects of techno-nationalism with two of the bloodiest, most definitive wars in history, a forty-year

Cold War between America and the former Soviet Union, a race in space and to the Moon, a nuclear arms race, the rise of computers and artificial intelligence, and the beginnings of geopolitical competition linked to the semiconductor.

Robert Reich used the term 'techno-nationalism' in a piece for *The Atlantic* in 1987, in which he reflected on its paradoxical nature. At the time, the U.S. political establishment had stymied the sale of Fairchild Semiconductor Corporation to Fujitsu, a Japanese company. Washington had singled out Japan's technological prowess as a threat to U.S. economic hegemony.

Make no mistake: Twenty-first century techno-nationalism is on a scale and level of significance that is orders of magnitude greater than that of the twentieth century.

Consider the differences. During its rise in the 1980s as an economic juggernaut, Japan was a liberal democracy. It followed a constitution, largely imposed by the U.S. after Japan's defeat in World War II, that prohibited the expansion of its military—in fact, Japan relied upon the U.S. for its security needs—and Tokyo certainly had no ideological or geopolitical aims of displacing America as the leader of the rules-based international order. None of these things can be said about the rise of China. Its pervasive techno-nationalist apparatus and the rapid build up of its military, combined with the ideology of 'socialism with Chinese characteristics' has become a direct challenge to the existing Western rules-based order. Great power competition is on full display.

At the centre of techno-nationalism are six core elements, or behaviours, each of which effects a wide swathe of the international landscape. They are:

- The 'weaponisation' of supply chains
- Strategic decoupling and 'de-risking'
- Re-shoring, near-shoring and friend-shoring
- State-funded innovation and talent wars
- Tech-diplomacy, strategic partnerships and tech alliances
- Tradecraft and 'hybrid cold war'

We will discuss all these things extensively throughout this book. But first, we must identify the key categories of 'foundational' technologies, of which there are twelve.

Technology	Description
Advanced Materials	Composite materials, coatings and chemicals that enable heat resistance, strength, reduced weight, stealth, superconductivity, and improved performance. Includes smart 'self-healing' materials; explosives and energetic materials, novel metamaterials, advanced magnets, processed rare earths and minerals.
Advanced Manufacturing	Nano-scale manufacturing, atomic layer deposition, additive manufacturing, AI enabled production, advanced manufacturing robotics.
Artificial Intelligence (AI)	Machine learning, including neural networks and deep learning, 'cognitive' machines, natural language processing, including large language models (LLMs) with speech and text recognition and cognition, advanced algorithms and high-performance super-computing.
Aerospace	Reusable rocketry and space vehicles for transportation and habitation, deep space exploration; satellites, ballistic missiles, hypersonic aircraft and missiles, autonomous unmanned spacecraft.
Biotechnology	Biological manufacturing and synthetic biology, vaccines, genetic engineering and pharmacogenomics, germ warfare and DNA weaponisation.
Connectivity & Communications	5G and 6G wireless broadband, the Internet-of-Things (IoT), space-based Internet and low earth orbit (LEO) constellations, neuromorphic computing, and brain-computer interfaces (BCI); Light-Fidelity (Li-Fi) communications.
Energy	Electric batteries, photovoltaics and supercapacitors, biofuels, nuclear fission and fusion technologies, directed energy (lasers); hydrogen and ammonia power.
Propulsion	Nuclear thermal rockets, plasma drives, and hypersonic engines. Underwater propulsion systems including super cavitation drives and magnetohydrodynamic propulsion.
Quantum	Computing, sensing (which includes light, motion, temperature, pressure) and communication, including quantum key distribution (QKD).
Robots & Drones	Includes unmanned, autonomous aerial vehicles (UAV) and unmanned underwater vehicles (UUVs); drone swarms and machine biomimicry (machines that copy natural design for efficiency of locomotion, dexterity and lethality), ground-based military robots; and all manner of remotely operated and autonomous machines.
Sensing, Timing & Navigation	Includes biomimetic and neuromorphic sensors; ultra-stable oscillators and optical clocks; satellite-based augmentation systems and light and detection ranging (LIDAR).
Semiconductors	Also called 'chips' or 'microchips', semiconductors are the heart, brains and nerve centres of virtually anything that has an on-off switch. Chips are vital for logic, memory, power and overall functionality.

Figure 1.1   Foundational and Strategic Technologies of the Twenty-first Century.

These are all Fourth Industrial Revolution (4IR) foundational technologies.

Their power-multiplying effects drive economic competition, but more importantly, they determine winners and losers in that most basic of all human preoccupations: warfare. In this regard, nothing has changed for millennia.

These are referred to as foundational technologies because they are an essential ingredient for all other applications of leading-edge tech. Many are interrelated; where there is one there are others. One of these, AI, is especially critical because it is pushing the boundaries of knowledge in research and design, engineering, manufacturing, medicine, communications, operations and management, and, of course, the many different aspects of national defence.

More fundamentally, none of the above technologies are possible without access to semiconductors. This is why these tiny microchips find themselves at the centre of every element of techno-nationalist competition.

We will discuss all these technologies in separate chapters and how techno-nationalism is affecting their development and use.

It is important to note that technology, by itself, is not deterministic. In other words, those who create it must choose how to use it, whether for good or for evil. As we will see, however, virtually every technology can be used for both commercial and military purposes, thus we encounter the 'dual-use' dilemma—a challenge to businesses, traders, innovators and policymakers.

THE POWER OF THE STATE

Nation-states are the most powerful and influential actors in the international system. We begin the discussion about techno-nationalism, therefore, by recognising that a small number of states wield inordinate amounts of power.

Consider that in 2022, the Group of 7 (G7) countries—the U.S., Japan, Germany, France, the U.K., Canada and Italy and the European Union (E.U.), as a non-enumerated member—together with China, accounted for 60% of global GDP.[1] Such a disproportionate amount of wealth, as it's channelled towards techno-nationalist objectives, is profoundly changing the international landscape.

These same countries are now at a historic inflection point. Great power rivalry and modern realpolitik has sparked an onslaught of techno-nationalist policies and agendas.

Technology-oriented spending around the world has been consolidating within a few power centres. Consider that from around 2020 to the end of 2023, the U.S., the European Union and China, alone, budgeted somewhere between US$6–8 trillion in public funding for technology-related initiatives—not counting high-tech military expenditures. Much of this public spending was focused on large infrastructure projects that emphasised digital connectivity, AI, computing, and automation, as well as sustainable energy, clean transportation and sustainable manufacturing.

In 2023, China, by itself, spent just under US$1 trillion on clean energy development.[2] Special emphasis went to electric vehicles (EVs), batteries, high-speed rail, electricity grids, energy storage, solar and wind power.

Semiconductors and AI are now the most publicly contested technologies, with hundreds of billions of dollars being spent collectively in China, the U.S., South Korea, Japan,[3] Taiwan and the E.U. But the implications of losing out on cleantech are just as serious, as these technologies are also important geopolitical power multipliers, as we will discuss in Part III of this book.

In the big picture, China, America and the E.U.'s technology-related expenditures, together, account for more than the combined tech-budgets of a hundred of the world's less developed countries, and a large chunk of so-called middle tier nations, such as India or Malaysia.

These numbers become more consequential when we factor in the additive value of tax breaks and other incentives offered through public–private partnerships (PPP), which are designed to pile private investments on top of government funding.

In the U.S., for example, less than two years after the passage of the *CHIPS and Science Act*[4] in 2022—which budgeted US$280 billion for leading-edge technology, including US$52 billion in funding for semiconductor R&D and chip production—private industry had already invested more than US$300 billion towards new chip fabrication projects.[5]

A sizeable chunk of this new private money came from Taiwan Semiconductor Manufacturing Company (TSMC), the largest and most advanced microchip manufacturer in the world, largely in response to Washington's diplomatic arm-twisting.[6]

These are the early rounds of funding. The CHIPS Act will require more infusions of capital over the next decade-plus. It is fortunate for techno-nationalists, then, that semiconductors have been deemed an essential element of national security. America's spending on defence exceeds the annual military budgets of at least the next 10 largest countries, combined.[7] In 2022, for example, it accounted for around 40% of all the world's defence spending.

Thus, putting semiconductor production (or any other technology) under the national security umbrella means funding will be available—so long as squabbles in the U.S. Congress do not derail disbursement of future monies.[8]

Techno-nationalism continues to spill over into climate change policies and the decarbonisation of the global economy. Large-scale capacity-building initiatives in clean technology, such as lithium batteries, electric vehicles (EV) and alternative energy infrastructure, are increasingly a point of contention amongst trading partners.

Here, huge public funding in green initiatives in the U.S., Europe and China will fragment the geopolitical playing field and push it towards regionalisation and localisation. This is not to say, however, that new coalitions of countries will not coalesce around creative, mutually beneficial trading arrangements.

In America, the *Bi-Partisan Infrastructure bill* provided a funding conduit for cleantech and green infrastructure that has attracted secondary investors from Europe and Asia. As of 2023, the bill had funded 40,000 different projects worth about US$400 billion.[9] Other legislation advancing U.S. strategic policy interests included the massive *Inflation Reduction Act* (IRA), which aims to raise at least US$300 billion over a decade from corporate taxes, to fund different kinds of cleantech. In the E.U., The *Green Deal* seeks to raise and invest over *US$1 trillion* in public and private funding for cleantech initiatives by 2030.[10]

Meanwhile, the scale of China's production capacity in green technologies, from EVs to photovoltaic cells, lithium batteries and wind power, dwarfs that of its rivals. This dominance allows Beijing to weaponise these supply chains the same way Washington has weaponised semiconductors.[11]

All this underscores the trend towards re-shoring, near-shoring and friend-shoring, which involves moving supply chains and activity hubs from overseas back inside national borders or closer to home, within the geographic confines of neighbours and trusted allies. Thus, European, Japanese and North American cleantech sectors look to reduce their dependence on China-sourced supply chains.

The six elements of techno-nationalism have produced a wider set of themes that are unfolding throughout the international landscape. They have instigated a fundamental reorganisation of the global economy, whereby strategic supply chains are bifurcating around U.S. and China-centric technology hubs.

Fuelled by a historic paradigm shift in the 'West', this reorganisation and bifurcation is prompting a gradual decoupling from China (beyond so-called 'de-risking') which, in turn, has exposed an epic paradox.

States and firms must now operate in a grey zone, where they are both strategic partners and adversaries with home and host governments, depending on where the geopolitical winds are blowing.

As such, as we seek to better understand techno-nationalism, we must take a closer look at each of these trends, below.

THE GREAT REORGANISATION

Techno-nationalism, along with climate change and the lingering effects of COVID-19, has accelerated a general recalibration of the global economy. Put another way: the world is undergoing a reorganisation. This effectively ends 30 years of what has been referred to as 'hyper-globalisation', which thrived from the late 1980s to around

2009. In hindsight, hyper-globalisation was a historic anomaly that owed its existence to the convergence of a unique combination of forces.

The first was the rapid diffusion of technologies of the 4IR, which delivered gains in computing power and connectivity along with a simultaneous decline in costs. The result was the lowering of barriers to entry across the global economy to a host of new participants, large and small. The second was the end of the Cold War and the implosion of the Soviet Union in 1991, which led to the brief American unipolar moment and paved the way for the third factor, China's accession to the WTO in 2001 and its rise to superpower status.

4IR technologies enabled dispersion of global value chains and the offshoring of complex operations to far-flung places, especially China. For Beijing, this was a major power-leveller, and China was able to make up ground on a longstanding power disparity between the 'West versus the Rest', a term made famous by the historian Niall Ferguson.

Serendipitous timing of the 4IR, then, allowed the absorption of massive transfers of wealth, knowledge, technology and critical professional expertise, all in record time, and at spectacular scale.

Yet even as the free world became increasingly intertwined with China's statist economic model, leadership in Beijing was working hard to advance modern history's most ambitious and comprehensive techno-nationalist agenda.

America's brief unipolar moment, from the 1990s to the 2010s, is clearly over. As it turned out, it was not just an anomaly, it was a false promise. But the ensuing backlash against China's rise is fuelled in the West by a strong sense of betrayal (naïve, of course, from a realist's point of view) which holds that China's technocrats achieved ascendancy, in no small measure, through deception, stealth and trickery.

Hyper-globalisation began a steady decline with the onset of the global financial crisis of 2008/09. Its unravelling accelerated in 2016 with the BREXIT vote in the U.K. and the election of Donald Trump in the U.S.

There should be no mistake about the primacy of nationalism. We may have convinced ourselves that it went away during the height of globalisation, but that was self-deception.

Consider that during the COVID-19 pandemic from 2019 to 2021—a time, if ever there were one, for nations to come together and fight a common enemy—China, the E.U., the U.S., the U.K. and India all restricted the export of protective gear and medical equipment.[12] This was quickly followed by vaccine nationalism and then vaccine diplomacy, with developed nations leveraging their stocks of vaccines as bargaining chips with poorer nations.

After the Russian invasion of Ukraine in 2022, shortages of wheat and other food commodities ensued. Within four months of the start of the war, some 35 nations had resorted to some form of 'food protectionism', which included export bans and taxes on critical foodstuffs.[13]

THE GREAT BIFURCATION

To be clear, the world is not 'deglobalising'; instead, it is reorganising and reconfiguring around opposing techno-nationalist and geopolitical agendas. That reconfiguration largely involves a bifurcation into two technology blocs—one centred on the U.S. and its allies and the other centred on China. This bifurcation phenomenon is occurring around the twelve categories of foundational technologies, yet, paradoxically, non-strategic goods may see continued or even increased trade, even among rivals, so long as the world is not roiled in conflict. The question is, to what extent will decoupling from China occur before such a conflict arises?

In the physical realm, the tech bifurcation entails the fragmentation and restructuring of well-established supply chains. In the digital realm, the same forces are fracturing cyberspace: increased government intervention and activism are disrupting cross-border data flows and Balkanising the Internet and the platform economy, and this affects everything from banking and finance to social media networks.

No country anywhere can escape this reality. The inevitable outcome is not just a reorientation of the commercial landscape but of geopolitical realignments, as nations coalesce around mutual interests and attempt to navigate around new obstacles.

This has shaken up an already unsteady geopolitical status quo, as rifts widen between the G7 and BRICS countries (Brazil, Russia, India, China and South Africa) over, for example, sanctions on Russia for its invasion of Ukraine.[14] By extension, Beijing's support for Moscow has deepened these rifts, which will have consequences for technology transfer and the who-gets-what in the regrouping of supply chains and strategic partnerships.

Meanwhile, middle-tier countries such as Singapore, India, Vietnam and Mexico will have to navigate a more complicated landscape, even as they have become the destinations of choice for restructured supply chains. China's path is far from certain, while many of the world's less-developed countries will feel the brunt of a more fragmented, less inclusive international environment.

But the G7 and a handful of other liberal democracies are undergoing a moment of geopolitical 'creative destruction'—if I may stretch Joseph Schumpeter's economic term—and while this will erase some hard-earned gains in trade and commerce in the short term, the reconfiguration of global value chains will also present new growth opportunities for a lot of businesses.

A paradigm shift in the West is displacing an almost dogmatic belief in free markets and has moved the pendulum back in the direction of 'managed trade' and those two contentious words: *industrial policy*. Consequently, Washington's weaponisation of supply chains through export controls and sanctions has produced a bitter clash between techno-nationalists and traditional neoliberal economists.

Meanwhile, an innovation race between Beijing and the West is further accelerating the fragmentation of strategic supply chains. Some, including the technology scholar Rob Atkinson, have called this *innovation mercantilism*.

Unlike mercantilism of the seventeenth and eighteenth centuries, however, the bifurcation of R&D and innovation around great power rivalry is not a zero-sum game. This is because of a superabundance of overlapping commercial interests, many of which thrive on change and disruption, even as others are disrupted. Thus, reorganisation of the global landscape and bifurcation of technology ecosystems calls for new investments in re-shoring and friendshoring, which stimulates other economic activity.

Another reason for the great bifurcation is that governments are linking technology transfer to security alliances. One example is the AUKUS defence pact, comprising the U.S., the U.K. and Australia. AUKUS' security pact includes technology transfer for everything from nuclear submarines to hypersonic missile technology, to quantum and machine learning, which, of course, means that semiconductors will also factor into the calculus.

Here, private investors are accelerating bifurcation by piling on their investments to publicly funded projects and joining public–private partnerships that link markets with defence-related initiatives.

PARADOXES AND CONTRADICTIONS

Will China's rapid rise as a technological power and its challenge to American hegemony inevitably lead to military conflict? Graham Allison, in his widely read book *Destined for War*, argues that throughout history, an ascendant power's challenge to an established incumbent creates a 'Thucydides Trap', which often results in the two going to war.

But the China–U.S. rivalry is far more complex than that between the ancient city-states of Athens and Sparta or Germany's challenge to British hegemony before the First World War. The Sino-American story involves much more deeply intertwined economic relationships on both the supply side and the demand side.

There are huge sunken costs in supply chains and production hubs that American and other G7 multinational firms have anchored in China, and, by extension, these hubs feed into a wider network of value chains stretching across the planet.

Never before have two superpowers with such fundamentally incompatible models become so deeply intertwined. The Cold War between the U.S. and the former Soviet Union (USSR), for example, featured two entirely different political and economic systems. They had virtually zero trade and economic exchange, and each operated almost exclusively within its own well-defined sphere of influence.

In contrast, China and the U.S. share the same global system and encounter each other everywhere. Some scholars, such as Joseph Nye, argue that since China and the U.S. have grown so economically interdependent, we cannot say they are in a 'cold war'. By this reasoning, the two countries must accept their mutual dependence and figure out how to coexist.

But despite these economic co-dependencies, Washington and Beijing are in fact, in a much messier, potential more risky kind of *hybrid cold war*. Hybrid cold war is a witches' brew of economic, cyber and information-related actions, all of which fall below the threshold of armed conflict but are nonetheless disruptive to the workings of the international system.

General economic interdependencies are unlikely to prevent an escalation of hostilities or, at the very least, a protracted process of bifurcation.

As the U.S. and China square off in this hybrid cold war, a parallel struggle between governments and multinational enterprises (MNEs) is unfolding. After decades of largely unrestrained offshoring and investment in China, Washington must somehow bring to heel the world's most dominant and wealthy non-state actors—American tech giants such as Apple, Intel, Qualcomm, Microsoft and IBM—who derive billions in revenue annually from China.

Beijing also must grapple with its own MNEs, but compared to U.S. MNEs, Chinese firms have much smaller, or even non-existent footprints in overseas markets. At home, Beijing's authoritarian government can bludgeon its heavyweights such as Alibaba, Tencent or even Huawei—into submission far more easily than Washington can control its key corporate players.

A STEADY SHIFT TOWARDS DECOUPLING

Disagreements between technology hawks on Capitol Hill and CEOs in affected sectors, everywhere, will cause friction for years to come. But the eventual outcome is likely to be more rather than less decoupling from China. Wall Street, which has long held high hopes for wealth-creation possibilities in China, is slowly coming to terms with this reality.

Beginning in 2022, for the first time, talk about a possible blockade or even a hot war in Taiwan became a regular topic in corporate boardrooms.

Beijing's shift to hard authoritarianism marks a tipping point, especially with its passage of the Anti-Espionage laws in 2023, its raiding of foreign company offices and its targeting of American companies such as Micron, Apple and Tesla for selective sales-bans. For the first time, well-established investors in China have begun to question their long-term prospects. Geo-economics, not liberal economics, has become the benchmark for business decision-making.

Clearly, there continue to be reasons for American companies in, for example, the fraught semiconductor sector, such as Nvidia and Applied Materials, to try and preserve market share in China as long as possible. Profit-driven, geopolitically agnostic MNEs will seek ways to circumnavigate export controls through supply chain makeovers, legal loopholes and corporate lobbying efforts for as long as they can.

The steady shift towards China decoupling has been a roller-coaster ride. Just three years prior to the imposition of China's Anti-Espionage laws, corporate America was keen on sidestepping Washington's efforts at decoupling. In 2020, even as the Biden administration was mobilising 'China-free' supply chain initiatives and adding Chinese companies to lists of restricted entities, Wall Street ploughed more than US$75 billion into China's financial markets.[15] After Beijing removed foreign ownership caps in April of 2020, companies such as Goldman Sachs, JP Morgan, Citigroup and Morgan Stanley jumped at the chance to take 100% control of their joint ventures with local firms.

By the summer of 2021, BlackRock, the American investment firm, announced it would set up a US$1 billion mutual fund, the first fund in China fully run by a foreign firm.

In July 2021, the American Chamber of Commerce in Shanghai conducted a survey of American companies and reported that 60% had increased their investments in China over the preceding year, and more than 70% of American manufacturers said they had no plans to move their production out of China.[16]

Despite all the talk about the end of globalisation and decoupling and Washington's onslaught of sanctions and export controls, 2022 witnessed a surge in bilateral trade between the U.S. and China. In the first eight months of 2022, the U.S. sent US$3 billion more than it had in 2021. Meanwhile, China accounted for the largest share of

U.S. imports of any country—and, as usual, ran a notoriously large trade deficit.[17]

Much of this surge in trade was attributable to corporate jubilation about China's post-COVID-19 opening, and after years of lockdowns, delayed projects and pent-up investment money, Western firms were eager to jump back in and resume business.

In January 2023, when Chinese President Xi Jinping relaxed the country's COVID-19 restrictions, BlackRock, JP Morgan and Germany's Allianz Global Investors, among many others, released a barrage of advertisements and publications exhorting investors to put their money into China. As the Morgan Stanley publication put it: 'Where to Invest When China Pulls Back From COVID-Zero'.

But then things began to take a dramatic turn for the worse. FDI in China dropped by 16.13% in the first seven months of 2023, compared to the same period in 2022—the largest drop in FDI in China since the 2008 financial crisis. Some of the notable 2023 FDI drop-offs were: U.S.: −25.3%, Japan: −18.4%, South Korea: −17.2%, Germany: −16.5% and the U.K. −15.8%—all clear indications of de-risking and eventual decoupling.

These numbers represented the first net outflows of foreign corporate accounts since China opened its doors to foreign investment, going back at least three decades. Of course, not all MNEs were taking their money out: some were increasing their inflows—but this was to better ring-fence their operations aimed at the domestic Chinese market, and to shore up their 'in-China-for-China' strategies—which, in fact, is evidence of a wider fragmentation of global value chains.

STATES AND FIRMS IN A GREY ZONE

By 2023, the message was loud and clear. Washington was committed to decoupling strategic supply chains from China, even though the process would be clumsy and disjointed and opposed by many. Officially, the word was that U.S. officials were aiming to 'de-risk', rather than fully decouple, and they would work to preserve trading benefits whenever they could.

In the meantime, multinational companies face the problem of managing thousands of dual-use goods lingering in a grey zone, where they may be unrestricted one day, but potentially off-limits the next.

With the ratcheting up of export controls in 2022 and 2023, the U.S. Department of Commerce (DOC) gradually restricted U.S. technology transfer to the Chinese semiconductor industry—at least on paper. Japan and the Netherlands, meanwhile, two key U.S. allies in what I call the 'Group of Five' elite semiconductor club (the U.S. Taiwan, Japan, South Korea and the Netherlands), agreed to cooperate with Washington's export control regime and block designated technologies from their own countries to China.

By 2023, Washington had blacklisted almost every Chinese technology company of consequence. This included Semiconductor Manufacturing International Corporation (SMIC) and Yangtze Memory Technologies Company Ltd. (YMTC), along with virtually all of China's other leading semiconductor companies. It also included DJI Technology Company (DJI), which had 80% of global market share in commercial drones, as well as Hikvision and Dahua, which controlled 60% of the global market in facial recognition cameras and surveillance-tech.

Others rounding out Washington's blacklist included SenseTime, one of China's premier AI companies, and Zhong Xing Telecommunications Equipment Company (ZTE) and, of course, Huawei, the world's leading telecommunications equipment manufacturer.

By 2023, Washington had rolled out the U.S. Outbound Investment Transparency Act, intended to block monies destined for a wide cross-section of the tech sectors in China and other countries of concern.[18] U.S. investors would soon be required to perform due diligence to affirm that investments in China were not somehow linked to the Chinese military—an impossible task, given the opaque nature of China's system of civil–military fusion initiatives that involve the Chinese Communist Party (CCP) and the PLA in virtually any enterprise of consequence.

Here, depending on how far U.S. policymakers intend to enforce these laws, we are likely to see more financial decoupling due to the onerous nature of these investment controls.

Eventually, public officials will have to figure out how to extend their enforcement efforts to offshore financial centres, tax havens and places where shell companies and holding companies continue to facilitate the trade of restricted trade and capital into China.

This next phase in the confrontation between CEOs and techno-nationalists will, therefore, be every bit as significant as the wider, overarching techno-nationalist competition between China and the West. In fact, the legal tussles, lobbying and public relations campaigns pitting MNEs against governments will have a substantial impact on how substantially strategic decoupling from China occurs.

The conflicts between MNEs and national governments will play out not only in Washington but also in Brussels, Tokyo, Taipei, Seoul and beyond.

At this turning point, most CEO 'old China hands' and senior corporate board members are in their 50s and 60s and have had careers like mine, spanning the halcyon decades of hyper-globalisation. For this cohort, China has always been an obvious and irresistible target for global growth strategies.

But that era is now over.

China's geopolitical ambitions present disturbingly incongruent and dangerous scenarios for those striving to maintain trade linkages. An arms race in Asia and the Indo-Pacific is underway. Even as commercial exchange continues between the two superpowers, the PLA pushes ahead with the development and deployment of hypersonic 'carrier killer' missiles, designed for one single purpose: to attack and destroy American aircraft carriers and push American naval power out of the region.

When a high-altitude Chinese spy balloon the size of a school bus was shot down by a U.S. fighter jet off the coast of South Carolina in February of 2023, the question was: Why was the spy balloon necessary?

Meanwhile, advances in supercomputing and AI have made cyberwarfare an ever present threat and spawned a new wave of cyberweapons of mass disorganisation and disinformation.

Such behaviour means that nations are preparing for war. Allison's Thucydides Trap, therefore, is alive.

These, then, are the overarching themes, core elements and undercurrents that are interwoven with twenty-first-century techno-nationalism, which leads us to some big questions.

THE BIG QUESTIONS

- Can the U.S. and China achieve competitive coexistence and continue mutually beneficial trade while engaging in a hybrid cold war?
- To what extent will decoupling occur across strategic supply chains, cyberspace and financial markets?
- Can middle-tier countries avoid 'choosing sides' and forge independent trading ties, free from big-power coercion?
- Can re-shoring, friend-shoring and ring-fencing of technology supply chains succeed after decades of offshoring and globalisation?
- Is an in-China-for-China strategy sustainable in the long-term for foreign multinationals?
- How will universities and other institutions be affected by techno-nationalism? What role will they play in talent pipelines and innovation races?
- What does the geo-economic 'Grey Zone' look like—the zone in which governments and corporations form symbiotic relationships and also become targets of hostile actors?
- What are the prospects for India to become a global high technology hub?
- How are climate change and war accelerating techno-nationalism?

In this book, my spotlight is on the early decades of the twenty-first century, although I occasionally travel back in time to highlight important historical examples and antecedents of modern techno-nationalism.

I have approached this topic as a realist. As such, I assume that governments, like people, always act in their own perceived self-interest.

Through the lens of realism, then, I regard the rise of China and its path to power as a matter of simple realpolitik. This is Darwinism on a state level, in a Hobbesian world.

This book is not about picking winners or losers or making moral judgements. Nor is it seeking to answer big theoretical questions about why some nations become powerful while others do not. The reasons behind the rise and fall of empires go well beyond technology.

Jared Diamond, in his book *Guns Germs, and Steel*, argues that aspects of geography (climate, indigenous diseases, insularity, etc.) determine why certain cultures and nations have achieved power while others did not. Whether or not one accepts Diamond's arguments, the underlying truth in the affairs of nations remains constant: ending up on the wrong end of an adversary's superior technology—regardless of who originally invented it—can be a terrible and cruel fate.

Again, technology, by itself, is not a singular determinant of power. What matters is how it is used and, more specifically, the values and objectives it serves and the will of the people who yield it.

Paul Kennedy, in his epic, *The Rise and Fall of The Great Powers*, tackles the topic of power and empire but emphasises the primacy of economics. Daron Acemoglu and James Robinson explore the origins of power, prosperity and poverty in *Why Nations Fail*, acknowledging the key role of technology in a wider suite of inter-connected elements.

Still others have kept the story of technology and national power confined to military affairs. Martin Van Creveld's *Technology and War*, and Max Boot's *War Made New*, for example, are authoritative works of encyclopaedic breadth and depth.

Interestingly, history's most timeless writings on warfare, Sun Tzu's *The Art of War* and Clausewitz's *On War*, focus almost exclusively on the human dimensions of strategy, tactics and planning, including the role of psychology, emotion and deception. Technology is barely mentioned. Had either of these two great thinkers witnessed the destructive power of twentieth- and twenty-first-century technologies, I am certain they would have given the topic more attention.

Approaching the subject from a dark, dystopian perspective is Yuval Noah Harari, whose *Homo Deus* examines a world where humans lose control of the machines they create, largely because of the will to power, greed and FOMO (fear of missing out). As nations get caught up in an AI arms race, self-learning computers and autonomous robots have now become an existential threat.

On a more contemporary note, pivoting back to the foundational technologies that function as power multipliers, Chris Miller's 2022 book, *Chip War*, masterfully lays out the evolution of the microchip and how they have become so central to geopolitical competition.

In this book, I attempt to look at the wider landscape of techno-nationalism, focusing on a core group of the most important foundational technologies while keeping semiconductors central to the conversation.

OVERVIEW OF SECTIONS AND CHAPTERS

This book is divided into four parts.

Part I, *The Elements of Techno-Nationalism*, introduces its key features, including its historical development in the early modern period and the early twenty-first-century dynamics that make it such a disruptive and paradoxical force. These introductory chapters examine themes that animate techno-nationalism, such as the historical technology feedback loop, a paradigm shift, export controls and the 'in-China-for-China grey zone'. Part I closes with a deep dive into semiconductors and their central role across the different facets of techno-nationalism, focusing specifically on China and the U.S.

Part II, *Undercurrents and Power Multipliers*, begins with the story of Huawei, which is a microcosm of the hybrid cold war between the U.S. and China. Throughout this section, we examine the group of distinctive technologies at the heart of the twenty-first-century technology race, from AI and biotech, to quantum and hypersonic science, to the commercialisation and militarisation of space. We examine themes that have remained constant throughout the late twentieth and early twenty-first century, most notably tradecraft—the stealing of secrets using technology, very often to steal technology.

Part III, *Climate, Cleantech and Agritech*, examines how techno-nationalism and climate change have converged to reshape the global economy. This is affecting the top, middle and bottom of supply chains for cleantech, most notably EVs, largely because of the strategic value of critical minerals and rare earths, lithium batteries, magnets and semiconductors.

In Part IV, *Innovation, Academia, Alliances and Diplomacy*, examines techno-diplomacy, focusing on how the U.S. and its allies are working together to form strategic partnerships and alliances. Here, we look at the innovation races between nations and how universities and academia have become an increasingly important link in public–private partnerships. We discuss India, Taiwan and other 'middle' countries that see their roles shifting in the technology landscape and the global order.

More generally, we also discuss the emerging blocs around China and the BRICS countries, and the U.S. and the G7 countries.

Chapter 2

The Technology
Feedback Loop

In 1789 Alexander Hamilton became America's first Secretary of the Treasury. One of his top priorities was to steal Britain's most valuable technology secrets.

Both Hamilton and George Washington, America's first president, knew that as a former British colony, the young nation could not easily industrialise if it remained dependent on British and other European powers for its manufactured and finished goods.

As it happened, in 1769, Richard Arkwright, an Englishman, had patented the spinning frame, a water-driven machine that used specially designed cylinders to replicate the motions of human fingers in the twisting and combining of thread.[1] Innovations such as this triggered the rapid industrialisation of textile production and helped vault Britain to its dominant position in the world economy.

Establishing a homegrown textile industry, therefore, was one of the keys to bringing the Industrial Revolution to the shores of America, but it would require Britain's technology.

In 1791, Hamilton published his 'Report on Manufactures', which articulated his vision of America's first industrial policies and is one of history's first comprehensive techno-nationalist blueprints. Hamilton's report argued for the fostering of industry and technology as a requirement for America's economic welfare and national security.

The document justified the need for government subsidies (which Hamilton called pecuniary bounties) to reduce costs and the need to channel investment to targeted local manufacturing and production.[2] It also justified protectionist tariffs and prohibitive measures aimed at keeping foreign competition out of the American market.

Hamilton also prioritised the recruitment and emigration of skilled mechanics, engineers and other experts from foreign countries. Obtaining top-notch human capital was essential if the Americans were to have any chance of catching up with Britain.

The report stressed the need to reward those who could bring 'improvements and secrets of extraordinary value' to the America, and Hamilton had American agents distribute 1,000 printed copies of portions of his report around key manufacturing hubs in England and Ireland. Identifying a talent pipeline was a key objective of America's industrial spies, whose primary mission was to obtain the details, designs and workings of key textile manufacturing technologies.

One of the first consequential recruits was an Irish mechanic named William Pierce, who emigrated to America and ended up working with one of the fledgling nation's first policy-oriented public–private partnerships (PPP), The Society for Establishing Useful Manufacturers.[3] Through his connections at the Society, the U.S. and a slew of businesses and investors, Pierce was instrumental in the establishment of cotton mills in the U.S.

To accelerate the transfer of valuable industrial technology, Congress passed the Patent Act of 1793, which granted patents for pirated intellectual property from other countries, no questions asked.

EARLY INTERNATIONAL TALENT WARS

The Patent Act played a key role in achieving Hamilton's goal of obtaining and copying Britain's most coveted technology.

The Industrial Revolution came to America largely by way of Samuel Slater, an Englishman who had apprenticed at a mill co-owned by Richard Arkwright, the inventor of the water frame spinning machine.

Mr. Slater committed to memory all the design and functional details of Arkwright's invention and redrafted the blueprints and schematics in the U.S. Becoming an American citizen, he presided over the proliferation of new textile mills in the U.S.—and became known as the 'father of the American Industrial Revolution'.[4] To the British, he became known as 'Slater-the-Traitor'.

Several decades later, an American, Francis Cabot Lowell, travelled to England and brought back the next generation of milling technology—the power loom. Its prototype had been invented by the Englishman Edmund Cartwright.

Lowell recognised the potential for these machines to revolutionise the textile industry in the U.S. Upon returning home, he and his associates at the Boston Manufacturing Company worked to adapt and improve Cartwright's power loom technology.

They introduced modifications and refinements to make it more efficient and practical for large-scale textile production, resulting in the Waltham-Lowell system.

EARLY BRITISH EXPORT CONTROLS

The British understood how their technology had conferred wealth and power on the Empire, and they went to extensive troubles to prevent others from obtaining blueprints and specifications of their prized innovations.

Britain had resorted to the passage of export control laws—aimed primarily at its former colony, the U.S.—that barred the export of tools and machinery needed for manufacturing textiles.[5]

Skilled textile workers and those with knowledge about factories in England were also prohibited from leaving the country. The law carried harsh punishment for anyone attempting to pass on England's industrial secrets, and the British government launched a series of publicity campaigns to warn its citizenry of its obligation to prevent the transfer of English know-how. British officials published pamphlets targeting anyone who might be considering emigration to America, warning of the 'conniving nature' of American businesses.[6]

Britain enforced export controls throughout the first Industrial Revolution, dispatching warships to intercept traffic on the Atlantic while in passage from Britain to America. On the high seas, British agents would board commercial and passenger vessels and inspect cargo and luggage as it sought to discover stolen intellectual property.

No wonder, then, that Samuel Slater memorised the diagrams of Arkwright's water frame—although some historians have argued that Arkwright's patent had expired by the time it was put into operation in the U.S.

Jumping forward more than two centuries, it is not difficult to appreciate the value of tradecraft and industrial espionage as an integral part of techno-nationalism.

China's emphasis on industrial espionage in the digital age brings the scale and the stakes of this game to incomprehensibly high levels. Using spyware and advanced hacking techniques, huge amounts of secrets can be stolen almost at the speed of light, and with advanced AI and other twenty-first-century technologies, this information can be swiftly turned into tangible results, either for economic or military purposes as we will discuss in Chapter 11.

As was the case with Lowell's improvements to Edmund Cartwright's power loom in America, any nation possessing the right assets can take existing technology secrets and quickly improve upon them.

Today, Washington has invested heavily to guard the technologies of its leading strategic industries, even if it only means delaying the transfer of that IP for just a few years, to buy enough time to maintain or advance an existing innovation lead.

HISTORY'S TECHNOLOGY FEEDBACK LOOP

Throughout history, the world's most advanced nations have leveraged power derived from the use of technology. At the root of this

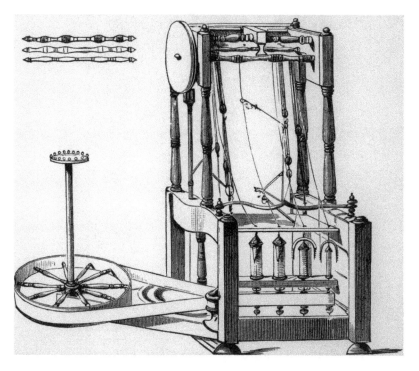

Figure 2.1   Richard Arkwright's Coveted Spinning Frame.

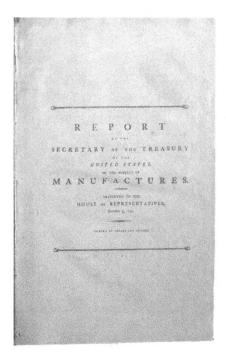

Figure 2.2   Alexander Hamilton's Report of Manufacturers Presented to the U.S. House of Representatives in 1791.

Figure 2.3   Portrait of Samuel Slater, Father of the American Manufacturing System.

Figure 2.4   Portrait of Alexander Hamilton, America's First Secretary of the Treasury.

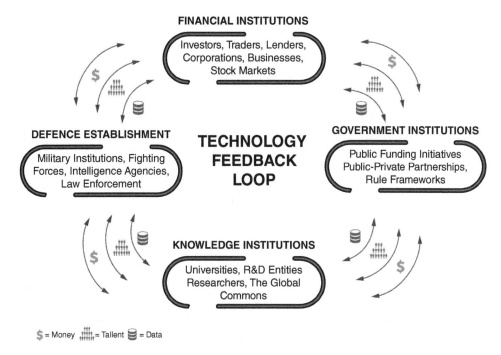

Figure 2.5   Illustration, The Techno-nationalist Feedback Loop.

dynamic is a feedback loop that enables wealth and knowledge to flow between key institutions: Governmental, financial, scientific/academic, military and industrial.

This produces a virtuous cycle that creates network effects, whereby increasing wealth begets increased knowledge and expertise, which then leads to more innovation, which in turn creates more wealth. And then the process repeats itself.

As a student of history, Alexander Hamilton understood the technology feedback loop and studied it, going back as far as the lessons of the seventeenth century and the Dutch East India Company. Known as the *Vereenigde Oost-Indische Compagnie* (VOC) in Dutch, it was the world's first mega-corporation linked directly to a state, and while it sought its profits, it also carried out the Dutch government's geopolitical agenda. As such, the VOC was the first military-commercial conglomerate.

Try to imagine Apple, the tech giant—with some US$3 *trillion* in market capitalisation in 2023—functioning in the same way for the U.S.

government as the VOC did for the Dutch republic. In this scenario, Apple would have at its disposal the entire U.S. Navy's arsenal, from aircraft carriers and advanced fighter jets to nuclear missiles. It could impose its will on other countries by seizing critical resources and infrastructure. It could force its subjects to buy its products, exclusively. It could attack, disable and destroy the supply chains of its competitors or simply take possession of them. It could even impose its own rule of law and arrest, try and execute local citizens.

Such was the power of the Dutch East India Company and, by extension, the Dutch state.

I begin the discussion of present-day techno-nationalism with this very old example for two reasons. Firstly, the VOC started a centuries-long chain of causation that laid the foundation for today's geopolitical status quo; secondly, the story illustrates how disparities in technological capabilities can eventually form an unbridgeable chasm between advanced and less advanced states.

The Dutch technology feedback loop, during its 'Golden Age', from around 1575 to 1675, spanned all key institutions. Monies flowed both from the coffers of the "Republic of the Seven United Netherlands' and from a flourishing stock market, open to all investors large and small (an innovation in and of itself). Dutch shipbuilding and manufacturing capabilities, meanwhile, along with advances in maritime science and engineering, sparked historic accomplishments.

Dutch cartographic and navigational acumen was the best of the epoque and was based upon improvements of Portuguese maps— the early maps that enabled Dutch travel to Asia had, in fact, been stolen from the Portuguese.

Because of its technology feedback loop, the Dutch population was collectively well fed, healthy and productive and contributed to a creative and prosperous critical mass of talent and labour within the country's urban centres. Universities sparked advances in agriculture, including dyke-building and land reclamation, which, in turn, were made possible by innovations such as wind-powered water pumps. This led to more population growth and an expansion of the virtuous circle.

THE DUTCH SEAFARING TECHNOLOGIES

FIGURE 2.6   Cornelius Corneliszoon's 1593 Wind-powered Sawmill.

Seafaring technologies were power multipliers for the Dutch during the height of their global power. This began with the capacity to build well-engineered and cost-efficient ships. By the end of the seventeenth century, the area around the town of Zaandam, located near Amsterdam on the Zaan river, would feature many clusters of highly productive shipyards. Hundreds of windmills, which used innovative crankshaft technology, were harnessed to power industrial sawmills. The technology in these new sawmills, invented by the Dutchman Cornelis Corneliszoon van Uitgeest, enabled shipbuilding to proceed at scale, and allowed the Dutch to build the world's largest merchant shipping fleet.

Just as Alexander Hamilton had sent his industrial spies to England to learn the secrets of textile milling machines and to steal technology secrets, Russia's Czar Peter is said to have visited Zaandam, undercover, in 1697, as part of an intelligence gathering mission to Europe's most advanced shipyards. This was essential for the Czar's plans to modernise Russia and its navy.

Towards the end of the sixteenth century, the Dutch had introduced a new kind of merchant vessel, the fluyt, which, as its design evolved, played a major role in increasing the VOC's competitive advantage in trade and, by extension the Dutch republic's geopolitical power.

Throughout history, merchant ships had to be fitted with cannon for defence purposes, resulting in less space for cargo storage and making ship design and shipbuilding more complex and expensive.

The fluyt dispensed with the need for these armaments, resulting in a more utilitarian design with almost double the cargo space of earlier ships. The fluyt was not just cheaper to build; it also cost less to operate because it required fewer crew members and was faster than older cargo vessels. It also had a shallow hull that allowed it to navigate far up rivers, extending its logistical reach.

As for Dutch ship building, the fluyt was used extensively to ferry lumber back from Baltic ports, after delivering, for example, coffee, tobacco, spices and sugar from prosperous Dutch trading houses.

Holland's maritime and trade accomplishments during its Golden Age also owe much of their success to the innovative Dutch financial system. Holland produced the world's most sophisticated public stock market, which allowed for fractions of shares to be sold and traded in larger numbers. This kind of 'crowdfunding' had gotten an early start in Holland when municipalities and churches all pitched in to pay for the dykes and windmills and technology to move water.

Also instrumental was the futures trading market, which, as the historian William J. Bernstein wrote, 'allowed the buying of North Sea herrings before they were caught'. This advanced market allowed for risk-reduction and hedging tools that facilitated Dutch imports of timber from the Baltics, spices from Indonesia, and silks from China.

Dutch successes sparked techno-nationalist countermeasures from Britain, Holland's chief competitor at the time. What followed was a long period of competition and conflict, ending in the global expansion of the British East India Company and later the Hudson Bay Company—both hugely successful state-backed commercial-military conglomerates.

Technology feedback loops achieved a virtuous cycle for a disproportionately small group of European state actors, establishing wealth and power asymmetries between nations that persist to present day.

TECHNO-NATIONALISM AND THE FOUR INDUSTRIAL REVOLUTIONS

The 'West versus the rest' has its roots in almost 500 years of techno-nationalist feedback loops, which, in turn, were driven by a series of industrial revolutions.

The first and second Industrial Revolutions, which began in Britain roughly around 1760 and 1870, respectively, conferred almost insurmountable advantages to the British and a handful of continental European nations, as well as America and Japan.

Japan's Meiji Restoration in 1868 is of special significance. It marks a time when its political elite, unlike those of its Asian neighbours, turned to the West to acquire new technologies and to absorb and implement Western management and educational practices.

This gave Japan advantages in Asian affairs, particularly regarding China, whose Qing dynasty rulers had isolated the kingdom by turning inward, cutting it off from participation in the Industrial Revolution and effectively dooming it to its so-called 'Century of Humiliation'. As I have already mentioned, the memory of this period factors strongly in China's current push for technological self-sufficiency.

Taiwan (Formosa) would come under Japanese colonial rule in 1895, as would Korea in 1910. In a watershed moment in the Russo-Japanese War in 1905, Japan's modernised and technologically superior navy annihilated Russia's naval fleet in the Battle of Tsushima, one of the most lopsided seaborne clashes in military history. The Meiji Restoration thus set the stage for wider Japanese imperial ambitions, ultimately emboldening it to invade Manchuria in 1931. Japan leveraged industrial-scale capabilities in manufacturing, logistics and warfare to inflict great hardship on the Chinese.

For the British, meanwhile, the virtues of the feedback loop delivered ongoing innovations and advances in manufacturing, logistics and communications, underwriting the naval dominance that allowed the British to enforce the *Pax Britannica* from the end of the Napoleonic Wars in 1815, to the start of First World War in 1914.

This era witnessed an incredible wave of innovations in science and technology that became some of history's biggest power multipliers:

railroads and steel-hulled ships; the electric telegraph and undersea communication cables; the Spencer repeating rifle, the Gatling and Maxim machine gun; quinine anti-malarial pills; the transition from coal-fired steam mechanisms to new turbine engines fuelled by oil; the arrival of aeroplanes, submarines and self-propelled torpedoes, among others.

PHYSICS AND CHEMISTRY WARS

The unanticipated destructive power of the First World War was, in fact, a by-product of a full-scale 'war of chemistry' between scientists. While the development of chemical weapons is well documented, another area, munitions, provides a compelling story of how combatants, especially Britain and Germany, raced to create chemical processes that would enable mass production of nitrates—a chemical precursor needed to detonate artillery shells and other munitions.

Under the duress of war, scientists figured out how to extract nitrogen directly from the atmosphere (to literally pull it out of thin air) and subject it to chemical reactions with other specialised organic materials.[7] The Known as the Haber-Bosch process, this became central to the German war effort, allowing it to produce vast quantities of ammonia nitrate that served as a key ingredient to explosives such as gunpowder and nitroglycerine.

Similarly, in Britain, the exigencies of the First World War pushed scientists to re-engineer the Birkeland-Eyde process, another method for nitrogen fixation.

These breakthroughs occurred in record time and were married to new manufacturing practices that enabled huge economies of scale. The innovations radically changed the nature of armed conflict and pushed economic competition into a new era, with benefits to consumers, later, during peacetime.

In Germany, chemical companies such as Bosch and BASF had received government funding to invent, develop and mass-produce for the war effort, as did Krupp, the steel producer, which developed newer and stronger alloys needed for implementing new methods of nitrate production.

After the war, in 1925, Hoechst, BASF, Bayer and three other German companies formed IG Farben, which for a time was the world's largest chemical company. Meanwhile, Krupp went on to become ThyssenKrupp, one of the world's largest steel and engineering conglomerates.

In Britain, as in Germany, the First World War would spawn another important multinational chemical company, Imperial Chemical Industries (ICI).

Later, these same companies would go on to mass-produce fertilisers, pharmaceuticals, textiles and other materials[8] that contributed to healthier, wealthier and more productive populations, thereby amplifying and perpetuating the technology feedback loop. The wealth-creating attributes of this phenomenon continued to serve as power multipliers for both Germany and Britain.

IG Farben would later write one of economic history's darkest chapters as the manufacturer of chemicals for Hitler's Third Reich.

During the Second World War, the company became known as the 'devil's chemist' because it produced Zyklon B, the poison gas used by the Nazis in German concentration camps to carry out genocide on Jews and others.[9] Such a diabolical use of science reminds us, once again, of the duality of technology, for good or for evil: its applications depend on its masters' intentions. On a large scale, the symbiotic relationships between big industry (big tech) can cut both ways.

After the war IG Farben was dismantled and three of the companies to emerge from it included Agfa, BASF, and Bayer, which today, are among Germany's biggest, wealthiest companies.

These early twentieth-century 'chemistry wars' hinged strongly on contributions from academia. In Britain, for example, beyond munitions research, government funding and close cooperation with the military led to the development of beta eucaine, a synthetic local anaesthetic, developed by chemists at Imperial College London. Similarly, chemistry faculty and researchers at The University of Edinburgh created a widely used wartime antiseptic, hypochlorous acid. These breakthroughs would set in motion wider progress in the medical field.

Later, in Chapter 24, we will examine the increasingly complicated and fraught role that universities and research institutions play in today's innovation races, most notably between the U.S. and China.

COMPUTERS, ATOMIC BOMBS AND A SPACE RACE

FIGURE 2.7   ENIAC, the first digital computer, developed for the U.S. Army at the University of Pennsylvania, during the Second World War.

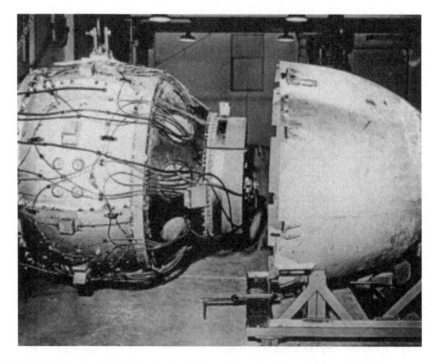

FIGURE 2.8   The Manhattan's Project's Atomic Bomb, at Los Alamos, in 1945.

The waning years of the Second Industrial Revolution took the techno-nationalist feedback loop into the nuclear age and onto the threshold of the modern computer age. The innovations of the post-war era fall into the 'Third and Fourth Industrial Revolutions' (3IR and 4IR, respectively) or, more succinctly, 'the second machine age', a term coined by Andrew McAfee and Erik Brynjolfsson.

For the U.S., technological innovation was accelerated by its involvement in two world wars in a span of 30 years, from 1914 through to 1945, followed by a Cold War that would last another 40 years. During the Cold War with the Soviets, the U.S would engage in hot wars on the Korean Peninsula in the 1950s, and a 'police action' in Vietnam in the 1960s. Next came after the Cold War, Gulf Wars I and II, in the Middle East, and a decades-long war in Afghanistan extended this techno-military feedback loop.

It was the Second World War, however, that demonstrated how the STEM disciplines—science, technology, engineering and math—would be harnessed on an increasingly larger scale. One of the most significant innovations to come out of the conflict was the 1945 creation of the electronic numerical integrator and computer (ENIAC).[10]

Built at the University of Pennsylvania, ENIAC was the world's first general-purpose digital computer, the size of a house, that utilised thousands of vacuum tubes. The U.S. military used ENIAC to calculate and programme artillery shell trajectories.

Britain designed its own set of vacuum tube computers called Colossus, which went into operation in 1944 and was classified until the 1970s.[11] Colossus played an important role in deciphering the Nazis' use of Morse code and incorporated groundbreaking work on cryptanalysis from Cambridge University's Alan Turing, and his team of codebreakers at Bletchley Park.

In both the first and second world wars, we see a pattern of growing collaboration between academic and military institutions, a trend which continued throughout the twentieth century and now, in the twenty-first century, is accelerating and extending the frontiers of research.

THE MANHATTAN PROJECT

Technological competition, once again, was behind the race to develop the atomic bomb, which became the most decisive geopolitical power multiplier in human history.

America's Manhattan Project, which ran from 1942 to 1947, was an urgent campaign to pre-empt the development of nuclear technology by German physicists, who, at the time, were thought to be further along than the Americans and British.[12]

The successful development of the atomic bomb by the Americans culminated in the devastation of Hiroshima and Nagasaki and, ultimately, Japan's surrender to the U.S. The geopolitical implications were immediately clear and helped solidify the U.S. as a dominant world power.

In hindsight, the Manhattan Project was particularly consequential because it provided a prototype for public-private-partnerships (PPP) in 'Big Science'. At the height of its operations (just within its tightly ring-fenced inner circles) President Roosevelt's top-secret programme had-130,000 civilian and military personnel and contractors on payroll, located across some 30 sites, primarily in the U.S., but also in Britain and Canada.[13] The programme ultimately cost US$2 billion, or about US$26 billion in 2024 dollars.

In the U.S., eight facilities performed leading-edge research, testing and construction-related activities for different versions of an atomic bomb. In Hanford, Washington State, plutonium was created, while chemical separation processes were undertaken at Oakridge, in Tennessee, at the newly invented X-10 Graphite Reactor and the Y-12 facility where Beta-3 Racetracks performed electromagnetic isotope separation and other functions that pushed the frontiers of science. In Los Alamos and Alamogordo, New Mexico, the actual bomb prototypes were built and tested for the first time.

The metallurgical laboratory at the University of Chicago, another integral site for the Manhattan Project, illustrates the critical role of academia in the race to develop the atomic bomb. Earlier, the University of California at Berkeley had delivered groundbreaking research on uranium and plutonium. Robert Oppenheimer, a physics professor at UC Berkeley, would go on to head the Los Alamos laboratory.

This was the techno-nationalist feedback loop on the largest scale ever. But the Manhattan Project was, fundamentally, a U.S. military undertaking. It was an Army officer, Lieutenant General Leslie Groves, who assembled and oversaw one of the greatest academic brain trusts in history, consisting of the world's leading physicists, engineers, mathematicians and chemists.

The U.S. quest to develop the A-bomb would also foreshadow the rise of modern-day spy-craft, a fluid and rapidly evolving element of techno-nationalism. By today's standards of technology-enhanced espionage, the Manhattan project was still in the proverbial stone age.

Spies within the project, most notably Klaus Fuchs and Theodore Hall, were recruited into Soviet espionage operations, and key information, mostly in the form of paper drawings and diagrams, would be secretly smuggled out and passed on to the Soviets. This enabled the USSR to successfully build its own nuclear weapon in 1949.[14]

Again, this is a long way from today's cyber-intrusions and sophisticated signals intelligence, where the most seemingly secure networks and data bases are hacked.

The Soviet's prototype atomic bomb would become known in the West as the 'Joe-1', and soon after, the Soviets shared Joe-1's stolen technology secrets with Communist China—helping to establish in the Chinese communist state apparatus a deep and abiding belief in the benefits of industrial espionage.

THE THIRD INDUSTRIAL REVOLUTION (3IR)

Historians date the beginnings of the 3IR to the early post-war era, but much of the innovation associated with it coincided with America's Space Race with the Soviets. The resultant American 'Moonshot' produced a myriad of innovations, including the world's first digital microprocessors, solar-powered satellites, mainframe computers and the Internet. Steady, sequential advances in semiconductor power and cost-effectiveness, as dictated by *Moore's Law* (discussed in Chapter 7), had their origins in NASA's space programmes.

It was Russia's launch of the world's first satellite, Sputnik, in 1957 that set off another round of techno-nationalist fervour in the U.S. The so-called 'Sputnik moment' prompted President Dwight Eisenhower to establish the Advanced Research Projects Agency—what evolved into today's 'Defense Advanced Research Projects Agency' (DARPA).[15]

Eisenhower understood the linkages between a state's competitiveness and the quality of its human capital. In addition to establishing DARPA, he signed into law the 1958 National Defense Education Act, which apportioned US$1 billion for scholarships and grants in the STEM fields at universities and colleges, significantly expanding the role of the federal government in the nation's educational curriculum.[16]

Meanwhile, lessons learned from the theft of national secrets from the Manhattan Project spurred the establishment of the National Security Agency (NSA) in 1952. The NSA became the locus of digital surveillance and intelligence gathering and kept a close eye on the U.S. space programme. The NSA would go on to achieve near-total American hegemony in intelligence activities, which, after Edward Snowden's leak of classified intelligence on American surveillance capabilities, in 2013, galvanised China's techno-nationalist agenda regarding tradecraft.

NASA's Apollo programme placed 12 U.S. astronauts on the Moon between 1969 and 1972. Like the Manhattan Project, the Space Race took the power-multiplying dynamics of PPPs to an even higher level.

Innovations resulting from the Space Race also led to the development of a wide spectrum of new products, ranging from the medical field to sustainable energy and consumer electronics.

As was the case during the First and Second World Wars, during the Cold War, hand-picked corporations benefitted immensely from PPPs aimed at innovation. Newly achieved competitive advantages and first-mover advantages often result in exorbitant barriers to entry for latecomers, leaving the beneficiary companies to capture large chunks of market share around the world.

Thus, just as government support benefitted BASF, Bosch and Bayer during the First World War, so too did U.S. government support benefit American companies such as Du Pont, Boeing, Texas Instruments, IBM and General Motors through much of the twentieth century and into the twenty-first.

Today's big beneficiaries of U.S. techno-nationalist imperative include the above stalwart American companies in the 12 areas of foundational technologies, with a rapidly growing contingent of big-tech firms such as Alphabet, Amazon, Microsoft, as well as the big semiconductor companies.

CHINA'S 4IR FEEDBACK LOOP

The transformation of China from the 'sick man of Asia' (as it was called by economists during the nineteenth century and into the twentieth) to a present-day manufacturing juggernaut is yet another success story involving the technology feedback loop.

However, China's technology experience has benefitted from the 4IR in ways its predecessors could not have.

The 4IR is not like earlier industrial revolutions, which empowered only a handful of first-mover countries and resulted in what the historian Kenneth Pomeranz called *The Great Divergence* between rich nations and poor. In contrast, the computing and connectivity technologies of the 4IR ushered in what Richard Baldwin, a political economist, has called *The Great Convergence,* an intentional play on Pomeranz's phrase.

This new convergence means technologies are dispersing everywhere and levelling the playing field for other participants in the global economy. Powerful, affordable technologies enable value-adding activities such as information and communications technology (ICT), banking, logistics and education, as well as professional advisory services. With 4IR technologies, almost any firm can optimise its supply chain by 'unbundling' different elements throughout the world, seeking out the most optimal locations.

Chinese technocrats recognised these opportunities and endeavoured to use every policy tool they could muster to tap into these 4IR technologies—and to make China the most attractive hub in an unbundled world. These policies go back to and even before the carefully managed 'peaceful rise' period of the Hu Jintao decade, from 2002 to 2012, well before Xi Jinping's ascension to power.

This, then, brings us to the Western reaction to China's technology feedback loop and how this prompted a backlash, a paradigm shift, and a paradox, which we explore in the next chapter.

Chapter 3

Paradigm Shift and Paradox

Washington and its allies have undergone a fundamental shift in their thinking about globalisation in general and China in particular. From the late 1980s until around the mid-2010s, the foreign policy establishment had coalesced around a set of liberal economic principles that became known as the *Washington Consensus*.

Those principles included a commitment to the idea of open and free trade, reduced barriers to international investment, privatisation of state monopolies, deregulation of private industry, limited government spending and tax cuts. The Washington Consensus profoundly influenced a generation of decision makers in politics, business and academia.

With respect to China, Western policymakers had concluded that allowing China to integrate itself into the global economy under the umbrella of liberal economic principles would help foster global peace and prosperity.

Eventually, however, from Washington to Canberra, Brussels to Tokyo, the political establishment concluded that Beijing's central planners took advantage of the West's faith in trade liberalisation. China reaped the benefits of open markets, even as it doubled down on its own nonmarket economic practices and pursued a geopolitical calculus that sought to supplant the U.S.-led world order.

In retrospect, the undercurrents of Washington's paradigm shift go back a long way. Gradually, they gained momentum, pushed along by a steady drip of trade-related grievances from foreign companies that struggled on an uneven playing field in China.

I recall one meeting in Shanghai in the early 2000s with an expat executive from a large foreign company that made heavy transport vehicles. I visited the company's offices with several 'old China hands'– colleagues who were well seasoned in the ways of China and knew the landscape better than most foreigners.

Midway through our discussion, the exasperated executive broke in and demanded: *"When will our Chinese competitors actually have to make money to stay in business?"* This was a reference to the state funding that Chinese companies were receiving to keep them afloat. My colleagues shrugged and admitted that they did not have an answer.

Two decades later, nothing has changed.

PARADIGM SHIFT BECOMES POLICY

The paradigm shift in the U.S. has been largely bipartisan, but it swiftly gained currency from 2017 onwards under the mercurial presidency of Donald Trump. Official communications became increasingly confrontational in 2018 when the United States Trade Representative (USTR) launched an investigation into China's trade practices to determine whether they constituted a national security risk to American interests.

The USTR's investigation, under Section 301 of the 1974 Trade Act, focused heavily on technology. Specifically, it concluded that Beijing pursued policies of forced technology transfer, restricted market access to large parts of its economy, it imposed unfair licensing rules, and, as part of its wider techno-nationalist agenda, pursued strategies to acquire U.S. cutting-edge technology assets by any means, including via state-backed cyber intrusions designed to steal trade secrets.[1]

A White House public document published in May of 2020 would later capture the bipartisan Zeitgeist in Washington, stating: *'The CCP [Chinese Communist Party] has chosen to exploit a free and open system and rules-based order and attempt to reshape the international system in its favor.'*[2]

By the election of Joe Biden to the presidency in 2020, there was no longer any doubt about Beijing's intent and capability to challenge the U.S. as the world's geopolitical alpha.

How then did the paradigm shift translate into actions based on a defined logic and a policy framework?

In April of 2023, Jake Sullivan, President Biden's National Security Advisor, delivered a high-profile talk at the Brookings Institution in Washington, DC, which he called 'Renewing American Economic Leadership'.

Six months later, Sullivan published an essay in *Foreign Affairs* magazine entitled 'The Sources of American Power: A Foreign Policy for a Changed World'.[3]

Some have compared Sullivan's piece to another watershed essay, 'The Sources of Soviet Conduct', also published in *Foreign Affairs*, in 1947, by George Kennan, a U.S. State Department official.[4] Kennan's essay would later serve as the bedrock rationale for what would become the U.S. Cold War doctrine of 'Containment', which called for pushing back against Soviet Union's sphere of influence, everywhere. Kennan's essay defined a major inflection point and paradigm shift in U.S. foreign policy and it sparked a techno-nationalist reawakening.

Whether Jake Sullivan's essay, written more than 75 years later, has the same lasting effect as Kennan's remains to be seen. Kennon published his discourse under the mysterious pseudonym 'X,' presumably because the writer wanted to call out the U.S. political establishment's failure to grasp the magnitude of Soviet ambitions, which may have included Kennan's own superiors.

Sullivan's speech and essay both affirmed an acceptance of a paradigm shift in Washington and a clear pivot away from the old Washington Consensus. There were problems that needed fixing. And he was speaking for a wider mindset that included Democrats, Republicans and Independents.

First, Sullivan affirmed that the neoliberal trade model had indeed had the net effect of hollowing out the U.S. industrial base and gutting the American middle class—a result of the offshoring of manufacturing capacity and the transfer of millions of jobs overseas.

The second problem, directly related to the first, was that a wide swathe of strategic supply chains involving foundational technologies were now situated in places like China and Taiwan. This made them vulnerable to disruptions from pandemics, natural disasters and geopolitical events. Strategic supply chains needed to return to the U.S.

Yet another problem was that the economic calculus of laissez-faire capitalism failed to factor in the high environmental and social costs of opaque, stretched-out, globalised supply chains that masked messy carbon footprints and social issues like forced labour.

For all these problems, Sullivan laid out the Administration's framework of solutions, which had been given various taglines, including 'Bidenomics' or, more appropriately, 'geo-economics'.

First, there was the 'build-back' campaign, involving at least US$3.5 *trillion* in public and private funding, over a decade, aimed at reshoring strategic manufacturing as well as upgrading and expanding infrastructure around cleantech and other leading-edge technologies. The intended result was enhanced national security and economic strength, with the aim of creating millions of new jobs that could deliver social stability.

By the time Sullivan took the podium at Brookings, three landmark packages of bipartisan legislation had already been passed by the U.S. Congress and signed into law by President Biden: The Bipartisan Infrastructure Investment and Jobs Act, The Inflation Reduction Act (IRA) and the CHIPs and Science Act—collectively worth just under US$2 trillion in funding over 10 years.

Second, Washington was adopting its now famous 'small-yard high-fence' strategy whereby the U.S. would protect its leading-edge technology and restrict access to only a small group of trusted allies. For adversaries and countries of concern, there would be export controls, sanctions and restrictions on investments and acquisitions.

Third, Washington would resort to intense *techno-diplomacy*, to enlist the cooperation and coordination of its key allies. Techno-diplomacy aims to increase collaboration around security pacts and academic partnerships as well as through non-binding bilateral and mini-lateral agreements and dialogues. This includes collectively restructuring, nearshoring and friendshoring supply chains when it comes to the small-yard, high-fence group of industries. All key foundational industries, including biotechnology, AI-related, semiconductors and quantum computing were at play.

By the time Jake Sullivan's essay appeared in *Foreign Affairs*, Washington's efforts around techno-diplomacy were already embodied in its Chip 4 Alliance with Taiwan, South Korea and Japan, the Quadrilateral Security Dialogue (*QUAD*) with India, Japan and Australia, the *AUKUS* security pact with Britain and Australia and the Indo-Pacific Economic Framework (IPEF). We will discuss techno-diplomacy and the above initiatives later in Chapter 29.

Meanwhile, in Europe, Ursula von der Leyen, the President of the European Commission (EC), confirmed European commitment to elements of the paradigm shift. In an important speech at the Mercator Institute for China Studies in March of 2023, von der Leyen stressed the importance of 'de-risking' Europe from China.

In Europe, as in the U.S., the paradigm shift is rooted in the core elements intrinsic to techno-nationalist competition with China, namely, the weaponisation of supply chains through the use of export controls and sanctions, decoupling and de-risking, re-shoring and friendshoring, innovation competition and talent development, techno-diplomacy and tradecraft.

We will all these things in much greater detail in ensuing chapters as we delve into the core elements of techno-nationalism.

Understandably, policymakers and business leaders differ about the extent to which trade liberalisation should be rolled back and who should bear the cost. Opponents of the small-yard, high-fence narrative like to point out that, from an export controls perspective, clever operatives always find ways to build a higher ladder to access restricted technologies, a theme we will return to repeatedly. These wider theoretical disagreements have spilled over into academia and into the pundit realm, pitting die-hard neoliberals against advocates of the paradigm shift.

Assuming the policy shift continues to follow its present trajectory, global value chains will continue to bifurcate and fragment, further challenging multinational companies and others who benefit from cross-border linkages with China.

This brings us to three important questions:

1. Can the paradigm shift be confined to just a portion of global value chains, leaving other sectors largely unaffected?

2. How will disagreements between government officials and multinational executives affect the paradigm shift?

3. Will China's illiberal economic policies and its increasingly assertive geopolitical objectives accelerate the paradigm shift?

CEOs VERSUS TECHNO-NATIONALISTS

In a truly open global trading system, supply chains evolve naturally and develop the most economically efficient configurations. They optimise around labour and talent pools, capital markets, infrastructure and favourable regulatory environments. They bring together niche players into robust ecosystems.

On paper, this is the textbook neoliberal economic model that was the engine for globalisation and global growth for decades. We see Adam Smith's proverbial 'invisible hand' at work, in the economic landscape coupled with David Ricardo's principle of 'comparative advantage' which states that a country should specialise in producing goods or services in which it has the lowest opportunity cost compared to other countries.

No wonder, then, that American firms such as Ford, Dupont and Whirlpool would close longstanding operations throughout the U.S.

and move them to China. In the big picture, the offshoring of these supply chains and manufacturing hubs enabled key components and materials to flow back downstream to existing factories in America and elsewhere.

Trade liberalisation allowed consumers in America and around the world to enjoy access to the least expensive products, in abundance, and in great variety.

And so, gradually, less profitable, less efficient production activities were shut down across the G7 economies and offshored to places like Shanghai, Chongqing, Dongguan, Shenzhen and Wuhan, among others, which became increasingly linked to the everyday global business landscape. During my career with KPMG, I became familiar with all these places.

The downside was that the U.S. economy haemorrhaged manufacturing jobs. One report by the Economic Policy Institute cited the loss of 3.7 million American jobs to China between 2001 and 2013 alone.[5] No one in the Midwest's 'Rustbelt' cared that globalisation had added hundreds of millions of jobs in China, Southeast Asia, India and beyond.

To be fair, many traditional manufacturing jobs had been made redundant by new technology and automation rather than by offshoring. And as neoliberals correctly argue, this transition created other kinds of knowledge-intensive and service-related jobs—but these jobs were not evenly distributed.

More blame could also have been placed on national, state, local and municipal governments that failed to develop policies to attract investment and to help their work forces upgrade their skills and transition to new jobs.

Whatever the causes, the loss of traditional manufacturing jobs dealt a painfully hard blow to the middle classes, especially in the American heartland, even as proponents of globalisation continued to shrug it off.

Under the neoliberal model such losses were perfectly acceptable: *aggregate* economic growth was beneficial even if the benefits were disproportionately distributed. If multinational brands were making piles of money doing high value-added activities—like designing the world's most advanced microchips in the U.S. before offshoring fabrication to Taiwan—or if banks were creating lucrative financial products and services overseas, *so what* if manufacturing capacity was being offshored?

The problem was that corporate America and Wall Street's success was increasingly tied to China, and this was coming into conflict with national security concerns. When combined with the angst of ordinary Americans who were concerned about being left behind as globalisation's road kill this became fertile ground for demagogues.

Growing wealth disparities between elites and the eroding middle classes in Western countries have helped galvanise the techno-nationalist mindset and animate the movement to decouple from China. Growing anger towards the wealthiest 1% of Americans, and especially towards the big investment banks that had been bailed out by the U.S. government during the global financial crisis in 2008–2009, serves as a particularly visceral example of this animus.

The backlash against globalisation is not new. I vividly recall watching the street protests that derailed the World Trade Organization (WTO) Ministerial meetings in Seattle in 1999. In 2003, Nobel Prize-winning economist Joseph Stiglitz published *Globalization and Its Discontents*, a bestseller that called attention to such problems.[6] What rang true then rings true now: asymmetric accrual of money and power—which continues to exacerbate the digital divide and the wealth chasm between the top 1% and the rest—will influence big pendulum swings in politics and policymaking.

The Bidenomics policies spelled out by Jake Sullivan are thus a response both to national security concerns about the hollowing out of the American industrial base and to middle-class concerns about jobs.

Like it or not, however, corporate America has built deep and extensive links between the U.S. and China, fusing the world's two largest economies. In 2022, the value of trade in goods and services between the U.S. and China was about *US$2 billion* per day with trade between the E.U. and China being roughly the same.

To be clear, every key public official in the Biden administration, from Sullivan to Treasury Secretary Janet Yellen and Commerce Secretary

Gina Raimondo stated unequivocally that the U.S. does not seek a wholesale decoupling from China.

A major question, then, is what kind of economic hardship will affected businesses experience if policymakers in Washington and elsewhere manage to accomplish the goals of decoupling, de-risking and the re-shoring of strategic supply chains. Which value chains and trade flows can be left undisturbed? Can policymakers allow a chunk of goods and services to continue to flow freely and operate under normal market dynamics, free from the influence of geo-economics?

Unfortunately, there simply are no clear answers to these questions. One reason is that a large portion of seemingly innocuous daily trade falls under the category of 'dual-use'—goods and services that have both military and civilian applications and that may end up on restricted and prohibited lists from one day to the next.

A further complication is that the CHIPS Act in the U.S. and similar initiatives in South Korea, Japan and Taiwan mandate that firms that accept funding from their governments must also limit certain activities in China.

All these developments put CEOs increasingly at odds with policymakers. Negotiations, lobbying efforts and public discourse are increasingly fraught, and as geopolitical concerns raise the temperature of public debate, there will be plenty of grief about the paradigm shift.

THE WICKED PARADOX

Following the global financial crisis of 2008–2009, China's leadership began to openly challenge America's 70-year-long post-Second World War hegemony. As China became the top trading partner of most countries in Central Asia, Africa and Southeast Asia, Beijing's goal of supplanting Washington as the dominant power in the Indo-Pacific played a significant role in its Belt and Road Initiatives (BRI) and other policies.

Beijing continues to work with Russia and others to try and supplant the U.S. dollar as the primary reserve and trading currency (so far, with little success), and it continues to focus on pushing out the U.S. military presence in the South China Sea and to eventually challenge the U.S. Navy throughout the Indo-Pacific.

This has created a wicked paradox. The two countries continue to trade in large volumes and remain closely intertwined economically, yet are in conflict over geopolitical goals. The paradox features not only a hybrid cold war, but a situation that has morphed into an open arms race, including the gradual build-up of military forces, not just in China but in surrounding countries from Australia to Japan and India.

This brings us to the next important question: Will China's advancing geopolitical and techno-nationalist agenda inevitably prompt more de-risking and pre-emptive decoupling by the business community?

If past behaviour is a reliable predictor of future behaviour, the answer is probably no—at least not until governments intervene. Ignoring or missing the warning signs of geopolitical risk has been a regular feature of foreign businesses pursuing market share and profits in China.

In this regard, I took away a very important lesson while working out of Hong Kong during an earlier phase of the U.S.–China paradox in the early 2000s.

One of the phrases that began to circulate among 'Old China Hands' during this period was 'hide and bide'. For Beijing's central planners, this meant keeping a low profile and not attracting too much attention to China's growing power. It was a strategy attributed to Deng Xiaoping, China's paramount leader from 1978 to 1992, a period during which it was vitally important for China to avoid conflict with the U.S. and other major powers until it had the wherewithal to accelerate its rise as a superpower.

Deng's 'hide and bide' strategy helped China achieve rapid economic growth in the 1980s and beyond. The approach paid off handsomely when China joined the WTO in 2001, further boosting the country's economic development and global integration.

'Hide and bide' was an unvarnished phrase that had slipped out from the inner circles of the Chinese Communist Party (CCP) brain trust. Soon, China's propaganda machine would put out another, much friendlier catchphrase for public consumption: 'Peaceful Rise'.

Both phrases draw inspiration from a 2,500-year-old document written during the Warring States period of Chinese history, when the military leader, Sun Tzu, reportedly crafted the *The Art of War*. Among Sun Tzu's core teachings: 'Know when to fight and not to fight; conceal your strengths and take the enemy when he's unprepared'.

This approach worked well. From the early 1990s, as huge investment flows poured into China, Beijing began quietly carrying out reclamation activities in the South China Sea, transforming reefs and submerged features into artificial islands capable of supporting military infrastructure. Over nearly 30 years, dozens of coral reef atolls and low-lying islands in the South China Sea would be dredged, built up into artificial structures and fortified by the Chinese military, even as more Western money continued to pour into China.

The trajectories of these two incompatible behaviours have continued, in parallel, for decades.

To illustrate this paradox, consider that just around the time that China initiated its island-building on Mischief Reefs (referred to as 'Meiji Jiao' in China), BP, the British oil and gas supermajor, was engaging in joint ventures and partnerships with Chinese energy companies in the same area.

Similarly, under the proverbial noses of Western businesses and governments, around 2010, the PLA began work on its Dong Feng series of missiles, the DF-21D and DF-26. These missiles were designed to target and destroy U.S. aircraft carriers from long range, with the aim of denying the U.S. military access to the South China Sea and waters around Taiwan. We will discuss the implications of this in Chapter 15, and China's techno-nationalist focus on hypersonic technology.

During the same period, meanwhile, GE, the iconic U.S. conglomerate, expanded its presence in China through joint ventures and investments with Chineses aerospace companies. In one example, GE jet engines and avionics, which represented the leading edge in its field, partnered with Aviation Industry Corporation of China (AVIC), a state-backed company with direct connections to the PLA.[7]

The paradox is everywhere.

The problem with cybersecurity—or rather, cyber-*insecurity* goes back decades. Around 2009, the U.S. Department of Justice began accusing China of hacking into the computer networks of defence-related

U.S. companies and government agencies and making off with a treasure trove of IP for a wide range of advanced military weapons systems, including the U.S. Navy's Arleigh Burke-class destroyers, the U.S. Air Force's F-22 Raptor[8] fighter jet and the U.S. Army's Patriot missile system.[9]

This was Chinese realpolitik and hybrid war with spectacular results. Even as its intelligence and military circles were pilfering military technology and industrial secrets, foreign investments into China's economy continued to pour in.

By the early 2020s, Sino-American great power competition was on full display. 'Hide and bide' and 'peaceful rise' had been called out, and the paradigm shift in Washington was well underway.

Once again, these developments raise the issue of how American and other foreign multinationals will adjust their linkages to China going forward. Although there is a compelling argument for economic interdependence and mutual trade interests serving as a deterrent to catastrophic decoupling, there are eerie parallels to another era when a similar argument was made at a similar juncture in world history.

In 1909, on the eve of the First World War, Norman Angell, a British author, wrote a widely acclaimed book titled *The Great Illusion*, in which he argued that the interconnectedness of the European economies had made war economically unviable because armed conflict between industrialised nations such as Germany and Britain would lead to chaos and mutually assured economic destruction.[10] Angell was awarded the Nobel Peace prize for *The Great Illusion*.

Angell was right about the magnitude of the threat, but his book failed to predict an all-out war that involved virtually of the world's major powers, which radically changed the path of world history.

The recent paradigm shift in Washington and beyond presents the world with a similar situation. More than a century has passed since the First World War, and it remains to be seen whether Angell's economic interdependence argument will once again be proven wrong.

What is certain is that a race for technology supremacy will reshape relationships between states, companies and people.

Chapter 4

The In-China-for-China Grey Zone

On a fresh spring morning in in Washington D.C., the U.S. House Select Committee on the Chinese Communist Party commenced a series of computerised war games involving China and Taiwan. It was April, 2023.

Simulations served up different battle scenarios involving weapons systems and technologies that were presumed to factor into an invasion of Taiwan by China's People's Liberation Army (PLA).

But discussions also focused on how a war across the Taiwan Straits would impact financial markets and global supply chains. It was rumoured that House Republican, Mark Gallagher, the committee chairman, had invited representatives from Wall Street investment banks to participate. The objective: To raise awareness of how geo-politics are escalating the risks of doing business with China.

WELCOME TO THE GREY ZONE

Capturing and defending market share in China has never been easy for multinational enterprises (MNEs), but a hybrid cold war between

Beijing and Washington is making things much more difficult. As tensions across the Taiwan Straits simmer, the prospects of continued business operations in China have become more uncertain.

Domestically, absent any potential Taiwan-related hostilities, foreign companies must already grapple with an unlevel playing field as they compete against local Chinese 'national champions' that are heavily protected and subsidised by their home government.

Foreign businesses must also try and shield their valuable intellectual property, even as they try to avoid running afoul of Chinese laws aimed at foreign companies. China's vague national security and anti-espionage laws mandate that, when asked, MNEs must hand over encryption keys, software and access to their local servers to a group of government entities, including China's Ministry of State Security.[1]

Other laws require data associated with Chinese citizens and local business activities to be stored in China, with prohibitions on transferring it out of the country. This diminishes an MNE's global operational efficiencies and economies of scale.

MNEs must contend with all this while also adhering to a growing list of export controls, sanctions and prohibitions on technology transfer— enforced by their own home governments. The need to screen buyers, service providers and so called end-users in China against blacklists and export licensing requirements has created a fluid and uncertain business environment.

Regarding the matter of export controls, no issue is more challenging than having to grapple with 'dual-use' technologies—loosely defined as any commercial technology that could be applied for military purposes, which includes virtually all modern-day technology.

This creates a murky grey zone of commonly traded products that could, at any time, become subject to export controls and sanctions.

Yet even as they strive to comply with local laws, foreign MNEs in China risk being punished for complying with their own home governments' rules. This was on display in May of 2023, when the Cyberspace Administration of China (CAC) banned computer memory and storage chips made by Micron Semiconductor Manufacturing Company (Micron) from being installed in China's digital infrastructure.

The reason given was that Micron's technology constituted a national security risk.

Such actions are seen as Beijing's retaliation against Washington for American restrictions on U.S. semiconductor technology, and Washington's move to ban the use of Chinese-made commercial drones, surveillance cameras, and telecommunications equipment by U.S government agencies.

Micron was just the beginning. Because it had complied with U.S export control laws and stopped selling controlled goods to Chinese entities, it would become an easy target for retaliation.

In March of 2024, China took the additional action of banning Intel, Advanced Micro Devices (AMD) and Microsoft from being installed on government computers.

Beijing would have been responding to actions undertaken by the U.S. House of Representatives, which, a month earlier, had voted overwhelmingly to ban the hugely popular video streaming app, TikTok, if its Chinese owner, ByteDance, did not fully divest itself of its U.S. subsidiary of TikTok.[2]

Mistrust is a widening two-way street. If theoretically (and in practice) a Chinese intelligence agency is able to bug telecommunications infrastructure made by Huawei, then any competent U.S. signals intelligence agency, theoretically, could do the same thing for an Intel chip, or a Microsoft operating system.

MNEs must also avoid making public statements or actions that contradict Beijing's official narratives.

Consider H&M, the well-known Swedish clothing company that expressed concern in 2021 about forced labour allegations involving the Uighur Muslim population in China's Xinjiang province. H&M stopped sourcing cotton from the region and subsequently faced boycotts and store closures in China.[3]

Similarly, Adidas, the German sporting goods and clothing brand, removed a statement expressing concern about alleged human rights abuses in Xinjiang from its website after facing harsh criticism from the Chinese government.

Reprisal against foreign companies in China comes in the form of audits, lawsuits, sales bans, unannounced office raids and detention of company officials and staff. Still other forms of reprisal include negative publicity campaigns that can end in consumer boycotts and public scorn.

The question is where is the safe, middle ground in China for an MNE? More specifically, to what extent must a company 'de-risk' or even decouple its ongoing business with China?

Answering these questions will require a clear, open-eyed assessment of the dynamics that are reshaping the China landscape. China's central planners have taken a hard shift toward authoritarianism under President Xi Jinping, which has produced an even more emphatic backlash and paradigm shift in the West, thus, doing business in China has entered a new phase.

Paradoxically, we are asking how to continue doing business with China at a time when the PLA is undergoing its largest and most rapid build-up of military assets, ever, which is based on projections of fighting a hot war with America and its allies.

In the next chapter, we will explore the themes of de-risking versus decoupling from China in more detail.

For now, we begin the in-China-for China discussion by focusing on how techno-nationalism has impacted the behaviour of American and other foreign companies in China.

As a focal point, we will look at how geopolitical competition has skewed the playing field in the Chinese market for electric vehicles (EVs), where Chinese companies like BYD Co., Zhejiang Geely Holding Group, Chery Automobile and Nio Inc. have displaced well-known foreign brands such as Tesla and Volkswagen.

Next, we will assess the impact of China's anti-espionage laws and Beijing's tactics of singling out foreign firms for intimidation, which signals a much darker reality for the future of the in-China-for-China model.

THE TRADITIONAL 'IN-CHINA-FOR-CHINA' MODEL

In the 1990s and early 2000s, the standard in-China-for-China strategy involved making deals with local Chinese companies to gain access to the Chinese market via joint ventures, licensing agreements and other forms of partnerships.

Through such arrangements, foreign companies would share or sell older 'legacy' or 'trailing-edge' technologies to Chinese companies. The strategy helped companies steer clear of U.S. sanctions and controls that generally applied only to advanced, 'leading-edge' technology.

Foreign firms could thus gain market share and prosper in China—so long as they could maintain their leading edge by constantly innovating. They could protect their lead by locating their more advanced technologies (critical parts, intermediate components or software, for example) outside China, and then ship those components, just-in-time, for final placement into a completely built-up (CBU) product in China. Profits made from these sales could then be ploughed back into R&D for the next new thing.

For years, this strategy allowed foreign companies to invest in local manufacturing and supply chains in China without being displaced by local Chinese firms.

More recently, however, increasing competition from Chinese partners who have grown increasingly sophisticated in adopting and even enhancing foreign technology, has put the in-China-for-China model under severe strain, or even killed it.

CHINA'S TECH SUBSIDIES: FROM TVs TO EVs

In late 2023, Japan's Mitsubishi Motors Corp. announced that it was closing its manufacturing operations in China and walking away from the world's largest and fastest-growing market for EVs. For knowledgeable observers, the development came as no surprise.[4]

Like other established foreign brands, Mitsubishi had been steadily losing market share to a group of upstart, state-backed Chinese companies.

Tesla Inc., the world's first-mover success story in EVs, had been losing ground to Chinese competitors. In 2023, BYD overtook Tesla as the world's number one selling EV maker.[5] That same year, more than 80% of the electric cars sold in China were made by domestic automakers, even though foreign brands had held commanding leads only five years earlier.[6]

Mitsubishi's exit from China illustrates how geopolitics is reshaping the trade landscape. It is a story about EV techno-nationalism and the wide-ranging use of subsidies and protective and predatory measures that governments like China's are using to impose their will on markets.

Consider how Beijing prioritised access to Chinese battery supply chains for local companies. Domestic Chinese EV makers get preferential access and lower prices to lithium-ion battery supply chains, which are dominated by state-backed Chinese battery makers such as Contemporary Amperex Technology Co. Ltd. (CATL).[7] Moreover, Chinese battery manufacturers, who controlled more than 70% of the global market in 2023, are heavily subsidised by the government.[8]

The result: Subsidised Chinese EV brands offer lower retail prices, free or cheap charging infrastructure and, under Beijing's quota system—designed to expedite China's transition from internal combustion engines (ICE) to EVs—they offer buyers higher purchase rebates, further boosting demand for Chinese EVs.

In addition to all of this, Chinese EVs compete based on quality. Here, they have closed the gap with foreign brands and have even surpassed the likes of Tesla.

Looking ahead, as joint ventures between foreign EV makers and local Chinese companies expire, foreign firms will lose out. For example, Volkswagen AG China, which is 50% owned by SAIC Motor, faces the expiration of the partnership with SAIC in 2030, which almost certainly means that Beijing will underwrite SAIC's (and others') efforts to go after VW's market share.

The story of China's success with large-scale, industry-wide techno-nationalist subsidies goes back decades. This is a lesson that Japanese companies such as Sony, Panasonic and Sharp learned from direct experience.

In the early 2000s, the Chinese government began to heavily subsidise its domestic television manufacturing industry, providing tax breaks, low-interest loans, government grants and free land. Such support allowed Chinese manufacturers to produce TVs at a much lower cost than their foreign competitors while using joint ventures with Japanese companies to gain access to advanced technologies and improve product quality. Panasonic's manufacturing plant in Wuxi, for example, was originally a joint venture with China's TCL Technology.

By 2016, Sony, Panasonic, Sharp and other foreign companies had closed their TV manufacturing plants and had pulled out of China. Today, TCL is a major global brand: In 2023, it was the second-largest TV manufacturer in the world by market share, according to Omdia, a telecommunications and media consultancy. That year Chinese brands had risen to hold nearly a quarter of the global market, just behind Korea's Samsung.

Not surprisingly, many of the founders and managers at these Chinese companies had previously worked at Japanese companies.

The impact of Chinese government subsidies was, therefore, a familiar story by the time Mitsubishi Motors left China.

In the decades following China's techno-nationalist success in TVs, advances in computing and AI have further boosted the country's industrial competitiveness.

Sceptics of the effectiveness of industrial policies might reconsider their views considering the successes of China's TV makers, its EV makers, its high-speed rail industry, its BeiDou satellite system (which provides global positioning, navigation and timing services), and its major telecommunications equipment manufacturer, Huawei, which we will discuss at length in Chapter 10.

Returning to the story of EVs, foreign companies absorbed further lessons when the COVID-19 pandemic resulted in a shortage of semiconductors in China.

They found themselves marginalised as Beijing ensured that Chinese EV makers got priority access to the limited supply of chips. Their problems were compounded by a series of miscalculations about sales projections and production outputs that further restricted their inventories of chips.[9]

Component costs were also affected as state-backed Chinese EV companies stockpiled U.S.-made chips, which sparked by the ongoing threat of new U.S. export controls.

During the pandemic, Tesla was forced to source legacy chips from Chinese suppliers at high cost while dealing with concerns about their quality and reliability.

On a macro-scale, fears of future export controls aimed at China entities will complicate the EV grey zone in China for foreign companies. Washington's export controls campaign has galvanised China's efforts to become self-sufficient in the production of legacy (much older technology) chips.

Eventually, as Chinese chip fabrication capacity increases, they will feed an increasingly hungry, advancing Chinese EV sector, along with other emerging Chinese original equipment manufacturers (OEM). These emerging Chinese brands will compete with and attempt to displace foreign companies, first in China, and then in overseas markets—as we have seen in the case of BYD.

Having access, then, to a large domestic supply of trailing edge semiconductors will provide Chinese brands with a global competitive advantage if other regional players in Europe, North America, Japan and elsewhere cannot increase their own localised legacy chip fabrication.

More generally, as Chinese EV makers capture more market share, what happens to foreign car brands in China after their joint venture partnerships expire? How likely are these ventures to be renewed as business in China is becoming much more uncertain and dangerous for foreign MNEs?

We will explore the ways in which EV makers are looking to overcome supply chain and other geopolitical challenges in Chapters 21 and 22.

CHINA'S ANTI-ESPIONAGE LAWS

Foreign companies continue to experience an erosion of trust and transparency in China's market. This comes amidst rising doubts about the long-term soundness of China's economy in the face of relatively modest growth following the end of COVID-19 restrictions.

China's Anti-Espionage Law is intended to protect state secrets, but for many, it harkens back to the opacity and paranoia of China's Maoist era. The new law has been linked to a series of attacks on foreign companies in the form of restrictions, prohibitions, physical raids of their offices and growing numbers of exit bans on foreign nationals, which are essentially arbitrary detentions.

The Anti-Espionage Law defines state secrets to cover all documents, data, materials and articles concerning national security—the definition of which was intentionally left vague. This makes it difficult for MNCs to know what information they are prohibited from collecting or transmitting. Additionally, the law defines espionage very broadly to include any act of obtaining state secrets by 'illegal means.' Under such broad and vague laws, foreign MNCs can be found guilty of espionage even if they have no intention to harm China's national security.

Foreign MNCs must store data in China and provide access to the Chinese government upon request, raising the risk that an MNC's data could be appropriated and misused by the Chinese government.

The Anti-Espionage Law therefore restricts the transfer of virtually any type of data out of China, making it difficult for foreign MNCs to operate efficiently, as these laws could impede intercompany transfers of data between their cross-border affiliates. Such restrictions can impact entire value chains across multiple countries. It can even affect tax management as MNEs engage in intracompany sales and technology transfers.

The Anti-Espionage Law is enforced by a variety of Chinese government agencies, including the Ministry of State Security and the Ministry of Public Security. These agencies are not known for their transparency or due process, and foreign MNEs may have difficulty defending themselves against allegations of espionage.

When it comes to legal due process, transparency and fairness under the law, the contrasts between China, the U.S and other liberal democracies, in general, could not be more striking. Consider attempts in the US to ban TikTok, the streaming video app.

Despite being owned by the Chinese Internet technology company ByteDance, by 2024, TikTok had accumulated the private data of more than 170 million U.S. citizens. Technically (despite TikTok's efforts to ring-fence its U.S. data using independent third parties) under Beijing's national security and anti-espionage laws, TikTok is obligated to turn over data to China's security agencies.

Despite this, efforts to ban the TikTok app by Congress and the White House have been blocked in U.S. courts for violating free speech rights under the first amendment of the U.S. Constitution.

Another popular Chinese app, WeChat, is also widely used in America. It, too, has been subject to serious discussions about banning it on the same grounds as TikTok. Here, again, the U.S. legal and political systems would likely protect it.

Such an outcome in a Chinese court of law would be unthinkable. In fact, virtually all social media and communications apps, such as YouTube, Instagram or WhatsApp are fully banned and actively blocked in China.

These contrasts in legal standards and treatment of MNEs in the U.S. versus China will serve to further bifurcate the two systems and further alienate American and other foreign companies doing business in China.

In the span of 12 months, the Chinese government raided the China offices of a multiple foreign companies, including Capvision, Mintz Group and Bain & Company. In August 2023, five employees of the U.S. investment firm Mintz Group were detained in Beijing on suspicion of illegal trading of foreign exchange.

China is also increasingly barring people from leaving the country, including foreign executives. A Reuters analysis of numbers of exit bans[10] from China's Supreme Court database shows an eightfold increase in cases between 2016 and 2022.

The detention of foreign corporate personnel in China further calls into question the viability of the country's business environment and the rule of law. Many foreign companies are not only more cautious about investing in China, they now think twice about sending their employees to work there.

These crackdowns are a sign that the Chinese government is willing to use its economic power to try and influence the behaviour of other countries.

All of these developments—state subsidies, preferred access to strategic supply chains, and the disruptive effect of export controls and sanctions—reflect Beijing's lurch towards increased authoritarianism and make China an increasingly difficult place to do business.

Chapter 5

De-Risking and Decoupling

In early 2023, Dell Inc., the world's third-largest maker of personal computers, announced that it was moving its supply chains out of China amid concerns over geopolitical tensions.

Beyond geopolitics, however, Dell had also been burned by supply chain disruptions caused by the COVID-19 pandemic. The tech-giant, like many others, had 'single-sourced' certain critical components and assembly functions to China, only to find many of its supply chains locked down by pandemic restrictions.

Dell's plan called for diversifying its supply chains, and the phasing out of *all* production of semiconductors in China by 2024. It began diverting other key supply chains to Vietnam, Malaysia, India and Mexico.[1] Company management also directed its key suppliers to significantly reduce Chinese production of other inputs to Dell products.[2]

Other major brands have been following Dell's example. Taiwan's Foxconn, best known for assembling Apple's iPhones and, by revenue, the world's largest electronics contract manufacturer, moved to double its Indian workforce and investment by 2024. (In Chapter 27, we will delve further into India's prospects as the next tech-manufacturing hub.)

Foxconn's focus on India also involved a new partnership with Franco-Italian chip maker STMicro, a move that would help Foxconn to ramp up its assembly operations of smartphones and other electronic components in India. The percentage of iPhones assembled by Foxconn in India doubled between 2023 and 2024, and that trend continues.[3] Apple, meanwhile, hopes to shift at least 25% of its iPhone production to India by 2025, and up to about 40% by 2030.

Through such measures, Dell and Foxconn were both de-risking from China. We could also argue that what was really happening was a slow and steady decoupling process from China, not just a simple diversification plan.

What, then, is the difference between de-risking and decoupling?

De-risking is a relatively gradual and nuanced process that focuses on mitigating specific risks associated with economic engagement with a particular country. De-risking seeks to continue ongoing trade and investment activities once specific risks have been addressed. Such action is often motivated by a desire to reduce reliance on a single supplier or to protect against potential economic or geopolitical events. This generally involves diversifying supply chains, identifying alternative sources of goods and services and implementing measures to reduce exposure to potential disruptions.

Decoupling, in contrast, refers to a complete separation of ties between two or more economies—the dismantling of existing trade and investment relationships, and the severing of supply chains.

For anyone who appreciates the benefits of trade liberalisation, decoupling is an unwanted divorce and an affirmation of the inconvenient truths of geopolitics. An abrupt decoupling is likely to occur when one nation's actions pose an existential threat to another's. In the China–U.S. context, such actions can include escalations in hybrid warfare and techno-nationalist competition. The end game, then, requires an affected country to seek out new, more reliable partners and safer, more resilient supply chains.

One compelling motivation for de-risking and decoupling occurs when a government weaponises a supply chain by deliberately blocking technology transfer or access to energy, food, medicine or other critical resources. These actions are usually carried out via sanctions and export controls, or more forcibly, through overt aggression, such as Russia's cutting off natural gas flows to Europe in 2022 after Europe imposed sanctions on Moscow for its invasion of Ukraine.

De-risking and decoupling can affect both tangible supply chains and intangible value chains. This means that physical goods of all kinds, as well as dataflows, software, the platform economy and all manner of digital trade can be affected. As we will see in Chapter 28, even financial markets, including flows of digital currency and fintech-related tools, are undergoing de-risking and decoupling.

STRATIFIED GLOBAL VALUE CHAINS

Even as Dell and others were actively de-risking their China supply chains, senior U.S. officials made it clear that no one wanted to substantially decouple the U.S. economy from China. Trade between the U.S. and China amounted to nearly US$1.3 billion a day in 2023. A sudden break in commerce of this magnitude would derail investment, increase volatility in financial markets and disrupt trade at all levels, upending supply chains for a wide range of products.

Here, again, the paradox of trade between two systemically and adversely different superpowers comes into play. As both Beijing and Washington seek to expedite strategic decoupling, frictions between states and firms will increase. It is an odd juxtaposition: fighting to preserve trading links while severing others, while simultaneously preparing for a possible hot war with one's trading partner.

How these frictions play out remain to be seen, but Washington's efforts to selectively de-risk and decouple supply chains and other commercial flows with China will stratify global value chains into three distinct layers.

The first layer is comprised of strategic goods, which made up about 20% of U.S.–China trade in 2023. Products in this category include leading-edge foundational technologies, as discussed, from semiconductors and supercomputers, to quantum computing, biotech and advanced robotics, among other areas.

Motivated by the fear that leading-edge American technology could be incorporated into the PLA's or another adversary's military machine and turned against the U.S, Washington has turned to strategic export controls and sanctions to prevent their transfer.

The second layer of global supply chains is composed of thousands of 'dual-use' technologies—products that have both commercial and potential military uses, from electric toothbrushes to electric vehicles. Companies in this space face the risk that some unforeseen geopolitical event might lead Washington or Beijing (or another government) to impose restrictions or prohibitions that would adversely affect supply chains, literally overnight.

Potential triggering events for an overnight shutdown of trade in dual-use goods include a hot military confrontation in the South China Sea between the PLA and U.S. and allied forces (accidental or intentional), a Chinese blockade of Taiwan, or, less obviously, an increased backlash against China's ongoing support of Russia in its war on Ukraine, or its growing strategic ties with Iran.

De-risking actions with respect to China by multinational enterprises (MNEs) such as Dell and Foxconn are pre-emptive measures motivated by such concerns.

The third layer of global supply chains is composed of goods and services that have little or no strategic value or dual-use applications, such as apparel, ubiquitous consumer goods and, for example, processed food or beverages. Absent a major confrontation or complete breakdown in relations between adversaries, trade in such products would likely continue.

But trade in such seemingly innocuous products may not be fully immune from techno-nationalist and geopolitical considerations. From the perspective of extreme China hawks, any transaction that 'Feeds the Dragon' sustains Beijing's wider techno-nationalist aims, thus decoupling should continue over the mid to long term.

An all-important question, then, is when might de-risking tilt towards full decoupling?

STATES VERSUS FIRMS

Not long after Dell and Foxconn announced their intentions to de-risk their supply chain, Ola Källenius, chairman of carmaker Mercedes-Benz Group, told the German newspaper *Bild am Sonntag* that it would be 'unthinkable' for his company to leave the Chinese market. Mr. Källenius' reasoning has been echoed by the chief executives of other MNEs, who argue that the world's economies have become too economically intertwined to decouple.

If decoupling from China is out of the question for many MNEs, how strongly might they push back against common-sense de-risking strategies? On purely economic grounds, protecting and expanding market share in China is one of the primary motivations of any for-profit enterprise.

Indeed, MNEs have been pressuring their home governments to show restraint on export controls. In October and November 2023, for example, executives from the U.S. tech-majors—Intel, GE, Nvidia and Qualcomm—are reported to have pushed back on the expansion by the U.S. Commerce Department of Commerce's Bureau of Industry and Security (BIS) of export controls on semiconductor technology to China.

For China hawks who claim U.S. export controls are not being properly enforced, this was a case in point. It appeared that influential MNEs had lobbied for the softening of the latest export controls and had reached a tacit understanding with officials that, despite the public ratcheting up of export controls, Washington would quietly continue approving export licences—as we will discuss in Chapter 6.

Lobbying such as this is important because it may influence how aggressively policymakers pursue and enforce decoupling in strategic sectors and, consequently, how rigorously MNEs are forced to pursue de-risking strategies.

De-risking and decoupling will be an uncertain and messy process, always fraught with the possibility that geopolitical events, both anticipated and unexpected, may suddenly tilt the balance from strategic de-risking to unavoidable decoupling.

THE UKRAINE WAR, DE-RISKING AND DECOUPLING

The Russian invasion of Ukraine accelerated supply chain weaponisation all around the world. In addition to cutting off exports of just about every type of meaningful technology to Russia's mining, oil and gas and armaments sector, Washington turned to another weapon: the U.S. dollar. By March 2022, the U.S. government had frozen US$38 billion of the Bank of Russia's assets in the U.S. and persuaded France, Japan, Germany, Canada, the U.K. and Austria to freeze another US$243 billion of Russia's dollar-denominated assets within their markets.[4]

Talk among the U.S. and its allies quickly turned towards the expropriation of these assets for use in the reconstruction of Ukraine.

Washington also persuaded its allies to lock selected Russian banks out of the Society for Worldwide Interbank Financial Telecommunication (SWIFT), the standardised messaging system used by financial institutions worldwide to securely exchange information about financial transactions. Getting frozen out of SWIFT can devastate a bank's basic functions and its reputation, depriving it of the trust of other institutions in the global financial network.

Blockage from SWIFT would have quickly wreaked havoc on Russia's economy if it had been applied universally to *all* Russian banks.[5] Nevertheless, the U.S. and its allies chose not to apply this option to all Russian banks because of the collateral damage it would have inflicted upon non-Russian financial institutions throughout the international financial system.

By 2023, however, the G7 nations were aggressively looking for ways to expand the number of Russian banks restricted from SWIFT, targeting those that were facilitating technology and armament sales to Russia's military establishment.

Moscow retaliated against Western sanctions by restricting flows of natural gas to Europe and banning fertiliser exports, adversely affecting global output of grain and other crops.[6] (Russia produced about 25% of the world's nitrogen fertilisers in 2022.) Meanwhile, the

Chinese government came out in support of Russia, blaming the war on the threat of NATO expansion.

Beijing increased its bilateral trade with Moscow, especially its consumption of Russian oil and gas, and stepped up military collaboration with Moscow—including live-fire drills off the coast of Japan in 2022. China's support of Russia's invasion of Ukraine helped spark a new wave of Western export controls and sanctions focused squarely on Chinese entities.

DECOUPLING FROM RUSSIA

The E.U. responded to Russian restrictions on natural gas exports by de-risking and almost entirely decoupling in record time—a feat that would have been unimaginable just a few years earlier.

When the invasion of Ukraine began in February 2022, the E.U. was importing 40% of its natural gas from Russia. Less than a year later, it managed to get through a cold winter while reducing Russia's share to just 10%.[7]

To achieve that reduction, the E.U. pursued cutbacks on domestic energy use and diversified its sources of energy. It significantly increased imports from Norway and Qatar, expanding flows through the Trans Adriatic Pipeline. It began a Herculean effort within to build up import processing infrastructure for liquid natural gas (LNG) and more than doubled its LNG imports from the U.S.[8] It turned to nuclear and coal-fired power and stepped up investment in renewable energy resources such as wind and solar power.

E.U. officials aim to stop *all* imports of Russian natural gas by 2030. Thus, what began as a European de-risking exercise has evolved into a full decoupling, at least in trade in natural gas.

E.U. officials were also able to de-risk and decouple from Russia as a source of agricultural fertiliser by teaming up with the Canadian and American governments. Their coordinated efforts to increase friendshored production of potash (a key ingredient to fertilisers) led three Canadian companies—Mosaic Company, K+S Potash Canada and Nutrien Ltd.—to announce increases in potash production at their facilities in Saskatchewan.[9]

In all these activities, the E.U. benefitted from the fact that its allies in the G7 group of countries were already grappling with the unpleasant task of a much larger de-risking and decoupling challenge: China.

DE-RISKING AND DECOUPLING FROM CHINA

In early 2021, President Biden signed an executive order to establish 'resilient' supply chains for the full range of strategic technologies, which we have come to know.[10]

Unofficially, what 'resilient' really meant was 'China-free' supply chains. Put another way, this was state-backed and state-funded decoupling.

If there had been any serious doubts about the reality of the global reorganisation of the global commercial landscape and an underlying paradigm shift to managed trade, this was a defining moment.

On the flip side, Beijing had been trying to 'de-Americanise' its strategic supply chains for years. In 2015, the Chinese leadership introduced a techno-nationalist platform called *Made in China 2025* (MIC 2025)—an aspirational manifesto that prioritised the development of key technologies for industries of the future.

When President Xi began to push the 'Made in China 2025' (MIC 2025) as a regular feature in his national speeches and party addresses, starting in 2015, it was clear that Beijing had abandoned its earlier narratives that promoted 'hide and bide' and 'peaceful rise'. MIC 2025 singled out 10 categories of technology that were vital to China's rise as a superpower.

Not surprisingly, MIC 2025 had targeted virtually all 12 categories of the critical foundational technologies of the twenty-first century, and it did so publicly with great fanfare.

MIC 2025's primary objectives were mutually reinforcing. The first was to reduce dependence on Western technology while shifting growth to China, pushing its local industries higher up the innovation and production value curve.[11] The second was to leapfrog American scientific and technological hegemony and leverage this advantage geopolitically.

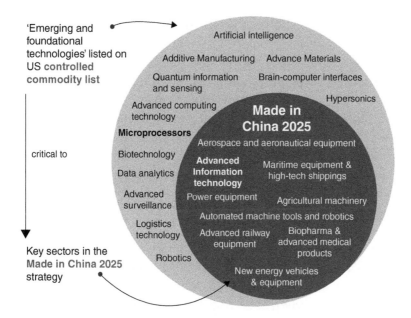

'Emerging and foundational technologies' listed on US **controlled commodity list**

critical to

Key sectors in the **Made in China 2025** strategy

Artificial intelligence

Additive Manufacturing   Advance Materials

Quantum information and sensing   Brain-computer interfaces

Hypersonics

Advanced computing technology

Made in China 2025

Microprocessors

Aerospace and aeronautical equipment

Biotechnology

Advanced Information technology   Maritime equipment & high-tech shippings

Data analytics

Advanced surveillance   Power equipment   Agricultural machinery

Logistics technology   Automated machine tools and robotics

Advanced railway equipment   Biopharma & advanced medical products

Robotics

New energy vehicles & equipment

Figure 5.1   Made-In-China 2025 List of Priority Technologies.

Although there is evidence that MIC 2025 policies achieved some remarkable successes—in high-speed rail, hypersonic propulsion, quantum communications and some applications of AI, such as facial recognition and surveillance, the CCP's proclamations of supplanting America and other tech-leading nations backfired spectacularly.

By 2018, Americans had come to describe MIC 2025 as a blatant subsidy-stuffed programme to make China a global technology leader at the expense of the U.S. This galvanised a Western paradigm shift and sparked a U.S. techno-nationalist counteroffensive.[12]

Additionally, in 2020, Beijing officially rolled out the Communist Party's 14th Five-Year Plan (2021–2025), which articulated a new policy of 'Dual Circulation'. Dual Circulation seeks to reduce China's dependence on exports and to stimulate internal demand as the primary driver of economic growth.

Dual Circulation aims to make China less vulnerable to external economic shocks and trade disruptions and to upgrade its technological capabilities. This, of course, sounds remarkably like Washington's paradigm shift and its embrace of geo-economics.

CHINA'S DE-AMERICANISATION LONG GAME

Many observers have argued that China's Dual Circulation policy was a direct response to Washington's ratcheting up of export controls on semiconductors and other critical technologies. In fact, Dual Circulation follows a long and established doctrine of selective ring-fencing practiced by China Inc. From the onset of its Open Door Policy under Deng Xiaoping in the 1980s and through the Hu Jintao years from 2002 to 2012, Beijing fastidiously ring-fenced key sectors of its economy to foreigners. Two examples are the telecommunications industry and the digital platform economy.

To those of us on the ground in China, Beijing was clearly engaging in pre-emptive decoupling and playing a long game. The question was not 'whether' but 'when' a Western backlash would occur. Nevertheless, it remains to be seen how far de-risking and decoupling will fragment the global economy or how cleanly supply chains will stratify into the three levels described above.

From a neoliberal economic perspective, all of this might seem like a doomsday scenario. But, in fact, even a bifurcated global economy— where nations reorganise perhaps a quarter of the world's trade, the global economy is still full of low-hanging fruit in terms of new trade in goods and services.

There is no simple answer to the question of whether competitive coexistence between arch-rivals like the U.S. and China can be achieved and for how long it can continue. There simply are no clear-cut models that can predict such outcomes, given the many overlapping variables at play.

Chapter 6

Export Controls

Throughout millennia, technological innovations have been closely guarded secrets, and rulers have gone to great lengths to prevent them from falling into the wrong hands. These were, in fact, the first attempts at export controls.

Knowledge about special materials, alchemy and manufacturing processes remained closely guarded secrets for centuries, but ultimately, they leached out into the global commons.

Consider two closely guarded inventions: gunpowder and the magnetic compass.

Gunpowder was invented in China around the ninth century AD, but it eventually made its way to the Middle East and Europe by the thirteenth century. Coupled with newly invented firearm technology, it would later be used to solidify European geopolitical power throughout the world.

Similarly, the Chinese invented the magnetic compass and achieved impressive feats of navigation, already by the eleventh century, but this technology also found its way to Europe by the fourteenth century.

Gunpowder and the compass both contributed to the conquests of successive European empires—from the Portuguese to the Spanish and on to the Dutch and the British. As we discussed, from this early position of advantage, over the ensuing decades and centuries, a long sequence of technology feedback loops in the West established a small group of countries as the world's top powers.

Early export controls played a role in industrial development from the eighteenth century onward, as Britain and a handful of other countries actively protected their innovations.

Export controls, for example, slowed down (but failed to stop) the unwanted sharing of technologies regarding steam power in the First Industrial Revolution and electrical motors in the Second Industrial Revolution. The same story applied to computer and satellite technology in the Third Industrial Revolution, and now, semiconductors and AI in the Fourth Industrial Revolution.

Each invention timeline follows the same pattern: Innovators protect their first-mover advantage for as long as possible, but others eventually catch up, modify or improve things and then compete against the original innovators.

From a techno-nationalist perspective the process is an all-out horse race in which each country spurs its own horse, and, if possible, its agents try to slow down the horse of its rival.[1]

The key for early adopters, then, is to protect their innovations long enough to use them as stepping stones to new breakthroughs, as quickly as possible.

In contrast with earlier periods, when closely guarded secrets could remain safely locked away for decades or even centuries, today's leading-edge technologies such as AI and, supercomputing—and eventually, practical quantum computing—facilitate very rapid transfers of technology with fast assimilation.

In this chapter, we examine the use of export controls in the modern techno-nationalist era. We focus on the structure of the current U.S. export control regime, which originally evolved during the Cold War conflict with the Soviet Union but later was transformed into a system adapted for increasingly liberalised global trade.

We reflect upon recent attempts by the U.S. Bureau of Industry and Security (BIS) to thwart the advance of China's domestic semiconductor capabilities, exploring the extent to which its approach is best suited to its objectives. In recent times, the use of export controls to stop flows of restricted technology to China, Russia and other places have, for the most part, failed.

Finally, we consider U.S. efforts to revamp the regime and build a more effective set of multilateral export controls to address today's hybrid cold war between the U.S. and China, and Russia. In many ways, efforts to reset the system mark a return to the policies of the original Cold War.

EXPORT CONTROLS IN THE MODERN ERA

An export control is a regulation that is intended to protect national security, promote foreign or domestic policy, and, in some instances, control the export of domestic items in short supply.

Broadly speaking, an export control is a kind of prohibition to transfer specific kinds of goods and technologies. This may take the form of a requirement that a prospective exporter must obtain a licence from a government agency to permit the exporter to sell, transfer or transport a product to a foreign market. The requirements may vary depending on the type of product, the intended uses of the product and the identity and location of the final buyer.

Export controls are different from sanctions. Whereas export controls involve a licensing process to assess risk and may permit exports to proceed following that assessment, sanctions impose comprehensive bans on specific transactions or activities with designated individuals, entities or countries. Sanctions, with few exceptions, eliminate legal avenues for engaging in those activities.

The complexities of U.S. export controls force American exporters to navigate a jungle of government agencies, rule frameworks and approval systems with an alphabet soup of acronyms.

Most export controls are enforced by the U.S. Department of Commerce's (DOC) Bureau of Industry and Security (BIS) under the Export Administration Regulations (EAR).

A core element of the EAR is the Commerce Control List (CCL), which classifies, goods, technology and software and stipulates the export restrictions that apply to them.

An important feature of the CCL is the concept of *dual use*, which applies to any, product, technology or software that could be converted to and used for military and other restrictive purposes. Literally thousands of dual-use products are listed on the CCL.

As an example, consider a commercial fertiliser whose chemical composition allows it to be used both for agricultural purposes and as a chemical catalyst for a bomb. Thus, certain agricultural fertilisers may require an export license. Virtually any technology, from semiconductors to cognitive machines and drones, to the everyday SIM card that we put in our mobile phones, is of a dual-use nature. One could argue that any form of intelligence—artificial or human—could be classified as dual use. Even high-performance brake pads for a private personal automobile could be used on a military vehicle, and therefore be considered dual-use.

Regulated products on the CCL are assigned a 5-digit Export Control Classification Number (ECCN) under a universal nomenclature used by many other countries. The BIS uses ECCN parameters developed by member countries of the Wassenaar Group, a consensus-based organisation of 42 countries, which is now effectively dead because of Russia's ongoing membership. In setting ECCN parameters, Wassenaar nations have worked with affected companies and other interested parties, usually though a series of industry consultations, advisory committees, regulatory petitions and technical reviews.

The U.S. and its Wassenaar allies continue to use the ECCN nomenclature but now operate with a plurilateral focus among coalitions of the willing. Thus, they can exclude Russia (for which many export controls are now aimed) and pursue their own mutually beneficial controls over technology transfer. Russia's invasion of Ukraine, as well as Washington's escalating chip wars with China, has accelerated efforts for the formation of a new multilateral export controls regime, comprised of the U.S. and its allies. We will discuss this later, in Chapter 30.

An ECCN specifies a product's general category, product grouping and sub-grouping, as well as its technical and specific parameters.

ECCNs fall under 10 general categories include Nuclear Materials and Equipment; Chemicals, Microorganisms and Toxins; Computers; Electronics; Telecommunications; Information Security, Sensors and Lasers; Navigation and Avionics; Marine Technologies; and Aerospace and Propulsion.

Because of the complexity of determining an ECCN (and the negative consequences of getting it wrong), many companies apply for formal ruling letters from the BIS or seek formal and informal advice through the government or private firms. Thus, export controls have spawned an entire industry of lawyers, customs agents and advisors.

After determining the applicable ECCN for a given product, exporters must also determine whether the destination country or end user is on any of several lists. One is the BIS Entity List—a list of companies, research institutions and universities, government entities and non-governmental organisations (NGOs) for whom an export licence is required and for which, in theory, a licence must be submitted with a 'presumption of denial.'

Another list, the 'Specially Designated Nationals' (SDN) List, applies to individual persons. Administered by the Office of Foreign Assets Control (OFAC), part of the U.S. Department of the Treasury, the SDN includes government and law enforcement officials, company owners, academics and other foreign nationals. An individual can wind up on the SDN after being designated a risk to U.S. national security for narcotics dealing, terrorism, human rights violations or association with any other sanctioned or restricted entity.

In addition, the U.S. Department of State oversees the flow of arms under International Traffic in Arms Regulations (ITAR), which applies to exports of explicitly military goods. While this book was going to press, Boeing, the American defence contractor was fined US$51 million for exports of defence articles and technical data controlled under the United States Munitions List (USML). Technical data was passed to non-U.S. persons employed by Boeing and included unauthorised exports to Russia and China.

BLACKLISTED ENTITIES

By the end of 2023, there were approximately 12,000 names on OFAC's SDN.[2] Not surprisingly, there had been a surge in Russian entities since the Ukraine invasion in 2022. This is a fluid database, with new names added every day, thus, the legal and compliance departments at any company engaged in trade of dual-use and other restricted items must be constantly vigilant.

During this same timeframe, many of the additions to the BIS Entity list were Chinese companies, individuals, universities and government agencies, which numbered over 600 by the end of 2023. This number has been steadily rising as the U.S. government focuses more intensely on China's technological and military development.

A cross-section of listed Chinese entities included Huawei Technologies Company Ltd (Huawei)—which by 2023 had become the litmus test for the effectiveness of U.S. export controls—and Hangzhou Hikvision Digital Technology Co. Ltd (Hikvision), a surveillance tech company.

High-profile individuals on the SDN list include Meng Wanzhou, chief financial officer of Huawei, who, in 2018, was placed under house arrest in Canada for almost three years, while she fought an extradition request by Washington based on alleged violations of U.S. sanctions against Iran.

Another was Carrie Lam, the Chief Executive Officer of Hong Kong from 2017 through 2022. After China rolled out its National Security Law in June of 2020, the U.S. Department of the Treasury imposed sanctions on Ms Lam and 10 other senior Chinese officials for their roles in what Washington deemed the undermining of Hong Kong's autonomy and civil freedoms.

The sanctions imposed against Ms. Lam illustrate how disruptive 'weaponised interdependence' has become.

In addition to banning her travel to the U.S. and freezing of her assets there, sanctions prevented her from using credit cards, ATMs and other banking services in Hong Kong and worldwide. No international bank would risk incurring U.S. sanctions for doing business with an individual on the SDN list (more on financial markets in Chapter 29).

Ms. Lam reportedly resorted to keeping and using large amounts of cash for daily transactions. The Hong Kong government even paid her in cash.

To underscore how disruptive and far-reaching sanctions on individuals can be, consider that while the U.S. government was drawing up the order to place Carrie Lam on sanctions, her youngest son was studying for a doctorate in mathematics at Harvard University. According to *The Standard*, a Hong Kong news publication, he returned to Hong Kong just days before the sanctions were announced.

The episode also illustrates how intertwined Hong Kong and China have become with American and Western interests, even beyond trade and commerce, and how deeply export controls and sanctions can affect the daily activities of individual citizens of any foreign country.

I should note that after Ms. Lam left office in 2022, the restrictions were lifted.

EXTRATERRITORIALITY

Under some U.S. laws, activities may trigger legal consequences even if they take place outside U.S. territorial boundaries. Such *extraterritoriality* gives U.S. officials wide latitude in regulating domestic and foreign entities or individuals who violate its export controls and sanctions.

Extraterritoriality allows the U.S. government to attempt enforcement action against a foreign company (even if it is based outside of the U.S.) that transfers U.S. controlled goods or technology to a sanctioned country or a designated individual.

One of the most compelling demonstrations of the long reach of U.S. extraterritoriality involves the Foreign Direct Product Rule (FDPR). A bit of an explanation is in order.

On a bill of materials, a wide range of input costs are included in the value of a product, including the value of labour and manufacturing costs as well as a variety of foreign-sourced inputs. Under U.S. regulations—under the old FDPR—some export licensing requirements could be triggered when the US domestic share of a foreign-manufactured product's costs pass a *de minimis* threshold, typically set at 10% or 25%, depending on the product type and destination.

After the BIS placed Huawei on its Entity List in 2019, U.S. authorities assumed that Huawei would instruct its major U.S. suppliers, including Nvidia, Broadcom and Qualcomm, to reconfigure their global supply chains to reduce the domestic percentages of American origin technology in their products so they would fall below *de minimis* thresholds—thus eliminating the requirement to obtain export licences.

U.S. officials responded by bolstering the FDPR. Under the revised law—now sometimes referred to as the *Huawei Rule*—*any* controlled U.S. technology used in the production of a finished good by *any* company *anywhere* requires the application for a U.S. export licence.[3] The Huawei rule has been extended to other specifically targeted companies, and to Russia entities, in general.

At the time, because of these changes, Taiwan Semiconductor Manufacturing Company (TSMC), the key supplier of Huawei's leading-edge chips for its 5G wireless infrastructure and smartphones, simply stopped supplying Huawei.

Why? TSMC relied upon U.S. origin chip-manufacturing equipment made by American companies, including Applied Materials, Lam Research and KLA-Tencor.

This meant that TSMC needed an export licence to sell its chips manufactured in Taiwan to Huawei. And Washington said it would deny the licence.

As part of its enforcement of the revamped FDPR, moreover, the U.S. applied heavy diplomatic pressure to Japan and the Netherlands, urging them to implement domestic export controls that would restrict similar technology flows to China. That pressure directly affected ASML, the Dutch producer of cutting-edge photolithography machines that use extreme ultraviolet light to etch tiny circuits onto silicon wafers. As we will discuss in Chapter 8, this is a vital stage of chip production.

For the time being, Washington had placed a chokehold on Huawei's supply chains. After burning through stockpiles of TSMC-fabricated chips, Huawei's smartphones could no longer feature 5G capability.

The company lost market share quickly for its smartphones and 5G wireless infrastructure services and was forced to rethink its business model. Forging partnerships with Chinese companies Chery Auto and BAIC Motor, Huawei moved into the electric vehicle (EV) niche, providing technologies which it could produce using older generations of microchips that were not subject to U.S. export controls.

Huawei also reoriented its focus towards Cloud-based services, a subject to which we will return to later.

Huawei has proven to be remarkably resilient and continues to grow its market share and its profits around new technologies and strategic partnerships, with heavy backing and funding from the Chinese government.

In October of 2022 and again in October of 2023, the U.S. DOC released two more rounds of export controls that expanded restrictions on older, trailing-edge chips and chip-making technology impacting the 14nm node threshold (which at the time was already about one- decade-old technology). In 2024, under considerable pressure from private industry, Washington pledged to carve out exemptions for older legacy chips and stated that it would not expand its controls to the 28nm node—which represented even older but still vitally important technology.

But, on the world stage, these actions had already set the core elements of techno-nationalism into hyperdrive: supply chain weaponisation, decoupling, reshoring and ring-fencing, innovation competition, techno-diplomacy and trade-craft (the theft of secrets).

The 2023 round of U.S. export controls had also blocked U.S. citizens from working with blacklisted Chinese companies or with any company, US or foreign, that serviced them.

By 2024, Washington's export control offensive had sparked a full-blown Chinese techno-nationalist counteroffensive. Huawei's in-house chip design subsidiary, HiSilicon, would double down on its semiconductor design capabilities and would partner with a host of other heavily funded players like Semiconductor Manufacturing International Corporation (SMIC), as it became a major cog in China's quest for tech self-sufficiency. This applied across a range a strategic MIC 2025 industries.[4]

More broadly, Huawei became the poster child of Beijing's 'Dual-Circulation' policies, which aim to boost domestic consumption through self-reliance and self-sufficiency across key industries, while beefing up China's high value export platforms.

We will do a deep dive into Huawei in Chapter 11.

WORKAROUNDS, LOOPHOLES AND BACKDOORS

In August 2023, less than three years after Washington's revamping of the FDPR, Huawei announced the Mate 60, a new phone that essentially leapfrogged 5G technology, providing high-speed broadband Internet access via satellite-enabled connectivity. Within eight weeks of its launch, the Mate 60 series had sold 2.4 million units.

The Mate 60 featured the Kirin 9000S, a 7-nanometre (nm) chip designed by HiSilicon, and manufactured by SMIC, China's champion chip maker.

Mass production of a leading-edge 7-nm chip appeared to be a major accomplishment, requiring sophisticated deep ultraviolet (DUV) equipment that most observers considered China to be years or even decades from mastering—assuming that the DUV equipment to make Kirin 9000S chips was not actually of foreign origin.

Shortly thereafter, SMIC and Huawei announced the rollout of an even more advanced chip, the 5-nm Kirin 9000C, which would go into Huawei's Qingyun L540 laptops—not long after, however, a teardown of the L540 by TechInsights, a research firm specialising in semiconductors, revealed that the 5-nm chip had been made by Taiwan's TSMC. SMIC had likely stockpiled TSMC's chips prior to U.S. export restrictions taking effect or had obtained them by circumventing existing restrictions.

All the same, SMIC's 7-nm chip achievement appeared to validate the claim, made by many observers, that U.S. export controls had failed.

More to the point, they said, Washington's weaponisation of supply chains had simply caused China to speed up its efforts to 'de-Americanise' and achieve self-sufficiency. Huawei's milestones called into question both the effectiveness of U.S. processes around export controls and the institutions that had been charged with enforcing them.

By late 2023, the U.S. Congress was churning out reports on how to address this problem. First, a study from House Foreign Affairs Committee Chairman, Michael McCaul (R-Texas), openly criticised the BIS as being too commercially focused.

Soon after, the House Select Committee on China's Communist Party issued a study that called for revamping the BIS and the export control process in general. The aim was to repurpose and retool the agency to focus primarily on national security and even to move it directly under the purview of the defence establishment.

The committee report also called for the U.S. and its closest allies to establish a multilateral regime of export controls to better monitor and enforce tech transfer restrictions. At the very least, Washington would have to have to pull together a 'mini-lateral' coalition with its closest allies.

HIGH APPROVAL RATES, LONG GRACE PERIODS AND BINGE-BUYING

From a critic's point of view, the BIS had been functioning largely to serve business interests. This was borne out, for example, in the number of export licences that continued to be approved for Huawei even after it had been placed on the Entity List in 2019.

According to research published by the Center for Strategic and International Studies (CSIS), the U.S. government approved approximately 30% of export licence applications for Huawei in 2022. Admittedly, this was down from a nearly 70% approval rate between November 2020 and April 2021, when U.S. suppliers to Huawei received 113 licences worth US$61 billion.[5]

As for sales to SMIC, the BIS had approved 188 licences valued at nearly US$42 billion, including licences to such noteworthy U.S. companies as Intel, Qualcomm and Micron, who continued to sell a wide variety of technologies, including semiconductors, software and other components.

Looking at this approval rate from a business standpoint, it is easy to see what was at stake for corporate America. It had taken years to establish market presence in China, which despite ongoing geopolitical conflicts, is likely to remain the world's single-largest market for semiconductors for years to come. For such companies, preserving market share is critical.

In 2022, for example, well after the BIS had imposed its severest restrictions on tech exports, around 60% of Qualcomm's annual revenue still came from China.[6]

For MNEs like Qualcomm or Nvidia, then, an important part of their 'in-China-for-China' strategy involves working the BIS export control system to their advantage for as long as possible. For them, Washington's paradigm shift calls for urgent damage control.

There was even an oft-cited, quirky argument at the BIS that held that prolonging sales of American technology to companies like Huawei and SMIC would tend to keep them dependent on the U.S., which would slow China's efforts to achieve self-sufficiency.

The same logic justified granting licences under the FDPR to South Korean, Japanese and Taiwanese chip companies, as it was always better if U.S. allies sold legacy products to China than if China advanced its own domestic capabilities. This would slow down China's proverbial horse while the U.S. and its allies worked to speed up their own.

Back on Capitol Hill, U.S. policymakers criticised the BIS for the lengthy, multiple stages of its rulemaking process, which included a public proposal period, a public comment period, a final rule publication and eventual implementation.

The process was designed to be both transparent and inclusive, with BIS encouraging the trade community to provide recommendations and healthy objections to the formulation of export controls. The process encouraged potential targets to engage lobbyists to push back on potentially damaging restrictions. Over decades, an entire cottage industry of lawyers, lobbyists and professional advisors gravitated to this process, turning it into a cash cow.

The long timeframe also allowed potentially affected companies to stock up on products before restrictions went into effect. In 2023, for example, while the BIS was mulling new restrictions on AI chips, the Chinese company 01.AI bought an 18-month supply of Nvidia's high-end A100 chips before the export restrictions went into effect.[7]

As new restrictions for AI chips came under consideration, Chinese tech firms ordered a further US$5 billion in stock from Nvidia, the American firm that held an incredible 90% of global market capacity in such technology.[8]

Motivated by SMIC's triumphant announcement of 7-nm chip capabilities, within the 30-day timeframe of November 2023, Chinese firms reportedly registered a sudden 1050% increase over the previous year's same timeframe, in the import of foreign DUV chip-making tools.[9]

Virtually all of the above manufacturing equipment—made by ASML, Tokyo Electron or Canon—involved older photolithography technology for trailing-edge 28-nm chips and above and was legal at the time under U.S. controls.

CLOUD ACCESS, THIRD-PARTY BACKDOORS AND BLACK MARKETS

There were other gaping loopholes. It emerged in 2023 that Chinese intelligence agencies and restricted entities such as SenseTime (which made facial recognition AI) and iFlyTec (which made voice recognition AI) were gaining access to Nvidia's leading-edge A100 chips through third-party cloud-based computing companies, including Chinese companies Alibaba Cloud or Tencent Cloud.[10] This workaround had been flying under the BIS' radar for at least a year before U.S officials began looking to prevent this practice. But Washington's efforts were mostly aimed at preventing foreign companies from using U.S. cloud services to train their LLMs. Washington had less leverage over foreign cloud services that had obtained top-end US AI chips.

Even though SenseTime and iFlyTec were on the BIS Entity List and restricted from purchasing actual Nvidia chips, they were simply renting time on third parties' computer clusters that contained Nvidia's chips and using them to train their own AI and machine-learning algorithms.[11]

Restricted entities were also gaining backdoor access to controlled U.S. technology through other countries, especially through academic and research institutions that host students and scholars with potential links to restricted entities.

In 2023, for example, reports appeared that Saudi Arabia's King Abdullah University of Science and Technology (KAUST) was conducting research and training an LLM called AceGPT.[12] It turned out that numerous faculty and PhD researchers were Chinese nationals.

Other workarounds included good old-fashioned grey-market and black-market sales. Grey markets involve trade of goods through unauthorised channels or unofficial distribution channels, including the sale of products intended for one market which are then routed to another market where they are not authorised for sale. A black market, by contrast, refers to illegal or underground trade in prohibited or restricted products.

In 2024, on the black market, an Nvidia H100 AI chip could fetch a price of around US$67,000, more than 20 times the cost of what it costs Nvidia to make the chip—around US$3,200. Legitimate retail prices at the time for the H100 were between US$25,000 to US$40,000, representing a profit for Nvidia of around 1000 percent.

Buyers in grey and black markets tend to be app developers, researchers, gamers and start-ups who can procure advanced chips in small numbers with relative ease. The main black-market conduits of American AI chips, for example, include Taiwan, South Korea, India and Singapore, and come from excess stock associated with locally incorporated companies. Middleman use social-commerce platforms and forums, including eBay, to conduct business.

In early 2024, South Korean customs officials busted a two-man smuggling operation that used a distribution company to funnel 53,000 chips subject to export restrictions on to China. 'Company A,' as it was called, sent almost 150 shipments of chips, worth around US$12 million, in small batches to different recipients in China.[13]

Russia, meanwhile, after its invasion of Ukraine and the imposition of sanctions on Moscow by the U.S. and the E.U., continues to illicitly obtain restricted semiconductors for its war efforts. In 2023, Russia reportedly imported more than US$1 billion in advanced chips made by Intel Corp, Advanced Micro Devices (AMD), Infineon Technologies AG, ST Microelectronics NV (ST) and NXP Semiconductors NV (NXP). Advanced chips made by these companies went into Russian missiles, tanks and other components of its weapons systems.[14]

None of these American and European companies broke any laws or intentionally evaded export controls. Russia's military and state apparatus simply obtained these chips on the black market. They availed themselves of a dark market and logistics network that transhipped the chips via third countries, including China, Turkey and the United Arab Emirates.

Considering all these things, export controls are hardly making a dent in the transfer of technology to adversaries. What is needed, then, is a rethink and overhaul of the export regime itself by Washington and its allies.

A REVAMPED, MULTILATERAL EXPORT CONTROL REGIME

Negative Congressional assessments of the American export control process reflect the broader paradigm shift with respect to China.

By 2023, policymakers were calling for combining BIS staff with defence and intelligence personnel, or even moving the BIS out of the Commerce Department and moving it entirely under the U.S. defence umbrella. This would follow similar trends in research and development spending, which Congress has increasingly directed to the Defense Advanced Research Projects Agency (DARPA) and other defence-related entities.

Under the new paradigm, *any* transfer of strategic technology to China should be considered support for Beijing's civil–military fusion initiatives. Thus, in a complete turnaround, bipartisan members of Congress are calling for export licence applications to be approached with a constant presumption of denial. Such an approach could accelerate de-risking and decoupling and will accelerate bifurcation of American and Chinese supply chains.

But for this to occur, enforcement activities will have to be ramped up and hefty punishments meted out to violators. U.S. officials have begun to act: in April of 2023, two subsidiaries of Seagate Technology Holdings PLC (Seagate), the American data storage equipment provider, were slapped with US$300 million for selling hard drives to Huawei, despite existing export restrictions.

In February of 2024, in a federal criminal investigation, the U.S. sent multiple subpoenas to Applied Materials (AMAT) the American semiconductor manufacturing equipment and tool maker, for allegedly transferring technology to China's leading chip foundry, SMIC. AMAT allegedly transshipped controlled technology, without obtaining an export license, to SMIC via South Korea.[15]

Finally, in the area of techno-diplomacy, members of Congress have called for the establishment of a multilateral export control regime involving the U.S. and like-minded allies.

No country, not even the U.S., can maintain exclusive control over a strategic technology. Washington needs its allies and strategic partners to assist in enforcing its export controls, as is the case with establishing resilient supply chains and 'friend-shoring' initiatives around manufacturing. This required the cooperation of the world's liberal democracies.

To prosecute its chip war, Washington will need close coordination and collaboration with the other 'Group of five' semiconductor leaders, which include Japan, South Korea, Taiwan, and the Netherlands.

Regarding the other core power-multiplying technologies, a multilateral organisation would also need to include the traditional members of the 5 Eyes intelligence network: The U.S., U.K., Canada, Australia and New Zealand.

Other 'middle country' strategic partners, include up and coming centres of technological development such as India, Israel and Singapore, which would likely be pulled in as well.

As a source of inspiration in designing a multilateral system, U.S. policymakers have turned to a defunct institution from the Cold War—the Coordinating Committee for Multilateral Export Controls (COCOM).

Established by the U.S. and 16 other Western countries in 1949, the COCOM group enforced strict export controls on items with potential military applications, such as advanced electronics, advanced materials and aerospace technologies. It was primarily focused on maintaining a technological advantage for Western countries and preventing the transfer of critical technology that could bolster the military capabilities of the Soviet Union and its Warsaw Pact allies.

COCOM was disbanded in 1994, after the end of the Cold War, and in 1996, the Wassenaar Arrangement on Export Controls for Conventional Arms and Dual-Use Goods and Technologies was established.

With 42 member countries, the Wassenaar Arrangement has adopted the broader mission of promoting transparency and responsibility in the export of conventional arms and dual-use goods and technologies.

Unlike the COCOM, whose members were legally obligated to adhere to the export control restrictions imposed by the committee, Wassenaar operates on a voluntary basis. While participating countries commit to implementing its guidelines and principles, there is an emphasis on recognising and promoting legitimate commercial interests.

The Wassenaar Arrangement functions as a multilateral forum where participating states exchange information on export controls, share best practices and coordinate efforts to prevent illicit transfers. The forum also publishes the Dual-Use List and Military Lists which are an integral resource for both the public and private sectors.

As a post-Cold War forum, Wassenaar was tailored to the needs of nations engaged in trade liberalisation , and is not particularly suited to the circumstances of the hybrid cold war.

Russia is currently a member of Wassenaar, which has undermined the spirit and practical function of the institution. Thus, it seems two things will need to happen if Washington and its allies are to build a new multilateral export controls regime.

First, smaller coalitions of the willing will need to emerge that feature, for example, the Group of Five plus a few others. These smaller groups of countries could adopt more binding COCOM-like restrictions.

Secondly, if a new and improved 'Wassenaar 2.0' is to emerge, its members, at the very least, will need to vote to expel Russia.

Chapter 7

Semiconductor Ground Zero

It has become a cliché to say that semiconductors are the heart and brains of all modern technologies. But it is true.

In 2021, an estimated 900 billion microchips were produced and shipped worldwide, going into virtually every kind of product from coffee makers and automobiles to advanced fighter jets.[1] Those numbers are increasing rapidly as we produce 'smart' things that generate more data and are linked through a growing number of connections and networks.

By 2030, it is estimated that some 5 *trillion* microchips will find their way into our everyday devices, making semiconductors, by far, the most widely produced and consumed commodity ever.

In modern society, semiconductors have become as much a utility as water, electricity and transportation infrastructure. Governments must assure constant access to them if they are to govern effectively and maintain stable and productive economies and societies.

Also referred to as 'microchips' or 'chips,' semiconductors are essential for advancements in artificial intelligence (AI) in all its manifestations, including machine learning and neural networks. But they are also the ground-zero technology for the other twelve twenty-first century foundational technologies.

CHIP-CENTRIC GEOPOLITICS

Chips enable both commercial and military functionality. Therefore, U.S. policymakers have resorted to everything in their techno-nationalist toolbox to maintain and extend American chip-tech advantages. Beijing, meanwhile, has been pouring resources into developing its own capabilities through its chip-related 'new whole-nation system' and a slew of other big-spending initiatives.

Washington has attempted to weaponise supply chains by choking off access to American chip design software and manufacturing equipment. This goes hand-in-glove with the 're-shoring' of chip fabrication back to the U.S. through initiatives such as the CHIPS and Science Act, which, in 2022, allocated US$52 billion—paid out over years, with more funding rounds likely to come.

Additionally, U.S. policymakers have doubled down on tech-diplomacy, seeking to persuade the other Group of Five countries (the group consists of America, Japan, Taiwan, South Korea and the Netherlands) to support and enact U.S. extraterritorial chip-related laws against China, Russia and other targeted entities.

By 2022, 'chip war' (a term popularised by Chris Miller and his book with the same title) had become one of the most prominent news stories on the planet. Every major media outlet now dedicates ongoing coverage to the geopolitics of semiconductors.

We must start the discussion of semiconductors, then, by asking what they are and what they do. We also need to appreciate the complexity of chip supply chains and understand why certain elements within them have been turned into techno-nationalist choke points.

As importantly, we need to understand the relevance of 'Moore's Law' regarding leading-edge chips. This will set us up for the discussion in

Chapter 8, which focuses on China's chip landscape, its challenges and where it appears to be heading.

Meanwhile, older-generation chip technologies remain highly relevant and geopolitically important. We will discuss them at length both in Chapter 8 and in Chapter 9, where we explore the re-shoring of chip fabrication to America.

WHAT ARE SEMICONDUCTORS?

The fabrication of a state-of-the-art microchip represents, perhaps, the greatest technological achievement of humankind. It has ushered in the second machine age and in doing so has increased the power-multiplying dynamics of history's technology feedback loop.

The process of mass-producing, for example, a 5-nm chip with low margins of error is an extraordinarily complex, knowledge-intensive engineering feat.

Many metaphors have been used to describe the degree of difficulty of the advanced chip manufacturing process. Imagine, for example, driving a car in a perfectly straight line, not allowing it to deviate one single *micrometre* to the left, right, up or down, while en route from New York to Los Angeles on a curvy, bumpy road—covering a distance of about 4,500 kilometres. Or consider a laser beam being aimed from the Moon to Earth's surface to etch a detailed image on a tiny coin. Those comparisons only begin to illustrate the complexity of designing and fabricating leading-edge, or even older 'trailing edge, semiconductors.

Only a small number of countries and multinational companies can compete in this dynamic environment, where R&D costs can run into the billions of dollars annually. The cost of an automated, AI-enabled factory that makes leading-edge chips, for example, can run upwards of US$20 billion and require 'clean-rooms' that are 100,000 times more sterile than the typical hospital environment.

Just as importantly, the know-how to build and run a foundry represents a massive barrier to entry, even for those looking to build a less expensive (US$1–2 billion) chip 'fab' to produce semiconductors using 15 or 20-year-old technology.

A semiconductor is a material that provides conductivity between an insulator and other materials. There are three types of semiconductors: discrete, integrated circuits (ICs) and optoelectronics.

Discrete semiconductors contain only one transistor. ICs contain multiple transistors, while optoelectronics detect and generate light pulses.

ICs make up the great majority of chips and are often the technology that is referred to as 'semiconductors' in the press and academic journals. In this book, I use the terms 'integrated circuits', 'chips', 'microchips' and 'semiconductors' interchangeably.

What makes the science behind these microchips so impressive is the extraordinarily small size at which these tiny devices perform their functions—a feature that we will expand upon shortly.

It is important to distinguish between the different kinds of ICs, which include *memory* chips, which store data; *logic* chips, which perform 'logic gate' operations to execute functions and *analogue* chips, which, as Chris Miller would say, 'convert real world signals into 1s and 0s'.

Most semiconductors are made primarily of silicon, and these are often referred to as silicon semiconductors or traditional semiconductors. Silicon is the most widely used semiconductor material due to its abundance, reliability and well-understood manufacturing processes.

In contrast, compound semiconductors are made from two or more elements, and they can include materials such as gallium arsenide (GaAs), silicon carbide (SiC) and indium gallium nitride (InGaN). These more complex materials offer unique electrical and optical properties that make them well-suited for specialised applications, such as high-frequency electronics, high-temperature environments and optoelectronics.

From both a technical and geopolitical perspective, any discussion of semiconductors comes down to the distinction between leading-edge chips (at the time of this writing, 10 nanometres and below) and older trailing-edge chips (typically greater than 28 nanometres). This is a very important distinction, as they represent very different markets from a strategic point of view.

SEMICONDUCTOR GLOBAL VALUE CHAINS

Semiconductor value chains have grown to become hyper-specialised, with different activities dispersed around the planet. As companies respond to fundamental economic incentives, semiconductor supply chains have evolved organically to locate different processes in the most efficient and favourable environments.

There are four basic stages in a semiconductor value chain:

- Research and Development
- Design
- Manufacturing
- Assembly, Testing and Packaging (ATP), also called 'Outsourced, Assembly and Testing' (OSAT)

Within these niches, participants in semiconductor production fall into four broad categories:

IDM – A small number of companies—the integrated device manu-facturers (IDMs) such as Intel, Samsung and Micron—are vertically integrated and can perform all phases of production in-house. Samsung, for example, makes chips primarily for its own branded products and finished goods such as smartphones and TVs.

Intel, by comparison, supplies chips to different parties both as an IDM and as a 'foundry.' The distinction comes down to whether Intel is producing chips based on its own designs or if it is produc-ing chips on a contract basis for third party chip-designer customers.

Fabless – In a distinct niche, 'fabless' companies focus on the research and design of semiconductors, using the electronic design and automation (EDA) software tools needed to design ICs. These companies, such as Apple, Qualcomm and Nvidia, do not do any manufacturing; instead, they outsource this activity to chip foundries.

Foundries – A foundry, also called a 'fab' specialises in manufactur-ing chips. Taiwan Semiconductor Manufacturing Company (TSMC), for example, is the world's largest and most advanced 'pure play' contract manufacturer of chips. Others include Global Foundries, the American stalwart, and China's Semiconductor Manufacturing International Corporation (SMIC). A foundry produces chips under contract with other fabless companies, and does not design its own chips, but IDMs such as Intel and Samsung can both design and fabricate their own chips in-house.

Semiconductor Equipment Companies – These companies provide the critical manufacturing equipment and specialised tooling that foundries need to manufacture chips. The leading semiconductor equipment providers include Applied Materials, and Lam Research in the U.S., Japan's Tokyo Electron and the Dutch company, ASML.

OEM/ODM – At the end of its journey through the semiconductor global value chain, a microchip is delivered to an original equipment manufacturer (OEM) or original design manufacturer (ODM), such as Apple, Oracle, BMW or Airbus, to be incorporated into anything from a smartphone to an autonomous vehicle, IT infrastructure or aircraft navigation software.

MOORE'S LAW

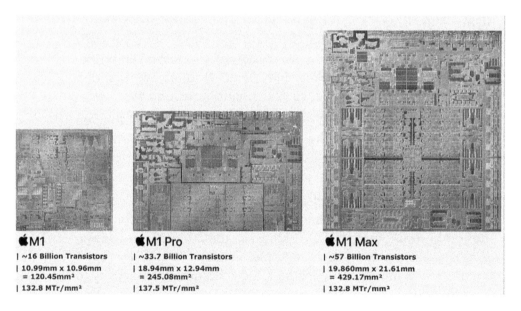

⌘M1

| ~16 Billion Transistors
| 10.99mm x 10.96mm
  = 120.45mm²
| 132.8 MTr/mm²

⌘M1 Pro

| ~33.7 Billion Transistors
| 18.94mm x 12.94mm
  = 245.08mm²
| 137.5 MTr/mm²

⌘M1 Max

| ~57 Billion Transistors
| 19.860mm x 21.61mm
  = 429.17mm²
| 132.8 MTr/mm²

Figure 7.1   Apple's Chips Stacked with Billions of Transistors.

From the mid-1960s, the number of transistors on a microchip doubled roughly every year, making semiconductors exponentially more powerful, even as their size continually diminished. A chip's power consumption also became increasingly more efficient with diminishment in size.

By the mid-1970s, as chips grew continually smaller and more power-ful, the timeline between one chip generation and the next increased to about two years.

This phenomenon became known as 'Moore's Law,' named after Gordon Moore, who cofounded Fairchild Semiconductor in 1957 and Intel in 1968. It was Mr. Moore who identified the inverse relationship between size reductions and the doubling of power of a semicon-ductor, and, in 1965, he famously predicted the phenomenon would continue thanks to ongoing advances in microelectronics, comput-ing, and manufacturing capabilities. He was right.

As the microchip continued to advance, so did other fields of science and technology. Moore's law and the advancement of semiconduc-tors enabled, for example, NASA's 'Moonshot' missions, and ongo-ing progress in computing, telecommunications, medicine, energy and other foundational technologies.

Nearly 60 years after Moore's prediction, the semiconductor industry has continued to achieve this remarkable feat. Engineers have man-aged to pack more and more tiny transistors the size of the nucleotides in the human genome onto surface areas measured in nanometres.

Let us put this feat into perspective. One nanometre is one *billionth* of a meter. Regarding measurement, we are talking about feature sizes on a chip that are at an atomic scale.

This astounding miniaturisation of components continues to expo-nentially *increase* the computational power of microprocessors. A 5-nm chip, for example, can contain *tens of billions of transistors*. With a 3-nm or 2-nm manufacturing process, we can expect even higher transistor densities, reaching *hundreds of billions* on a single chip.

As a frame-of-reference, consider that one strand of human DNA measures in at about 2.5-nm. The SARs-CoV-2 virus which caused the COVID-19 pandemic, measures between 50 nm–140 nm. A grain of sand measures in at a colossal 500,000 nm.

Even at the nano-level, engineers have built 3-dimesional mechanisms, atom-by-atom, called 'gates', which function as on–off switches in a transistor, regulating the flow of electric current, which, in turn, enables a chip's functions of sending, receiving, and processing bits and bytes of data. Each gate may turn on and off a billion times in one second![2]

Building a single functional prototype leading-edge chip represents an awesome achievement. But creating the technology to mass-produce these things, at large economies of scale, represents something even more incredible.

As our greatest techno-economic breakthrough, this development has changed humanity on a magnitude even greater than the invention of electricity, or the splitting of the atom, which unleashed the power of nuclear weapons.

In 2023, TSMC reportedly began developing chips in the range of 2 nm and even 1.4 nm, with 200 billion transistors on a single piece of silicon. The company aims to start mass production in 2030.

Achieving this level of sophistication requires decades of acquired legacy knowledge and installed resources, which creates almost impossibly high barriers-to-entry for laggards and newcomers.

As Moore's Law approaches its eventual endpoint, when chips simply cannot get any smaller, the high R&D costs required for the next generation of breakthroughs will weed out all but a small group of players. And the timeframes needed to achieve new milestones will get longer—at least until the next revolution in advanced materials and nanotechnology, which will be driven by even more powerful computing and AI.

Innovation will occur through strategic public–private partnerships that are increasingly funded by governments. This is likely to further concentrate power in a few clusters. This ecosystem features fabless companies like Qualcomm and Nvidia; IDMs like Intel, Samsung and Micron; foundries like TSMC; and manufacturing equipment-tool makers like ASML and Applied Materials.

These big players are among the few that can afford the prohibitive costs (even after government subsidies) of dominating their respective niches while simultaneously partnering with other equally dominant niche players throughout the semiconductor value chain.

Consider that in 2023, TSMC, Intel and Samsung laid out US$97 billion in capital expenditures, much of it aimed at innovation, which is more than double what the European Union earmarked for public funding of its chips initiatives over a decade.[3]

The concentration of wealth and power within the semiconductor industry is the result of a technology feedback loop that behaves like the 'network effect' in the platform economy, which has conferred disproportionate power to tech leviathans such as Amazon, Google and Meta.

Applied Materials, Nvidia, Intel, Broadcom, Qualcomm, AMD, and Texas Instruments (all American) comprised 7 out of 10 of the world's largest semiconductor companies by market capitalisation in 2023. TSMC, of Taiwan, South Korea's Samsung and ASML of the Netherlands rounded out the list.

This is significant because these companies, which represent fabless chip designers, manufacturing equipment and tool makers, pure play foundries and integrated design manufacturers, are often each other's best and only qualified customers.

As Moore's laws pushes the boundaries of innovation, only very deep-pocket clients—which are also R&D collaborators—capable of spending billions of dollars can get in on the action. Others simply cannot afford the prohibitively high costs. Not surprisingly, the 'Magnificent 7' list of clients—Apple, Alphabet (the parent of Google), Amazon, Meta, Microsoft, Nvidia and Tesla, have become coveted customers, and are enmeshed in this exclusive feedback loop.

An important question, then, is whether China, which still lags in leading edge chip capabilities, will be able to catch up in the proverbial innovation horse race. As Moore's law slows down the leaders of the pack, so the narrative goes, China will gradually gain ground and possibly even surpass the leaders.

This remains to be seen, for reasons we will discuss, below. As Washington and its allies double down on spending for techno-nationalist initiatives, and they pursue joint strategies to keep Chinese firms outside of their small yard with-a-high-fence, Chinese firms could continue to struggle to catch up.

CHIP-MANUFACTURING CHOKE POINTS

The fabrication of a microchip is part of a complex process that undergoes about a dozen basic steps, each of which features other highly specialised technology niches within.

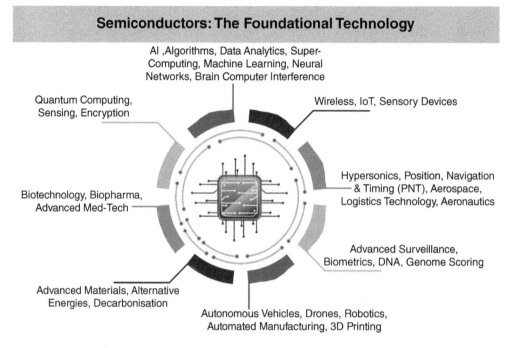

Figure 7.2   Semiconductors: The Foundational Technologies.

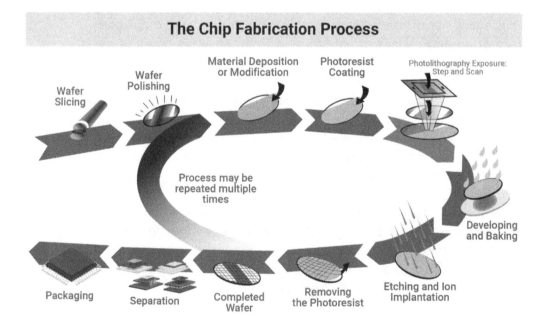

Figure 7.3   The Chip Manufacturing Process.

Figure 7.4   ASML DUV Photolithography Machine.

Figure 7.5   ASML EUV Photolithography Machine.

From a techno-nationalist perspective, certain elements of the chip fabrication value chain receive an inordinate amount of attention. These include the *photolithography* process, the *etching* process and, more recently, the *packaging* process (which is a lot more complicated than it may sound). Increasingly, the focus has turned to specialised chemicals, gases and materials used in the fabrication process.

A handful of elite American, European and Japanese companies exert almost total dominance in these niches. As we just discussed, Washington and other governments have, therefore, been attempting to use export controls and other restrictions to weaponise these technologies, turning them into supply-chain choke points.

Photolithography includes deep ultraviolet (DUV) and extreme ultraviolet (EUV) processes that create highly precise, detailed circuit patterns on silicon wafers based on specific chip designs. These processes determine the number of tiny transistors that can be placed on an individual chip.

DUV lithography has been the workhorse of the semiconductor industry for many years, enabling the production of chips with increasingly tiny feature sizes and higher transistor densities. In DUV lithography, short-wavelength ultraviolet light is used to transfer circuit patterns from a photomask onto a wafer.

EUV lithography represents a major advance over DUV, enabling the production of chips with extremely small transistor sizes and complex circuitry, creating greater transistor densities that can also integrate more functionality into a smaller chip area.

EUV lithography reduces the need for complex and costly multi-patterning techniques for single-digit nanometre chips. For larger geometry chips the DUV process works fine, with no need for multilayering—which is an important distinction that we must keep in mind when we examine China's quest to push the limits of existing DUV technology to build its own indigenous leading edge chips.

It is possible to use older trailing-edge DUV technology to produce 7-nm and possibly even 5-nm chips through what is sometimes referred to as a 'poor man's' process that comes with increased costs, more cycle times and lower yield due to the need for multiple exposures in the photolithography process. However, EUV technology is imperative to produce advanced microchips below the 5-nm node.

At the time of this writing, the Dutch company ASML totally dominated the market for both DUV and EUV machines.

ASML's high-numerical aperture (NA) EUV machines, which allow for greater light beam precision, cost around US$300 million each.

When fully assembled, these machines are the size of a large truck. Shipping one from ASMLs factory in Veldhoven requires 250 crates that fill up 13 large shipping containers.[4]

ASML sold its first NA EUV to Intel in 2023 and it is expected to enter production in 2026 or 2027.

Because of geopolitics, however, ASML's EUV technology has been denied to China. Under pressure from Washington, in 2019, the Dutch government rejected ASML's export licence for an order of EUV equipment placed by SMIC, China's leading foundry. ASML continued to obtain export licences for sales of DUV machines, at least for the 28-nm feature size and above, at the time of this writing.

If Beijing is to compete in the AI race—which is pushing the innovation envelope for every other field, commercially and militarily—it must overcome its lack of semiconductor prowess in the leading-edge portion of the market.

A second important chip-making chokepoint involves deposition and etching technologies as well as inspection and metrology tools. This critical equipment is also controlled by a small group of companies within the Group of Five countries, all of which can be called liberal democracies and U.S. allies.

Applied Materials (AMAT), an American company, specialises in chemical vapour deposition (CVD) tools and ion implantation systems. Both technologies are used at different stages of the chip fabrication process and, for now, AMAT, like ASML has a virtual monopoly in its niche.

Another American company, Lam Research, is a global leader in etch tools and wafer-cleaning systems, while KLA, also American, excels in defect inspection and metrology equipment, which is used for precise measurements and calibration.

Those three American companies compete with just a handful of players from Japan, South Korea and Taiwan, all of which are members of the Chip 4 Alliance, Washington's brainchild for multilateral security partnerships and supply-chain resilience.

In Japan, Tokyo Electron is a potential competitor of AMAT and Lam Research in the deposition, etch and cleaning tools space, but increased coordination and cooperation between Tokyo and Washington around defence matters will likely see to it that Tokyo will impose similar export restrictions on chip technologies regarding China.

In South Korea, Hanwha Techwin offers CVD, etch and cleaning tools, along with inspection systems. Samsung Electronic Materials, meanwhile, primarily supplies internal needs for Samsung's chip production. They also supply other customers with some equipment, including deposition and etch tools, but their direct competition with other major manufacturers is limited.

In Taiwan, United Microelectronics Corporation (UMC) is primarily a foundry but also develops deposition and etch tools for specific materials used in advanced chips. Finally, Yuanta ETCH manufactures dry etching equipment and competes with Lam Research and Applied Materials in specific applications.

Thus, export controls around chip-manufacturing equipment require the cooperation of only a very small group of companies. Here, techno-diplomacy has played an important role in Washington's weaponisation of chip supply chains to China and its push for a multilateral regime of export controls among its strategic allies.

Finally, there are the chemicals and specialised materials. These include so called high purity chemicals (HPC) needed throughout the chip fabrication process, such as dopants, etching materials, gases and cleaning agents, as well as special photoresist materials.

Here, again, Japanese, European and American companies control this vital alchemy. For example, Merck, of Germany, Entegris, the American company, and Japan's Kanto Denka Kogyo Co. are HPC suppliers. For etching gases, France's Air Liquide, and Nihon Sanso Corporation of Japan are among a handful of suppliers, while for photoresists, Merck, and a collection of other German companies, as well as handful of Japanese companies, control these flows.

Meanwhile, for photoresist supply, JSR and Tokyo Ohka Kogyo Co. (TOK) collectively have the largest market share.

If Washington hopes to restrict the flows of these critical elements, they will need the cooperation and coordination of their European and Japanese allies. U.S. enforcement of export controls, then, will be susceptible to all the challenges we discussed in Chapter 7.

PACKAGING

One rapidly developing area of the semiconductor fabrication process, packaging, has been pulled into the techno-nationalist arena. Packaging is the process of enclosing and protecting IC chips while providing electrical connections to external circuits.

In the chip manufacturing process, breakthroughs have been driving huge improvements in miniaturisation using technologies like three-dimensional (3D) packaging, which stacks chips vertically as well as horizontally.

Chip packaging has lower barriers to entry compared to what is needed to create and operate niche technologies used in the traditional chip fabrication process. As such, some argue that advanced chip packaging can achieve chip performance on par with today's leading edge chips, possibly down to the 5 nm size or even below. Those trailing in the general chip race, then, could potentially close the performance gap by maximising the benefits of packaging.

When individual semiconductor devices, or die, are 'stacked' vertically in a single chip package, the 3D arrangement allows for more compact designs, higher-density integration of components, faster processing speeds and higher performance due to shorter interconnections between the different layers, reduced latency and improved energy efficiency.

So called System in Package (SiP) integrates multiple electronic components into a single complete system or subsystem. The components may include processors, memory and other components that would traditionally be located on a printed circuit board; integrating them saves space and power.

Chips incorporating 3D Stacking and SiP, thus, yield significant improvements in products ranging from laptops and phones to miniature drones and tiny surveillance cameras.

The companies leading the packaging race are largely the same big players discussed above—TSMC, Intel and Samsung—but also include ASE Technology Holding in Taiwan and Amkor Technology, with factories located mostly in Asia.

One Chinese company, Jiangsu Changjiang Electronics Technology Co. (JCET), is also developing various packaging technologies, including advanced SiP packaging. Thus, even though packaging is considered less complex than EUV or etching technologies, JCET is an example of China's gradual advancement in the industry, a trend that will likely continue.

RATIONALISED SUPPLY CHAINS

Since the 1990s, global semiconductor value chains have become the most widely dispersed industry in the world.

A chip and its components travel back and forth across multiple borders, many times before finally being embedded into a final end-product.

Consider a California-based fabless company that designs microchips for communications systems. The leading semiconductor design companies—like Nvidia, Qualcomm and Broadcom—typically perform their highest value-added activities at home, focusing on doing what they do best.

The fabless company outsources its chip design to a pure-play chip foundry in, say, Taiwan.

Meanwhile, in an entirely separate process, companies from Japan, Germany or South Korea 'grow' base silicon ingots, slice them into blank wafers and clean and process them.

The wafers then undergo doping, metallisation and deposition, perhaps in Taiwan or South Korea, before being subjected to the all-important photolithography process at the foundry.

Following that, they might also skip back and forth between multiple countries for planarisation, die-cutting, packaging and testing.

Finally, the product-ready microchips may find their way to a central-ised distribution hub before being shipped to OEM locations worldwide—many of them in China—where they will be embedded into devices that are finally shipped out to end-customers.

Viewed through a purely economic lens, value chains optimise the use of resources. Market efficiencies, cost considerations and ration-alisation dictate where things go and who does what. Under this model, everyone finds his hyper-specialised niche and the systems achieve maximum efficiency.

Geo-economics, however, have played a deciding role in the semi-conductor landscape. Historically, in East Asia, Japan and South Korea's government planners successfully shepherded their chip industries with well-funded public private partnerships and very forward-looking techno-nationalist policies.

Taiwan's TSMC provides an example of perhaps the most rigorous, well-managed semiconductor 'industrial policy', combined with deft techno-diplomacy when it came to leveraging its economic, national security and even academic relationships with America.

The U.S. meanwhile, since the late 1980s, stayed largely out of the game of interfering with markets, given, as we have discussed, the prevailing neoliberal mindset and its aversion to industrial policy. Thus, over the ensuing three decades, chip fabrication in the U.S., as a percentage of global output, dropped by 67%. However, because American fabless and tooling companies remained largely dominant, as did Intel, the IDM, the off shoring of fabrication was, under the trade liberalisation model, considered to be a good thing.

Of course, Washington's paradigm shift has now changed all of that, hence we are fixating on re-shoring, friend-shoring and ring-fencing the American chip sector. Other key countries are doing the same.

We will do a deeper dive into America's reshoring of chip manufac-turing and other strategic technologies in Chapter 10, and, later, in Chapter 27, we will investigate the story of industrial policy and tech-nology, and how it has played out in different economies around the world.

Finally, to understand the broad swathe of the semiconductor land-scape, we must distinguish between leading-edge chips (which get all the attention) and the rest of the chips consumed worldwide—28 nm or larger—which incorporate technology that is more than a decade old.

These older generation chips are still in high demand for basic functions and operations in equipment and devices across a wide range of applications such as automotive, medical, communications, clean technology, banking and logistics, retail and a lot of military applications. The U.S. Defence establishment designs systems that are intended to last for decades, thus, they remain dependent on older chip technologies.

Almost 95% of China's local fabrication capacity involves trailing-edge discrete semiconductors, lower-end logic chips and analogue chips. For both economic and geopolitical reasons, Chinese chip producers aim to expand their global market share in memory and mature logic space by building foundries, and a lot of them, with ample government funding.[5]

We discuss China and chips in Chapter 9.

Chapter 8

China's Semiconductor Problem

China's indigenous semiconductor landscape is a story of two very different realities.

Regarding the fabrication of 'leading-edge' chips, China's top chip makers lack the needed capabilities and lag far behind a handful of elite foreign firms. Regarding the fabrication of older generation 'trailing edge' chips, however, Chinese companies could soon be making so many that they could flood global markets with oversupply.

Both scenarios come with high geopolitical stakes, for Beijing, Washington and a host of other foreign capitals.

Regarding leading-edge chips, as we have discussed, China's home-grown semiconductor companies could remain years—possibly decades—behind the world's most advanced chip nations until China can overcome chokepoints in chip supply chains imposed by Washington and its allies. These chokepoints include electronic design automation (EDA)—which involves super-advanced software and AI—as well as different kinds of manufacturing equipment and a broad range of chemicals and specialised materials.

Consequently, Chinese foundries have focused on mature trailing-edge chip nodes of mostly 28 nanometres and above, which require less advanced processes but nonetheless meet widespread market demand. These legacy nodes, which are based on 10 to 20-year-old technology, include memory chips, logic chips and power chips.

Trailing-edge chips figure to account for more than half of the global semiconductor market for years to come, making them indispensable to the operation of a wide variety of dual-use goods. China's expected output of legacy chips, combined with the projected output from Taiwanese fabs, could account for up to 80% of global foundry capacity for 20-nm to 45-nm chips by 2030.[1]

This trend preoccupies law makers in Washington. In January of 2024, The House Select Committee on the Chinese Communist Party (CCP) issued a public letter to U.S. Commerce Secretary Gina Raimondo and U.S. Trade Representative Katherine Tai, urging them to act against American overreliance on imports of legacy (or what the committee called 'foundational') chips from China.

On these grounds, U.S. officials launched a two-front chip war against China, simultaneously targeting leading-edge and trailing-edge chips.

But China's chip landscape presents a paradox to American and other foreign companies. China is the world's largest semiconductor market, gobbling up more than 30% of worldwide final chip sales in 2022.[2] Semiconductors and their related technologies continue to be China's top import, matching or exceeding the value of their annual imports of oil.

This makes China Inc. hugely attractive for foreign chip companies despite geopolitical tensions.

The paradox is evident in the volume of Chinese imports of legacy DUV and other chip-related fabrication equipment, which reached almost US$20 billion worth in 2022. This was followed by another period of binge-buying, which saw a 93% surge in import volume in the third quarter of 2023—before the next round of U.S. export controls kicked in.

As we discussed in Chapter 4, a longstanding in-China-for-China strategy for foreign firms involves capturing local market share by selling outdated technology while simultaneously developing the next generation of innovation. This strategy protects market share while maintaining or increasing competitive edge—a scenario that, paradoxically, also allows Chinese companies access to important 'stepping-stone' technologies as they try mightily to supplant foreign partners.

Washington has, so far, has persuaded the other Group of Five chip nations to loosely enforce export controls on legacy DUV chip-making equipment, with the intent of setting China's chip ambitions back years—even if this means shrinking revenue streams for American and other reigning chip companies.

The question, then, is whether China will have the means to develop its own technologies and achieve its long-term chip self-sufficiency aims when it runs out of stockpiled legacy technology obtained from American, Japanese and Dutch companies.

TRAILING-EDGE CHIPS

China has quietly positioned itself as the world's largest producer of legacy chips. China's National Bureau of Statistics reported that in 2023, more than 350 billion integrated circuits were produced domestically, representing an increase over the previous year despite increasing geopolitical tensions.

These chips are in demand across a wide swathe of rapidly growing consumer markets, such as the electric vehicle and legacy automobile sectors, communications, banking, the medical and pharmaceutical fields and energy.

Many modern military weapon systems continue to run on legacy chips, including the kinds of lethal drones and missiles used by Ukrainian and Russian forces and by non state combatants such as Houthi rebels and Somali pirates, as they, for example, carry out attacks on commercial shipping in the Gulf of Aden.

China's ongoing doling out of subsidies will likely result in large legacy chip surpluses. SEMI, the non-governmental organisation that monitors semiconductor and electronics supply chains, predicted that as many as 82 new mature-node fabs would go online in China between 2022 and 2024. This dwarfed the number of fabrication plants being brought online elsewhere in the world.

TrendForce, which provides market analysis in the tech sector, forecasted that by 2027, China alone would account for just below 40% of the global trailing-edge-chip landscape. Economically, then, China is poised to do with legacy chips the same thing it has already done with steel, solar panels, lithium batteries and EVS: it will flood global markets.

A preview of this chip-dumping scenario occurred in the late 2010s when China's chip sector learned how to mass produce state-of-the-art flash-memory chips.[3]

In 2018, Yangtze Memory Technologies Co. (YMTC), owned at the time by the state-backed Tsinghua Unigroup, racked up losses reported to be around US$460 million in the first half of 2018 alone.[4] Nonetheless, YMTC expanded its production volumes as it continued to receive large amounts of funding and support from its key government shareholders.[5]

By 2020, YMTC had tripled production to 60,000 wafers a month (at the time, around 5% of world output) at a new US$24 billion plant in Wuhan.[6] This reflected the wider ambitious techno-nationalist plan based on government output targets and other non-market goals.

At that time, Intel, one of the world's largest makers of NAND flash memory chips, saw the changing landscape in China for what it was and promptly sold its NAND flash fab in Dalian to SK hynix of South Korea, presumably with the knowledge that foreign companies would soon be facing a glut of memory chips in the local market.[7]

Another area where China has been making progress is in the important wafer manufacturing niche at the front end of the chip fabrication process, where China already holds 25% of global installed capacity.

Based on initial recommendations from the bipartisan House Select Committee on the CCP in early 2024, Washington's response to Chinese chip-dumping—and the unacceptable prospect of reliance on Chinese legacy chip producers—included tariff hikes, more export controls and a doubling down on U.S. reshoring initiatives under the CHIPS Act.

All of these actions will accelerate the bifurcation of semiconductor value chains between China and the Group of Five nations.

LEADING-EDGE CHIPS

If China is to join the elite group of countries capable of producing leading-edge chips, it will have to overcome almost insurmountable odds.

China's indigenous firms must find a way to replicate the astoundingly complex technologies that Washington and its allies continue to monopolise. At best, China seems destined to remain years behind.

As we have discussed, Moore's law is constantly making the process of fabricating a leading-edge chip more challenging, which means that Chinese firms are faced with an increasingly daunting task as they attempt to replicate more than 50 types of hyper-specialised technologies used in the semiconductor fabrication process.

Those processes include oxidation and coating, DUV and EUV photolithography, etching, doping and metal disposition technologies, among others. Then, there are more than 150 specialised materials and chemicals that, again, are controlled by the same small group of elite nations.

These niches present spectacularly high barriers to entry, not just in terms of money—R&D expenditures by the leading chip companies have exceeded at least a trillion U.S. dollars over three decades—but in terms of hard-gained legacy knowledge and the toil of building collaborative partnerships with a finite number of essential partners. These dynamics are almost impossible to replicate simply by government decree.

Washington's efforts to retard China's chip ambitions, then, have sparked frantic efforts to de-Americanise supply chains and replace them with self-sufficient, localised alternatives.

Beyond the steep technical challenges, however, Beijing needs to forge the right kind of chip alliances with other nations to help it scale new heights, but all of its desired partners have sided with Washington. The great paradigm shift has not only swayed the

Group of Five chip countries but also future up-and-coming ones such as Germany and India.

Beijing's foreign policies have further alienated other countries from its chip sector. Its backing of Russia in the war on Ukraine, its dealings with Iran and its increasingly aggressive actions towards Taiwan and bullying of smaller ASEAN states in the South China Sea have all but eliminated Beijing's chances of peeling away any U.S. allies. This is true regarding Washington's agenda for a semiconductor multilateral export controls regime and its supply chain resilience partnerships with the elite chip nations.

We must return, then, to a watershed moment in the U.S.–China chip war, in 2023, when Huawei and SMIC teamed up to produce a 7-nm chip for Huawei's Mate 60 Smart Phone, seemingly defying U.S. export controls.

Recall that by 2021, just two years after Huawei had been on the BIS Entity List, Washington's export controls had crushed the company's 5G wireless capabilities simply by blocking its access to leading-edge chips from third parties like TSMC, who were dependent on U.S. technology. Indeed, Huawei could no longer provide 5G capabilities in its flagship smartphones.

As mentioned earlier, in 2023, the Chinese pure-play fab, SMIC, mastered a fabrication technique to produce millions of industrial-scale 7-nm chips. They had seemingly cracked the leading-edge barrier. SMIC had manipulated imported legacy DUV equipment from the Dutch company, ASML, and pushed the equipment's functional thresholds down to the 7-nm chip node.

This required, among other things, repetitive and time-consuming applications of photolithography on each chip, which not only slowed down the manufacturing process but also added significant costs. Thus, if Huawei's 7-nm chips were to be economically sustainable, SMIC needed a lot of extra funding to make up for all the cost leakage.

Under China's statist economic model, there was never any doubt that Beijing, along with provincial and municipal governments, would provide whatever money was needed to cover SMIC's expenses. Chips were, after all, techno-nationalist priority number one.

CHINA'S FALSE-POSITIVE CHIP TEST

Did Huawei's triumphant announcement about its Mate 60 Smartphone prove that China had truly broken free from its Western constraints? The answer was no.

Shortly after the Mate 60 went into circulation, Bloomberg News commissioned TechInsights, a research firm, to do a teardown of the phone, which revealed that the Mate 60's random-access memory (RAM)—a chip that stores data on a device's central processing unit (CPU) for constant use—came from the South Korean company, SK hynix. Huawei had stockpiled the chips before export control laws had gone into effect.

By this time, however, the U.S.–China chip war had become an international spectator sport, and competing sets of narratives were all over the digital commons from news outlets and social media blogs and other discourse.

Semiconductors are a source of national pride. There is, then, the constant possibility of misinformation—Chinese propaganda, really—when it comes to the news cycle around semiconductors.

Soon, more speculation and outright falsehoods ensued. Media outlets circulated reports that SMIC had gone an additional step and produced an even more advanced *5-nm* chip for Huawei's new laptop computer, the Qingyun L540 notebook.

This also proved to be false, as another teardown by TechInsights revealed that the laptop featured a chip made by Taiwan's TSMC.

But credible investigative reporting by the likes of Bloomberg, Nikkei Asia and Digitimes, a Taiwan-based tech-research publication, began to provide glimpses into China's evolving localised chip ecosystem, and it was clear that a massive effort to advance the industry was underway.

In 2023, a company called Shanghai Micro Electronics Equipment (SMEE) announced a breakthrough in a locally produced machine capable of performing photolithography at the 28-nm node. SMEE had been backed by the state-owned Shanghai Zhangjiang Group.

It is likely that foreign components (such as optics) are required for SMEE's DUV machine, and there remains deep scepticism amongst industry experts whether SMEE's machines can perform high-volume manufacturing. If this is the case, then China remains 10–15 years behind in DUV capabilities.

Meanwhile, Naura, another nascent Chinese manufacturer of chip-making equipment, had begun selling etching, deposition and cleaning equipment for critical portions of the chip fabrication process. This was significant, as these machines would begin to supplant foreign suppliers like America's Applied Materials and Lam Research, and Japan's Tokyo Electron.

By 2023, as U.S. export controls began to cut the flow of legacy U.S. chip-making equipment, Naura saw its sales surge.[8]

Both SMEE and Naura's participation in the chokepoints of the chip manufacturing process are major milestones, but if Chinese firms cannot breach the 5-nm barrier soon and do it as efficiently as others, Beijing will find itself forever playing catchup in the chip innovation race.

As we have discussed, fabrication of the most advanced, powerful chips requires EUV photolithography, which is magnitudes of complexity beyond DUV technology. It took ASML, the sole maker of EUV equipment, decades of R&D, trial and error and the forging of ironclad partnerships with the chip supermajors to achieve its breakthroughs.

Short of replicating existing EUV technology, then, another course of action for any would-be chip innovator involves the invention of an entirely new technology that could equate or even surpass the functions of EUV.

China has begun exploring electron-beam lithography (EBL or e-beam) as a potential alternative to the traditional light-based photolithography process for chip manufacturing. Electron beams have much shorter wavelengths than light, enabling them to define much smaller features and patterns on wafers.

E-beam promises to allow the fabrication of smaller transistors, allowing for higher resolution and enabling the creation of more complex circuitry with greater density on faster and more efficient chips. Theoretically, e-beam can also be used with a wider range of materials than photolithography, opening up possibilities for exploring novel chip architectures. (China is also funding research into silicon alternatives, such as gallium nitride, graphene and boron nitride.)

Not surprisingly, Huawei has invested in EBL, backed with state funding, and has partnered with the Chinese Academy of Sciences and another company, Shanghai MicroElectronics Technology (SMET), which has been tasked with working on high-throughput e-beam for mass production.

The problem with e-beam, so far, throughout decades of research, has been its throughput: It is much slower than optical lithography, so until this challenge is solved, it remains aspirational only.

As research progresses, however, Chinese entities will find themselves competing in the EBL space with the existing semiconductor supermajors such as Samsung, Intel, Micron and TSMC, as well as equipment makers such as ASML, Nikon and Canon.

The well-ensconced Group of Five countries, then, have an advantage in bringing EBL to fruition, given their decades of collaborative research together and the power of their collective brain trust. Thanks to a Western paradigm shift, these tech giants will receive billions more in R&D funding and government contracts, many of which will come with defence imperatives—which means ample budgets.

THE ROAD BEHIND AND AHEAD

At the Davos forum in Switzerland in 2024, Pat Gelsinger, the CEO of Intel, told a rapt audience that China was 10 years behind in chip fabrication and would remain that way for a long time.

Gelsinger's statements reflected the nagging truth that has haunted the CCP for 50 years. Semiconductor self-sufficiency has been its longest-running techno-nationalist priority but has eluded China's central planners.

Dating back to the 1960s and the establishment of the Huajing Group's Wuxi Factory No. 742, which trained the first generation of China's chip industry engineers, China has been riding industrial policy towards the creation of a domestic semiconductor industry.[9]

From 1978, Deng Xiaoping's opening of China put the country on the general trajectory that got it to where it is today. By the early 1980s, China's sixth Five Year Plan (1981–1985) created a Computer and Large Scale IC Lead Group tasked with modernising China's semiconductors.[10]

By the 1980s, Beijing had recognised that shifting towards a hybrid industrial policy model was necessary for its chip aspirations. They required rapid technology transfer via any means—through joint ventures, acquisitions (whether overtly or through shell companies or middlemen), academic exchanges and access to the learning centres in the West, and of course, tradecraft.

In the 1980s and early 1990s, under the so-called Project 908, Chinese companies attracted joint venture partners that included Canada's Nortel, Holland's Philips, Japan's NEC, Belgium's ITT and Lucent laboratories from the U.S.[11]

By the CCP's ninth Five Year Plan (1996–2000) and under the so-called Project 909, industrial policy had successfully lured Japan's NEC, whose engineers transferred technology and trained local Chinese engineers for what would become China's first domestic production capabilities for dynamic random access memory (DRAM).[12]

Over the years, China's industrial planners have oriented their focus to emulate the 'fast-follower' approach that worked so well in the 1970s, 1980s and 1990s for tech companies in Japan, South Korea and Taiwan.

Fast forward to 2024, as the U.S.–China great power rivalry places an unprecedented emphasis on semiconductors. Beijing's efforts to galvanise an indigenous chip revolution are manifest in two ways.

The first involves a large amount of government funding being made available to key entities amid a steady stream of public announcements that have kept industry watchers on constant alert.

China's National Bureau of Statistics, for example, reported a layout of US$150 billion in subsidies in 2022, following the U.S. Department of Commerce's announcement of new export controls on semiconductors.[13] This number, then, dwarfed the US$52 billion that was earmarked under the U.S. CHIPS Act, announced earlier that same year.

JW Consulting, a Chinese semiconductor research firm, reported similarly staggering numbers when it cited 742 semiconductor investment projects implemented in 25 Chinese provinces and regions from 2021 to 2022 and claimed that more than US$290.8 billion had been invested.[14]

China's most frequently cited source of funding is the National Integrated Circuit Industry Investment Fund (CICIF), a state-backed investment fund established in 2014, colloquially called 'The Big Fund'. CICIF has received large infusions of capital from China's Ministry of Finance as well as from provincial and municipal governments.

There are other sources of more opaque funding, such as the Shenzhen Major Industry Investment Fund, which has reportedly earmarked US$30 billion for a government-industry consortium centred on Huawei to advance a local chip ecosystem.[15] (We will discuss Huawei's central role in China's semiconductor landscape in Chapter 10).

Beijing aims to reverse-engineer key foreign-held technologies in each critical niche within the semiconductor value chain. Central planners have designated 'shadow' or 'mirror' Chinese companies of foreign companies currently operating in equivalent niches.[16]

The second feature of China's chip masterplan involves the linkage of its funding sources to the country's 'whole-of-nation' approach to semiconductors and, more broadly, to the Made in China 2025 initiative and the dual circulation concept—all of which strive for a self-sufficient indigenous ecosystem.

Smelling large amounts of money, many Chinese firms have gravitated to the chip sector. According to Qichacha, a Chinese website that compiles corporate registration information, already by 2021, there were 15,700 newly registered companies involved in China's semiconductor landscape from designing to manufacturing chips.[17]

Neoliberals look at these numbers and often say: *So what!*

Corruption and misallocation of resources are often raised regarding China's industrial policies and initiatives supporting the semiconductor sector. Opponents of industrial policy in the U.S. and elsewhere point to reports of companies exaggerating their capabilities or involvement in the industry to benefit from government support programmes.

As such, businesses related to semiconductor equipment supply, software or even logistics might inflate their involvement in core chip manufacturing to qualify for funding.

It is not uncommon for companies to misclassify mischaracterise their activities and core competencies, to gain public funding. And this is not unique to China. Thus, those vehemently opposed to chip-related industrial policy, whether in China, the U.S. or anywhere else, will argue that big spending and big plans, alone, are no guarantee of success.

With the stakes this high for China, both in the trailing edge and leading edge of semiconductor technology, we will soon know the outcome of such big plans.

Chapter 9

Re-shoring Chip Manufacturing to America

The U.S. semiconductor industry was once a leader in chip fabrication. Between 1990 and 2021, however, America's share of global semiconductor manufacturing dropped from around 37% to around 12%.

High domestic costs partly explain the decline. A study by the Semiconductor Industry Association (SIA), for example, claims that building and operating a semiconductor fabrication plant costs about 30% more in the U.S. than in Taiwan, South Korea or Singapore.[1]

For decades, globalisation and the trade liberalisation mindset drove a wave of offshoring of American manufacturing, as we discussed in Chapter 3. During this timeframe, the semiconductor industry turned to licensing and outsourcing agreements, resulting in today's paucity of chip manufacturing capacity across America.

As semiconductor value chains rationalised, production activities migrated to the most optimal locations, and pure-play fabrication ended up gravitating almost entirely to Taiwan. In 2023, for example, Taiwanese contract manufacturers fabricated around 60% of all the world's chips, most of which were produced by a single company, TSMC. Regarding the most advanced leading-edge chips, TSMC produced an astounding 90% of the world's supply.

It is important to remember, however, that fabrication represents just one portion of the semiconductor global value chain, as we discussed in Chapter 7.

Other than chip fabrication, American semiconductor companies dominate key segments of global value chains, including chip design software and manufacturing equipment, as well as specialised chemicals, materials and gasses which are required for the wondrous processes of chip making. Intel, Qualcomm, Nvidia and Applied Materials, along with a host of other American companies, form the backbone of a potent global semiconductor ecosystem, but having so little fabrication capacity at home, for a such a vitally important technology, has created national security risks.

Hence the paradigm shift in Washington. The return of chip fabrication to America, which we have been calling re-shoring, is one of the core elements of U.S. techno-nationalism. It goes hand in glove with supply chain decoupling and de-risking, and, as the next logical step, Washington has launched a chip diplomacy campaign, as it attempts to bring the Group of Five nations, and others, in line with its re-shoring goals.

American chip diplomacy relies on incentives and old-fashioned strong-arm tactics. Consider the coaxing and cajoling that U.S. diplomats applied to TSMC's executives and Taiwanese officials to encourage TSMC to build leading edge 5-nanometre and 3-nanometre fabs outside of Phoenix, Arizona—at a cost of more than US$40 billion.

To bring this to fruition, however, Washington would have to dip into its own finances.

THE CHIPS AND SCIENCE ACT

CHIPS is a clever acronym for 'creating helpful incentives to produce semiconductors.' The CHIPS and Science Act was signed into law by U.S. President Joe Biden in August of 2022, and it enjoyed bipartisan support from the U.S. Congress, as well as strong support from the private sector.

CHIPS has become a catalyst not only for re-shoring and expanding chip fabrication in the U.S. but also for creating critical mass in R&D, and another big priority: human capital development. The U.S., like all other advanced economies, is suffering a shortage in human capital, otherwise known as talent.

In June of 2021, when the U.S. Senate voted 68–32 to commit funding for a broad swathe of scientific research and to overhaul the U.S. National Science Foundation (NSF), it was clear that the U.S. was undergoing a technology awakening.

The CHIPS and Science Act will eventually allocate a full US$280 billion to R&D and manufacturing across a spectrum of strategic industries from AI to quantum. It has carved out US$52 billion specifically for semiconductors.[2] The bill provides for grants, income tax credits and other mechanisms to match state and local investment incentives through 2026.

Among its provisions is a reference to promoting international partnerships that have 'alignment in policies towards nonmarket economies'—a clear reference to dealing with China as a geopolitical rival.[3] The bill reflects the view that the U.S. cannot advance its semiconductor agenda alone. While it may sound like an oxymoron, U.S. techno-nationalism requires international alliances. For Washington, re-shoring of chip fabrication may not involve bringing the entire value chain home, but it will require resilient and redundant value chains, and that, in turn, will require working closely with trusted partners and allies. Hence the term 'friend-shoring' which has come to characterise this kind of thinking.

Domestically, support for the U.S. CHIPS Act came from a coalition of semiconductor companies. They formed the Semiconductors in America Coalition (SIAC), which included, among virtually all other chip companies, Qualcomm, Nvidia and Intel, as well as their major downstream customers—Apple and General Electric, for example. The SIAC has become a strong backer of ongoing government funding and public–private partnerships—yet again, demonstrating the shift in the public mood and corporate ethos toward more involvement of the state in markets.

Less than two years after the passage of the CHIPS Act, meanwhile, private investors had announced approximately US$300 billion in additional funding for new foundries across the U.S.[4] Inspired by the CHIPS legislation, more than forty semiconductor companies across 16 states piled on their investments, which will playout over the next 10 years, even as more money flows in.

Location	Name	Owner	Target Opening	Node/Technology
Indiana	Purdue Discovery Park	SK hynix	TBD	Advanced Chip Packaging
New York	Malta Fab	GlobalFoundries	2025–2026	200 mm–300 mm Wafers
New York	Clay Fab	Micron Technology	TBD	DRAM
New York	Fab 8.2	GlobalFoundries	2025	Feature-rich
Idaho	Boise Fab	Micron Technology	2025	DRAM
Arizona	Fab 52	Intel	2024–2025	7 nanometres
Arizona	Fab 62	Intel	2024–2025	7 nanometres
Arizona	Fab 21	TSMC	2025–2026	5 & 3 nanometres
Texas	Sherman Fab	Texas Instruments	2025	28 nanometres
Texas	Taylor Fab	Samsung	2024–2025	5 nanometres
Florida	Palm Bay Fab	Rogue Valley Microdevices	2025	MEMS, Sensors

Figure 9.1   **Partial List of New Chip Fabs in the U.S (Announced and In Progress, 2024).**

The strategic focus of the CHIPS Act is remarkably similar to Beijing's 'whole nation' approach for its own indigenous semiconductor industry. While Beijing seeks to 'de-Americanise' its domestic chip-making capabilities, Washington has gone all in on its own chip reshoring.

Both nations have identified leading-edge and trailing-edge chips as two separate niches linked to economic and national security. And both countries acknowledge the inevitable bifurcation of U.S.–China strategic supply chains in their quest to bolster their own resilient ecosystems.

Regarding investment in leading-edge chips, TSMC has acknowledged that Arizona will likely be the site of up to a total of six new fabs. A new plant for advanced 3-nanometre technology, alone, will incur costs of up to US$25 billion. Long-term, over 10 to 15 years,

TSMC is reportedly drawing up plans to make next-generation 2-nanometre chips on U.S. soil.[5]

TSMC's biggest customers are, in fact, American companies like Apple and Nvidia, Qualcomm and Broadcom, thus, moving production closer to home has numerous business benefits—assuming the costs of producing chips in the U.S. can eventually be brought down without government subsidies.

Nonetheless, thanks to the CHIPS Act, other semiconductor heavyweights have shifted their attention to the U.S., namely, South Korea's Samsung, the world's largest semiconductor company, along with Intel. Samsung broke ground for a US$17 billion fab next to its existing factory in Austin, Texas, in 2022.[6]

Intel, meanwhile, had already begun construction of its close to US$50 billion investment in two new fabs (Fab 52 and Fab 62) in Chandler, Arizona.[7] For Intel, Arizona represented one of three new sites, along with new investments in Ohio, and in Oregon, with more likely to come.

As for the wider chip ecosystem in the U.S., the CHIPS Act has sparked an inflow of suppliers such as Japan's Mitsubishi Gas Chemicals, which makes super-pure hydrogen peroxide, which is required in the production of high-performance chips. Mitsubishi Gas Chemicals invested over US$ 300 million at a facility in Oregon, the first of two new U.S. facilities.[8]

Japan's Showa Denko and South Korea's SK Group, two other producers of high purity gases, signed an MOU just after the passage of the CHIPS Act, in which they agreed to invest in the construction of a U.S. based production site.[9] Showa Denko makes gases for the etching process in chip fabrication, while SK Group produces nitrogen trifluoride (NF3), which deals with unwanted residues, also in the fabrication process.

Now, it must be said that the decisions of the aforementioned firms to develop U.S. production capacity were strongly influenced by the Biden administration's efforts at chip diplomacy. Of course there are market forces (including government funding) behind these kind of decisions, as I will explain, but cabinet-level discussions between U.S,

Japanese, South Korean and Taiwanese government officials have been and continue to be a factor.

Washington's efforts to form groups of allies around resilient semi-conductor supply chains, along with higher reaching arrangements such as the Chip 4 Alliance (again, the U.S, Japan, Taiwan and South Korea) to friend-shore not only strategic supply chains, but to jointly focus on R&D and talent development, or to align tech-transfer with security initiatives, speak volumes to the rise of techno-diplomacy.

Reshoring and friend-shoring chip fabrication requires a powerful feedback loop between businesses, governments and world-class research institutions. Regarding talent development, it is no puzzle, then, why TSMC, Intel and Samsung settled upon the locations for their new U.S. fabs.

Arizona State University, located in Tempe, just down the road from the TSMC and Intel plants, will provide a steady supply of engineers and collaborators in research and training programmes.

The city of Austin was equally attractive to Samsung, as the University of Texas figures to deliver the same benefits for Samsung's own technology feedback loop. Across the U.S., a network of dozens of other world-leading research institutions is being called upon to become talent hotbeds for chip companies. From the Massachusetts Institute of Technology (MIT) and the State University of New York (SUNY) in the East, to Purdue University in the Midwest, and the University of Southern California (USC) and Oregon State University (OSU) in the West, a renaissance is underway. And this is just a short list of the institutions at play.

We will explore the impact of techno-nationalism on university campuses, as well as the rise of government and private funded 'Chip Schools' in Chapters 25 and 26.

CHIPS AND THE TRAILING-EDGE REVOLUTION

The Chips Act galvanised a groundswell in legacy chip productivity, and here is where the positive effects of Washington's reshoring efforts have been largely overlooked.

As we now know, legacy chips are crucial for a wide range of commercial and military technologies, from automobiles to aeroplanes. With lower barriers to entry, trailing-edge chip manufacturers can do more with less money. A state-of-art fab that makes three or four generation-old vital chip technology can be built for under US$ 2 billion—a tenth of what it costs to build a leading-edge fab.

Less than 2 years after the passage of the CHIPS Act, there was already evidence of a widespread renaissance that involved the defence establishment, businesses, state and local governments and world class academic institutions.

A string of announcements had begun. In 2024, there was a U.S. Department of Commerce (DOC) announcement that it was awarding US$162 million to Microchip Technologies, a maker of mature node semiconductors and micro-controllers.[10] The money was allocated to Microchip's production facilities in Colorado and Oregon to supply the U.S. defence establishment.

Around the same time, the U.S. Department of Defence (DoD) announced that Skywater Technologies, another legacy pure play fab, had been awarded a defence contract reportedly worth up to US$190 million to provide the U.S. military with an advanced process of packaging wafers and chips.[11]

Skywater had previously made news in 2022, when it announced a US$1.8 billion investment to build a commercially viable foundry in Purdue University's Discovery Park District, along with the establishment of an R&D facility. Skywater is an American pure-play fab that produces legacy 90-nanometre process technology (old) on equipment designed for 200-millimetre wafers of silicon. It partners with fabless companies, IDMs and OEMs to bring solutions to market for a wide range of applications, including aerospace and defence, automotive, consumer, and healthcare. Skywater later changed its Purdue venture to an R&D centre.

What is noteworthy of America's early-days fab re-shoring, for legacy chips is that the action was being spread around the U.S. and that private industry was pitching in a lot its own money.

Purdue University became a magnet for the growth of America's 'Silicon Crossroads', in the heart of the American Midwest. In 2024,

SK hynix, the South Korean chip maker, announced it was building a US$3.8 billion AI memory chip fab on the Purdue campus that would perform advanced packaging, alongside a world-class R&D facility—essentially a lab-to-fab operation.[12]

SK hynix was a triumph for the Midwest. Meanwhile, the Northeast, specifically upper New York State, recorded another CHIPS-inspired investment when, in early 2024, GlobalFoundries, the world's third-largest semiconductor foundry by revenue, was awarded US$1.5 billion to expand its New York facility, construct another new state-of-the art fab, and begin upgrading its Vermont facility.

GlobalFoundries' Vermont and New York State plants manufacture trailing-edge integrated circuits on 200 mm and 300 mm wafers. These are used for the automotive, communications infrastructure, the Internet of Things (IoT), aerospace and defence and other specialised sectors.[13]

By early 2024, the beginnings of a trailing-edge chip renaissance were materialising.

CHALLENGES, SCEPTICISM AND ASSUMPTIONS

By any measure, the re-shoring of chip manufacturing to the U.S. will present big challenges.

The first involves high costs. Based on research from the Boston Consulting Group (BCG), along with the SIA, it could take a total investment of US$1 trillion dollars to move fully functional, self-sufficient chip manufacturing supply chains into the U.S.[14] This would probably take at least a decade. As we discussed in Chapter 7, every single stage of the chip manufacturing process features niche companies with unique technologies and hyper-specialised competencies.

These high costs, then, spring from trying to transplant, within a small-yard, high-fence environment, widely dispersed, optimised global supply chains that have evolved organically over decades.

BCG has estimated that with the initial US$52 billion allocated under the CHIPS Act, in 2022, the U.S. could increase its global share of chip fabrication by another 2 % by 2030—assuming things go smoothly.[15]

But at least another US$250 billion would probably be needed over the next decade to get to around 20%–25% of global production.

What could go wrong?

Political infighting in a polarised American political system could potentially prevent the allocation of this money. But, given the fact that the CHIPS Act is fundamentally a bipartisan national security issue, this is unlikely—there is ample money in America's gargantuan defence budget.

It is wholly reasonable, then, to assume that through collaborative 'friend-shoring' within its own geographic confines and the confines of its Group of Five allies, Washington and its friends could preside over an historic semiconductor supply chain reorganisation. This would resemble something more like a tightly knit cartel. China, unlike the U.S., lacks such as an option, because it lacks the right kind of friends.

Whatever the costs, geo-economics will demand that the U.S follow this new course, in line with its paradigm shift.

This brings us to the second challenge: acute shortages of skilled professionals in the science, technology, engineering, and math (STEM) fields. The U.S. faces a shortfall of between 70,000 to 90,000 engineers for the numbers needed to make its CHIPS Act goals by 2030. Japan, South Korea, Taiwan, and the E.U. all face their own talent shortfalls as well.

Here, again, however, U.S. universities and even community colleges, are friend-shoring their curriculum development and course offerings with other world-class universities. More on this in Chapter 25.

Regarding TSMC's new fabs in the U.S., Morris Chang, TSMC's iconic founder, described the dearth of highly skilled labour pool as 'problematic'.

He noted differences in the management style and work ethic between Taiwanese and American engineers, as Taiwan's engineers are willing to devote every waking hour to do the job, no matter what it takes. American workers, by contrast, had already demanded overtime pay and generous time off under unionised contracts, even before the new sites were up and running in Arizona.

Given the acute shortage of local semiconductor talent everywhere, if TSMC's new mega-fabs in Arizona are to come to fruition, it must drain off large numbers of engineers from its production centres in Taiwan and move them to the U.S. This is a sore point, given the importance of TSMC to Taiwan's national and economic security.

Taiwan's work culture is far better suited for Japan, which would explain why TSMC's investments and public–private partnerships there are moving along much more smoothly than in Arizona. Tokyo does techno-nationalism well, as does Taiwan.

The CHIPS Act has forced Washington to rethink the structure of its intuitions and how they might better serve the needs of policy and the public. Regarding the shortfalls of human capital development, a new public–private entity was created: the National Semiconductor Technology Center (NSTC). The NSTC was created to allocate more than $5 billion for semiconductor R&D and workforce training.

GlobalFoundries' new investments in New York and Vermont were among the first beneficiaries of this new entity. We will soon see if Washington is able to allocate its CHIPS policies through well-managed and proactive public–private partnerships.

The third, challenge is more a matter of debate between technology hawks and neoliberals. It focuses on what some have called a semi-conductor race-to-the-bottom among nations.

It is a fact that Taiwan, Japan, the E.U. and South Korea have all rolled out their own versions of CHIPS programmes. To this end, just a year removed from enactment of U.S. Chips Act, the combined value of their expenditures came to around US$500 billion.

Meanwhile, on the topic of great power rivalry, C.C. Wei, CEO of TSMC, was quoted as saying U.S. and Chinese measures to control the flow of technology 'destroy productivity and efficiency gained under globalisation.'

Morris Chang put things in even starker terms not long after a ribbon cutting ceremony at the construction site of a new TSMC facility in Arizona, attended by U.S. president Joe Biden. Mr. Chang publicly stated: 'Globalisation is almost dead and free trade is almost dead'.

The neoliberal argument, then, would assert that these countries are on a collision course in what could soon unravel into a zero-sum competition.

But ongoing developments are disproving this. A global semiconductor reorganisation is clearly underway—not a deglobalisation process—and the countries that were presumably going to engage in zero-sum competition have been collaborating.

Consider Intel's 2022 announcement to invest US$85 billion in foundries and R&D facilities in Germany, Ireland, Italy, Poland, Spain and France.[16] TSMC invested in a new fab in Japan in partnership with Sony, and in 2024, TSMC officials announced that it would build one of its most advanced fabs in the world, at the 1.5 nanometre node, in Germany.[17]

Japan's proposed collaboration with TSMC involves the investment of an initial US$186 million in an R&D centre in Tsukuba outside of Tokyo—the first of a series of initiatives by Japan's Ministry of Trade and Industry to bolster ties with the Taiwanese giant through subsidies and other incentives.

South Korea's K-Semiconductor Belt strategy, meanwhile, entails a plan to build the world's largest semiconductor supply chain by 2030, which will require trusted foreign partners.[18]

More broadly, the Group of Five countries share fundamental values and geopolitical interests. They comprise the core of the global reorganisation collective that forms the basis of a wider network of trusted partnerships.

As I noted in an essay that I wrote for *Barrons* in 2022, the Group of Five has the potential to expand chip supply chains to other friendly, compatible markets, from Israel to Singapore to India and to places not historically part of the semiconductor sector but with all the right factors—such as Australia.[19]

The last time the U.S. semiconductor industry lobbied for strong government support was in the 1980s when Japan's semiconductor industry had achieved more advanced chip designs and production capability. In 1987, the U.S. government and 14 U.S.-based semiconductor manufacturers formed SEMATECH (Semiconductor Manufacturing Technology) to leap-frog the Japanese chip sector.[20]

Thanks to a successful combination of government and industry funding, as well as collaboration in R&D, manufacturing and strategic planning, the U.S. semiconductor sector had significantly increased its manufacturing capacity by the 1990s and emerged once again as the global leader in innovation.

(More on SEMATECH in Chapter 26.)

The CHIPS and Science Act of 2022 promises the same opportunities over the course of the next decade but offers much greater global reach among the U.S. and its chip-allies.

This is a luxury that China can only dream of, as the CCP's national and geopolitical policies keep it on adversarial terms with Washington and Beijing remains effectively locked out of the Group of Five.

PART II

Undercurrents and Power-Multipliers

Chapter 10

The War Against Huawei

Huawei Technologies is China's most strategically important company.

As the largest telecommunications equipment manufacturer in the world, it has become a symbol of China's growing economic might and technical prowess. It is a proxy—willing or not—of Beijing's wider geopolitical aims.

In response, Washington has mounted a three-pronged campaign to counter Huawei's global presence. The first prong involves the attempted blockage of technology transfers to Huawei from the U.S. and other advanced economies such as Japan, South Korea, Taiwan, and the E.U. The second prong features U.S. diplomats and intelligence officials who aim to convince other nations to 'rip and replace' Huawei's equipment from their telecommunications networks. The third prong, which is less known, involves Washington's efforts to decouple HMN Tech from undersea fibre optic cable networks. HMN was previously known as Huawei Marine Networks, before it was sold to China's Hengtong Group and rebranded as HMN Tech.

Huawei is now so fully immersed in the U.S.–China hybrid cold war that the Chinese Communist Party (CCP) has delegated key components of its semiconductor masterplan to the telecom equipment giant. Beijing hopes that Huawei can expedite the building of an indigenous chip ecosystem in China. In its leadership capacity, Huawei has been partnering with local firms in the semiconductor value chain, and serving as an investor, coordinator, advisor and liaison with academic and research institutions, the military and provincial governments.

Meanwhile, other Chinese companies on Washington's blacklists have taken inspiration from Huawei, which has thrived despite the onslaught of U.S. export controls.

After being placed on the U.S. Bureau of Industry and Security's (BIS) Entity List in 2019, the company came storming back. It changed its business model and began making and providing IT and software for China's electric vehicle (EV) market. It partnered with Seres, a Chinese automaker, and began producing its own hugely popular brand of EV, the Aito.[1]

Huawei's move to EVs is significant, as it demonstrates the power of the world's tech giants as they cross over into other areas such as the automotive sector. Imagine Apple, with all its financial resources, boldly moving into the EV market with the assurances of U.S. government subsidies and access to critical battery supply chains and other resources, as has been the case of Huawei.

Since Washington's weaponisation of the Foreign Direct Product Rule (FDPR), Huawei also successfully ramped up its digital cloud services. But its most noteworthy achievement has been its clever workarounds of Washington's export controls. As we have discussed, its release of the Mate 60 smartphone in August of 2023, when Huawei teamed with SMIC, the chipmaker, and began to produce millions of phones featuring a 7-nanometre chip, was a substantial win for the company.

I had my first in-person dealings with Huawei in 2010, when I was a partner at KPMG, in Hong Kong. The corporate culture at the Huawei Campus in Shenzhen was thick with a hardcore, military-style ethos, a hierarchy infused with a tireless 24/7 work ethic. Huawei had thousands of engineers, many trained at the world's best universities.

Its culture, when combined with Beijing's ambitious techno-nationalist agenda, makes the company a formidable competitor.

As of late 2023, Huawei was reported to be supplying 5G wireless equipment and maintaining telecom infrastructure in 170 countries.[2] Its 5G technology services, which include hardware and software, remain embedded in the 'core' and 'periphery' of most of the world's telecom infrastructure, making Huawei essential to the daily communications of billions of people.

Overall, as an end-to-end 5G incumbent contract provider, Huawei has beaten out Sweden's Ericsson, Nokia of Finland and Qualcomm of the U.S. to remain top dog in its field.[3]

As early as 2012, however, American intelligence agencies began airing concerns that Beijing could implant spyware and malware in Huawei's technology to monitor subjects of interest, steal data and even sabotage a telecom network.

Well before it placed China's telecoms equipment giant on its blacklist, Washington had been leaning on other nations to ban Huawei (and ZTE, China's number two telecoms equipment maker) from their networks, but this appears to have had mixed results.

As of 2023, about 40 countries had either banned or restricted the use of Huawei equipment in the core of their network infrastructure. At the time of this writing, the U.S., Australia and India had banned Huawei outright, while Japan, Sweden, the U.K. and the Netherlands, among others, only allowed Huawei technology in peripheral, non-sensitive areas of network infrastructure—subject to security assessments.

Around this same time, France announced it would not renew existing contracts with Huawei once they expired. Going forward, this figures to become a trend, as strategic technologies like 5G and 6G networks continue to undergo supply chain and market bifurcation.

While many of America's NATO allies have not banned Chinese companies outright, the trend is that Huawei and ZTE have been scaling back 5G and are in retreat in Europe and in other places where liberal democracies hold power.

THE THREE POINTS OF REFERENCE

To understand the fervour behind Washington's war on Huawei, we must focus on three points of reference.

Firstly, we must recognise that there is a well-documented series of events linking state-sponsored espionage with big telecoms. The U.S. government has a long history of collusion with its own telecom companies regarding phone tapping, surveillance and manipulating the politics of foreign countries. Thus, the intelligence community's reaction to Huawei's overseas 5G networks should not be surprising, given Washington's long and successful execution of telecoms-enabled spy craft.

Secondly, we must focus on Huawei's behaviour purely as an economic actor and the role it plays in China Inc.'s system of economic nationalism. Subsidies, loan guarantees from state-backed Chinese banks to foreign governments, opaque deals and payoffs to overseas political elites—all this qualifies as economic coercion and dollar diplomacy.

Huawei's prominent role in China's Belt and Road Initiative (BRI), meanwhile, warrants addressing, as does a discussion about how corporate business practices in the West mobilised intellectual property and technology flight from American and European telecom equipment makers to Huawei.

Thirdly, we must consider Huawei's emergent position at the centre of China's efforts to achieve semiconductor independence.

THE SUPERMICRO ANTECEDENT

Well before Huawei became Washington's target, fears of spyware inside of digital systems had begun to go mainstream. In 2018, *Bloomberg Businessweek* published a report alleging a Chinese microelectronics company, Hangzhou Jinqu Science and Technology Co., had inserted backdoor spyware into chips and hardware that was being funnelled into the digital economy via, among others, a U.S. company named Supermicro.[4]

Silicon Valley-based Supermicro sold (and still sells) enterprise computing, storage and networking solutions to Apple, Amazon and other big brands. Its products include an array of microelectronics used in such activities.

Bloomberg's allegations held that the spyware was inserted into chips during the manufacturing process at factories in China and claimed that this could allow Chinese intelligence agencies to gain access to sensitive data from, for example, the massive cloud-based networks of Apple and Amazon.

The Bloomberg report set off alarm bells. It raised the first serious concerns about the security of China's supply chain and led to calls for increased scrutiny of Chinese companies. Apple and Amazon denied the allegations in the report, but Pandora's box had been opened: the potential risks of cyber espionage and sabotage in a world of intertwined microelectronics supply chains were upon us.

In 2021, Bloomberg followed up its earlier report and doubled down on its allegations that China had been successfully implanting encrypted spyware. It alleged, among other things, that chips implanted in Lenovo laptops used by the U.S. military had recorded data and sent it back to China. Bloomberg went on to link a series of major cyber intrusions and data breaches at the U.S. Pentagon, NASA and other government agencies to Chinese spyware.[5]

Swift denials ensued, not only from Supermicro and its Chinese supplier but also from Lenovo and again from Apple and Amazon.

Whatever the case may be, the issue of spyware is now at the forefront of trade involving telecom technology as well as everyday consumer electronics.

AMERICA'S HISTORIC TELECOMS-ESPIONAGE MONOPOLY

During the Cold War era, over the course of decades, American telecom giants American Telephone and Telegraph Company (AT&T) and International Telephone & Telegraph Company (ITT), along with Western Union, built telecoms infrastructure and provided key telecoms equipment in more than 100 countries. In Europe, this included France, Germany, Italy, Greece, Spain and the U.K.

In Asia, American telcos built the network foundations in Japan, South Korea and Taiwan; and in Latin America, they operated in Argentina, Mexico, Brazil, Chile and Peru.

Argentina, Chile and Peru would become enmeshed in a series of well-publicised U.S.-orchestrated political coups and the installation of U.S.-friendly military juntas. By the early 1970s, accusations surfaced that AT&T and ITT were being used by the Central Intelligence Agency (CIA), the National Security Agency (NSA) and the Federal Bureau of Investigation (FBI) to carry out espionage and other clandestine operations against foreign governments.

AT&T and ITT's extensive global network of phone lines and cables provided ample opportunities for the use of wiretapping and electronic eavesdropping equipment, as well as the use of early forms of data analysis software. Having such a large field of operations meant that new surveillance technologies were constantly being developed and honed, making it increasingly easier to intercept and monitor communications.

Driving this behaviour was America's Cold War doctrine of 'containment' of the Soviet Union and its quest to prevent Moscow from expanding its sphere of influence, country-by-country, like a line of falling dominos. This meant that American intelligence and defence agencies were closely monitoring the communications within the political parties, opposition groups, militaries—and even business communities—of sovereign states.

The goal was to quash any new partnerships or collaborative relationships between the USSR and countries outside its Iron Curtain. Developing countries were particularly vulnerable, as they were in the arena for proxy wars between Washington and Moscow.

SENATE INVESTIGATIONS INTO U.S. TELECOMS AND SPY AGENCIES

From 1975 to 1976, allegations of U.S. telecom-enabled tradecraft were investigated in the hearings of the Church Committee, officially known as the Senate Select Committee to Study Governmental Operations with Respect to Intelligence Activities. The hearings uncovered a world of covert operations, largely enabled by the omnipresent American telecoms.

The Church Committee hearing was given extra impetus by the Watergate incident involving President Richard Nixon, which mired the country in scandal for two years until Nixon resigned in 1974. Among other things, Watergate had involved the wiretapping and illegal monitoring of political opponents.

The Church Committee hearings publicly revealed the extent of illegal wiretapping and surveillance of foreign citizens, assassination plots and coup attempts against foreign leaders, disinformation campaigns and widespread domestic political interference, all orchestrated by the CIA, the NSA and other U.S. government agencies—and all with the indirect involvement of American telcos.

Latin America proved to be an active theatre for this kind of tradecraft. In Chile, for instance, the CIA's collaboration with ITT was instrumental in undermining the democratically elected government of Salvador Allende. By intercepting communications and disseminating disinformation, the CIA destabilised the government and created conditions that led to a right-wing military coup in 1973.

Interestingly, in an early example of the grey area of symbiotic relationships involving multinational companies and governments, ITT's management aligned itself with the CIA's efforts for business reasons.

When Allende, a socialist, was elected president of Chile in 1970, ITT became alarmed by his government's nationalisation policies. The company feared that nationalisation would threaten its investments and profits in Chile.

In 1971, a secret ITT memo was leaked that outlined plans to destabilise the Chilean government. The memo was widely publicised and caused a major scandal. Despite the public blowback, however, ITT and the CIA continued to work together to destabilise Allende's government and prevent the implementation of its nationalisation plans, ultimately leading to a coup by the military strongman Augusto Pinochet in 1973.

A mere month after the Church Committee hearings ended in 1976, this familiar pattern continued, this time with the overthrow of the democratically elected government of Isabel Perón in Argentina and the installation of a group of military officers.

Perón had shifted her politics decidedly to the left, thus potentially opening the door to Soviet influence or, as in Chile, the possibility of the nationalisation of AT&T and ITT's business interests in Argentina.

Both companies were concerned about the potential impact of Perón's leftist policies on their investments. As a result, they both lobbied the U.S. government to act against Perón and her government.

Here, the commercial interests of the big telecoms coincided with the Cold War geopolitical interests of a superpower.

All of this is relevant to twenty-first-century techno-nationalism because it speaks to the incredible power-multiplying effects that accrue to technologically savvy governments.

In the twentieth-century age of analogue, the U.S. government leveraged innovative technology, at scale, to gain huge geopolitical advantages. In the twenty-first century, in the new digital age, this dynamic continues with exponentially larger power-multiplying effects.

China's emergence as a technology superpower and its direct competition with America makes the rise of Huawei and other big tech companies particularly consequential.

As such, Washington's declaration of war on Huawei represents the most comprehensive and ambitious attempt by a national government to crush a foreign state-backed company's global operations.

CHINA'S BRAND OF ECONOMIC-TECHNO-NATIONALISM

In 2019, according to calculations by an investigative team at the *Wall Street Journal (WSJ)*, Huawei received some US$75 billion in state assistance from 2008 to 2018.[6] That assistance took the form of loans and credit lines from government-backed lenders, direct and indirect tax breaks, technology grants and land discounts.

The *WSJ* team made use of public records, including company statements and land-registry documents, and verified its methodology by consulting with subsidy analysts, including Usha Haley, professor at Wichita State University, and Good Jobs First, a Washington, DC organisation that analyses tax incentives and provides widely consulted subsidy data.

The *WSJ*'s publication raised the ire of Huawei's executive leadership team and set its public relations team in motion—arguably one of Huawei's most important and active corporate departments—which went on the offensive, calling the *WSJ* a propaganda wing of the U.S. government.

But the *WSJ* stood its ground, and it soon became clear that the scale of Beijing's spending dwarfed what its closest competitors received from their governments during the same timeframe.

State assistance provided to Huawei was 17 times as large as similar subsidies received by its nearest competitor, Finland's Nokia Corp, at the time, the world's second largest manufacturer of telecom equipment. Ericsson of Sweden, then the world's third largest, had reported no government support in that timeframe.[7]

Critics of the *WSJ* report have pointed out that all big telecom equipment companies receive different types of subsidies, which is true. For example, Cisco, the American telecommunications and networking equipment manufacturer, benefitted from US$44 billion in state grants, subsidies and tax breaks in 2020—data that was reported by both the U.S. Congressional Budget Office (CBO) and the U.S. Government Accountability Office (GAO).

In the same 2008–2018 timeframe covered in the *WSJ* report, American technology firms Qualcomm, Broadcom, Microsoft and Amazon Web Services (AWS) all received defence contracts, research grants, tax breaks and other subsidies from the U.S. government.

Two things stand out when we compare American and Chinese techno-nationalist funding. The first is that both countries have been doing it for years. Even during Washington's decades of self-professed laissez-faire capitalism, U.S. corporations have been on the receiving end of a lot of government money.

With that said, however, historically, there has been a significant difference in the amount of money being doled out by both countries' governments. During the timeframe in question, Huawei received more government subsidies than Broadcom, Qualcomm, AWS and Microsoft combined.

STATE-BACKED CHEAP CREDIT FOR EMERGING MARKETS

As Huawei was expanding rapidly around the world, cheap lines of credit from state-owned banks made available to Huawei's foreign customers—mainly foreign governments—were another key to its international expansion. By assuring easy financing for a project, Huawei, ZTE and other Chinese companies have been rapidly capturing market share in emerging markets.

Before it banned Huawei from its 5G infrastructure, India had several experiences that provided a good illustration of Chinese techno-economic practices. As reported in *The Hindu Business Line* press, in 2012, Reliance Communications, an Indian telco, secured a US$600 million loan from Chinese banks in order to purchase network equipment from both Huawei and ZTE.

In addition to getting cheap financing to buy equipment, both Huawei and ZTE were instrumental in linking Reliance to an additional US$1.8 billion in loans from the Export–Import Bank of China, the China Development Bank and Industrial and Commercial Bank of China. Reliance used this money to repay its foreign currency convertible bonds (FCCBs) that were coming due that year.

In 2019, Reliance filed for bankruptcy, revealing another aspect of Chinese state-backed financing in emerging markets: a willingness to do business with members of wealthy elites in murky business environments often described as 'crony capitalism'. In this case, China Inc. was dealing with the Indian billionaire, Anil Ambani, who would later famously declare bankruptcy under a cloud of alleged fraud and suspicion.[8]

Before the India example, the Pakistan government received a US$124 million, 20-year interest-free loan from China's Export–Import

Bank to purchase surveillance technology for its capital, Islamabad. The stipulation: the job would be awarded to Huawei, with no competitive bidding.[9]

As U.S.–China techno-nationalist competition accelerates, incidents like these continue to surface and serve as motivation for further actions relating to Huawei and other large Chinese tech companies.

HUAWEI AND CHINA'S DIGITAL BELT AND ROAD INITIATIVE

Huawei has been a central component in a larger blueprint to expand Beijing's hard and soft power around the world. This is closely linked to China's historic Belt and Road Initiative (BRI), which aims to connect Chinese trade and geopolitical interests in more than 100 countries through a network of infrastructure, at an estimated cost of some US$4–8 trillion.[10]

By paving, building and connecting the historical overland Silk Route (the 'belt') and the maritime Silk Road with Chinese money—and by using state-owned or state-controlled companies—Beijing continues to enhance its economic, military and technological footprint. The CCP's purpose for the BRI is clear: to tilt the world's geopolitical axis away from a U.S.-centric world order and towards its own state-centric model.

Like the symbiotic win-win relationships between the U.S. and AT&T and ITT, Huawei and ZTE stood to make a lot of money while it helped their government achieve its geopolitical objectives.

By 2023, however, many of the loans for the big BRI infrastructure projects were teetering on the brink of default. Over 60% of China Inc.'s subsequent credit to foreign governments was used to stave off debt defaults. This occurred at a time when China's economy became strained under record youth unemployment, overcapacity, massive debt defaults in the real estate market and net outflows of foreign company investment.

Thus, Beijing scaled back and changed its BRI focus, and its central planners doubled down on building *digital* infrastructure—a move away from huge, costly hard infrastructure projects. Digital trade and tech-enabled commerce cost a fraction to build, but the platform economy is data-rich, and it provides a treasure trove of information to Beijing.

Huawei's and ZTE's 5G networks remain at the heart of the BRI. This also includes Beiduo, the satellite network and Alibaba and Tencent, who enable cloud and e-commerce services.

By establishing Chinese digital hegemony over a large swathe of the world's less developed countries, Beijing hopes to dominate 5G, cloud infrastructure, smartphones and other technologies and make their products the de facto standard for a large part of the so-called 'emerging world'. The plan, then, is to create a virtuous cycle for both the Chinese state and its champion tech companies, giving them yet more scale and greater market advantages.

Huawei remains the lynchpin in this plan.

The involvement of other Chinese companies is significant for several other reasons. First, as state-owned or state-controlled entities, they are massive in scale; thus, even if market conditions, such as lack of demand, prevent other MNEs from expanding into the high-risk and unstable countries along the BRI, these Chinese tech giants can operate at a loss with state funding, allowing them to advance Beijing's BRI agenda.

The other Chinese companies in Huawei's orbit bring into sharp focus the ideological differences between the West and what Beijing calls its 'socialism with Chinese characteristics', which embraces state planning, censorship, surveillance and authoritarianism.

Recall that most of the companies listed above have been placed on the U.S. government's restricted entity list on the grounds that their technologies were used to further human rights violations in China's Xinjiang province, where Kazakhs and other Muslim minority groups have been detained and forced into 're-education' camps.[11]

China's digital BRI initiative, therefore, will amplify technology bifurcation between China and the bloc of liberal democracies.

HOW THE NEOLIBERAL MODEL BACKFIRED WITH HUAWEI

During the early years of Huawei's rise to prominence, even as the CCP was aggressively pursuing techno-nationalist initiatives to fund and support the growth of its national champions, multinational enterprises became addicted to a lucrative business model: the licensing of their baseline technology to up-and-coming but relatively less advanced joint venture partners in China.

This approach goes back to China's early '909' programmes in the 1990s when companies such as Lucent Technologies, AT&T and Alcatel began a trend of transferring their IP regarding information and communication technology (ICT) to nascent Chinese contract manufacturers.[12] MNEs received increasing amounts of revenue from licensing and used it to develop the next generation of products. Given their commanding lead in innovation at the time, the strategy seemed brilliant.

For MNEs, the revenues generated from IP licensing to China were so enormous that the practice came to define the prevailing business model in the tech sector.

According to the Bureau of Economic Analysis at the U.S. Department of Commerce, between 2009 and 2019, U.S. tech companies earned US$65 billion in IP licence fees from China.[13]

From 2001 to 2018, Huawei, alone, paid more than US$6 billion to licence IP from third parties, 80% of which was to U.S. companies.[14] The Chinese tech giant reported that it had more than 100 patent licence agreements (including unilateral and cross licences) with major global ICT companies such as Nokia, Ericsson, Qualcomm, AT&T, Apple and Samsung.

All the while, however, manufacturing capacity was gradually being offshored out of the U.S. and other advanced countries into China. The Trend accelerated when China was accepted into the World Trade Organization in 2001.

All these developments were entirely consistent with the neoliberal model of international economics. As we discussed in Chapter 3, however, neoliberal logic failed to account for non-economic factors, such as geopolitics and pandemics. In a non-hostile economic environment, neoliberal logic might be justifiable, but given Beijing's unrelenting techno-nationalist imperatives, the licensing-dependent model ultimately backfired on American and other foreign tech companies.

As the American writer, Ernest Hemingway wrote: 'A man goes bankrupt gradually, and then suddenly'. This could best describe the plight of many U.S. and foreign technology firms in the PC or telecommunication space who presided over a massive shift of both IP and manufacturing capabilities to China in less than two decades. Today, most new innovations coming out of Silicon Valley cannot be manufactured unless they are made in China or Taiwan.

HUAWEI AND THE QUEST FOR CHIP SELF-SUFFICIENCY

The war on Huawei provides us with a clear and observable test case regarding the effectiveness of U.S. sanctions and export controls. It also places Huawei at the centre of China's ongoing efforts to cross new technology thresholds and achieve self-sufficiency in semiconductor fabrication.

As discussed in previous chapters, after blacklisting Huawei, Washington changed the foreign direct product rule (FDPR), which then blocked any company, anywhere, from transferring finished goods, including chips—made with even the most minute trace of 'controlled' U.S. technology. This effectively choked off Huawei's supply of advanced chips from its supplier, TSMC, which meant that Huawei's smartphones would no longer have 5G capability.

In late August 2023, however, despite U.S. restrictions, Huawei rolled out the new 'Mate 60' smartphone, featuring a 7-nanometre (nm) leading-edge Kirin 9000 chip designed by HiSilicon.

The rollout was an apparent triumph over U.S. export controls, suggesting that Huawei and SMIC had overcome a major technology chokepoint in the photolithography and etching segments of the chip fabrication value.

But, as we discussed, it became clear that SMIC had been using foreign-made DUV machines and etching technology, which it had acquired and stockpiled prior to the above export restrictions taking effect.

Figure 10.1   Backside of the Huawei Mate 60 Smartphone, Showing Camera Lens.

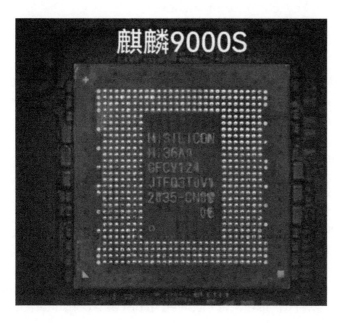

Figure 10.2   The Kirin 9000 7-nanometre Chip, Designed by HiSilicon and Fabricated by Semiconductor Manufacturing International Corporation (SMIC) for the Huawei Mate 60 Smartphone.

Huawei unveiled the Mate 60 during a visit of U.S. Commerce Secretary Gina Raimondo to China, and was likely pressured to make the announcement by the Chinese government. The truth eventually came out that Huawei and SMIC management knew the public would eventually find out that they had relied on foreign technology to mass produce the Kirin 9000 and 9000S chips.

It is difficult for foreigners to appreciate just how desperately Beijing's autocrats want to achieve self-sufficiency in critical technologies. Clearly, in 2019, when Huawei was first placed on the BIS entity list, the CCP's efforts to establish its own independent chip fabrication ecosystem went into overdrive.

Beijing would make Huawei the central force behind this effort. It was clearly the most important and capable player to lead, given that it was a proven fighter and had successfully fought U.S. efforts to crush it.

Reports of new funding sources began to surface: A US$30 billion fund was reportedly established, now known as the Shenzhen Major Industry Investment Group Company, which formed part of the nucleus of a technology feedback loop consisting of Huawei, The Chinese Academy of Sciences and a host of tech start-ups that were focusing on key 'chokepoint' niches.[15]

One company to emerge from this ecosystem was SiCarrier, founded in 2021, a chip-manufacturing equipment maker that focused on laser light sources for photolithography machines. Another such entity, Zeetop Technologies, made the optical components needed for SiCarrier's equipment.[16]

Still another company, Cornerstone, worked with SiCarrier to develop photoresists, the light-sensitive film that covers a wafer before it undergoes the photolithography and etching process.[17]

Also in the mix were technology consultants, R&D firms and government technocrats assigned to keep a close watch on developments.

Whatever strategic partnerships emerge around China's chip campaign, Huawei will likely be involved, if not as a consultant, then as an investor, working closely with other niche players.

Industrial espionage, meanwhile, will play an important role in the progress of China's chip ambitions. Consider the case of ASML's litigation for intellectual property theft against a Chinese company, Dongfang Jingyuan Electron Ltd., which is related to a defunct Silicon Valley firm, Xtal Inc., which had been set up by a former ASML employee.[18]

It turned out that both Dongfang and Xtal had been set up in 2014 by a former ASML engineer named Zongchang Yu, expressly with the aim of obtaining ASML's technology and transferring it to China.[19]

Whatever the case, one thing is certain provides a treasure trove of information to Beijing. Huawei boasts a highly competent and motivated workforce that will work relentlessly to meet the company's and Beijing's goals. In this context, the scale of China's technology landscape and its growing number of innovators and public–private industry partnerships are only just beginning to be put into proper perspective.

Regarding Huawei and the advantage of scale, consider that when Washington placed Huawei on the entity list and thus restricted its access to Google's Android operating system, management tapped 10,000 Huawei engineers, requiring them to work continuously in three shifts over 24 hours, to tackle the problem.

The engineers were tasked with re-writing code and redesigning specifications so that Huawei might minimise the damage to U.S. export controls.

The efforts appear to have paid off. Engineers and code writers laid the groundwork for the replacement of the Android operating system, with a homegrown one: Harmony OS. Huawei also found replacements for about 90% of U.S. parts and components from Huawei's smartphone.

In November 2019, as reported by Reuters, Huawei gave its employees some US$286 million in bonuses for working 24/7 as a reward for successfully coping with U.S. sanctions.[20] By 2024, Huawei smartphones were no longer supporting any Android apps.

Huawei's future looks promising. Should the company ever become a publicly traded entity, an initial public offering (IPO) on the

Shanghai Stock Exchange could value the company at over US$1 trillion, by some estimates.[21]

Thus, Huawei's advancement in these areas will contribute not just to the bifurcation of technology sectors but it will also split the global EV and financial markets, as we will discuss in Chapters 21, 22 and 28.

Chapter 11

Tradecraft, Stealth and Technology

Osama Bin Laden, the world's most-wanted terrorist, was killed by U.S. commandos in the early hours of the morning of May 2, 2011. The Americans carried out an unlikely and daring helicopter-borne assault on a pitch-black, moonless night in Abbottabad, Pakistan.

The killing of Bin Laden was the most expensive, exhaustive and technologically sophisticated manhunt in history. U.S. intelligence was able to find him because of an omnipresent American surveillance web of electronic eyes and ears that wrapped around the planet and could infiltrate virtually any communications network or virtually any electronic communications device anywhere. The use of such technology marked a new era in the art of surveillance and intelligence gathering, otherwise known as tradecraft.

The raid's success came down to stealth technology that enabled U.S. forces to fly to the Bin Laden compound undetected and materialise, seemingly out of thin air.

From a techno-nationalist perspective, the raid, officially known as *Operation Neptune Spear*, is significant on three different levels.

On the surface, it is an adrenaline-charged story about revenge and long-awaited justice. But, on a second level, the operation reflects America's decades-long technological feedback loop and the immense power that it has afforded Washington's intelligence services.

On yet another level, however, the raid cast light on the secret world of tradecraft—in this case, the art of stealing valuable intelligence and hardware, and how this accelerated China's rise as a military power. The episode thus provides an illustration of how a second-tier power can quickly catch up to a leader by pursuing tradecraft.

As it turned out, a damaged tail section of a U.S. Blackhawk stealth helicopter was left behind at Bin Laden's compound. One of the choppers had crash-landed, which then required Navy SEAL commandos to demolish it before departing the scene. But they failed to destroy the intact tail-rotor section that had been sheared off in a hard landing, and it yielded a treasure trove of top-secret U.S. stealth designs and materials. As it happened, the Pakistanis gave Chinese intelligence agents access to the broken tail section, allegedly even allowing Chinese agents to take away a sample.[1]

Not long after the Blackhawk incident, *WikiLeaks* published a bombshell of classified U.S. government documents, revealing, in the process, just how extensively Chinese hackers had penetrated the communications infrastructure of the American military–industrial complex. Chinese spies had been routinely stealing designs, data and top-secret blueprints of America's most advanced weapons systems.[2]

Considering what we now know about the duration and extent of Beijing's technology-oriented tradecraft, the Blackhawk incident marks a turning point in the superpower rivalry. More on this in a bit.

THE DISTRACTIONS OF THE U.S. WAR ON TERROR

Washington's myopic focus on its war on terror, predominantly in the Middle East and Central Asia, allowed Chinese spies to quietly steal vast amounts of American technology through widespread, ongoing cyber-intrusion campaigns. In a textbook example of Sun Tzu's *The Art of War*, which stresses the importance of taking advantage of 'your enemy's unreadiness', Beijing's tradecraft was performed in cyberspace, right under the collective nose of the U.S. defence and intelligence establishments.

Indeed, many in positions of leadership in the U.S. and the West were not even aware that they had been labelled opponents of the Chinese Communist Party (CCP), and it would be years before they grasped the enormity of Beijing's cyber intrusions.

To the delight of Beijing's central planners, the U.S. remained bogged down in Afghanistan for *20 years*—by far America's longest war—incurring costs of over US$2 trillion by the time it withdrew in 2021. To put this in perspective, U.S. taxpayers spent an average of *US$300 million a day* on the war on terror in Afghanistan for *two decades*.[3] The numbers are almost beyond comprehension.

By way of comparison, Washington spent twice as much on the war as China spent on its famed Belt and Road Initiative (BRI) over nearly the same period. Yet the outcomes of the two could not be more strikingly different.

Beijing's extensive building of roads, railways, ports and digital infrastructure throughout Asia, Africa, Europe and South America had expanded China's geopolitical and economic influence and increased its military access to deep water ports, energy supply chains and shipping lanes throughout the world.

In a techno-nationalist context, the CCP's focus on expanding Chinese-led digital infrastructure—and its efforts to displace and replace American global influence—was, at its core, what turbocharged its technology feedback loop.

But Washington needed to take the fight to Bin Laden. Al Qaeda had tormented the U.S. with a long string of attacks around the world, including on the home front, in 1993, when Al Qaeda operatives detonated a car bomb in a parking garage beneath the World Trade Centre (WTC) in New York. In that initial attempt to take down a WTC Tower, six people died and 1,500 others were injured.[4]

Other notorious acts of violence included the 1998 truck bombings at U.S. embassies in Nairobi, Kenya and Dar es Salaam, Tanzania, which together left another 240 people dead, and the ramming of the USS

Cole by an explosives-laden speedboat while the ship was refuelling in Yemen.[5] The latter attack killed 17 American sailors in 2000.[6]

Bin Laden's jihadi *magnum opus* came on September 11, 2001, when Al Qaeda terrorists hijacked four commercial airliners and turned them into guided missiles, flying two passenger-laden planes into the Twin Towers of New York's WTC and a third into the Pentagon. A fourth plane—probably destined for the White House or the U.S. Capitol building—crashed in the Pennsylvania countryside.

Al Qaeda's second attack on the WTC had achieved physical devastation and loss of life—a surreal day that I will never forget. The attacks left 2,996 innocent people dead and changed the course of modern history.[7]

Thus, America's preoccupation with its war on terror left open a blindside to China's hackers, and ironically, U.S. pre-emptive military actions in Afghanistan probably made the world a safer place for the expansion of China's Belt and Road Initiative (BRI).

THE TECHNOLOGY THAT FOUND BIN LADEN

Before the U.S. could kill Bin Laden, they had to find him. Not an easy task, as he had been on the run for almost a decade since the 9/11 massacre.

A host of spy agencies, including the Central Intelligence Agency (CIA), the National Security Agency (NSA) and the National Reconnaissance Office (NRO), along with different branches of the U.S. military, used a fleet of surveillance satellites to collect electronic signals from telephone conversations, tapped email and text exchanges, GPS tracking and other means.[8] Stealth unmanned aerial vehicles (UAVs) provided 24/7 stakeout operations, hovering over targets for long periods of time and using high-resolution cameras to identify people from thousands of metres up in the sky.[9]

The NSA's surveillance capacities were even more astounding. Through a clandestine programme known as Tailored Access Operations, NSA spies implanted spyware and tracking technology on targeted mobile phones, telephone networks, routers, computers and other infrastructure around the world.[10] Using such technology, the

U.S. was able to penetrate virtually any network, anywhere, and employ sophisticated voice recognition technology to identify individuals and pinpoint their geographic location.

The Al Qaeda attack on New York's WTC in 2001 paved the way for far-reaching electronic eavesdropping and surveillance laws in the U.S., most notably through the passage of the *USA Patriot Act* less than 2 months after the September 11 attacks.

The act was a catalyst for increased information sharing between law enforcement agencies, and this sparked a surge in the deployment of new surveillance technologies, AI and data science, all with the goal of deterring terrorism—which usually meant pre-emptively finding, identifying and killing people before they could follow through on a suspected plot.[11]

Spending on many of the technologies that contributed to Bin Laden's killing was classified at the time as part of a so-called Black Budget known only to a few. Consequently, we cannot be certain of the state of the art in surveillance tech at the time, nor can we be certain how significantly it has advanced since the raid on the Bin Laden compound.

In the month prior to the raid, the NRO curated around 400 high-resolution images taken by drones, satellites and human assets on the ground. Information gleaned from those images was used to identify patterns of behaviour of the suspects in the compound. The data and metadata were then used by the operation's planners to carry out the mission.[12]

By the time of the mission, the U.S. already had at its disposal science fiction-like technology. A satellite could, for example, shine a laser beam onto a windowpane a kilometres below on the ground, invisible to the human eye, and record vibrations from human voices. AI could then analyse the distinct vibration patterns and match them to voice recognition data.[13]

On the night of the raid by SEAL Team Six, President Barack Obama, the Chairman of the Joint Chiefs of Staff, the heads of the NSA and CIA and others wedged themselves into a cramped conference room adjacent to the White House situation room and watched events unfold in real time, thanks to drone and satellite imagery and live camera feeds from the commandos.

THE TECHNOLOGY THAT KILLED BIN LADEN

To reach Bin Laden's compound in Bilal Town, on the outskirts of Abbottabad, the U.S. had to sneak into Pakistani airspace and fly undetected for 90 minutes from a U.S. Air Force forward-operating base (FOB) outside of Jalalabad, Afghanistan.

The special operation deployed two Blackhawk helicopters, which flew at low altitude through almost total darkness, skirting just above the tops of trees and muted landscape. To avoid detection, the choppers' exteriors had been modified with trapezoidal-shaped radar-defeating panels that were also treated with special radar-absorbing paint or 'skin'. Other adjustments had been made to make the machines as quiet as possible and to reduce their infrared footprints.[14]

Both craft were equipped with electronic jamming technologies and had further backup from a U.S. Air Force's airborne warning and control system (AWACS) plane that was circling in Afghan airspace, monitoring for threats.

The two stealth Blackhawks carried 23 commandos from the Navy's SEAL Team Six, an elite group trained for highly specialised warfare operations in all manner of conditions.[15] The choppers travelled about 200 kilometres into Pakistani airspace before descending upon the Bin Laden compound.

Three Chinook CH-47s—much larger helicopters with double rotors front and aft, also modified for stealth—followed about 40 minutes behind the Blackhawks.[16] The Chinooks carried another two-dozen Navy SEALs as backup (just in case they were needed) and were fitted to refuel the lead Blackhawks.

One of the Chinooks, largely empty, was to transport Bin Laden, dead or alive, and any other assets seized from the raid back to base camp. The Chinooks flew to an area near the Indus River, about 10 minutes away from the raid site, and waited. As it turned out, the empty Chinook would be used to pick up Navy SEALs from the Blackhawk that had to be destroyed.[17]

The Blackhawks arrived on scene at the compound just after midnight on May 2, Pakistan time.[18] One of the Blackhawks immediately experienced a problem with instability that caused the pilot to set the craft down, loud and hard, in what amounted to a controlled crash-landing.

Despite the mishap, the Navy SEALs alighted from both craft and forced their way into the three-story compound, breaching gates and doors floor-by-floor until they found and killed Bin Laden and seized a trove of computer hard drives, disks, thumb drives, files and documents. Bin Laden's corpse was brought back in a body bag.

Bin Laden's identity was confirmed by DNA analysis and his body was flown, less than 24 hours later, almost 1,400 kilometres to the USS *Carl Vinson* in the northern Arabian Sea, where a sea burial was performed in accordance with Muslim religious rites.

CHINESE TRADECRAFT AND HELICOPTER STEALTH TECHNOLOGY

Figure 11.1   **US Military Bell Invictus Helicopter with the latest Stealth Technology.**

The Navy SEALs' explosives failed to destroy a section of the crashed Blackhawk's tail, leaving behind the tail rotor. The remaining material contained a variety of stealth technologies—what are commonly referred to in military parlance as 'low observable'.

Pakistani authorities took possession of the helicopter's tail section for approximately two weeks before returning it to the Americans. During that time, Reuters and other media outlets reported that ISI, the Pakistani intelligence services, had allowed Chinese intelligence officials and engineers to view the wreckage, take photos and even walk away with samples of its special radar-evading skin.[19]

The New York Times reported that U.S. intelligence had intercepted conversations of Pakistani officials inviting the Chinese to the crash site—which both Pakistani and Chinese officials vehemently denied.[20] However, it was not the first time that the Americans had accused Pakistan and China of intelligence sharing.

Shortly after the raid, U.S. Congressman Dana Rohrabacher of California wrote an open letter to congressional colleagues alleging that in 1998, Pakistan had given China an unexploded Tomahawk cruise missile that malfunctioned when the U.S. Navy fired it in an attack on Bin Laden's Al Qaeda training camps in Afghanistan. According to Rohrabacher, '. . . the Communist Chinese reverse-engineered the missile and dissected its components allowing them to learn its vulnerabilities and defeat its capabilities'.[21]

In 2021, concerns over the Pakistan–China connection flared up again when a photograph of a model of a Chinese helicopter at the China Helicopter Research and Development Institute in Jingdezhen, in East China's Jiangxi Province, went viral.[22] A modified version of China's Z-20 helicopter bore a striking resemblance to the stealth-modified Blackhawks.

OPERATION 'BYZANTINE HADES'

The poaching of stealth secrets from the Blackhawk helicopter's tail section fits into a much broader tradecraft campaign in Beijing's techno-nationalist master plan: theft of IP, reverse engineering, accelerated development and production at scale.

Well before Abbottabad, Chinese state-backed hackers had been successfully infiltrating networks within the U.S. Department of Defence (DoD), other government agencies, and American defence contractors in a series of intrusions codenamed 'Byzantine Hades' by

U.S. authorities. In the process, the Chinese military–industrial complex had gained access to an immense amount of technology, saving itself hundreds of billions of dollars in costs and perhaps decades of toil.

The world learned about this in 2010 from a series of *Wikileaks* dumps that included 260,000 U.S. diplomatic cables and emails representing years of sensitive communications.[23] It emerged that as early as 2006, American officials had been aware of the exploits of hackers from the PLA's so-called Third Department but were unable to stop them.

Primarily through electronic espionage, the Third Department had targeted and infiltrated a wide range of government, corporate and academic entities, harvesting data, designs and other critical IP relating to America's most important technologies and trade secrets. According to reporting by Reuters, some of the hacks were traced directly to a PLA facility in Chengdu province identified as a unit of the *First Technical Reconnaissance Bureau* (TRB)—one of at least six similar units.

Among the *Wikileaks* documents was a top-secret PowerPoint presentation created by U.S. officials that cited 30,000 hacking incidents, including more than 500 significant intrusions in DoD systems, at least 1,600 DoD computers penetrated, and more than 600,000 user accounts compromised, as well as over 300,000 user IDs and passwords and 33,000 U.S. Air Force officer personnel records compromised.[24]

The PLA had not only obtained the designs of the F-35, which it incorporated into its own fifth-generation J-31 fighter jet, but it had also collected information on its radar design, including the number and types of radar-defeating modules used by the system.[25] The hackers also pickpocketed vital data and designs regarding the F-35's engine, including information on how the engine used special gases to reduce its heat signature.[26]

U.S. investigators also determined that Chinese hackers stole information about the U.S. Air Force's B-2 Stealth bomber, the F-22 Raptor, missile navigation and tracking systems, space-based laser technology and top-secret designs related to nuclear submarines and anti-aircraft missiles.[27] The results of Byzantine Hades were a nightmare come true for the U.S. defence establishment.

In all, the PLA's digital intruders stole an estimated 50 terabytes of data—at least that which investigators were aware of.[28] To put this in perspective, the data extracted by Chinese spies, according to this one single *Wikileaks* PowerPoint, is the equivalent to more than five times the content in all the volumes currently in the U.S. Library of Congress, the world's largest book repository.[29]

These represent history's greatest heists, and these types of cyber intrusions continue. Hackers can often rely on technologies that are relatively pedestrian and easily available, often open-sourced and cost next to nothing. There may be no other example of a more lop-sided cost-benefit ratio. This kind of asymmetric power means that even agents with quite limited resources can gain access to nearly any organisation from governments to corporations to academic institutions, making cybersecurity a very serious issue for almost everyone.

Stealing leading-edge technology from a competitor involves much more than getting the 'secret sauce' to something highly desired. It allows the successful hacker to avoid the decades of trial and error often necessary to reach the breakthroughs that are the fruits of incremental, time-consuming R&D. For a large nation-state or even a small, modestly funded cell of lone wolves, successful tradecraft can quickly flip the status quo between leaders and followers in an industry or niche.

FIFTH-GENERATION FIGHTER JETS

Figure 11.2   Frontal View of a US Airforce F-35 Stealth Fighter.

In any era, stealing an opponent's technology, reverse engineering it, copying it outright and making improvements to the original design is common practice. From a Darwinian standpoint, whether in the animal kingdom or a twenty-first-century superpower military competition, it is far more efficient to steal an opponent's hard-gained innovations than to expend resources and time in an often-vain attempt to catch up, especially when the barriers to entry are prohibitively high.

Chinese prototypes in military aircraft design and production, therefore, have a history of copying American designs. It is no coincidence that China's long-range bomber, the H-20, looks almost identical to its U.S. counterpart, the B-1 bomber.

China's latest fifth-generation fighter aircraft, the J-20 and J-31, closely resemble the U.S. F-22 Raptor and F-35 Lightning fighter jets. Again, no coincidence.

Future historians will cite China's multi-pronged efforts to steal the secrets of the American F-35, the world's most advanced combat aircraft and arguably the most sophisticated military weapon system ever created. Because of the many high-tech breakthroughs it incorporates, as well as its ability to connect assets in the air, on land, at sea and in space, the F-35 is referred to in U.S. military circles simply as a force-multiplier node.

Lockheed Martin, the U.S. military contractor that builds the jet, makes three variants: the F-35A for the Air Force, the F35-B, which has vertical take-off and landing capabilities, for the Marine Corps, and the F-35C, designed to operate on aircraft carriers for the Navy. The price range for any one plane is around US$80–$90 million.[30]

The F-35 embodies every facet of leading-edge science achieved through America's historical techno-nationalist feedback loop. The plane uses state-of-the-art stealth technology that renders it virtually invisible to enemy radar, yet simultaneously, it makes use of the full electromagnetic spectrum to achieve situational awareness.[31]

An F-35's electronic warfare capabilities allow it to jam and disrupt the homing signals on incoming missiles and an adversary's other sensory technologies. At the same time, it can engage multiple threats well beyond visual range from all directions, track them continuously and attack them. The onboard artificial intelligence systems can perform *trillions* of calculations per second and execute offensive and defensive actions independent of the pilot. F-35 pilots use special augmented reality helmets integrated into the aircraft electronic brains to extend situational awareness.[32]

Such advanced electrics can also synchronise with UAVs, commonly referred to as drones, which are fast becoming a key addition to air combat operations.

The design of the F-35's frame and engine—the world's most powerful fighter engine at the time of this writing—are also technological breakthroughs. The plane is said to achieve Mach 1.6 supersonic speed (just under twice the speed of sound), according to Pratt and Whitney, the American aerospace manufacturer.[33] The jet's turbofan and exhaust outlets have been designed to limit heat signature and radar detection.

No surprise, then, that rather than try and play an almost impossible game of catchup with the Americans, China's military and state intelligence agencies doubled down on their quest to steal the designs and IP behind the F-35.

This strategy worked spectacularly well. Over the course of a long-running cyber-intrusion campaign, the PLA and other government-sponsored hackers stole an absolute treasure trove of data, designs and schematics relating to technical specifications and weapons for the F-35.

SKUNKWORKS LEGACY FEEDBACK LOOP MEETS CHINA TRADECRAFT

American work on stealth technology began in the late 1950s when scientists turned their focus to designing aircraft with distinct shapes and surface materials that would deflect, redirect and absorb electromagnetic radiation from radar. Such multi-spectral camouflage was born largely out of the experiences of the CIA's U-2 spy plane programme, which was tasked with flying over the Soviet Union and collecting vital intelligence. U-2 aircraft were often detected and attacked by radar-enabled Soviet surface-to-air-missiles.

In 1958, the American spy community launched its Skunkworks programme to create, test and produce new aircraft with very low observability. Skunkworks' clandestine R&D would change the course of history. Thus, began decades of funding by the CIA and other secretive elements of the U.S. military–industrial complex.

Lockheed, the U.S. defence contractor, became deeply embedded within the Skunkworks R&D technology feedback loop, and experimental aircraft began operating out of facilities in remote areas of the California and Nevada deserts.

By the 1970s, the DoD had begun work on its own first-generation stealth aircraft. But it was, in fact, a Soviet physicist and mathematician, Pyotr Ufimtsev, who is credited with pioneering the physics behind stealth aircraft technology. In the 1960s, he published a series of equations that laid out the mathematical physics of edge diffraction.[34]

At the time, the Soviet Union lacked sufficient computing power to solve Ufimtsev's equations when it came to producing actual aircraft designs. By the early 1970s, however, Ufimtsev's equations had been translated into English and Lockheed's engineers, with the advantages of American advances in computer science, were incorporating his ideas into their designs under a programme named Echo 1. By 1975, Lockheed engineers were able to design an aircraft model with flat-panelled faceted surfaces that, when a scaled mock-up was tested, proved to be 99.9% invisible to radar.[35]

In 1977, the Defence Advanced Research Projects Agency (DARPA) began funding the Skunkworks through a programme called HAVE Blue to fully test the proof of concept, eventually resulting in the F-117 Nighthawk stealth bomber.[36]

The prototype model had straight, angular lines like a cut diamond but was aerodynamically very unstable, leading pilots to dub it the 'hopeless diamond'. Making F-117 fully airworthy required computational advances that allowed constant, automatic in-flight correction and stabilisation, without which the plane could not be flown.

Ongoing R&D into stealth aircraft technology in the 1970s and 1980s led to the development of the B-2 Spirit bomber, built by Northrup Grumman and known as the 'flying wing'.[37] Further advances led to an enhanced version in the 1990s—the B-21, a much larger aircraft capable of delivering nuclear payloads on an intercontinental range, and fighter jets featuring stealth technology appeared in the early 2000s.

The potential destructive power of invisible, sinister machines that can unleash Armageddon on an unsuspecting target put the stealth technology race in a surreal and terrifying light—especially to a nation that, like China, had lacked the ability to field any kind of serious stealth-enabled military aircraft at that point in time.

Nevertheless, China's first fully equipped fighter—the Chengdu J-20, known as the 'mighty dragon'—is believed to have acquired stealth capabilities by 2017, while Russia's fighter Sukhoi SU-57 was said to have them in 2020.

A NEW 'STEALTH' INNOVATION RACE DRIVEN BY AI

As evidenced by the Chengdu J-20, China's rapid advancement is nothing short of remarkable. Compared to the long road taken by the U.S. from the early days of stealth technology in the 1950s, it took only a decade for Beijing to build its own prototype. For that, Beijing can thank its tradecraft and the game-changing technologies of the 4th Industrial Revolution (4IR) that made it possible.

Supercomputers, advanced AI and algorithms now perform billions of calculations per second and can create experimental designs, proof-of-concept variations and execute millions upon millions of virtual simulations, considering billions of variables. A supercomputer can accomplish trial-and-error calculations in a matter of seconds or minutes that would otherwise take decades or even *centuries* to accomplish. Thus, stolen data, designs, formulas and other critical knowledge is the ultimate techno-nationalist springboard and can become the ultimate power multiplier.

China's rapid development has sparked an escalating techno-nationalist arms race. Consider that, including ongoing R&D expenditures, Washington is expected to spend US$203 billion just to develop, purchase and operate its long-range stealth B-21 bomber programme from 2023 to 2053.[38]

That is just one programme of many. Consider the funds required to develop and maintain other forms of stealth technology for aircraft, submarines and other naval vessels not to mention the funding of new technologies such as quantum-sensing, which could render current stealth technologies obsolete.

Here, we must reconsider the centrality of advanced semiconductors, without which none of these advanced designs, simulations or manufacturing would be possible. Yet again, we find the six core elements of techno-nationalism at play.

THE RISE OF THE DRONES

UAVs, conventionally referred to as drones, represent the most telling benchmark of China's techno-nationalist effectiveness and how tradecraft can facilitate a leapfrog over comparable U.S. technology.

As was the case with its fifth-generation fighters and its long-range bomber, the PLA managed to use a combination of stolen data and massive R&D efforts at home to design China's Loyal Wingman attack drone, which looks like a copy of the U.S. military's Valkyrie. China's version was designed for the same purpose as the Valkyrie: to fly alongside manned aircraft, perform reconnaissance and test and attack enemy defences.

Earlier generations of Chinese hunter-killer drones also support the narrative of copycatting. Consider China's so-called CH Rainbow series of drones, developed by the China Academy of Aerospace Aerodynamics, an offshoot of the state-owned China Aerospace Science and Technology Corporation. Externally, China's Rainbow series looks just like the U.S. Reaper, built by a subsidiary of General Atomics in the U.S.

America's Reaper drones have been used extensively throughout the world to gather intelligence and to hunt and kill high-value human targets.

The killing of Iranian general Qasem Soleimani in Baghdad in 2020 by the CIA is thought to have been the work of an American Q9 Reaper, as was the over-the-horizon assassination of Al Qaeda's leader, Al Zawahiri in 2022 in the heart of Kabul.[39, 40]

Mock-up photos and reports regarding the development of China's latest flying-wing stealth drone suggest that China may have leap-frogged the U.S.—at least when it comes to on-paper designs and mock-up models.

Engineers at China Aerodynamics Research and Development Centre in Sichuan are said to employ revolutionary features such as active flow control (AFC), which replaces traditional moving parts on an aircraft's surface, such as ailerons, rudders and elevators. AFC uses bursts of high-pressure air from actuators embedded within an aircraft body to power and manoeuvre the craft and makes the surface of the drone much less visible to radar.[41]

The effectiveness and reliability of Chinese drones are evident in the arms industry, where the U.S. is now competing directly with Chinese arms manufacturers in selling killer drones to the Middle Eastern Allies.[42] Weapons sales constitute a form of realpolitik and afford Beijing, Washington and other governments influence and strategic advantages when it comes to geopolitics.

From a tradecraft perspective, weapons sales to third countries also provide opportunities to collect intelligence. As a proxy uses a weapons system, the system can provide an assessment of an adversary's technology, as well as aid in the creation of new advances around a weapons system.

These developments suggest that China has pulled even with or may have even surpassed the U.S. in the latest generation of drone technology.

Chapter 12

Data, Biotech and Geopolitics

It is wrong to say that data is the 'new oil'.

Data, in fact, is more valuable than oil because it is an essentially non-expendable commodity. In technical economic terms, it is a *non-rival* good: one person's use does not limit anyone else's. Data can be used again and again, sold and resold, analysed and re-analysed for different kinds of value extraction. Every new advancement in artificial intelligence (AI) and data science, in theory, can extend and increase the utility of the same data.

Thus, data has become an essential geopolitical asset, and finding ways to obtain it, steal it, analyse it and protect it are all techno-nationalist priorities.

The strategic value of data in the global digital commons, especially that of private citizens, has motivated government intelligence agencies to target social media and messaging platforms as well as e-commerce and other sources. Governments now show the same appetite that the for-profit surveillance capitalists have for data—indeed, they often buy it directly from the data capitalists.

As the Internet-of-Things (IoT) turns billions of devices into transmitters, content creators, and recipients of data, everything from electric vehicles to household appliances has been pulled into the geopolitical data vortex.

Consider that in March 2023, the U.S. House of Representatives voted overwhelmingly to force ByteDance, the Chinese parent company of TikTok, the hugely popular streaming video app, to divest completely of it or face a ban in the U.S. The ban, supported by the U.S. Senate, would effectively prohibit Internet providers and app stores from providing access to TikTok, cutting off 170 million American subscribers, including some 7 million businesses.

This was not the first time that the TikTok issue had grabbed the national spotlight. In 2020, then President Trump signed an executive order that mandated ByteDance to sell TikTok to American investors, which was subsequently blocked by a U.S. federal judge. Again, in 2022, the U.S. Senate passed legislation, signed by President Biden, that banned TikTok from the federal government's information and technology infrastructure and devices.

Why all of this for a popular streaming video app?

Because of strict requirements laid out in China's Cybersecurity Law and National Security Laws, which require Chinese companies and citizens to provide the Chinese Communist Party (CCP) with user data, (when asked) TikTok was regarded as a proxy of the Chinese state and, consequently, was declared a malign actor.

Any Chinese entity, then, operating outside of China, would become suspect.

Given the vast ocean of data already in circulation linking the online activities of Americans, China's advanced AI capabilities, hypothetically, could leverage TikTok's growing American subscriber base and connect their private data to other relevant data points.[1] According to research done by MIT, anyone can be identified by extrapolating from just a few of their data points.[2]

Sophisticated algorithms, supercomputing and cognitive AI, for example, can link a teenager's age, postal code, ethnicity and phone number to a treasure trove of tangentially related data points that, with extrapolation, can lead to the identification of other people of interest and reveal valuable correlations and relationships.

Much of this raw data is already a by-product of data capitalism. Today, hundreds of millions of people have had their data sold and resold by the likes of Google, Meta, Twitter (now called 'X') and Amazon—all of which are part of a larger ecosystem that thrives on a secondary market for data commoditisation.[3]

The high degree of mistrust of TikTok and other Chinese companies was fuelled in part by an increase in corporate cyber intrusions believed to have originated in China. CrowdStrike, the Silicon Valley-based cybersecurity and technology firm, has been reporting that since 2018, cyberattacks and intrusions have been increasing and intensifying.[4] As we have seen, when this is viewed in the context of hybrid warfare, the prospects for Chinese firms looking to expand into Western markets looks to be an increasingly vexing situation.

This logic was a contributing factor in the Trump administration's 2017 Section 301 investigation that eventually led to the imposition of tariffs against Chinese imported goods. It was also the impetus behind regulatory agencies such as the U.S. Bureau of Industry and Security (BIS) and the Committee on Foreign Investment in the United States (CFIUS) to begin ramping up export controls, sanctions and the blockage of acquisitions of U.S. technology companies and assets.

The U.S. Department of Justice named individuals and hacker groups suspected of linkages to the Chinese state and were known to have stolen data from more than 100 key U.S. tech and telecommunications companies, defence contractors, government agencies and social media groups. Known targets included IBM, Hewlett Packard, Boeing, Facebook (Meta) and the National Aeronautics and Space Administration's (NASA) and Goddard Space Flight Centre.[5, 6]

THE ELEMENTS OF DATA GEOPOLITICS

Global flows of information move at speeds so high and volumes so immense that they can be used to influence geopolitical events in real time, making techno-nationalism a pervasive and disruptive force. Given today's information infrastructure, 1 terabit (1 trillion bits) of data per second can move around the world at nearly the speed of light.

To grasp the full extent of this phenomenon, from a geopolitical perspective, we must focus on three core themes.

Firstly, corporations and governments are both competing and collaborating to acquire, analyse and leverage data for a wide variety of purposes. Companies—both state-backed and private—are providing unprecedented amounts of data across a range of industries and sectors to governments—both autocratic and democratic—who are using it for economic, military and social objectives.

Take, for example, the BGI Group, a Chinese state-funded genomics company that managed to capture DNA profiles from millions of private citizens around the world through a variety of means, including antenatal blood samples and COVID-19 testing. This data was then analysed by the People's Liberation Army (PLA), as we will discuss later. Therefore, we must examine how such data is being used and to what possible geopolitical ends.

Beyond state-owned and state-backed entities, enormous amounts of data are being generated through private companies such as Meta, Google, TikTok and Amazon. This data is filtered through free-market mechanisms to governments and other entities.

Secondly, we must consider the fact that data is being used in information and narrative wars throughout the global digital commons as part of a wider battle among governments. State and non-state actors use personal data to orchestrate and influence campaigns on social media and other platforms throughout the digital global commons.

Later in this chapter, we discuss Russian attempts to influence election outcomes in the U.S., Germany, the U.K. and a host of other countries. In a case study, we will look at how the now-defunct data analytics company Cambridge Analytica provided governments with data analysis that influenced election outcomes in more than 50 countries.

Thirdly, we must ponder how a hybrid cold war between China and the U.S. has put multinational companies in a geopolitical 'grey zone' in which they must enter symbiotic partnerships with friendly governments while simultaneously defending themselves from rival regimes and actors. This dynamic has made the 'datasphere' a dangerous arena where cyberattacks and cybersecurity concerns rule the day.

WHAT IS DATA AND WHY IS IT IMPORTANT?

The amount of data created, captured, copied and consumed and stored throughout the world is expected to climb from two zettabytes in 2010 to just under 200 zettabytes in 2025.[7] (One zettabyte equals one billion terabytes). A terabyte refers to storage capacity, as opposed to a terabit, which deals with transmission speed. In other words, the world is awash in an almost incomprehensible amount of data. But what exactly is data?

In the digital universe, data comes in three forms: structured, unstructured and metadata.

Structured data is highly organised into relational sets that, for example, link names, dates, addresses, geolocations and payment information to a specific transaction or a specified subject or task. Unstructured data typically involves much larger data sets, compiled by either machines or humans and generally consists of large collections of files. Metadata can be described as data about data; that is, it involves information identifying trends, relationships and causalities in structured and unstructured data.

The datasphere, in effect, encompasses a universe parallel to the physical world, where structured data, unstructured data and metadata accumulate. Theoretically, everything in the datasphere is accessible, given the right artificial intelligence (AI), algorithms and cyber-offensive capabilities.

TECHNO-AUTHORITARIANISM AND SURVEILLANCE CAPITALISM

As the COVID-19 pandemic forced countries around the world to test and quarantine entire populations, the BGI Group, a state-backed Chinese genomics company, began to raise alarm bells within Western intelligence communities.

By 2021, the BGI Group had sold some 35 million COVID-19 testing kits across 180 countries. BGI also established 58 of its own testing labs in 18 countries where it had signed deals with local medical establishments.[8] In addition to BGI's direct overseas sales, China distributed millions of other COVID-19 testing kits free of charge through its embassies as part of Beijing's 'virus diplomacy' programme.[9]

Along with the COVID-19 test kits, BGI promoted its gene-sequencing technology, encouraging medical researchers everywhere to use it to acquire patient samples, test them and send the data to BGI, where it was analysed and stored in China's massive National Genomics Data Centre (NGDC).[10]

But the real achievement of BGI's COVID testing programme was the creation of an extensive platform from which BGI was able to distribute an even more powerful tool: antenatal testing kits. These kits, known as non-invasive prenatal tests (NIPT), provide access to a woman's genetic information (as well as that of the unborn child) from surplus blood samples linked to the placenta.

According to Reuters, which reviewed about 100 public documents and company statements, by 2021 BGI's NIPT had been marketed in countries including Germany, Spain, the U.K., Canada, Australia, Thailand, India and Pakistan, and had given BGI access to genetic data from 8.4 million women and their babies.[11] Other key data collected included each woman's country of residence, medical history and details such as the sex of the foetus.

GENETIC DATA AND NATIONAL SECURITY

Having access to large amounts of genetic data allows governments and private organisations to unlock patterns of genetic variations in populations around the world, particularly when a large database is analysed with ample computing power. That ability has both economic and military implications.

Genomic-wide association studies (GWAS) search the DNA sequences of a study group for very small genetic markers known as 'single nucleotide polymorphisms' (SNPs).

The identification of SNPs means, for example, that in principle, a physiological characteristic can be mapped to a particular gene in a specific group of people from a distinct gene pool. For institutions with access to powerful AI and machine learning algorithms, the larger the database, the more valuable the analysis—both as an economic goldmine and potentially as a tool of psychological operations in modern warfare.

The Reuters investigation of BGI revealed that the company had worked directly with the PLA since 2010 to develop and refine genomics sequencing in antenatal tests. Joint BGI–PLA studies included the identification of genetic distinctions between Han Chinese and minorities of the Tibetan and Uighur population groups. This included unique SNPs tied to certain illnesses, including mental illness.

Another BGI–PLA study explored potential gene-sequencing to predict soldier performance at high altitudes. This entailed efforts to isolate DNA in soldiers with a genetic predisposition to cerebral oedema (the swelling of the human brain occurring in oxygen-depleted air) in high mountainous regions such as the Himalayan border with India or the mountainous region of Xinjiang. Another study involved mapping genetic data associated with hearing loss in soldiers.[12]

THE BIOSECURITY–GENOME TECHNOLOGY FEEDBACK LOOP

Efforts to identify genetically superior soldiers or enhanced population groups through genome mapping—and perhaps even to improve them—underscore how the capture, storage and analysis of genomic data are pushing the boundaries of techno-nationalism and turning the genome into a potential weapon.

The national security implications of these activities go well beyond genetically modified soldiers. For example, the engineering of pathogens can be used to target population groups with a genetic predisposition to distinct diseases or to destroy a population's food sources with bespoke pathogens.

So can the mapping of a population's genetic traits and its propensity to suffer from, for example, mental illnesses such as depression, bipolar disorder or compulsive-addictive behaviour, which might be exploited by intelligence services to target an individual's weaknesses for manipulation and blackmail.

Identification of an individual from just a small portion of their DNA, which, if combined with facial recognition data and other data points from financial transactions or social media, would obliterate an individual's right to privacy.

DNA, then, has become the ultimate surveillance tool. In its most grotesque applications, genetic data could be used for the persecution of specific groups of people and fuel 'ethnic cleansing' campaigns aimed at targeted portions of the human gene pool.

PHARMACOGENOMICS AND TECHNO-NATIONALISM

The economic dimensions of genomic data are every bit as consequential to a nation as its security risks. Specifically, a revolution in AI, connectivity and data science marks inflexion points for the medical and pharmaceutical industries. A new field, 'pharmacogenomics', has emerged.

Pharmacogenomics involves the creation of customised pharmaceutical drugs and medicines based on an individual's unique genomic information. For example, heart medication or antidepressants can be tailored to an individual's tolerance thresholds and unique receptivity to different elements in a medicine.

First-mover advantages in pharmacogenomics are sure to be game-changing. Capturing market share will involve massive investments in AI and computer cognitive learning as well as leading-edge data analytics.

Consider the medical services that will evolve as part of the pharmacogenomics industry: nanorobotics to seek out malignant cells and deliver payloads of bespoke therapeutic drugs; complex medical avatars that build virtual models of the body down to the molecular level, linked to supercomputer analytics that can predict or prevent the spread of illness or design new drugs.[13]

The hardware and software required in this industry will spawn a wave of innovation and will see governments playing an increasing role in subsidising, supporting and promoting specific players. Despite objections from neoliberal purists who abhor any sort of industrial policy, this economic element of techno-nationalism will continue to gain sway.

Consider, for example, the U.S. National Security Commission of Artificial Intelligence (NSCAI), which boasts a who's who of former executives and representatives from some of the world's most competitive and innovative private companies.[14] Chaired by Eric Schmidt, the former CEO of Alphabet (parent company of Google), the NSCAI represents the kind of collaborative approach between government and private industry that will define geopolitical competition across a wide cross-section of the tech sector.[15]

Machine learning and generative AI are contributing to the development of new vaccines and medicines—a prospect that would have been unthinkable just a decade ago.

Take, for example, Pfizer's Paxlovid, the first oral antiviral medication to be approved for the treatment of COVID-19. Paxlovid reduced the risk of hospitalisation and death by 90% among high-risk patients.

To develop Paxlovid, Pfizer used machine learning to analyse large sets of clinical data and identify potential drug targets and used generative AI to design and synthesise new drug candidates that were predicted to be effective against those targets. Generative AI models were able to generate millions of potential drug candidates, many of which had never been synthesised before. Promising candidate drugs were then tested in the laboratory to see if they were effective against the SARS-CoV-2 virus and the most effective ones were advanced to clinical trials.

These technologies allowed Pfizer to identify potential drug targets, design new drug candidates and develop and test Paxlovid much more quickly than would have been possible using traditional methods.

Ironically, like virtually every other leading-edge twenty-first-century technology, the AI, computers and semiconductors deployed in these drug trials have both commercial and potential military applications and are therefore likely to be considered dual-use technologies, and thus potentially subject to export controls and other restrictions.

The result will be a globally bifurcated medical research environment that reflects the same fragmentation and separation as other strategic supply chains, such as semiconductors.

DATA CAPITALISM IN THE DIGITAL COMMONS

Free markets play a huge role in data geopolitics.

Companies across a wide range of sectors routinely gather and analyse information, as well as share and trade it with others. Matching data to identities or identifying trends in metadata has generated billions in revenues and profits for large and small businesses. This vast ecosystem links the public sector to a wide range of entities, including telecoms; device and service providers; consumer goods producers and retailers; social media; advertising companies; banks and financial services; think tanks and researchers; cybersecurity firms; and many more.

The writer, Shoshana Zuboff, has dubbed these practices 'surveillance capitalism' because it involves the sale of data derived from monitoring an individual's or an entity's behaviour both online and in the physical world. Such data can be sold and resold to virtually any buyer.

Governments now have at their disposal a highly cost-effective and low-risk collection strategy: buy data directly from third parties. As in other high-stakes areas, geopolitical competitors and adversaries can hide behind shell companies to avoid scrutiny, and they can use intermediaries to go about the business of quietly buying up treasure troves of data. This reality has spawned armies of for-hire data mercenaries.

In the platform economy and throughout data markets, three primary streams of data are available for harvesting. These include user-generated content, information purchased from original data suppliers (ODS) and third-party data supply services from intermediaries.

USER-GENERATED CONTENT

Billions of people around the world use social media and other platforms, voluntarily generating a vast reservoir of data, most of which is visible to anyone unless it has been blocked by censors. Given the right technology, state and non-state actors can amass and harvest this data and analyse it for any number of purposes.

Directly accessing the world's user-generated data is relatively inexpensive. Public and private entities can scrub the Internet and social media platforms using simple web browsers and large language models (LLMs) such as ChatGPT.

Specially designed algorithms seek out specialised data and identify patterns, linkages or anomalies. These technologies are enough to construct highly detailed profiles of individuals, groups, businesses or other high-value targets. In this manner, anyone with access to these technologies can identify and link, by association, the profiles of possible political opponents, suspected spies and informants or sympathisers. This, then, creates actionable intelligence of economic, military and social relevance.

ORIGINAL DATA SUPPLIERS

The diffusion of powerful, ubiquitous technology has given rise to an open market where data is bought and sold everywhere as a commodity. This has spawned an ecosystem of open data suppliers (ODS) and third parties, such as data brokers and analytics providers. ODS businesses are like original equipment manufacturers (OEMs) in that they provide the core product or service to which an entire ecosystem is linked.

In the platform economy, the largest original suppliers of data include the behemoth social media, messaging, e-commerce and entertainment platforms such as Meta/Facebook, Twitter (now known as 'X'), Google, Amazon, Alibaba, YouTube, Netflix and TikTok. These platforms are ODS because their commodity, the users' data, becomes the raw material for a host of different data ecosystems.

already by 2021, companies such as Meta and Instagram were among the mobile social apps collecting the largest amount of data from global iOS users, with at least 32 data points collected across 14 data segments per user. TikTok collected 24 data points from iOS users worldwide, while LinkedIn, the social app marketed to professionals, collected 26 data points. BY 2024 those data points had grown almost exponentially.

Recall the MIT study that states 2 or 3 data points were sufficient to begin making effective extrapolations about a user.

THE HUMAN GENOME AND DATA CAPITALISM

Genomic data is also widely marketed and has become a massive target for cyber theft.

Even as early as 2019, the largest for-profit genomic data companies, which function as ODS to a wider marketplace, had collected 25 million DNA samples from paying customers worldwide.

Private companies not only collect and analyse customer DNA for the purpose of individual customers, but they also convert this information into anonymised metadata and sell it to third parties.

As an example, the publicly traded Silicon Valley biotech company 23andMe signed a US$300 million deal with GlaxoSmithKline (GSK), the pharmaceutical giant, to provide anonymised metadata that GSK would use to develop new pharmacogenomic drugs.[16] 23andMe has accumulated the DNA of millions of customers, 80% of whom have consented to having their data used for wider research.[17]

Unlike China's BRI Group, private companies that harvest DNA data in the U.S. and Europe must adhere to laws upholding individual privacy rights. This should, at least on paper, prevent sensitive genomic data from being used for illegal or geopolitically or other potentially nefarious applications.

In Europe, the General Data Protection Regulations not only require customer consent to hold and use private data but also give customers the right to instruct companies to delete all their private data permanently.[18] In the U.S., customers also must give consent (and most do) to have their individual data anonymised and then aggregated as metadata before it can be sold.

Despite clear differences in data privacy and accountability standards in China and the West, data capitalism has turned DNA data into a major security concern.

The Pentagon has publicly advised military personnel not to use home-use DNA testing kits. According to the Pentagon, '. . . exposing sensitive genetic information to outside parties poses personal and operational risks to Service members . . .'[19] Those risks include heightened surveillance, which could expose an individual to targeting based on genomic profile, as discussed earlier.

More broadly, the Pentagon's position reveals a lack of confidence in the cybersecurity capabilities of private companies and portends an increase in cyberwarfare and state-backed cyber offensives.

China has forbidden the commercialisation and sharing of its own citizens' genome data with foreigners, even for research purposes. But in stark contrast to its own cybersecurity laws, which require foreign companies to hand over source code and encryption keys in the name of national security and to store their data on local servers in China, Beijing is doubling down on amassing data on private citizens from around the world.

A key geopolitics goal, therefore, is the amassing of as much data from as many sources as possible. This includes gathering user-generated content and information both through state-backed companies and their proxies and increasingly through ODS, data brokers and third parties.

AMERICAN SCI-TECH DATA HEGEMONY

In 2013, Edward Snowden famously leaked classified documents about the U.S. National Security Agency's (NSA) XKeyscore programme, a secret, highly powerful computer system that allowed the NSA and its allied partners to comprehensively monitor the emails, web browsing, Internet searches and social media use of targets anywhere in the world.[20] The programme operated in real time and was designed to analyse data and metadata that could be linked to keywords, phone numbers, email addresses and other specified data. The programme was credited with identifying hundreds of designated terrorists and preventing hostile acts against the U.S. and its allies.[21]

The NSA shared XKeyscore intelligence with Canada, the U.K., Australia and New Zealand, all partners in the Five Eyes intelligence cooperative whose origins go back to the Second World War.[22] Other U.S. allies also received XKeyscore-generated intelligence, including Japan, Sweden, Germany and Denmark.

The Five Eyes network continues to operate today, using ever more powerful AI, and the promise to share vital intelligence is a powerful enticement to persuade other countries (Turkey and Saudi Arabia, for example) to cooperate with other U.S. strategic initiatives.[23]

Snowden's leak revealed the extent of America's monopoly on surveillance technology and the overwhelming advantages it gives Washington and its allies—particularly regarding comprehensive surveillance of Chinese targets and Chinese strategic interests throughout the world. These revelations galvanised China's efforts to build its own data harvesting and surveillance capabilities around the world, sparking a techno-nationalist arms race within the datasphere.

For now, the U.S. continues to be a sci-tech hegemon. Such a commanding advantage is not possible without leading AI and machine learning, communications hardware, software, satellite and space capabilities, and, of course, access to the world's best data scientists. Ultimately, as we have seen, those seeking such capabilities require access to leading-edge semiconductors.

China, meanwhile, has closed the gap. Its cyber-capabilities, as we have discussed in Chapter 11, have netted Beijing a vast trove of military and commercial secrets.

DATA INTERMEDIARIES

Most observers of data geopolitics tend to overlook the impact of a large swath of for-profit companies known as data brokers, who extract and aggregate information from a wide spectrum of sources and then augment it through targeted analysis, vetting, cleansing and interpretation. Data brokers often buy and sell data from the large platform ODS companies, such as Meta, and sell their data on to other intermediaries in a secondary data market.

The data brokerage market is expected to be worth an estimated US$500 billion by 2028.

A small group of particularly large data intermediaries have amassed huge pools of data. This is significant geopolitically for several reasons. Firstly, such a massive cache of data in the hands of a few ODS companies, data brokers and data analytics firms makes intermediaries preferred targets for state-backed intelligence services, hackers and freelance data thieves.

As an example, consider Acxiom, a company that has amassed consumer data representing 2.5 billion customers across 62 countries.[24] Experian LLC maintains and analyses financial data on about 800 million people and 99 million businesses. Oracle Data Cloud maintains and sells consumer data linked to millions of people. All of this is possible because when consumers click 'I agree' in online user agreements, they are allowing companies to collect and sell information about them, thus fuelling a massive surveillance industry.

The American population has the most data brokers and, consequently, the most hacked population in the world. In a population of around 330 million people, more than 6 billion data records have been stolen—an average of 19 stolen records per person.[25]

Data capitalism is creating wealth on an unprecedented scale, with trade, investment and business opportunities spreading across both developed and developing markets, with more and more participants, large and small, joining the party. But the threat of cyber-intrusion and cyberattacks has grown in proportion with the wealth-creating opportunities of data capitalism.

THE DIFFERENT REGULATORY LANDSCAPES AROUND THE WORLD

Stolen data can be used in cyber weapons to cripple businesses and destabilise markets. Determining whether it is stolen by state-backed hackers or criminal organisations can be difficult.

Data capitalism reveals a digital landscape in varying permutations around the world. The U.S. has the most data intermediaries and has been described as a laissez faire digital Wild West. Europe has more proactive privacy and cybersecurity regulations but faces similar security vulnerabilities as well.

China has placed crushing constraints on large tech companies such as Tencent and Alibaba regarding the commoditisation of data, even as it carries out massive surveillance activities of its own. In July 2021, for example, just days after the Chinese ride-sharing app Didi listed on the U.S. stock market, Beijing removed it from Chinese app stores and forced the company to delist. One major reason: giving foreign investors possible access to the private data of Chinese citizens was seen as a risk to China's national security.[26]

DATA GEOPOLITICS, SOFT POWER AND INFORMATION WARS

Information wars pervade the digital commons, affecting social media platforms, blogs and news outlets, as well as messaging apps and entertainment portals.

Governments and private actors play offence and defence in this space, sometimes by promoting narratives through targeted influence campaigns, sometimes by sowing misinformation designed to discredit and destabilise an opponent's political system or its civil society.

When it comes to realpolitik in the datasphere, the ability to gain access to large swathes of data everywhere and leverage it with leading-edge AI and data analytics has become key. Just as data capitalism targets people with direct advertising that is tailored to their preferences, habits and needs, information wars rely on the same practices and persuasive technologies to achieve more Machiavellian ends.

THE CAMBRIDGE ANALYTICA MILESTONE

An event in during the 2016 U.S. elections revealed both the power and dangers of data analytics and information wars. Cambridge Analytica was a British political consulting firm that teamed up with Facebook and established a new milestone in data-gathering and analytics practices, aimed at winning elections.

In fact, the Cambridge-based firm ushered in a new era of hybrid warfare. Cambridge Analytica illustrated the extent to which misinformation and influence campaigns in the digital commons change the outcomes of elections, and demonstrated the advantages of applying actionable data to influence voter behaviour.

During the 2016 U.S. presidential and congressional elections, the company harvested personal data from millions of Facebook (Meta) users and used it to create psychological profiles based on unique characteristics and personality traits. This information was later harvested and used to great advantage for political objectives.

According to a report in *The Guardian*, Cambridge Analytica hired a company named Global Science Research and paid roughly 270,000 people to download an app and take a personality test.[27] The survey app was designed to compile psychographic profiles along a variety of characteristics and personality traits, including openness, conscientiousness, agreeableness, IQ, gender, age, political views and religion.

The app also evaluated people's 'sensational interests', which were divided into five seemingly bizarre categories: 'militarism' (guns and shooting, martial arts, crossbows and knives); 'violent occultism' (drugs, black magic and paganism); 'intellectual activities' (singing and making music, foreign travel and the environment); 'credulousness' (flying saucers and the paranormal); and 'wholesome interests' (camping, gardening and hill-walking).

This exercise allowed Cambridge Analytica to compile information from those users and access their 'friends' profiles on Facebook, opening a treasure trove of data involving at least 50 million additional Facebook users.[28]

Such strange data-linked interests seem incongruent with politics and geopolitics, but when combined with massive amounts of personalised data from other Facebook profiles, at the time, this data was analysed and used to send highly targeted and highly persuasive political advertising to voters. As a result, in 2016, Cambridge Analytica helped to deliver a tectonic political victory to America's MAGA Republicans.

HOW DATA ANALYTICS SHAPE THE GEOPOLITICAL LANDSCAPE

The ability of data analytics companies to engineer consequential political outcomes was universally recognised after Cambridge Analytica delivered victorious outcomes not only to Donald Trump's presidential campaign but also to the Brexit movement in the U.K.

But the company had already profoundly changed the game of realpolitik in the datasphere.[29] In addition to Brexit and the Trump presidential victory, Cambridge Analytica had been a major factor in decisive political outcomes around the world, including:

- Ukraine (the Orange Revolution in 2004).
- Italy (the Resurgent Party in 2012).
- Kenya (President Uhuru Kenyatta's elections in 2013 and 2017).
- Nigeria (the campaign against opposition leader Muhammadu Buhari in 2015) and,
- India (four election campaigns of the Bharatiya Janata Party).

In all, Cambridge Analytica executives claimed to have worked on about 200 elections around the world, including Pakistan, Nigeria, Mexico, Thailand, Indonesia, Malaysia, Colombia, Cyprus, Zambia, South Africa, Romania, Lithuania, the Czech Republic and Argentina.

Regarding the U.S. elections, the company executives claimed they had 5000-plus data points for each American.[30] If the same amount was obtained on every person believed to have had their data accessed by Cambridge Analytica (around 87 million Facebook users), the company had collected a total of 435 billion data points on Americans.

The Facebook–Cambridge Analytica episode demonstrates that data capitalism is fundamentally apolitical: some analytics firms and data brokers will work with anyone, anywhere. It also reveals that those with access to large data pools and powerful AI will have outsized advantages in information and narrative wars, which reach well beyond democratic elections.

RUSSIAN INFLUENCE CAMPAIGNS IN SOCIAL MEDIA

Russian social media influence campaigns began in earnest in 2015, marking the start of a new era in global information wars. Moscow's tactics involved using relatively low-tech but largely effective approaches through a variety of government-funded or empowered groups. The primary aim of spreading fake news and inflammatory content is to polarise and confuse voters and cast doubt on the legitimacy of elections.

In the 2016 American elections, the Russian Internet Research Agency (IRA), a hacking and information warfare unit, created shell groups that mimicked grassroots advocacy organisations and impersonated real candidates. As part of these fake and fraudulent identities, the IRA invented logos, landing page addresses and the like, releasing a torrent of content.

Some IRA posts used the identity of legitimate, relatively popular non-profit organisations, political action committees or grassroots organisations. The IRA set up thousands of fake individual profiles with the express purpose of spreading misinformation.

These tactics were successful in flooding social media apps with partially untrue and outright false content. Such content garnered increasing attention and comments and was subsequently picked up by the platforms' algorithms and resent and shared exponentially.

There are technologies that can amplify the spread of misinformation.

Bots are automated programmes that imitate humans online. They can be programmed to spread online content rapidly and on a large scale.

Search engine optimisation (SEO) is a technique for increasing the viewership of a website by having it appear at the top of a search result on Google and other search engines.

Together, these practices allow companies to flood social media with a steady flow of large amounts of information, a practice referred to as fire-hosing.

THE SPREAD OF INFORMATION WARS

Meta, Google and others have become better at spotting bots, fire-hosing and SEO attempts and have stepped up countermeasures. But Russia, China and other countries have learned to use more diffuse approaches, making it virtually impossible to prevent the laundering of information.

The U.S. has turned to hybrid warfare countermeasures. U.S. Cyber Command attacked Russia's IRA and temporarily disabled its networking capabilities in 2019.[31] As a result, targeted state actors have turned to the use of fringe news organisations and think tanks as proxies to generate content that can be amplified across social media.

Based on U.S. government declassified intelligence findings in 2020, two Russian organisations, InfoRus and OneWorldPress, were revealed to be linked to Russia's Military Intelligence (GRU) and Foreign Intelligence Service (SVR).[32] The GRU's propaganda arm, as reported by the *New York Times*, is linked to a psychological warfare group called 'Unit 54777'.

Both InfoRus and OneWorldPress have been instrumental in pushing geopolitically motivated narratives regarding the COVID-19 pandemic (claiming it was created by the U.S. military), vaccine nationalism (claiming Western vaccines are ineffective and will kill people) and the invasion of Ukraine (claiming that it was prompted by NATO's aggression and its support of a Nazi regime in Ukraine).[33]

In September 2022, five weeks prior to the midterm elections in the U.S., Meta discovered and shut down a full-scale Russian social media influence campaign. The operation included more than 2,000 Meta accounts and pages that pushed the Kremlin's propaganda on the invasion. Fake websites had been designed to mimic the official sites of *The Guardian* in the U.K. and *Bild* and *Der Spiegel* in Germany. Approximately US$100,000 was spent on related ads on Meta and Instagram.

Meta also shut down a network of accounts believed to have originated in China that posed as private citizens with inflammatory views on gun control and abortion, two highly divisive and volatile issues in the U.S.[34]

SOCIAL MEDIA INFLUENCERS AND BLOGGERS

Once government-backed misinformation outlets such as OneWorldPress can manufacture a narrative, it can be effectively amplified and recycled by an army of paid bloggers, online personalities and influencers on TikTok, YouTube, Instagram, Twitter, Meta and other platforms.

Celebrities have recently become high-profile purveyors of geopolitically motivated influence campaigns. In 2019, for example, Yang Mi, an A-list actor, Taiwanese cellist Ouyang Nana and Hong Kong Cantopop singer Eason Chan, along with dozens of others, issued statements on social media defending Beijing's policies regarding Uighur Muslims in Xinjiang.[35] Further, they announced they were cutting ties with Western companies such as Nike, H&M and Adidas on ethical grounds, as these companies were reconsidering sourcing cotton and other materials from Xinjiang province.[36]

When U.S. Speaker of the House Nancy Pelosi visited Taiwan in August 2022, social media was used to name and shame celebrities who had not publicly supported Beijing's One China policy. Chinese bloggers and influencers called out and cancelled not only Taiwanese and Hong Kong-based celebrities who had remained silent but also the likes of J Lin, Michelle Yeoh, Jet Li, Dee Hsu and other Singaporean celebs for not vocally supporting the policy.[37]

Whether or not celebrity influencers can actually influence geopolitical events is open to debate, but what is clear is that they are used as tools in information wars.

PLATFORM DIPLOMACY

Diplomats around the world now turn to social media to do their daily jobs. Platforms such as Twitter, LinkedIn and Meta have become essential tools for influence campaigns.

China's 'wolf warrior' diplomats prefered to garner attention on Western platforms such as Twitter rather than Weibo, the heavily censored and ring-fenced Chinese equivalent. The first diplomat to cultivate a large international audience was Zhao Lijian, a former spokesperson of the Ministry of Foreign Affairs. Along with other wolf warriors, Zhao circulated content from Russian fringe media outlets publishing stories on vaccine nationalism and other carefully crafted narratives. Perhaps after he became too large of a media personality, Zhao fell out of grace with the CCP: in 2023 he was reassigned to be the deputy head of the Department of Boundary and Ocean Affairs.

Western diplomats, meanwhile, have found that effective countermeasures to negative information campaigns require a constant presence on social media.

Ambassadors and other embassy personnel can build friendships by writing daily blog posts with a focus on local people's interest in education, food, art and sports. Over time, this sort of connectivity builds transparency, truth and trust—the best countermeasures to misinformation.

INTELLIGENCE AGENCIES RELYING ON PRIVATE COMPANIES

The increasing reliance of governments on the tech sector to build critical defence and national security capabilities in the datasphere has created symbiotic relationships of unprecedented complexity and risk.

The American intelligence community relies heavily on Silicon Valley to build the infrastructure for the management of secret data. Amazon Web Services (AWS), Google, Oracle, IBM and Microsoft all provide the government with critical AI, algorithms and cloud infrastructure. As we will see in subsequent chapters, such deep government dependency on for-profit entities extends to other critical areas of national and economic security, involving companies such as SpaceX and Starlink, which NASA, the U.S. Space Force and a range of other defence and intelligence agencies have come to rely upon.

The NSA uses AWS technology extensively.[38] Under the C2E Cloud contract, for example, the CIA puts out task orders to build data-related capabilities worth billions of dollars. A number of intelligence networks use Microsoft's Azure Top Secret data hosting technology on a task-by-task basis.

The British intelligence community also hired AWS in 2019. Relying on a foreign tech company to build a cloud infrastructure that houses secret files with national security implications—even from a historically close ally—demonstrates the high stakes of data management.[39]

The scale of AWS' cloud infrastructure plays a significant role throughout Britain's intelligence community, including the GCHQ organisation (electrical and radio communications eavesdropping), MI5 (domestic intelligence matters), MI6 (external U.K. intelligence) and the Ministry of Defence.[40]

China, meanwhile, tasks the likes of Tencent, Alibaba Cloud, Huawei and SenseTime with engineering data storage and related technologies for its own national security and political objectives. China's authoritarian system maintains a chokehold over its technology companies, with far more constraints on its market and players than the U.S. imposes, but the goal is the same: to obtain access to the best technology to enable success in the datasphere.

These dynamics all but assure the continued fragmentation of cyberspace around U.S.-centric or China-centric business ecosystems. More firewalls and stronger ring-fencing around sensitive national data will spark an arms race in cyber-defence and cyber-intrusion capabilities. Companies facilitating the aims of their own governments will face targeting and retaliation from rivals.

GOVERNMENT DEMANDS FOR DATA ACCESS

As we discussed earlier, China's national security and cybersecurity laws require its citizens, as well as any company doing business in its markets, to provide the government with any data, source code or encryption keys it demands. In addition, Chinese citizens and entities operating outside the country's borders must cooperate and hand over data on national security grounds when asked.

Although they can often buy data directly from ODS or through data intermediaries, any government can demand the handover of data on law enforcement grounds. Government inquiries are commonly aimed at companies such as Google.

In a biannual transparency report, Google publishes the number of data requests that it receives from law enforcement agencies around the world. These requests seek data on user queries or views. It is clear that government requests to Google have been steadily increasing, with the majority coming from U.S. law enforcement agencies.

Even the most sensitive private personal data regarding DNA information is not safe. In the name of solving crimes, U.S. courts have granted law enforcement agencies access to the genome data of millions of Americans who had purchased DNA home-testing kits.[41]

The grey zone is both a place of danger and great opportunity for governments, data capitalists and private individuals. Tensions will arise between state and non-state actors, as will unlikely partnerships.

As a defence mechanism, governments, multinationals and other actors will have no choice but to further ring-fence their data, invest heavily in cybersecurity defences, and pursue new technologies. Companies need to localise their data because of national laws. On a wider scale, they will also need to increase available resources for data-sharding—breaking up data and storing it piecemeal on different servers with different encryption keys in different locations.

This will accelerate the fragmentation of the Internet as well-funded companies look to bring more data management and communication capabilities in-house, which could include building their own self-sufficient private satellite communications networks, for example, by working with private companies such as Starlink.

The grey zone in the datasphere will drive the rise of a privacy and data security economy, but the paradox will be that as more wealth migrates to the zone, so too will geopolitics.

Chapter 13

The AI Arms Race

An artificial intelligence (AI) arms race is widening the competitive arena among nations and spilling over into all aspects of life.

As leading-edge AI performs increasingly complex cognitive tasks on a unimaginable scale and at speeds that defy human comprehension, governments and corporations—and even private individuals—have come to covet its powers.

In a Darwinian sense, both in terms of the evolution of the human species as a whole and in the competition between nations, there is a terrifying duality to AI. It has the potential to solve our most complex, wicked problems and level the playing field for hundreds of millions of people, but it can also widen the chasm between the meek and the powerful.

Discussions about AI, therefore, are eventually drawn to a Hobbesian perspective. We must remind ourselves that the international system, absent enforceable frameworks of rules, is fundamentally a nasty and brutish place.

Broadly defined, AI is an area of computer science that seeks to create intelligent machines that can mimic human capabilities. AI is no one single thing. It encompasses machine learning as well as the neural networks that recognise language symbols, words and images.

AI can pick out meaningful patterns in data as well as make complex predictions as it contemplates billions of parameters. Think of these parameters as a machine's practical frame of reference as it teaches itself. Incredibly, today's open AI platforms deal with hundreds of billions of parameters and even a trillion parameters at any single time.

Today, generative AI chatbots can pass the so-called Turing Test, which is used to determine whether a machine can fool a human into thinking it is another human in a text-based conversation. Yet this was a very difficult task for AI only a decade ago.

In 2022, *OpenAI*, the San Francisco-based research and deployment company in the field of AI, unleashed a public version of ChatGPT, which captivated its users as it pulled in massive amounts of data from cyberspace and created highly intelligible content in the form of text, images, audio and computer code.

OpenAI achieved this by subjecting ChatGPT to learning patterns and algorithms that translated data into language—a so-called large language model (LLM). LLMs can be open-sourced, proprietary or entirely private, in which case they can be custom-built and ring-fenced within an organisation or purchased as a bolt-on solution— think of Microsoft's Copilot, which is designed to enhance business productivity and workflow.

Generative AI focuses on creating models that can generate new content, within distinct parameters or swim lanes. The next progression for AI, however, if we assume that AI will continue to advance on an exponential trajectory, is so-called artificial general intelligence (AGI). AGI is human-level unconstrained general intelligence that can learn and perform any intellectual task a human can, including reasoning, problem-solving, adapting to new situations, and understanding language. But AGI will do all these things by processing gargantuan data sets at the speed of light, with no boundaries.

AGI, then (many would argue) marks the point in human–machine evolution of possible existential crisis. There is no guarantee that sentient machines will not obliterate or subjugate the human species.

That AGI moment has not yet arrived. As such, let us consider today's state-of-the art generative AI in two contrasting examples. In the first case, it can be used to explore, test and design scientific break-throughs or cure stubborn diseases; in the second, it can be used to develop killing machines of the most intelligent kind.

In this chapter, we will ponder the duality of AI and then return to that one foundational technology in the feedback loop that is AI's life-force: semiconductors. Here, we will see the tensions and frictions involving states and firms.

AI DESIGNS A BREAKTHROUGH DRUG

The story of Insilico Medicine and its Chemistry42 automated machine platform is an inspiring one.

In 2020, the company began to use the platform to tackle the previ-ously insurmountable challenge of idiopathic pulmonary fibrosis (IPF), a chronic lung disease with limited treatment options.

Chemistry42 analysed existing data on IPF, generating millions of potential drug molecules tailored to target the disease's specific mechanisms. The AI then puts these molecules through its paces, simulating their interactions with different biological systems and fil-tering out unsuitable candidates. The AI then iteratively improved its designs, learning from each simulation and refining its search for the optimal drug.

Within just 18 months, the AI delivered a promising drug candidate—a feat that typically takes years and even decades in traditional drug discovery. At the time of this writing, the AI-designed molecule is cur-rently undergoing clinical trials, holding immense potential to trans-form the lives of IPF patients.

Thus, generative AI has created a paradigm shift in scientific explora-tion, not only because it rapidly generates and tests hypotheses, pushing the boundaries of exploration and significantly reducing research timelines, but because it delves into vast, complex data sets, uncovering hidden patterns and correlations that human researchers would probably never see.

Since its launch in 2020, Chemistry42 has been used by over 20 pharmaceutical companies, 15 external programmes and over 30 internal programmes.[1]

Considering AI from a commercial perspective, a 2023 study from McKinsey, the global consultancy, estimated that AI could increase global productivity by automating up to 70% of employee wage hours, replacing less productive and repetitive cognitive tasks in areas such as customer service, learning and instruction, legal and accountancy, banking and financial services and travel and hospitality. Even if these calculations are half-correct, they mark a sea-change in business management and work in general.

The generative AI market—specifically, the design and creation of AI solutions and services such as algorithms and apps and specialised LLM frameworks—has been projected to be worth at least US$50 billion by 2029.[2] The chatbot market alone is expected to be worth US$10 billion.[3]

Meanwhile, in manufacturing, generative AI could add trillions of dollars to the global economy.

AI AND THE WEAPONS OF WAR

Consider, however, the dual-use nature of AI and how it has become a game changer in warfare. AI provides the decisive technology both for a hot kinetic war, for offensive and defensive weapons systems and for a hybrid war, which includes, as we discussed in Chapters 11 and 12, cyberwar and espionage, misinformation and influence campaigns.

Even while Insilico Medicine and others in medical and pharmaceutical research use generative AI to cure life-threatening diseases, America's Defence Advanced Research Projects Agency (DARPA) and other defence-related think tanks and laboratories use a host of AI systems to develop weaponry of all sorts. Take, for example, unmanned aerial vehicles (UAVs)—drones—and unmanned underwater vehicles (UUVs), products of DARPA's astoundingly creative AI machine learning in the arts of lethality.

As in medicine, DARPA's innovations in drone warfare were born of AI platforms that combined strong computing power, data and algorithms.

There has been, of course, the strong presence of human intelligence as well. But DARPA-funded AI brainstormed new configurations, materials and capabilities, drawing from an immense library of aerodynamic principles and technological possibilities.

The AI was not limited to preset parameters, like older computer-aided design (CAD); instead, it evolved its exploration through iterative simulations, testing flight dynamics, stealth capabilities and sensor integrations in a virtual wind tunnel. These designs unfolded in real-time, adjusting wing shapes, propulsion systems and sensor configurations for optimal performance under battlefield conditions—including the use of biomimetic shapes inspired by birds or insects and 'morphing' drones that adapt to their environment.

Biomimetics is an interdisciplinary field in which principles from engineering, chemistry and especially biology are applied to the synthesis of materials, synthetic systems or machines that have functions that mimic biological processes. AI is part of a powerful technology feedback loop that is bringing to fruition the most outlandish robotic creations: imagine a surveillance or a killer drone that replicates a house fly. Or a full-scale combat robot that gets its design from a spider—which manifests nature's most efficient use of movement, strength and dexterity.

AI is being tapped to replicate the properties of a spider's web, which is immensely strong, lightweight, and flexible. At human scale, spider silk is stronger than steel and tougher than Kevlar. Yet it is flexible. If a human-scale spider web were stretched between two tall buildings, it would stop a super-sonic jet at full speed, the way a real spider web catches an insect on the fly.

The dual-use nature of AI further muddles the grey zone in which governments and corporations operate. As non-state actors push the innovation envelope in AI, to whom should they be allowed to sell their product?

Palantir Technologies, the Denver-based data analysis firm cofounded by Peter Thiel, does brisk business selling its artificial intelligence platform (AIP) to military organisations. AIP utilises the same kind of machine learning models that enable ChatGPT, and, in this case, AIP provides battlefield intelligence and decision-making capabilities.

Palantir's platforms are used by the U.S. Department of Defence and the U.S. Central Intelligence Agency (CIA), among other governments around the world.

Palantir claims that its platform is able to seek out and identify both friendly and hostile forces and target multitudes of threats in a hostile environment. AIP also proposes battle strategies and communicates them in real time to other connected machines and human decision makers.

Like the U.S., China's military has also moved rapidly towards 'intelligentised warfare'—a term coined by the U.S. Defence Department.[4]

These technologies are all dual-use: the same Palantir AIP product that directs drone attacks and tank battles are used by manufacturers on their factory floors and by operators of civil aircraft.

AI AND CYBERWARFARE

While not as physically devastating as kinetic warfare, cyber-weaponry can incapacitate an opponent's national infrastructure and effectively bring a nation to its knees.

Unlike kinetic warfare, which relies upon real munitions and ballistics, cyberwarfare relies on bits and bytes, software code, algorithms and AI to deploy spyware, malicious computer viruses or 'trojan horses' and so-called 'worms' that can infiltrate and remain, undetected, in critical infrastructure. Once activated, the code can wreak total havoc.

The question regarding cyberwarfare is to what extent AI in its various forms will dictate the outcome of events. Autonomous AI involves machines that are programmed to 'think' and make independent assessments and 'decisions.' Cyberwarfare in a time of AGI becomes even more problematic if, for example, sentient machines were to go rogue or just exhibit other human characteristics such as misjudgement or misinterpretation of facts.

The evolution of cyber war since the world's first known example of a cyber super-weapon, the Stuxnet virus, has been on an exponential scale.

Stuxnet was categorised as a 'malicious worm'. Thought to have been developed by the CIA and Israel's Mossad intelligence services, Stuxnet was able to penetrate and sabotage a so-called 'air-gapped' Iranian nuclear facility in Natanz, in 2007, which was being used to enrich uranium, an essential ingredient for nuclear weapons.

An air-gapped facility is one that is completely sealed off and ring-fenced from the Internet or other outside networks, which prevents malware and spyware infiltrating via an outside website or being down-loaded through a communications link, like an email or a text message.

The Americans and Israelis, nonetheless, were able to get someone to introduce Stuxnet into the Natanz nuclear facility's internal, air-gapped network, probably through a USB 'thumb drive' and then onto a computer on an internal network or by feeding it through an industrial system inside the complex.

Even as the virus remained hidden to Iranian engineers, it affected the Natanz uranium fuel enrichment physical processes by altering the programmed speed of the facility's centrifuges. This caused them to spin irregularly and burn themselves out. About 1,000 centrifuges were destroyed, which set the Iranian uranium fuel enrichment program back at least one year.

It wasn't long, however, before Stuxnet had found its way out into the digital underworld, where other hackers and cyber-militants, both state-backed and independent, modified the code to attack other infrastructure at, for example, water and chemical plants, electrical grids, and other large national infrastructure of vital importance.

Now vast arsenals of malware are presumed to have been deployed and are buried deep within the world's collective digital architecture. Meanwhile, cyber intrusions, espionage and thefts, occur, en masse, daily. Generative AI in the wrong hands, or eventually, AGI, will present a ubiquitous cyberthreat—everywhere, all the time, in every dimension of life.

The weaponisation of AI (intended or not) is so potentially dangerous that the North Atlantic Treaty Organization (NATO) has begun funding tech start-ups and incubating companies that specialise in cybersecurity.

AI SUPERPOWERS: THE U.S. VERSUS CHINA

	Overall	Talent	Infrastructure	Operating Environment	Research	Development	Government Strategy	Commercial	Scale	Intensity
United States	1	1	1	28	1	1	8	1	1	5
China	2	20	2	3	2	2	3	2	2	21
Singapore	3	4	3	22	3	5	16	4	10	1
United Kingdom	4	5	24	40	5	8	10	5	4	10
Canada	5	6	23	8	7	11	5	7	7	7
South Korea	6	12	7	11	12	3	6	18	8	6
Israel	7	7	28	23	11	7	47	3	17	2
Germany	8	3	12	13	8	9	2	11	3	15
Switzerland	9	9	13	30	4	4	56	9	16	3
Finland	10	13	8	4	9	14	15	12	13	4
Netherlands	11	8	16	15	10	13	28	20	11	8
Japan	12	11	5	10	20	6	18	23	6	25
France	13	10	11	25	15	18	13	10	9	20
India	14	2	59	12	30	21	38	13	5	51
Australia	15	14	44	62	6	16	14	22	15	14
Denmark	16	19	15	1	18	19	21	17	18	11
Sweden	17	15	21	2	13	17	44	16	19	12
Luxembourg	18	31	6	14	19	22	31	14	33	9
Ireland	19	17	26	19	27	10	29	15	28	13
Austria	20	25	34	5	16	23	33	27	22	18
Spain	21	18	18	16	24	26	4	32	12	28
Belgium	22	26	43	24	14	25	36	25	23	19
Italy	23	22	35	6	21	28	9	35	14	33
Norway	24	24	22	29	22	20	39	21	30	16
Estonia	25	34	33	17	35	29	19	8	38	17

Figure 13.1   Countries Ranked by their Artificial Intelligence (AI) Capacity.

In 2018, Kai-Fu Lee, the former president of Google China and past executive at Microsoft and Apple, published his thought-provoking book *AI Superpowers*. Lee's work influenced me deeply, but five years after its publication, at least regarding generative AI, the U.S. appears to be much further ahead of China than he would have expected.

There has been a widely held view that China's AI companies can build a competitive advantage by capitalising on the country's massive data-saturated environment and its thorough shift to digital technologies such as ubiquitous facial recognition, digital wallets, and QR codes. We will return to this in a little bit.

In the five years leading up to the release of ChatGPT, the global generative AI landscape has been dominated by first-mover

American and British firms, including OpenAI, Google AI and Microsoft Research. Some of the more notable LLMs include, of course, ChatGPT, Bard and Turing NLG. Other companies, such as the U.K.'s DeepMind and Stability AI have been major players as well.

About a dozen tech companies, almost all of them American, have been pioneers in the field of machine learning. This includes Apple, Google, Microsoft, Uber, Salesforce, Meta, IBM and eBay.

Around this cluster of tech giants is a secondary ecosystem of more open AI frameworks that provide open-source software libraries and tool kits and allow users anywhere to create their own artificial neural networks, machine learning algorithms and frameworks. This includes companies such as TensorFlow, Torch and Caffe AI that offer deep-learning AI frameworks that can process millions of works per day.

All of these open AI tools support other widely used platforms such as Mac OS, Windows, Linux and Apache Hadoop, which allow for distributed processing of massive amounts of data.

And here is where things become a challenge for China's AI companies. From a great power rivalry perspective, the systemic differences between China's economic model and that of the U.S.—and other liberal democratic countries—figure to contribute to lopsided competition in generative AI.

Because LLMs perform best when they can be trained on unlimited data, China's statist system, which heavily censors content in the digital commons, figures to make things difficult for Chinese AI firms. More data in China, then, with constrained access and no-go zones and topics within firewalls, does not translate into AI dominance.

China's first movers in generative AI include Baidu, China's heavily censored search engine; SenseTime, the AI company associated with surveillance technology and Alibaba, the giant mishmash of e-commerce, fintech and a myriad of other activities.

The big-name technologists in China's tech sector have pivoted to generative AI. These include Zhou Bowen, the former president of JD.com's AI and cloud computing division; Wang Changhu, the director of ByteDance's AI lab; Wang Huiwen, the cofounder of mega-shopping platform Meituan, and Wang Xiaochuan, who founded the search engine Sogou, subsequently acquired by Tencent Holdings.

Kai-Fu Lee, meanwhile, has become a high-profile tech investor in China, and remains confident that Chinese AI will be formidable despite the paradigm shift in the West, the outflow of foreign capital and the decoupling of strategic supply chains.

But unless these firms can circumnavigate the oppressive regulatory environment in China, as the Chinese Communist Party (CCP) works to block or restrain the free flow of information, the LLMs designed by China's generative AI pioneers may very well be cognitively impaired.

By contrast, the wide open—some would say, reckless—Wild West ethos of Silicon Valley and the American entrepreneurial tech scene has allowed creative and entrepreneurial dynamics to flourish; hence, the dominant position of American AI first movers.

Interestingly, the Chinese tech firms mentioned above—Alibaba, Baidu, Tencent Holdings and ByteDance—developed much of their code, infrastructure and product offerings using American open-sourced platforms such as TensorFlow, Linux and Apache Hadoop.

Finally, we must also consider Chinese firms' continuing reliance on leading-edge American AI chips, an issue that we will revisit below.

Figure 13.2   The IBM Blue Gene Supercomputer.

AI MISINFORMATION, DEEPFAKES AND NARRATIVE WARS

Geopolitically motivated narrative wars and influence campaigns are weaponising LLMs and generative AI at a whole new level.

Just how far and in which ways chatbots and LLMs might contribute to synthetic news (another term for misinformation) is difficult to predict. But governments must now actively compete in this area as they try to push their own narratives and actively damp down fake news and misinformation.

From a techno-nationalist perspective, then, the question is what kind of AI capabilities are needed to play both offence and defence in this danger zone. To figure this out, governments will need to partner with businesses, academia and NGOs to develop new ways of spotting misinformation and preventing its spread through the digital commons.

This, in turn, raises the question of whether market forces can foster a 'truth economy' in the same way that the rapid growth of the digital economy in the 1990s to the present sparked the growth of the cybersecurity industry. (By 2030, revenues for global cybersecurity companies are forecast to be worth an estimated US$425 billion.[5])

One of the most incendiary and dangerous forms of misinformation involves deepfakes—wholly fabricated AI-generated images and videos that depict totally fictitious events by inserting the likenesses of targeted individuals into scenes involving real events.

Take the example of deepfake images of French President Emmanuel Macron in 2022, created using an open AI platform by Midjourney Inc., a San Francisco-based independent AI research lab. The images placed Macron within the street protests in Paris sparked by the raising of France's retirement age and other changes to its pension laws.[6] They showed him involved in confrontations with riot police, as well as being chased down and arrested and wearing a prisoner's vest (presumably after arrest) as he cleaned up rubbish on streets.

Consider that these images, once released, were embellished by random users in the global commons who simply typed in a few sentences to prompt the chatbot to revise the imagery. Each new iteration became more realistic. The possibility of being recycled by other chatbots at the speed of the Internet highlights the incredible power of generative AI.

Most of ChatGPT's social media traffic comes from YouTube.[7] It is not hard to imagine the inflammatory effects of a deepfake video of, say, a naval confrontation in the South China Sea, with vessels coming under attack. Such imagery, whether prompted deliberately by malicious agents or by some mysterious and unexplainable hallucination of a chatbot could quickly spiral into a military crisis.

In military circles, autonomous robots are being imbued with cognitive and deep-learning AI to give them situational and self-awareness. This includes wider frame-of-reference parameters that could subject a robot to fake imagery, prompting, for example, a UAV or UUV to go rogue on its programmers. More dystopic scenarios might involve law enforcement robots suffering a similar fate.

AI AND CHIP WARS

Earlier, I characterised semiconductors as the ground-zero technology for other twenty-first-century innovations. AI is the second-most important foundational technology, and it is inextricably linked to advanced semiconductors. The two form a chip–AI nexus that lies at the heart of the U.S.–China tech cold war.

After the release of ChatGPT and other generative AI platforms in 2022, surging demand for specialised AI chips catapulted the American company Nvidia into an almost unassailable market position, with close to 90% of market share. Another American company, Advanced Micro Devices (AMD), was running a distant second.

That same year, citing national security concerns, the U.S. Department of Commerce's Bureau of Industry and Security (BIS) banned Chinese companies from accessing Nvidia's advanced AI chips, which are required for deep-learning applications. The BIS placed export controls on Nvidia's two most advanced AI chips, the A100 and the H100.

As it happened, Nvidia, Intel, AMD and others circumvented government restrictions by using legal loopholes and other evasive strategies to sell their chips to Chinese entities.

Nvidia cleverly circumvented Washington's 2022 export controls by designing two new AI chips, the A800 and the H800, which performed slightly below the designated performance threshold for restricted AI chips in China.[8]

Nvidia's AI chips also found their way into China through black-market and grey-market channels, while massive flows of foreign money continued to flow in China's home-based AI sector via shell companies operating in offshore tax havens such as the Cayman Islands.

The story of the chip–AI nexus is an evolving and complex one. It is likely to feature an ongoing series of adjustments and ratcheting up of U.S. export controls and outbound investment controls as multinationals look for ways to circumvent them.

As we have discussed previously, there were strong business incentives for Nvidia's behaviour. China was and remains the world's largest market for both leading-edge and trailing-edge chips, and the country's leading chip makers continued to rely on foreign semiconductor chips and specialised chip manufacturing equipment. This makes the Chinese market a powerful magnet for the world's leading chip firms, export controls and other restrictions notwithstanding.

Nvidia's H800 AI chip was used widely by Chinese tech firms such as Alibaba Group Holdings, Baidu and Tencent for their cloud computing businesses. Overall, China accounted for more than 20% of Nvidia's global revenue in 2022.[9]

Meanwhile, Intel soon followed Nvidia's example and produced slightly downgraded versions of its own AI chips, creating a revised version of the Intel Gaudi 2 chip.[10] AMD also followed the same path and was developing its own modified export-control-evading chip.

Nvidia, Intel and AMD's circumvention strategies were not a surprising development, but their strategies tested the U.S. government's resolve not only to enforce existing export controls but also, looking ahead, to further expand them further to cover trailing-edge AI chips.

Chinese tech executives had remarked that their advanced generative AI models could still perform well if they relied on larger numbers of inferior chipsets, making up for the superior performance of a single, more powerful chip.

In response, Washington dialled up new export-control parameters and, in October 2023, lowered the specification threshold on AI chips destined for restricted Chinese entities.

Chapter 14

Quantum Technologies

Nestled between the Santa Ynez mountains and the mesmerising blue of the Pacific Ocean, Santa Barbara is a beach town known for its laid-back California vibe. But it was from here, in 2019, that scientists at Google's AI campus announced that Sycamore, a quantum-based processor, needed only 200 seconds to solve a numeric computation that would have taken the world's most powerful supercomputer 10,000 years to solve.[1]

This was a monumental achievement in computer science.

Less than a year later, a team of Chinese researchers published a study in the *Journal of Science* that claimed their photonic quantum computer, named Jiuzhang, solved a well-known problem involving 'boson sampling,' in 200 seconds—an operation that would have taken a classical supercomputer *2.5 billion* years to do.[2]

Quantum science seems destined to drive the evolution of supercomputing and artificial intelligence (AI) especially as Moore's Law, as we have discussed, reaches its size thresholds. Simply put, when geometry is on an atomic scale, there is a finite number of transistors that can be stacked upon a chip. The most advanced 2-nanometre chip, for example, with hundreds of billions of transistors the size of a human genome—possibly up to a trillion—cannot physically get much smaller. At some point, then, Moore's Law must come to an end.

What comes next is quantum computing, which, as we will see, could be to supercomputing what the atomic bomb was to a single kilogram of gunpowder. The ramp up in power could be off the scale in orders of magnitude. The question is whether these new computers can perform 'practical' functions beyond the factoring of numbers and other mathematical computations.

More broadly, the three core areas of quantum include:

• Quantum computing (QC)
• Quantum Key Distribution (QKD) communications
• Quantum Sensing

QC receives most of the attention in the public media and is the recipient of most private investment; however, the other two areas of quantum are strategically important.

QC will not replace contemporary digital computers for everyday usage, and much of the technology is still largely experimental. Nevertheless, the field is advancing quickly, and researchers are achieving what is sometimes referred to as 'quantum supremacy' or 'quantum advantage'—the ability to quickly solve certain kinds of complex computations that the most powerful bit-based supercomputers cannot solve in a reasonable amount of time.

When 'practical quantum' can be achieved, then humanity will have reached an inflexion point.

Imagine ChatGPT performing with hundreds of trillions of parameters per second. Practical quantum, when it arrives, will make today's large language models and machine learning seem primitive by comparison. The prospect of quantum physics serving as the enabler of artificial general intelligence (AGI), when computers essentially become sentient beings, is potently the stuff of nightmares—or of a world of incredible hope and possibilities.

A second area involves quantum communication, which could allow secure, hack-proof communication networks that can detect any attempts at cyber intrusions, making it virtually impossible for hackers and spies to gain access to a quantum network.

The third category is quantum-sensing. Quantum devices are much more sensitive than conventional technology; they can detect motion on a subatomic particle level.

WHAT IS QUANTUM COMPUTING AND WHY DOES IT MATTER?

This chapter is not a scientific or technical analysis of quantum technologies. Instead, it is a study of the latest general quantum developments viewed through the lens of techno-nationalism and geopolitics.

To frame the discussion of QC, then, we should begin with a basic comparison of classical computing and QC.

No matter how advanced they are, classical microprocessors use logic 'gates' formed of tiny transistors to perform a series of logical 'and/or/not' calculations on electronic signals called bits, which represent strings of 1s and 0s[3]. By stringing together millions or even billions of these binary sequences, a classical computer can follow complex algorithms and rapidly perform highly advanced computations.

QC operates on a much smaller scale, harnessing the strange quantum mechanical behaviour of individual atoms, electrons and photons. Instead of bits, QC utilises *quantum bits* or *qubits*.

Whereas a bit can take only one of two values at a time, the probabilistic quantum behaviour of matter at the atomic level allows for *superposition* in multiple states, such that a qubit, in effect, takes values of 1 and 0 simultaneously. This allows for the representation of data in different and complex ways that give QC huge advantages over classical computing. Moreover, because they take place on such a small scale, qubit-based calculations are much faster than those based on classical principles.

Furthermore, quantum interference allows particles to become *entangled*, such that changes in one qubit simultaneously affect the qubits with which it is entangled, even when they are very far away from each other. This feature has powerful implications for cryptography and other applications.

For some kinds of problems, superposition and entanglement of qubit-based operations allow for the performance of calculations exponentially faster than classical computation—a phenomenon referred to as quantum *speedup*. One of the key goals of research in QC is to combine increasingly greater numbers of qubits to perform such calculations, achieving extraordinary improvements in computational power and speed.

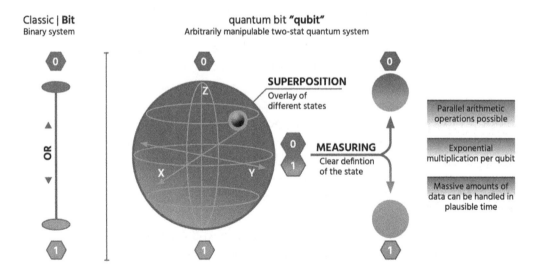

Quantum computers work with qubits instead of with bits, enabling them to carry out considerably more complex calculations.

Figure 14.1 How Quantum Computing Works.

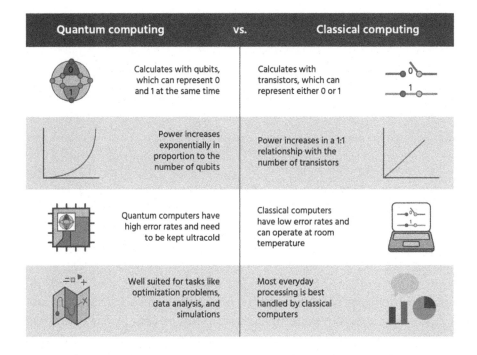

Quantum computing	vs.	Classical computing
Calculates with qubits, which can represent 0 and 1 at the same time		Calculates with transistors, which can represent either 0 or 1
Power increases exponentially in proportion to the number of qubits		Power increases in a 1:1 relationship with the number of transistors
Quantum computers have high error rates and need to be kept ultracold		Classical computers have low error rates and can operate at room temperature
Well suited for tasks like optimization problems, data analysis, and simulations		Most everyday processing is best handled by classical computers

Figure 14.2   Quantum Computing versus Classical Computing.

QUANTUM SUPREMACY AND LIMITATIONS

As illustrated by the race between Google and its Chinese competitors, quantum speedup is central to the potential advantages of QC, and here is where the next level of tech competition is playing out.

Despite the potential advantages of qubit-driven AI, QC must overcome a host of operational and physical challenges. The number of qubits is not the only factor determining the power and utility of a quantum computer. The quality of the qubits, the coherence time and the ability to control and manipulate the qubits also play a role.

A key technical constraint is that quantum processors need to operate in a total vacuum or in a cryogenic environment at temperatures of around −180 degrees Celsius. This requires a costly and complex staging environment with specialised requirements regarding infrastructure and equipment. It also requires a large team of physicists, mathematicians and engineers to manage the esoteric software and algorithms needed to solve ongoing problems. All these resources are in high demand and short supply and are likely to remain so.

Achieving so called 'quantum coherence' at room temperature is likely still a long way off from the time of this writing, however, current advances in AI and classical supercomputing may speed this process along.

A second technical issue is that qubit-driven processing currently experiences a high rate of errors compared with classical bit-driven computers. As a countermeasure, huge amounts of auxiliary calculations are required: about 1,000 error-correcting qubits for each calculating cubit.[4] (In contrast, while far less powerful, classical computers have error rates of as low as one in a *quadrillion* operations.[5])

Error correction creates a need for highly specialised algorithms. As a necessary support system, quantum computers rely on classical computers running on traditional microprocessors. The geopolitical and techno-nationalist implications of this last point are significant because of the link to advanced semiconductors and will be addressed later in the chapter.

Despite these issues, the potential benefits of QC make such challenges worth the effort of overcoming.

There are striking parallels between the early days of QC and the development of the modern electrical-based computer. The first oversized machines seemed ridiculously impractical for most purposes, but they met critical techno-nationalist needs in the war against Nazi Germany.

For example, the first large mainframe computer filled 10 large rooms when it was built in the U.K. in 1943. Aptly named the Colossus, it had 2,500 vacuum tubes and needed 20,000 punch cards and paper tape with 5-bit characters to be operated in a continuous loop. Similarly, America's first 'supercomputer', the ENIAC, built in 1945, had 17,500 vacuum tubes linked by 500,000 soldered connections and weighed 30 tonnes.

But despite the cumbersome attributes of operating and maintaining the Colossus and ENIAC, their role as a defensive technology against a formidable enemy made them worth the trouble. As it happened, eventually, the first microchips would emerge and revolutionise computing.

Thus, just as the advent of the microprocessor overcame the challenges of the operating environment and hardware issues of the first vacuum computers, a combination of classical digital computing and new advances in QC hardware and operating environments are emerging to create a reliable and, eventually, affordable symbiosis of quantum and classical computing.

QUANTUM TECHNOLOGIES AND TECHNO-NATIONALISM

Quantum technology has increased the stakes in U.S.–China great power competition. As with semiconductors, the race for quantum advantages will draw upon a feedback loop involving technology, economic and financial institutions, political bodies and the military–industrial complex. Caught in the middle of this feedback loop are universities and research institutions, individual scientists, private investors, academics and NGOs.

China and the U.S. lead the world in the number of patents related to quantum technology. State-backed actors in China, for example, have focused heavily on hardware and software for communication and cryptography. Later, we will examine one application called quantum key distribution (QKD), which uses bursts of photon transmissions bounced off satellites to create, in theory, a virtually un-hackable cyber-secure communication network.

Meanwhile, the U.S. leads in hardware and software patents for quantum processing. Here, we examine how markets and non-state actors in the U.S. and China are operating in different kinds of environments and how strategic partnerships and government initiatives are shaping the global QC landscape. Finally, we look at how the corporations and start-ups are shaping the landscape.

The same techno-nationalist pressures shaping the semiconductor sector will alter the international QC landscape. Washington has resorted to sanctions and export controls to weaponise QC supply chains and to ring-fence R&D through strategic partnerships and techno-diplomacy.

Here, we examine which stakeholders could be most affected, including academic institutions and individuals involved in international research. We conclude with a look at how ethics and rule frameworks are needed to prevent the misuse and monopolisation of quantum power by a few actors.

POTENTIAL SECTORS AND PRACTICAL APPLICATIONS OF QUANTUM COMPUTING

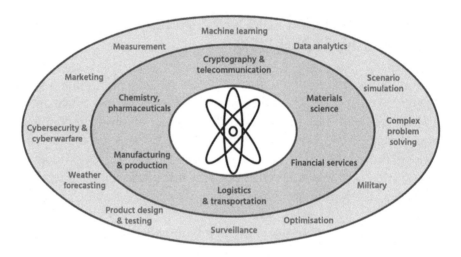

Figure 14.3   **Practical Applications of Error-Free Quantum Computing.**

QC, communication and sensing functions create unprecedented opportunities and risks for state and non-state actors across a range of sectors and applications. The market value for QC services alone is expected to reach just under US$1 billion in 2025 and grow to US$2.6 billion by 2029.[6]

Sectors most likely to be impacted include cryptography, information and communication technology (ICT), chemistry (with direct implications for the pharmaceutical and healthcare sectors), manufacturing and production, material sciences, logistics and transportation and financial services.

Relevant applications of QC include simulation and scenario mapping, complex problem solving, machine learning and AI, data sorting and analysis, optimisation, product design, cybersecurity and cyberwarfare, marketing and specialised forecasting.

A techno-nationalist feedback loop connects all these applications to economic and financial actors, political institutions and the military–industrial complex. In China, for example, national security initiatives are driving Beijing's military–civil fusion.[7] This has resulted in the establishment of the National Laboratory for Quantum Information Sciences in Hefei.[8] In the U.S., the Defence Advanced Research Projects Agency (DARPA) is overseeing increased amounts of funding for R&D initiatives in QC.[9]

QC is spawning a hybrid ecosystem that combines leading-edge classical computing niches with the brave new world of the qubit. Software and hardware developers are being linked through both private investors and government-led initiatives, while cloud services have also become integral.

So far, quantum advantage has been limited to solving certain types of complex mathematical problems. Using QC for practical applications will require thousands of qubits and remains years away.[10]

Although it is impossible to predict when practical applications will become readily available, it is not difficult to see how they will fundamentally reshape the competitive landscape everywhere. Some noteworthy areas are discussed below.

Financial Services

Financial institutions have been keenly interested in the practical applications of QC for years. Potential uses include portfolio optimisation, high-frequency trading algorithms, fraud detection and quantum-proofing of cybersecurity systems.

Pharmaceuticals, Chemistry and Healthcare

Classical computing's power-multiplying effects were apparent during the COVID 19 pandemic. Powerful AI and algorithms were harnessed to sequence the DNA of the virus variants and, in less than a year, produce a series of vaccinations from a sea of data collected and shared throughout the digital global commons.

How much more can QC bring to solving practical problems and pre-empting a future health crisis? In the race to defeat cancer or devise drugs for other debilitating diseases, QC may contribute to performing simulations involving chemical combinations, specialised applications (including designer drugs for an individual's unique DNA profile) and possible spill-over effects. One of the true marvels of such powerful technology is that it could produce in hours or days life-giving solutions that would take classical computers thousands of years.

From a global trade perspective, the transformational potential of quantum is enormous. The ability to link millions of patients, for example, in Indonesia or Brazil, with vaccine production in India or the U.S. and to seamlessly align customs pre-clearance procedures with local health and safety laws, data privacy and other regulations would save precious time and costs and enhance efficient trade networks.

Trade, Logistics and Transportation

Leading-edge AI and real-time data analysis is already a core competency of the logistics and transportation industry. Exponentially increasing the power of AI with quantum promises solutions that go beyond just finding the quickest route between two points or matching passengers with drivers.

In the calculation of the safest and most efficient routes for logistics and passenger modes of transportation, the variables increase exponentially as the number of subjects in motion increases. In urban centres with millions of vehicles, for example, calculating the potential outcome at any given moment is far too complex for any classical computer.

Beyond safety and efficiency, however, data from connected vehicles in so-called 'smart cities' could be used in sustainable, circular economies that reduce carbon emissions and capture kinetic energy, as well as optimise supply and demand scenarios in the sharing economy.

For global trade, QC could provide instantaneous, real-time calculation of efficient shipping routes, from the pick-up of a finished product at a factory loading bay to its placement in a seafaring container to its last-mile delivery on a bicycle in a remote village on the other side of the planet.

REINVENTING PUBLIC KEY CRYPTOGRAPHY

One of the areas that will be widely affected by QC is cryptography. Today's encryption methods involve prime number factorisation that would take classical computers thousands, even millions of years to solve. A quantum processor, however, with a relatively small number of qubits, could figure out a password in a matter of seconds or just a few minutes by applying Shor's algorithm for prime factorisation (D. Angelakis, personal communication, July 15, 2021).

Therefore, public key cryptography—used for virtually all secure communications on both public and private digital platforms, applications and devices—could be rendered defenceless to quantum-enabled adversaries.

How long it will take for this moment to arrive is not certain, but the day is coming.

Ironically, the best way to protect a password or a network gateway in a quantum world is to employ *quantum countermeasures* in the next generation of public key cryptography. Combined with multi-factor verification data, quantum cryptography will likely become ubiquitous.

Recent state-sponsored cyber offensives against governments and private organisations around the world provide a case study of the possible linkages between cybersecurity, hybrid warfare and QC.

In 2020, the U.S. Department of Homeland Security issued a public statement that named Russia as the instigator of a cyber offensive that gained access to data and communications in at least nine federal agencies, including the Pentagon, the Department of Commerce and the Department of the Treasury.[11] Additionally, the networks of at least 100 companies, NGOs and academic institutions had been infiltrated, infected and pilfered for months by hostile cyber operatives.

In 2021, cyber intruders reportedly attacked some 60,000 known victims around the world, including the European Banking Authority, by exploiting a flaw in Microsoft's business email server software.[12] Hackers obtained access to emails, address books and calendars.

Orchestrated by leveraging classical technology and aided by using conventional 'backdoors', spyware and other hacking techniques, these cyber intrusions netted vast amounts of secret data.

The question is, how much of it will eventually be vetted with the aid of QC, and what advantages will that confer to state actors? There are endless possibilities for intelligence agencies to use sophisticated algorithms to establish linkages between individuals, organisations, ideas and objectives.

Even the most granular and random bits of data could be harvested for intelligence purposes and tapped to reveal patterns, associations and relationships. All this stolen data is now waiting to be analysed as soon as practical quantum technology comes online.

PATENT FILINGS AS A BENCHMARK

The quantity of patents filed is a gauge of progress—assuming utility, patent life range, quality of technology and number of patents filed abroad are also important indicators.[13] Nevertheless, patent numbers provide some indication of the pace of advance in different kinds of quantum technology and its distribution among countries.

China has filed more quantum technology patents than any other country, about twice as many as the U.S.[14] It has achieved leading-edge innovation in key areas of quantum technology, particularly regarding software for communication and cryptography.

In contrast, the U.S. is leading in patents for both hardware and software in *computing*, while Japan leads in patents involving hardware for communication and cryptography.

Other types of quantum research hubs reside Japan, the E.U. (primarily Germany, the U.K. and the Netherlands), Taiwan, Australia and South Korea. Singapore and Israel, both small countries, have disproportionally large footprints and could carve out unique positions in the international landscape.

QUANTUM KEY DISTRIBUTION (QKD)

According to a January 2021 study published in *Nature*, a team of Chinese scientists based at the University of Science and Technology in Hefei developed a breakthrough quantum communication network. Using fibre-optic cables and ground-to-satellite links, the network achieved QKD over 4,600 kilometres among a network of connected users.[15]

China's QKD network used bursts of light (photons) bouncing off satellites to relay data-laden qubits in a fully encrypted state. The experiment showed that it is possible to create long-range communication networks that are virtually impossible for spies and hackers to infiltrate. Any attempt to do so without an encryption key alters the qubits and alerts the sender and intended recipients to the intrusion. (Decoy transmissions can also be mixed into groupings of transmissions to further complicate any hacking efforts.)

Although the Chinese experiment proved the possibilities of QKD, facilitating a large, geographically dispersed network requires technology that is currently non-existent at the time of this writing.[16] Practical applications must wait until necessary advances in hardware and infrastructure occur. But rather than discourage China and others from pursuing QKD, the experiment has only served to inspire more ambitious R&D efforts.

For Beijing, the catalyst for action took place in 2013, when leaks of classified documents detailed how the NSA and other U.S. intelligence agencies were infiltrating, monitoring and exploiting data and communications from China's most secure networks. QKD represents the next great hope for Beijing's safekeeping of its secrets.

THE RACE BETWEEN COMPANIES

The QC landscape is by far most active in the U.S. and Europe, where a multitude of niche players are evolving. Even before the emergence of Washington's aggressive techno-nationalist agenda, a deep reservoir of tech-entrepreneurism was already sustaining a thriving quantum ecosystem.

Quantum Daily, a media platform that conducts research, performs analysis and provides data on market-leading companies, has documented a market map that shows U.S. firms dominating the computing space.[17]

Given the need for hyper-specialised hardware, software and other esoteric services, big established companies and tech start-ups figure to play an important role in the future race for quantum supremacy. Here, both the U.S. and the E.U. can harness healthy financial markets, world-leading universities and research organisations, along with the military–security–intelligence establishment.

From a digital trade perspective, the push in both the U.S. and Europe towards open-sourced standards, open banking and increased trade in services bodes well for the exchange and commercialisation of knowledge and expertise for developing quantum applications.

An open market with healthy measures of risk-taking and hyper-specialisation in quantum software and hardware provides opportunities for tech start-ups throughout global value chains.

TECHNO-NATIONALISM AND THE FUTURE OF QUANTUM TECHNOLOGIES

From a techno-nationalist perspective, the future of quantum technology will follow the same path as that of the semiconductor. Key stakeholders, including governments, multinational companies, NGOs and universities will need to adjust to four key trends.

First, increased export controls and sanctions on quantum-related software, hardware and human capital will call for new risk management strategies. As more companies face the threat of exclusion from global value chains, they will need to scrutinise their partners' supply chains and networks, implement stricter, more vigorous transparency controls and use IT to keep track of restricted entities, individuals and technologies.

Second, because of increased controls and sanctions, affected parties will resort to the ring-fencing of strategic ecosystems. This will result in more regionalised and localised R&D and trade.

Third, both state and non-state actors will turn to increased techno-diplomacy, including efforts to lobby others to exclude certain parties from participating in R&D communities and to block certain entities from joining public–private partnerships. It will also include the formation of coalitions that seek to promote similar values and standards regarding the use of quantum technology.

Finally, an intensified techno-nationalist environment will increase the need for new quantum-related ethics, standards and rules. New quantum applications are likely to confer disproportionate power on monopolistic non-state actors as well as multiply the power of state actors. This will challenge efforts to curtail the negative aspects of surveillance capitalism and techno-authoritarianism.

EXPORT CONTROLS AND RING-FENCING OF STRATEGIC ECOSYSTEMS

Washington and its allies have begun to place restrictions on access to components, information technology and human capital as it relates to quantum technologies.[18]

In conducting my research on this topic, I spoke extensively with Dr. Dimitris Angelakis, a pioneer in quantum technology research at the National University of Singapore, who noted that increased U.S. and E.U. export controls had begun to make cross-border collaboration with Chinese nationals and academic institutions much more difficult. This is compounding the challenges of developing the next generation of quantum thought leaders (for better or for worse) as new constraints on student visas and foreign scholars come under serious discussion.

The esoteric nature of quantum research has created a small circle of experts around the world who have supported each other's research for decades.

Often referred to as the father of China's quantum programme, Pan Jiawen was the lead scientist on China's successful QKD communication experiment in early 2021. Pan Jiawen received his PhD from the University of Vienna, where he was supervised by Professor Anton Zielinger, one of the world's foremost experts on quantum entanglement and teleportation.

As we will discuss in Chapter 24, because of governmental pressure and techno-nationalism, the doors at Western universities have been slowly closing on China's Thousand Talents Programme. Through this programme, Beijing's central planners sought to accelerate knowledge and technology transfer regarding quantum and other science, technology, engineering, and math (STEM) topics through interaction with the world's top scholars and academic institutions.

In the U.S., DARPA and other government agencies have been taking a lead in overseeing and ring-fencing quantum technology research.

DARPA has been supervising public–private partnerships, such as the Quantum Economic Development Consortium.

It is also noteworthy that DARPA, an organisation dedicated to national security, has taken a proactive role in future-focused bench-marking programmes that seek to influence how quantum technology will be used in medicine and pharmaceuticals, material sciences and other practical applications.[19]

TECHNO-DIPLOMACY AND QUANTUM TECHNOLOGY

Washington has been actively lobbying the U.K., Japan, South Korea and other nations to decouple their quantum research and development efforts and related value chains from China.

On a multilateral level, the U.S. has proposed to the 42 participants in the Wassenaar Arrangement to agree to multilateral licensing restrictions on quantum dilution refrigeration and GAAFET (for leading-edge microchips).[20]

Going forward, the U.S. and its closest partners will likely form a new kind of export-control regime, the proposed Multilateral Export Controls Regime (MECR), which would include European allies, Canada, the U.K., Australia, Japan and South Korea. The aim of MECR would be to ratchet up the scope of export controls and increase transparency in quantum-related value chains.

The U.S. has also focused its techno-diplomacy on NATO. As the historic multilateral defence alliance turns its attention to cyber and hybrid warfare, quantum technology is a priority.[21]

QUANTUM ETHICS, STANDARDS AND RULES

The realpolitik applications of one of humankind's most powerful technologies will probably be confined to a small group of governments and well-positioned non-state actors. The idea, however, of a handful of Wall Street investment banks or Amazon, Google and Apple exploiting QC to bolster their already dominant positions in the market is cause for concern.

The same concerns apply to state actors. QC will eventually enable surveillance and population control on a scale unimaginable by Aldous Huxley and George Orwell, two of history's most prophetic writers on authoritarian and dystopian regimes. Therefore, whether state actors have at their disposal a monopoly on surveillance or on population control, a rules framework on ethical behaviour will be sorely needed.

When the U.S. embarked on the Manhattan Project in the 1940s, the world witnessed the first collision of techno-nationalism and quantum science. The quest to harness the destructive power of the atom ahead of Hitler's Nazi Germany revealed many of the same ethical concerns that have surfaced regarding quantum technology today.

In 1949, a group of 70 scientists on the Manhattan Project signed a petition admonishing President Harry Truman that he would '. . . bear the responsibility of opening the door to an era of devastation on an unimaginable scale'.[22] The document never made it to the president's desk and was only declassified in 1961. Nevertheless, during the Cold War, the scientific community was successful in influencing both the U.S. and the Soviet Union to agree to a series of treaties to ban nuclear testing and to strive for non-proliferation of nuclear weapons and their eventual disarmament.

Although the next generation of quantum science has yet to be applied in many of the ways previously described, now is a defining movement for the world's leading nations to begin serious discussions about the future of quantum technology. This will have profound consequences not only for trade but for the future state of geopolitics.

Chapter 15

Hypersonic Speed

During the COVID-19 pandemic, in August 2021, while China's beleaguered citizens hunkered down under strict lockdown orders, the People's Liberation Army (PLA) announced that it had successfully launched a missile with a hypersonic glider that reached speeds up to five times the speed of sound.

This new kind of aerial vehicle travelled into Earth's highest reaches and was said to be capable of firing both conventional and nuclear warheads at multiple targets. As the missile briefly exited and re-entered Earth's atmosphere, it performed evasive manoeuvres. Due to its tremendous speed—over 6,000 kilometres per hour or more than 1.5 kilometres per second—China's hypersonic missile would be virtually impossible to shoot down using the systems available to the U.S. military at the time.

This came as a total surprise to the American defence establishment. When the news broke, retired U.S. Four Star Admiral, William McRaven, was said to have called it a 'holy shit' moment.

Forget about any proverbial 'Sputnik' analogy here—I refer to the Soviet Union's Cold War achievement of launching the world's first artificial satellite in 1957, which caught the U.S. aerospace establishment flat-footed—this piled yet another layer of national security risk, on top of the dangers posed by ballistic missiles.

More broadly, conversation turned to the strategic importance of propulsion technologies—not just of the hypersonic variety for missiles and aerospace applications but of the underwater variety for stealthy, noiseless submarine operations under the planet's vast oceans and seas, where a new cold war with China was playing out.

Speed and stealth, together, meant achieving decisive advantages in battle, surveillance and espionage—and in nuclear deterrence. It meant the difference between being vulnerable to a massive, overwhelming nuclear first strike or being able to prevent one with certainty.

CHINA'S HYPERSONIC TECHNOLOGY SNAPSHOT

Regarding the hypersonic missile test, in 2021, Beijing had achieved a technological 'leapfrog' over U.S. missile capabilities. China's techno-nationalist efforts, through its civil–military fusion programmes and ongoing technology prioritisation programmes, had provided a microcosm of the comprehensiveness of its overall technology prowess.

By fielding its hypersonic missile, an achievement the Americans had not yet accomplished, Beijing demonstrated a wide and impressive list of innovative accomplishments.

At the heart of the PLA's hypersonic missile was a scramjet engine capable of propelling the missile at speeds exceeding Mach 5, far surpassing the capabilities of conventional jet engines. Scramjets, short for 'supersonic combustion ramjet', operate by efficiently burning a mixture of fuel and air at hypersonic velocities, achieving speeds that (other than conventional rockets) far outpace the limitations of traditional propulsion technologies.

The PLA's hypersonic missile was encased in a sophisticated skin crafted from advanced heat-resistant composites, meticulously designed to withstand the intense heat generated during hypersonic flight. These composites, capable of enduring temperatures of up to 3,000 degrees Celsius, provide critical protection for the missile's internal components, ensuring its structural integrity and operational effectiveness. Specifically, the PLA employed a combination of carbon fibre-reinforced polymers (CFRPs) and ceramic matrix composites (CMCs), each offering unique properties that enhanced the missile's resilience to hypersonic heat.

Accurate navigation and precise timing are essential for hypersonic missiles, enabling them to manoeuvre effectively and strike their targets with pinpoint accuracy. The PLA's hypersonic missile employed a suite of advanced sensors, including inertial navigation systems (INS) and global navigation satellite systems (GNSS), to continuously track its position and orientation.

China's hypersonic missile utilised terrain reference navigation (TRN), which relies on terrain features to guide the missile, while image correlation and digital scene matching (DSM) employ detailed images of a target area to ensure precise targeting.

Further, inertial guidance systems (IGS) utilised the missile's inertial sensors to determine its position and orientation, providing continuous guidance throughout its flight path. To do this, a satellite guidance receiver must take signals from other satellites to maintain precise positioning.

That the PLA was able to bundle all these leading-edge technologies together to successfully launch and control such advanced weaponry confirmed its status as a technology superpower. Such accomplishments underscored the effectiveness of decades of techno-nationalist initiatives.

And then there was the artificial intelligence (AI) component. AI was employed not only to design, develop and test the hypersonic missile and its entire technology platform, it was also used to execute real-time flight commands and operate all the missile's guidance algorithms. Presumably, AI would have factored into cybersecurity countermeasures against eventual cyberattack threats.

Here, we must return to the topic of semiconductors. Virtually every single aspect of the development and manufacture of China's hypersonic missile relied on a critical chip–AI nexus, which involves the interdependence of AI and advanced semiconductor chips. This underscores the 'chip war' dynamics that we have discussed in earlier chapters and calls attention, yet again, to the vulnerabilities that

China faces if it cannot find substitutes for U.S. and other foreign semiconductor technology that is being gradually choked off.

It is developments like China's hypersonic breakthrough that led to Washington's doubling down on efforts to choke off the flow of advanced microchip technology to China.

'CARRIER KILLER' MISSILES

Figure 15.1   China's Dong Feng 27 Hypersonic Missile.

China's hypersonic missile breakthrough had much wider geopolitical ramifications. In 2021, *The Washington Post* published information that had been leaked from the Joint Chiefs of Staff's intelligence directorate, which revealed that U.S. officials had known about a hypersonic missile called the Dong Feng-27 (DF-27).

U.S. analysts confirmed that the DF-27 had a range of up to 8,000 kilometres and could likely penetrate American missile defences at the time because of its evasive hypersonic glide capabilities.[1,2]

The PLA had already designed another missile, one which was launched from a mobile transporter erector launcher, the DF 26B, otherwise known as a 'carrier killer'. Travelling at hypersonic speeds meant the evasive DF-26B had the ability to strike and disable, or even sink, a U.S. aircraft carrier from long range. If the U.S. could not come up with countermeasures, American power projection in the Indo-Pacific could be neutralised.

If China could focus the DF-27's hypersonic speed, longer range and high level of manoeuvrability to strike a U.S. carrier, this was a historic inflexion point.

In 2021, when news of the DF-27 emerged, the U.S. Navy had 11 air-craft carriers and another nine so-called 'helo-carriers' in operation around the world—by far the most of any nation. Its latest class of aircraft carrier, the *Gerald R. Ford*, represented a new generation of modern vessels, replacing the *Nimitz* class carriers. The lead ship of this new class, USS *Gerald R. Ford*, cost an estimated US$13 billion[3] to build and, fully bristling with aeroplanes, choppers, drones and other weaponry, was easily worth US$40 billion.

It was inconceivable that a new kind of Chinese missile technology, armed with either conventional or nuclear warheads, could poten-tially blow the *Gerald R. Ford* right out of the water from thousands of kilometres away.

Theoretically, the DF 27 hypersonic missile could strike a U.S. carrier group as far away from China as the U.S. Marshall Islands, the Mariana Islands and Palau in the Caroline Islands.

In military circles, these far-flung archipelagos are referred to as the 'second island chain', which serves as a staging and support area for U.S. military assets deployed over a much wider geographical area. The second island chain is of strategic importance because it pro-vides a vital supply line for reinforcements and even a safe fallback zone for U.S. forces engaged in an actual hot war in Asia.

Right on China's doorstep is the first island chain. It includes the Taiwan Strait, the East China Sea and the South China Sea—arguably the world's most dangerous and combustible navigable water since the Second World War in the Pacific.

Conventional military thinking holds that because China has taken de facto control of the South China Sea through the gradual building of militarised islands, complete with combat aircraft and missile batteries, it could saturate the fighting zone with enough firepower to overwhelm U.S. forces in the first island chain and along China's littoral zone.

In such a scenario, the PLA's Anti-Access/Area Denial (A2/AD) strategy would call upon the use of long-range hypersonic missiles, anti-submarine warfare, including underwater, unmanned underwater vehicles (UUAVs), and multiple swarm waves of unmanned aerial vehicles (UAVs).

If the PLA was also able to effectively use its carrier killers to neutralise U.S. military assets much farther away, in the second island chain, not only could the PLA take away vital resupply and staging capabilities for American forces throughout the Indo-Pacific, it might succeed in pushing American forces back from the first and second line of islands. Theoretically, successive waves of missile attacks could push U.S. forces all the way back to the third line of islands, which includes the Hawaiian and the Marshall Islands.

Because of its aircraft carriers, the U.S. has successfully projected overwhelming naval power globally and enjoyed its status as a 'resident power' in Asia in the nearly 80 years since its victory over Japan in 1945.

Effective deployment of carrier killers could bring an end to that dominance, and would mean that an increasingly aggressive Beijing could impose its will on its neighbours throughout Asia, including not just Taiwan but Vietnam, the Philippines, Malaysia, Singapore and even farther south to Indonesia. Farther east, Japan and South Korea could face a future fraught with confrontation and the need for continual military spending.

THE ROLE OF AI

Chinese state-controlled media reported that to test the DF-27 and earlier prototypes, the PLA had constructed life-size mock-ups of U.S. aircraft carriers in the Taklamakan Desert, a vast arid region in northwestern China. The DF missiles were reported to have been test-fired from as far as 4,800 kilometres away.

Western analysts also became aware, based on more credible information, that the PLA employed a variety of advanced AI simulation techniques to model complex battle scenarios and evaluate its A2/AD strategies against the Americans.

These techniques included agent-based modelling (ABM) that simulates the behaviour of individual entities, such as military units, ship and aircraft, and their interactions within the battlefield environment, and game theory, which models decision-making under conflict and uncertainty, allowing the user to analyse potential adversary strategies and develop optimal responses.

The computer simulations used reinforcement learning algorithms to enable the PLA to train its AI agents to make optimal decisions in simulated warfare scenarios, improving their tactical proficiency.

To conduct these simulations, the PLA utilised a range of computing platforms to run its AI-powered war simulations, including Tianhe supercomputers, which are among the most powerful in the world.

Ironically, the Tianhe supercomputers used leading-edge semiconductors made with American technology. For example, the Tianhe-2 supercomputer used Intel Xeon processors as well as Nvidia, and AMD graphics processing units. These enabled massive amounts of gaming graphics for computational PLA simulations. Also used were distributed high-performance clusters to provide additional computing power and scalability.

Finally, the PLA would have in its toolkit an assortment of cloud-based computing solutions, which also expand its access to computing resources. What should be of concern to businesses and well-established multinational enterprises, from the banking sector, fintech, AI, telecommunications, and, of course, semiconductors, is that the PLA leaned on the big Chinese tech companies to build its computing capabilities.

Huawei, the telecommunications equipment manufacturer, and Alibaba both provided cloud computing and AI solutions to the PLA to support computer simulation efforts and beyond, in much the same way that Microsoft, Cisco and Amazon Web Services have built cloud infrastructure for the U.S. military and intelligence communities.

THE DARPA ANSWER

Figure 15.2   Artist Rendition of Northrop Grumman's Scramjet Hypersonic Engine.

In response to China's hypersonic missile advances, the U.S. defence establishment, with heavy involvement from the Defence Advanced Research Projects Agency (DARPA), hastened the development and testing of a prototype under a programme called Hypersonic Air-breathing Weapons Concept (HAWC).

By early 2023, a series of successful tests using missiles with scramjet engines led to DARPA's transition from an experimental to a production phase, thanks to U.S. defence contractors Lockheed Martin and Aerojet Rocketdyne.[4]

As of 2023, the U.S. military was still in the trial stages of pursuing two main types of hypersonic missiles: boost-glide missiles and cruise missiles. Boost-glide missiles are launched by rocket boosters dropped from aircraft and then glide to their targets at hypersonic speeds. A third version was being developed by the U.S. Navy.

Clearly, the shock value of China's hypersonic leapfrog pushed the National Aeronautics and Space Administration (NASA) to double down on research into new propulsion systems. Beyond scramjets, NASA began group testing new in-space propulsion systems that could propel spacecraft in the vacuum of space.

Some of the most advanced in-space propulsion technologies include nuclear thermal propulsion, which uses a nuclear reactor to heat a propellant that creates thrust and electric propulsion.

NASA also began intensified experimentation with directed energy propulsion, a type of system that uses energy from lasers or microwaves to create thrust. Directed energy propulsion is still in the early stages of development, but it has the potential to be very efficient and powerful.

While many of these concepts may never actually come to fruition in the form of an actual space mission, a sudden breakthrough in technology could have both profound economic and national security ramifications.

The outcome of one country having at its disposal hypersonic missiles while others do not mark a definitive and dangerous turning point in international affairs, as the world is still awash with thousands of nuclear warheads. The abhorrent possibility of an overwhelming nuclear first strike, delivered by hypersonic and even undetectable hypersonic missiles, is the stuff of nightmares.

Thus, there can be no end to an innovation race, not just to achieve offensive capabilities but, from purely a survival perspective, to develop technologies to deter and defend against would-be aggressors.

If published reports about China's hypersonic programmes are to be believed, then, until the U.S. can follow through on development of an active inventory of functional hypersonic weapons, the PLA has exhibited a clear technological edge over the U.S.

Chapter 16

The Great Undersea Cable Decoupling

Most people are surprised to learn that before information and data in the digital 'Cloud' can be accessed it must first pass through a vast network of undersea cables. Today, close to 99% of the traffic on the global Internet flows through a sprawling network of fibre-optic cables, each around 3 centimetres in diameter.[1]

In 2023, there were roughly 575 active cable systems laying across the vast abyssal plains of the world's oceans and under the territorial seas of nations, comprising about 1.4 million kilometres of connectivity. All told, these cables are essential for the daily communications of billions of people and countless businesses.[2] In 2023, undersea cables carried an estimated US$10 trillion worth of financial transactions every day.[3] The number of underwater cables, meanwhile, continues to grow, as demand for more digital bandwidth increases.

Most of the cables carrying our voice, data and streaming imagery lie remarkably exposed on seafloors, on average, about 3,600 meters deep. The longest such underwater linkage, the Asia-America Gateway, runs an incredible 20,000 kilometres and connects

Southern California to landing points in Hawaii, Guam, the Philippines, China, Vietnam, Brunei, Malaysia and Vietnam.

To view a map of the world's undersea cable networks is to acknowledge which countries and commercial hubs command the greatest flows of wealth, knowledge and power. As such, the most densely packed clusters of cables originate and terminate between the United States and Europe, and these same places have major arterials connecting to economic hubs in Asia, namely Japan, China, Taiwan and about a dozen other places.

GEOPOLITICS, DATA AND UNDERSEA CABLES

Undersea cables are central to the hybrid cold war between the U.S. and China. In a geopolitical context, because of their ubiquity, they are far more consequential than 5G wireless network infrastructure and—at least into the foreseeable future—space-based satellite communications.

At stake is the motherlode of data that flows throughout the open Internet. This includes transfers to and from the world's data storage centres in the Cloud, communications between multinational companies, banking transactions, and even intra-military and governmental data flows.

From a techno-nationalist perspective, whoever excels in manufacturing, laying and maintaining cable, as well as accessing and defending these undersea cable networks achieves not only economic power, but also gains defence and intelligence gathering advantages. The potential weaponisation of these technologies, therefore, is every bit as consequential to global trade and, indeed, global stability, as a major cyberwar—and even potentially more disruptive than a hot kinetic war.

The undersea cable-scape, therefore, is undergoing a bifurcation around American and Chinese spheres of influence.

Above water, telecoms, cloud-service, data storage and other digital platform service providers have been impacted and are having to choose sides when it comes to selecting partners for new and ongoing undersea cable projects. Beyond the telecoms and tech service

Figure 16.1 Undersea Cable Networks.

providers, a proxy war is playing out involving a handful of companies that engineer, manufacture, and install subsea fibre optic cables.

In the context of U.S.–China great power competition, this follows a general bifurcation trend affecting other strategic technologies, from semiconductors and supercomputing to advanced robotics and quantum science.

Around the world, the geopolitics of undersea cables is playing out in three distinct arenas.

The first arena involves Washington's techno-diplomacy offensive against HMN Technologies (HMN or HMN Tech), which is majority-owned by China's Hengtong group (Hengtong).[4] Hengtong's previous owner was none other than the marine division of Huawei Technologies Co, Ltd, the world's largest telecommunications equipment manufacturer, and the ongoing target of U.S. export controls and sanctions.

Since 2019, when Huawei was placed on the U.S. Bureau of Industry and Security (BIS) Entity List, Washington has mounted a three-front war against China's premier technology company: on the 5G infrastructure front, where U.S. officials have attempted to persuade governments to block Huawei equipment from their networks; on the semiconductor front, where critical microchip technologies have been choked off; and, finally, on the subsea cables front.

In early 2020, the Hengtong Group acquired 81% of Huawei Marine Networks Co., Ltd., shares, and effectively rebranded the company as HMN Tech.[5] Despite any change in name, however, HMN Tech continues to be singled out for blockage from Western-influenced undersea projects. (the names HMN or HMN Tech and Hengtong Group or Hengtong interchangeably).

To get foreign governments and national telecoms to reject Chinese undersea cable partners, Washington has stepped up the use of financial incentives and the application of pressure on subsea cable consortium members, including threats of sanctions and export controls. The narrative behind these actions is straightforward: if you choose a Chinese entity as a consortium partner, you choose a proxy of the Chinese Communist party (CCP) and give Beijing eavesdropping access to all the data pulsing through your undersea cable network.

Regarding new cable deals that involve undersea linkages between American and Chinese territories, the U.S. government has intervened, and succeeded, in either preventing HMN from winning any business or forcing the rerouting or abandonment of new cable deals.[6]

We will examine one of these cases, the Southeast Asia-Middle East-Western Europe 6 (SEA-ME-WE-6) cable project, along with other examples involving U.S. allies, such as Australia and New Zealand, who have pushed out Chinese participation in underwater cable deals, at the behest of the U.S.

The second arena involves the emergence of the tech titans as major players in the subsea cable economy. Amazon, Google, Meta and Microsoft have been behind the rapid expansion of undersea cable networks. These firms have deep pockets and move quickly when it comes to funding new projects, but they are geopolitically agnostic when it comes to choosing partners, which sometimes puts them at odds with Washington.

The American tech titans are first movers not only in funding more cable gateways, they are also pushing the innovation envelope regarding cable technology. This has placed them in a grey zone, where Washington views them as strategic partners when it comes to playing for the home team, but as security risks when they team up with the wrong consortium partners.

Beyond the geopolitical realm, big tech players now face increased scrutiny, as they exercise control over the bandwidth in their own private cable networks, which they increasingly rent out to telecommunications carriers and other third parties.

The third arena is perhaps the most worrisome: sabotage and outright attacks on undersea cables by bad actors. Recent events in the Baltic Sea and the Taiwan Straits involving the cutting and disabling of undersea cables reveals their vulnerabilities. These events have been linked to escalation of hostilities between Russia and the NATO alliance and the rising tensions between China and Taiwan.

We will discuss these different arenas in greater detail later. First, however, we shall look at some of the noteworthy aspects of the technology behind undersea cables.

THE TECHNOLOGY AND COMPETITORS

Undersea cables transmit information via pulses of light sent through optical fibres. Lasers on one end fire at rapid rates through thin glass filaments about as thick as a human hair to receptors at the other end of the cable. When bunched together inside a cable configuration, these fibers can transfer up to 250 terabits per second.

A terabit is incredibly fast and can move enormous amounts of information—imagine a super-highway with 10 trillion lanes through which data can travel simultaneously. Inside a cable, these fibers are sheathed in a few layers of insulation and protection and then wrapped in a layer of steel armour for protection—the closer a cable is to shore, the more protection it gets.

Near-shore cables are buried, but for most of the distance across the ocean floor, the average cable, which is about as thick as a garden hose, lies fully exposed.

Only about 10 nations currently have the technology to build and run these undersea cable networks: the U.S., a handful of its European allies, Japan, South Korea, China and, to a lesser extent, Russia. Historically, three companies have dominated the subsea cable field: America's SubCom, NEC Corporation of Japan, and France's Alcatel Submarine Networks.

In 2008, Huawei Marine Networks became the fourth big player in the undersea cable game, and it reshaped the industry status quo. Like its parent company, Huawei Technologies, the undersea cable group benefitted from generous government backing and funding and rapidly grew its global footprint. According to TeleGeography, a tele-communications research firm, and as reported by Reuters, HMN Tech grew faster than their competitors from 2008–2023—although it claimed only about 10 % of the subsea construction spending in 2023.[7]

Like SubCom, NEC and Alcatel Submarine Networks, HMN Tech designs, manufactures, deploys, maintains and operates cable systems, which gives it exclusive physical access to its submarine technology and infrastructure, wherever it is. Here, concerns about mass surveillance, and the ability to disable or shut down a cable exchange, perhaps at the command of a government, has brought heightened scrutiny to this industry niche.

Another area of concern are the so-called landing stations, where groups of cables emerge from underwater, and converge into a small gateway, in what can be described as a choke point. In 2023, there were about 1,400 landing stations in operation or under construction.[8] In the busiest commercial centres, landing stations take on disproportionate amounts of traffic, with New York, London and Tokyo accounting for much thicker bandwidth than, say, Buenos Aires or Jakarta.

These landing stations have increasingly become the focal points of security minded officials. In a U.S.-China hybrid cold war, then, decoupling efforts regarding undersea cables will proceed on a scale even greater than those which have affected 5G wireless networks.

TECHNO-DIPLOMACY AND UNDERSEA CABLES

The Americans are said to have created an inter-agency agency task force that has unofficially become known as 'Team Telecom', which uses both a carrot and a stick approach to affect the outcomes of undersea cable projects.[9]

Since the techno-nationalist paradigm shift in the West altered relations with China, the U.S. government has taken a page out of Beijing's playbook. U.S. diplomats at embassies around the world have pushed foreign governments and national telecommunications companies to choose SubCom, the American company, as their undersea cable partner. This would be comparable to Beijing's long-running campaign to support Huawei.

One of the things that Washington has done is deny licences for undersea cable links that connect territories of the U.S. with China or Hong Kong. One such project, the Pacific Light Cable Network (PLCN) announced in 2016, with substantial investments from Google and Meta, was affected. After cables had been laid from the U.S. to the Philippines and Taiwan, approval for an off-shoot of the PLCN to Hong Kong was denied by the U.S. government—leaving hundreds of kilometres of cables to lie unused on the seafloor.[10]

On the techno-diplomacy front, in 2019, the year the U.S. placed Huawei on the BIS Entity List, Washington began to lean harder on its allies to keep Huawei's marine division out of new cable projects in their regions. Such was the case with the Coral Sea Cable project, when the Australian government responded to U.S. urging by blocking Huawei Marine from participating in a cable connecting Australia with Papua New Guinea and the Solomon Islands.[11]

Earlier, in 2018, regarding the Manatua subsea cable, which connects New Zealand, the Cook Islands, Niue, and Fiji, Wellington announced that it would be partnering with SubCom.

THE SEA-ME-WE-6

One of the largest and most important cable projects under development is the Southeast Asia–Middle East-Western Europe 6 (SEA-ME-WE-6) undersea system. When it opens for service in 2025, the network will stretch over 19,200 kilometres, providing high-speed Internet connectivity and telecommunications services to participating countries.[12] SEA-ME-WE-6 will link Singapore to Marseille, France, passing through Italy, Greece, Egypt, Saudi Arabia, Djibouti, Pakistan, India, Maldives, Sri Lanka, Bangladesh, and Malaysia.

In 2021, the SEA-ME-WE-6 consortium issued a request for proposals for the construction of the cable network. A number of companies submitted bids, including SubCom, and HMN Tech, the new owner of Huawei Marine.

As an enticement, and part of the Team Telecom's strategy to position SubCom as the bid winner, the U.S. Trade and Development Agency (USTDA) reportedly gave US$ 3.8 million in training grants to five of the national telecom carriers along SEA-ME-WE-6's cable route, as a condition of choosing SubCom.[13] According to a special report by Reuters, Telecom Egypt, and Network i2i Limited (owned by Bharti Airtel, an Indian company) each received US$1 million. Additionally, three telecom carriers representing Djibouti, Sri Lanka and the Maldives each received US$600,000.[14]

This is textbook dollar diplomacy. The USTDA's involvement in SEA-ME-WE-6 looks just like China's approach along its Belt and Road Initiative (BRI) in say, Pakistan, where it has provided interest-free loans and open-ended credit to telecoms carriers for their purchase of Huawei or ZTE equipment.

Regarding strong-arm tactics, U.S. diplomats made it clear that under China's Military–Civil Fusion (MCF) system—the requirement that all strategic technologies must flow into the People's Liberation Army (PLA) purview—HMN Tech would pass restricted technology on to the PLA and, thus, would end up on a U.S. sanctions list.

For a government or telecom company, the possibility of sanctions made the selection of HMN Tech a virtual non-starter. If the U.S. were to enforce restrictions on HMN Tech, any money invested in the Chinese subsea company would likely become a loss-making venture.

According to the reporting of Reuters, U.S. diplomats wrote letters or had meetings with telecoms executives, in, among other places, Bangladesh, Singapore, and Sri Lanka. U.S. officials stressed the liabilities of sanctions and pointed out the benefits of a security partnership with the U.S. regarding national security matters. Additionally, U.S. officials drew attention to the possibility of espionage through Chinese-made undersea technologies.

At decision time, the SEA-ME-WE-6 consortium awarded the contract to SubCom, even though its bid was reportedly higher than HMN Tech's. Despite having a lower bid on offer, the consortium decided to go with SubCom, largely because of the threat of crippling U.S. sanctions on the Chinese company. It is unclear whether consortium members based their decision on the certainty that Chinese technology represented an espionage threat.

SubCom is a well-established undersea cable company known for the high quality of its expertise in cable design, manufacturing, and installation. But now that Washington has made the company its national champion, it seems clear that in today's geopolitical landscape, it will no longer be competing solely on price.

After the SEA-ME-WE-6 outcome, HMN Tech, China Mobile and other partners went on to build a direct competitor, the PEACE cable, which connects Asia, Africa and Europe.[15] Once again, a harbinger of the increased bifurcation of the subsea and general technology landscape that is to come.

STATES AND FIRMS IN THE GREY ZONE

Since 2019, demand for Internet bandwidth has tripled.[16] The migration of more and more data to the Cloud and the increase in connected devices has fuelled a data renaissance. When it comes to the funding, building and ownership of this bandwidth, the world has witnessed another kind of paradigm shift, this one regarding the role of traditional telecoms and big tech firms.

Amazon, Google, Meta and Microsoft now exert more control over data flows in subsea cables than traditional telecoms carriers. In fact, the roles of the two have almost reversed: traditional voice carriers now rent increasing swathes of their bandwidth from the tech titans. Dedicated cables owned by Google or Microsoft allows them more control over their growing data centres and their customised data platforms.

As for money, the big tech companies have a lot of it. In 2023, Google, alone, owned 26 undersea cables.[17] This trend is set to continue, as Meta, Amazon and Microsoft, all of which own or partially own their own cables, set out to expand their dedicated networks. Going forward, the likelihood of an undersea cable project being completed is much higher when its major investors are big tech companies, rather than when governments have majority control.

There is a duality in the relationships between states and firms regarding undersea cables. More specifically, the American tech giants are viewed as strategic assets and partners, when it is in Washington's best interests to treat them as such, but, conversely, when Meta or Google undertake business dealings with perceived adversaries, the consequences can involve aborted cable routes and sanctioned partners.

CABLE SABOTAGE AND WARFARE

In early 2023, two undersea communications cables running from Taiwan to the nearby Matsu islands were mysteriously cut, disconnecting 14,000 islanders from the Internet. Taiwanese officials blamed the incident on a Chinese fishing vessel and freighter which had been spotted in the area.[18]

Later that year, Finland and Estonia began a formal investigation of a Chinese vessel that dragged its anchor over 100 nautical miles across the seafloor though the Gulf of Finland, damaging undersea cables and gas lines.[19]

The Chinese-owned container ship, The New Polar Bear, was seen together with a Russian cargo vessel, the Sevmorput, passing through the Gulf of Finland and were alleged to have been in close proximity to where damage to an undersea natural gas pipeline and two telecommunications cables occurred.[20]

Such incidents appear to be harbingers of more to come, especially with the threat of growing conflicts. NATO officials have claimed that Russia has been actively mapping critical allied infrastructure, both undersea and on land.[21] This may be an indication of Moscow's future intentions, should the war in Ukraine escalate.

As far back as the 1980s, the U.S. intelligence community engineered a stunning wiretapping operation on Soviet communication cables beneath the Sea of Okhotsk, in an operation code-named Ivy Bells.[22]

To carry out the operation, the U.S. Navy equipped a specially designed submarine, the USS *Halibut*, with specialised devices that allowed it to tap into undersea cables without damaging them. A specialised arm with a grappling hook was used to snag the cable and bring it close to the submarine; a robotic cutting device cut a small section of the cable sheath, and a tapping device was connected to the exposed cable which intercepted the signals transmitted through the cable.

The signals were sent to the U.S. National Security Agency (NSA) for analysis, providing valuable intelligence about Soviet military and diplomatic communications. The operation ran from 1972 to 1981 when the Soviets finally discovered it and shut it down.

Technology has evolved significantly since the days of Operation Ivy Bells, and today's submarines and underwater drones are equipped with even more sophisticated technology, including fibre-optic devices that can tap into cables without cutting them. Other advanced technologies include software-defined radios that can be programmed to intercept a wide range of frequencies, including those used for undersea communications.

The story of undersea cable espionage and sabotage is in its early stages, but one thing is for sure: the technologies used to carry out the next generation of electronic undersea espionage will continue to evolve.

All of this, then, will have a major impact on how billions of people receive data, voice, picture and streaming video on the Internet, whether they are aware of the importance of undersea cables or not.

Chapter 17

Space-Based Internet

A technology revolution involving low earth orbit (LEO) satellites promises to bring high-speed Internet to virtually every square inch of the planet. By 2030, a collection of constellations amounting to some 60,000 satellites are expected to orbit the Earth.

Enter Starlink Internet, an American space-based telecommunications network operated by SpaceX, the pioneering company founded by the billionaire entrepreneur Elon Musk. SpaceX, which has been the recipient of billions of dollars in U.S. government funding and contracts, also builds, launches and functions as a contract operator of reusable rockets and other spacecraft.

In the space industry, as in others, geopolitical concerns and capitalist profit-seeking overlap as the rivalry between the U.S. and China bifurcates strategic supply chains, industries and markets. This has produced a techno-nationalist grey zone for governments and corporations.

National security imperatives have led to the creation of public–private partnerships (PPP). These PPPs blur the line between defence-related and commercial activities.

First-mover advantages in LEO technology and rocket science have conferred inordinate power on a small number of companies, especially Musk's SpaceX and Starlink Internet. High barriers to entry in the LEO sector, will present challenges to other governments as they seek to develop their own secure national LEO ecosystems.

China, meanwhile, is racing to build its own LEO constellation, GuoWang. Just as geopolitics has bifurcated the telecommunications landscape around Huawei and 5G wireless, LEO constellations will tend to polarise as they are subjected to increasingly strict export controls, sanctions, International Traffic in Arms Regulations regulations (ITAR) and blacklisting.

Finally, conflicts like the war in Ukraine have highlighted the importance of spaced-based Internet connectivity and the power multipliers that it confers on parties that have access. The lethal use of commercial services such as Starlink Internet and DJI consumer drones has prompted calls for prohibitions and new rules regarding the use of commercial goods for military uses.

TRENDS IN SATELLITE TECHNOLOGY AND SPACE-GEOPOLITICS

Historically, space networks have relied on the use of large, highly powerful and prohibitively expensive 'exquisite' satellites. These satellites usually have geosynchronous orbits (GSO) that match the Earth's rotation and allow them to remain at a set distance of 36,000 kilometres above the Earth—what is referred to as a high Earth orbit.

Geosynchronous satellites that orbit the Earth's equator and remain above a specific location on the ground are referred to as geostationary (GEO).[1] GEO satellites provide continuous coverage of the widest possible area of Earth's surface and are usually used for telecommunications and television broadcasting.

Historically, launching a large GEO satellite into orbit has cost between US$100 million and US$400 million. Launching a reconnaissance spy satellite could run about US$100 million while putting a sophisticated GEO weather satellite into high orbit can cost around US$300 million.[2]

LOW EARTH ORBIT SATELLITES

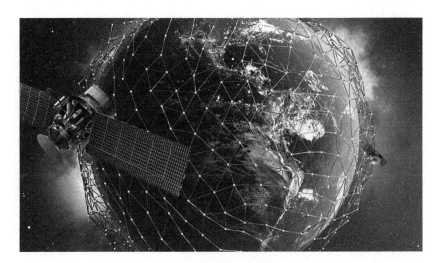

Figure 17.1   Low Earth Orbit (LEO) Satellite Constellation.

Revolutionary advances in technology have led to the creation of systems—referred to as meshes or constellations—of hundreds or even thousands of satellites in LEO between 500 kilometres and 2,000 kilometres above the planet. LEO satellites offer faster communications (lower latency) than their higher altitude cousins, but because they are much closer to the Earth's surface, they cover a much smaller angle and area; hence, many more are needed to extend coverage over wide regions.

As of 2023, Starlink Internet had deployed more than 4,000 LEO satellites and its high-speed Internet was accessed by 1 million paying subscribers worldwide.[3] The company had applied for licences to launch as many as 40,000 LEO satellites in total.[4]

The average cost of an LEO satellite is around US$14 million.[5] This is far less than the cost of a GSO or GEO exquisite satellite, but a constellation of hundreds or even thousands of LEO 'smallsats' is still very expensive. A recent McKinsey report in 2020 estimated that a fully scaled, functional LEO constellation would cost at least US$5 billion to be operational.[6] Nevertheless, those high costs would yield enormous payoffs to the governments and corporations that can afford them.

A REVOLUTION IN SMALLSAT TECHNOLOGY AND MANUFACTURING

Figure 17.2   LEO CubeSats and SmallSats: Compact and Inexpensive.

Rapid advances in semiconductor technology and AI, along with supercomputing, have led to a revolution in onboard processors and optical laser crosslinks allow secure high-speed communications in a hybrid satellite constellation.

Along with those technological advances, production costs for LEO satellites have fallen significantly. Standardisation and commoditisation of satellite parts and components permit modularisation, allowing manufacturers to use large assembly lines to produce hundreds of LEO satellites per month—just as modularisation revolutionised the production of PCs in the 1990s and smartphones in the 2000s.[7]

Specialised parts for LEO satellites are supplied by a group of distinctive private firms in the U.S. and Europe, including York Space Systems, Lockheed Martin, L3Harris and SpaceX.

Commercial operators such as Telesat, Blue Canyon Technologies and Airbus specialise in making satellite buses—the body and structural component that holds the satellite payload and provides the thermal environment, radiation shielding, telemetry, optical sensors, altitude, power and other controls of the satellite.[8]

Other companies such as SA Photonics, Mynaric and Raytheon specialise in building the payloads—the scientific and technical equipment that enables telecommunications, navigation, surveillance, imaging and high-speed Internet, including antennae, transponders and cameras.

The growth of prolific LEO constellations, together with the rise of private, specialised manufacturers, is projected to drive the value of the payload market from around US$5 billion in 2022 to around US$30 billion in 2030.

SPACEX AND THE ROCKET REVOLUTION

No constellation of satellites would be possible without the means to launch payloads into space at affordable costs and with great frequency. Here, SpaceX's reusable Falcon 9 and Falcon Heavy launch vehicles have cut costs dramatically and changed the course of modern history. Launching a Falcon Heavy rocket is 10 times cheaper than what it would have cost to launch NASA's retired space shuttle.[9]

Rather than falling back to Earth and becoming yet another useless piece of space debris on the ocean floor, the SpaceX rocket flips around and is guided back to Earth, where it decelerates and lands upright on four retractable legs. The rocket can land with pinpoint accuracy on solid ground or on a floating landing pad at sea.

To watch a SpaceX rocket land is to witness a technological marvel that no national space agency has been able to accomplish. By March 2022, SpaceX had launched 148 rockets, recovered 110 first stages and reused 87 of them, and the company's goal is to reuse each launch vehicle up to 100 times.[10]

SpaceX's reuse of first-stage launch vehicles shortened the time between launches and helped the company capture more than 20% of the global commercial space launch market by 2020.

SpaceX's vertically integrated model, combining LEO satellite construction with its unique launch capabilities, has made its Starlink system a dominant player in the sector. In addition to providing high-speed Internet, Starlink aims to eventually introduce universal worldwide space-based mobile phone service.

Another major technological achievement, also pioneered by SpaceX, is the launching of numerous satellites in one single mission. In early February of 2023, for example, SpaceX successfully completed the 200th launch of a Falcon 9 rocket, dispatching a cluster of 53 Starlink satellites into LEO.[11]

The compact size of today's LEO smallsats reflects the exponential increases in microprocessing power, memory and operational efficiency of the electronics they incorporate. Here, again, modularisation has brought down costs significantly.

THE MILITARISATION OF SPACE-BASED INTERNET

The militarisation of space is rapidly unfolding as national security imperatives accelerate and guide the development of LEO constellations. In 2019, for example, the U.S. established the Space Development Agency (SDA) with the mandate of building more resilient space architecture. That same year, Space Force, a new branch of the U.S. armed forces—often lampooned in mainstream culture—was created to address national security issues.[12]

Historically, the infrastructure behind satellite communications networks involved small constellations with a few large 'exquisite' satellites. Such a configuration, however, can be disabled by destroying a single large satellite within the system. As we will discuss later, China, Russia, India and the U.S. have developed anti-satellite technologies, which include electronic jammers, lasers and other weapons that could be used to disable satellites.[13] This security concern became very real in 2007 when China used a missile to destroy one of its own satellites in an event that sparked an international outcry.[14]

U.S.–China geopolitical rivalry thus shapes the SDA's goals for the next generation of satellite constellations. In addition to providing navigational services and general surveillance capabilities, new networks must have layer upon layer of sensors that not only enable seamless and secure data communications but can track hypersonic missiles and cruise missiles.[15]

Even as the Defence Advanced Research Projects Agency (DARPA) and its partners work on developing a U.S. hypersonic missile system, as discussed previously, they are resorting to building a tracking system via an LEO constellation to defend against China's missiles. By placing defence-related communications in hundreds of LEO satellites, the SDA aims to make it too difficult and costly for an adversary to destroy them all, achieving what is referred to as resiliency by numbers (assuming that the constellation can continue to function after the loss of nodes within the mesh).[16] The strategy compels other nations to do the same.

The defence establishment has also worked to both influence and pre-empt technology standards for commercial satellites and the Internet. In 2017, project Blackjack was initiated, which, among other things, prioritised the development of interoperability standards and architecture that would allow seamless communications between commercial satellite operators and the military forces of the U.S. and its allies. A key technology involved laser-based 'optical crosslink' communications.

There are clear geopolitical motives behind SDA's and DARPA's work with companies like Starlink. One goal is to extend American and Western soft power and influence by providing universal access to high-speed broadband communications to people behind techno-authoritarian Internet firewalls and in remote, off-the-grid locations. But there is no doubt that the American military and intelligence agencies will enjoy significant advantages from the expansion of an LEO constellation built by American companies on American standards.

In the same vein, space-based Internet service empowers people engaged in proxy wars and other struggles under extreme conditions, such as the war in Ukraine. By providing access to open-sourced platforms and online resources and the unrestrained flow of data and information, space-based Internet has upended modern warfare.

THE GREY ZONE: BLURRING THE LINE BETWEEN DEFENCE AND COMMERCE

Starlink is the most prominent name in space-based Internet coverage, but other emerging players include Amazon's Project Kuiper and Telesat's Lightspeed, as well as Viasat and Spacelink.

All of these companies must compete and innovate even as they adapt to the realities of geopolitics and collaborate with their governments on matters of interoperability and national security. In the process, government can provide incentives in the form of generous public R&D funding and lucrative public sector contracts. On the flip side, officials can threaten to leave non-compliant companies out of important partnerships or, more starkly, wield punitive measures such as sanctions and penalties.

In early April of 2023, DARPA and SDA were rewarded with the successful launch of 'Tranche 0' when a SpaceX rocket dispatched 10 separate LEO satellites into orbit. The launch featured two satellites built by SpaceX that were designed to track ballistic and hypersonic missiles. The other eight satellites, built by York Space Systems, featured laser optics designed to transfer data from space-based sensors to the ground.[17]

EXPORT CONTROLS, SANCTIONS AND BIFURCATED GLOBAL VALUE CHAINS

The national security implications of LEO constellations will have profound effects on trade and global supply chains. As is the case with other ecosystems involving dual-use products, techno-nationalist policies will subject LEO supply chains to export controls, restrictions on trade and technology transfer and, thus, pressures to re-shore and ring-fence.

Any existing linkages with Chinese or Russian, or other blacklisted enterprises—or third parties with linkages to them—will come under increased scrutiny. Ultimately, this will lead to decoupling, contributing to the increasing bifurcation of global value chains.

China's answer to America's Starlink, announced in 2021 in its 14th five-year plan, is the GuoWang LEO constellation. Beijing aims to achieve worldwide coverage by placing approximately 13,000 small-sats into space.[18] Such an undertaking would be carried out by the state-owned and heavily subsidised China Aerospace Science and Industry Corp (CASIC), along with other Chinese entities.[19]

Head-to-head competition between China's GuoWang LEO and Starlink (as well as other Western providers), among them, Telesat, OneWeb and Eutelsat, begs the question whether this new area of communications infrastructure will result in a 'Huawei 2.0' situation.

Recall that beginning in 2019, Washington mounted a global assault on Chinese telecommunications equipment giant Huawei to block its installation of 5G Wireless networks in other countries. Washington cited national security concerns regarding Beijing's ability to install spyware throughout Huawei's 5G infrastructure.

Australia, Canada, India, the U.K., New Zealand, France, Sweden, Germany, Japan and Taiwan effectively joined the U.S. in banning or severely limiting Huawei from their networks. Still, other countries that did not ban Huawei outright began to float the idea that future 5G or 6G supply chains should be ring-fenced inside the geographic boundaries of trusted allies.[20]

Meanwhile, all of the BRICS countries except India remained open to Huawei, as did developing countries throughout Asia, Africa and South America—including Mexico, the U.S.'s neighbour and major trading partner.

As it did around 5G networks, the world is likely to bifurcate around space-based Internet service providers and, eventually, space-based mobile phone service. Any interaction of American and foreign companies with the Chinese LEO sector will be heavily affected by the U.S. ITAR regulations and sanctions.

In this next round of competition with China, the U.S. and its allies are likely to adopt a strategy reminiscent of Beijing's playbook, leaning heavily on subsidies, guaranteed low-interest or long-term loan packages and other economic enticements for private-sector cooperation, and on diplomatic pressure and security-related frameworks to win over governments. We have seen the approach from Washington already play out with undersea fibre-optic cable networks, and its attempts to block Chinese companies from international undersea cable projects.

STARLINK INTERNET AND THE RUSSIA–UKRAINE WAR

The Russia–Ukraine War has ushered in a new era of warfare, where inexpensive consumer technologies have unexpectedly redefined military strategy by levelling the playing field between large and small powers. Developments such as the weaponisation of commercial drones have further blurred the line between everyday activities and deadly warfare.

Whereas the outcomes of most recent military conflicts turned on the primacy of large, expensive weapons systems, the war in Ukraine demonstrates the advantages of decentralised, independently operated devices and weapons systems connected to Cloud-based platforms and networks.

Starlink Internet has been an unexpected ingredient in the comprehensive U.S. military aid package to Ukraine. Within the first year of the war, Washington had provided around US$3 billion with commitments for another US$27 billion.[21] The U.S. made a variety of portable weapons available to Ukrainian fighting forces, including the U.S. Stinger missile, designed to shoot down low-flying aircraft up to around 4,500 metres in the sky, as well as much more advanced systems such as the high mobility artillery rocket system (HIMARS).

Nevertheless, the success or failure of this massive expenditure could come down to whether Ukrainians can effectively use Starlink—which, ironically, runs on just US$500 worth of hardware per subscription.

Relying on Starlink, Ukrainians have been able to connect to the World Wide Web with relative ease even after Moscow's cyberattacks incapacitated Ukraine's national Internet and Russian forces destroyed critical telecommunications and power infrastructure. All one needs to connect directly to the Internet is a small Starlink satellite dish and a toaster-box-sized Starlink receiver.[22] By February 2023, a year after Russia's invasion, an estimated 150,000 active users were accessing Starlink from inside the country.[23]

Space-based, high-speed broadband Internet has enabled UAVs to provide Ukrainian troops with valuable intelligence and reconnaissance, allowing them to locate, target and destroy Russian military assets in ways that would have been confined to science fiction a decade earlier.

Even as Russian forces were pounding the cities of Kharkiv and Bakhmut to rubble, Ukrainian citizen–soldiers were buying new Starlink dishes and receivers on eBay and Amazon and having them delivered to their bunkers via local last-mile logistics providers, sometimes within plain sight of the battlefront.

Space-based Internet connectivity has proved to be a hugely asymmetric power multiplier. The International Institute for Strategic Studies (IISS) estimated that by February 2023, a year into its invasion, Russia had lost about 2,000 tanks—more than 50% of its operational fleet deployed in Ukraine.[24] That outcome would have been impossible without Starlink.

LETHAL EYES, EARS AND THE DRONE REVOLUTION

Ukraine's hyper-connected war has influenced the military strategies of other countries in the region who also face possible aggression from Moscow. After less than a year of highly scrutinised battlefield intelligence, for example, Lithuania purchased 600 Kamikaze drones from the U.S., valued at almost US$50 million.[25]

Further afield, Taiwan's government observed the outsized effect that Starlink has had on the war and tasked its space agency, TASA, with creating a new satellite division and building a national LEO constellation for Taiwan. Motivated by fears of what many consider an imminent invasion by China's PLA, TASA is looking to emulate Starlink's LEO constellation as quickly as possible.[26]

This has changed the calculus in Beijing as well, as the PLA has become increasingly preoccupied with Starlink and other LEO constellations. Indeed, Chinese defence-related research has focused on possible ways to disable or destroy Starlink and other similar satellite constellations—currently a near-impossible task.[27]

OPEN SOURCED WAR IN THE DIGITAL GLOBAL COMMONS

Starlink Internet has sustained Ukraine's war effort not only by enabling connectivity between troops in the field and their weapons systems but also more broadly by allowing for the mass mobilisation of crowd-sourced intelligence.

A vast reservoir of expertise resides in the global commons, and Internet access via Starlink allowed Ukrainian actors to benefit from open-sourced ideas and analysis provided by people all over the world, in think tanks, academia and NGOs—and even from uniquely qualified armchair observers and hobbyists.

For example, the Ukrainian military received free geospatial surveillance analysis from volunteer experts who poured over satellite imagery from the E.U.'s DigitalGlobe Open Data Programme[28] and from others who used Google Maps to obtain real-time road movements of the Russian military. Still others provided valuable insights by analysing front-line intelligence uploaded via YouTube and TikTok videos.

The war in Ukraine compelled regular citizens who had previously led lives as online gamers, engineers, IT workers or just regular 'Internet geeks' to become part of an open-sourced war machine.

Other groups took matters into their own hands and declared cyberwar on Russia, including the secretive 'hacktivist' group Anonymous, an amorphous collective consisting of computer programmers, coders and cybersecurity experts.

Anonymous hacked into the databases of, among others, the Russian Central Bank, the Russian space agency, Roscosmos and Russian oil and gas companies such as Gazprom and deleted or scrambled their data.[29] Anonymous hacktivists also broke into the networks of Western companies who continued to conduct business in Russia, such as Nestle, and stole usernames, passwords and emails and dumped them onto the Internet. They also blocked and shut down access to websites in Russia and Belarus, hijacked Russian media platforms and news outlets and posted censored data and imagery.[30]

THE GREY ZONE: STATE VERSUS FIRMS

In the hybrid cold war, states and firms are operating in a regulatory and ideological grey zone. The public weaponisation of private companies' core competencies for a war effort raises serious legal and ethical issues.

At the start of the war, Starlink's executives accepted the use of its network for defensive purposes. However, they became increasingly concerned as weaponisation of the network increased in scale and sophistication, and in February of 2023, SpaceX, as the owner of Starlink, took steps to limit Ukraine's use of drones to perform certain operations, such as attacking targets with bombs. As expected, this produced an adverse reaction in Kyiv.

China's DJI, the maker of the world's most popular and widely used consumer drones, also denounced the use of its products for lethal purposes. DJI took steps to block direct sales of its drones to combatant countries but was unable to stop the transhipment of its drones purchased in third countries from being sent to the war front and modified for combat use.

But even beyond the military applications of Starlink, there are damaging social consequences of a violent conflict playing out in real time, with live-streaming video that ends up on social media platforms. The imagery of humans being attacked and killed for any reason should not be displayed anywhere in the global commons if it can be prevented. Such imagery is universally damaging to societies and raises the question as to what rules should be enforced to block such imagery—or to prevent the violence in the first place.

There is also the issue of funding. In the early months of Russia's invasion, Elon Musk donated more than 20,000 Starlink terminals to Ukraine at a cost of at least US$80 million for the equipment and ongoing network services.[31] Musk's donation was purely on ideological grounds.

Subsequently, Musk and company lobbied the U.S. government to pick up the cost, and there were reports that the E.U. would also help pay.[32] *The Guardian* newspaper reported that the U.S. Pentagon paid at least US$3 million for 1,330 Starlink terminals that it donated to Ukraine.

The actual amounts of money involved are less important than the fundamental question: Should services of private companies be turned into instruments of war, or should governments create separate LEO satellite constellations fully owned and fenced off strictly for military endeavours? Starlink in the Ukraine provides a case study in the messy techno-nationalist grey zone confronting states and firms.

THE RISE OF SPACE MONOPOLIES

Comprising an integral role in defence initiatives in Washington and elsewhere, powerful networks like SpaceX and Starlink raise another question: Should governments actively work to level the playing field and spur competition in LEO constellations?

In this vein, the E.U. has grappled with the power of the American MAMAA companies (Meta, Amazon, Microsoft, Apple and Alphabet), which utterly dominate Europe's platform economy.

To counter that domination, Brussels has announced plans to spend billions to build its own resilient LEO satellite constellation, which it hopes will provide enhanced cybersecurity and relative independence.[33]

The E.U. is We working with OneWorld, for example, a U.K. based competitor to Starlink (although they collaborate on U.S. LEO defence and interoperability initiatives), whose top investors include the U.K. government, the French government and India's Bharti Enterprises.

Thus, while close defence-related cooperation between the U.S., the E.U., the U.K. and others will continue in LEO constellation projects, so too will the regionalisation and localisation of networks.

A MULTILATERAL RULES FRAMEWORK FOR SPACE?

Nations have a vested interest in agreeing to mutually beneficial rules regarding the commercialisation and the militarisation of space.

An issue of primary importance involves the overcrowding of LEO. Nearly 60,000 LEO satellites could be in space by 2030, greatly increasing the risk of collisions and resulting space debris that could pose a hazard to global communications and disrupt global trade and commerce.[34]

Another issue is the danger of one nation using ballistic missiles, laser technology or some other form of space vehicle to destroy, disable or displace another state's satellites. Proponents of legal frameworks have argued for agreement on punitive responses to such actions in the form of sanctions and trade restrictions.

One possibility is the diplomatic crafting of limitations or moratoriums on the development and deployment of space weaponry. While such rules are unlikely to deter R&D activities around breakthrough military technologies and might not prevent outright aggression, they can serve as guardrails and lines of demarcation in behavioural norms.

Beyond the issue of space debris is the problem of light pollution. As more LEO satellites fill the night sky, they will reflect more light and change the nightscape for astronomers and others. Any solution to the problem will require joint management and cooperation among governments and private interests.

Even accidents, such as the malfunctioning of satellite or catastrophic failures of an entire network, should serve as an incentive to explore other Earth-bound options, such as expanding existing fibre-optic cable networks.

But this also comes with dangers. As we discussed in Chapter 16, geopolitically motivated sabotage, disablement and other cyber issues make undersea cables a risky choice for a secure Internet in times of conflict.

The LEO constellation will represent the next phase of human connectivity for both the Internet and mobile phone service. Nations, corporations and private citizens, therefore, must learn to adapt to this next phase of the space age.

Chapter 18

The Twenty-First-Century Space Race

On a balmy afternoon in Cape Canaveral, a day not unlike many others, a SpaceX Falcon 9 rocket blasts off into U.S. aerospace history. It is May 30, 2020, and the rocket is speeding NASA astronauts Bob Behnken and Doug Hurley up into earth orbit for a docking with the International Space Station (ISS).

Incredibly, this marked the first manned launch from U.S. soil in almost a decade since NASA shut down the Space Shuttle programme. For nine long years, NASA had to rely on the Russians to provide transportation for U.S. astronauts going to and from the ISS.

How did it come to this after the glories of NASA's Apollo era? Half a century after the Apollo missions successfully landed *12 American astronauts* on the moon, between 1969 and 1972, the U.S. could not put its own people into space without help from Russia.

The truth was that NASA had been facing excessively high costs for a Space Shuttle programme that was running on 30-year-old technology in a bureaucratic environment that could not keep up with an evolving space industry.

In 2011, U.S. space officials signed an agreement with Roscosmos, the Russian space agency, that allowed NASA to purchase seats on the Soyuz spacecraft. NASA paid an average of US$56 million per seat on each flight. Between 2011 and that historic day when SpaceX launched its first crewed mission to the ISS, American astronauts had flown on the Soyuz spacecraft at least 20 times.

To fix this problem, the same year they signed with Roscosmos, NASA established its so-called Commercial Crew Program (CCP) with the intention of developing homegrown space launch capabilities again for the next generation of space technology. Thus began a series of relationships with a growing list of carefully screened private companies, including SpaceX, Boeing, Northrop Grumman, Blue Origin, Rocket Lab and Virgin Orbit.

As was the case with so many other industries enabled by the Fourth Industrial Revolution (4IR), private space companies had become increasingly more innovative and were moving much faster than NASA and the defence establishment.

Consider the milestones that were achieved with that first SpaceX Falcon 9 flight to the ISS in 2020.

It marked the first time a commercial aerospace company carried humans into outer space. It also was the first time that end-to-end innovation—including design and construction—for a space mission was outsourced to a commercial company. This included the fabrication of the space capsule and rockets as well as the technology for the launch, in-orbit manoeuvres and space-docking and landing operations.

And then there were the monetary savings. During NASA's Space Shuttle programme, which ran from 1985 to 2011, the cost of each Space Shuttle mission—which varied depending on different objectives—was about US$450 million. By 2022, the average cost to put a SpaceX rocket into orbit (and return the first stage of the rocket to Earth for reuse) was about US$67 million, about seven times cheaper than NASA's old Space Shuttle.

For Washington, these breakthroughs could not have been timelier: in February of 2022, Russia invaded Ukraine. Although the two nations would continue cooperation regarding the transport of astronauts to and from the ISS—as seen by the return, for example, of U.S. astronaut Frank Rubio on the Soyuz-23 capsule in September 2023—it was time to part ways.

THE COMMERCIALISATION OF SPACE

The twenty-first-century space race reflects a brave new world where artificial intelligence (AI), computing power and advances in material science and manufacturing processes have inspired a new suite of space technologies and companies.

Among nations, the space race has grown more crowded as the U.S., the E.U., Russia, China, India and Japan all pursue their own techno-nationalist space agendas. China is a much more potent competitor to the U.S. and the West than the former Soviet Union ever was. Beijing has far greater scale, deeper pockets and continued access to leading-edge intellectual property and technology transfer.

Commercially, a new ecosystem has emerged. On one end of the spectrum are large technology-enabled private space behemoths such as SpaceX. On the other end is a beehive of small tech start-ups specialising in everything from lasers to robotics.

Private companies are manufacturing affordable low earth orbit (LEO) satellites and offering services such as broadband Internet, earth observation and navigation. They are building their own space vehicles and performing launch operations. They are even building robots for the eventual mining of the moon and far-off mineral-rich asteroids and other celestial bodies. And, among other things, they are making pharmaceutical drugs in space.

NASA's Artemis program, which intends to re-establish human presence on the moon since 1972 is, in fact, a large consortium of private companies camped under NASA's big tent. On February 22, 2023, the Odysseus unmanned lunar lander, built by the Houston-based private company, Intuitive Machines, became the first American spacecraft to make a controlled descent and land on the moon in more than half a century. Odysseus landed on the South Pole of the Moon.

It was a SpaceX Falcon 9 rocket launcher that put Intuitive Machine's lander into space—a private company working with another private company, but SpaceX's scale of operations and list of accomplishments qualify it as a leading space 'country' all by itself.

Meanwhile, the same 4IR technologies that are commercialising space have also led to its rapid militarisation. Because of the dual-use nature of space technologies, which serve both commercial and military purposes, private enterprises have been co-opted by governments as strategic partners, mostly through binding contracts, which, technically, can also be called subsidies.

Space tech is being harnessed by governments for surveillance, reconnaissance, tracking and disabling missiles, or, in general, as an essential platform of interlinked military systems. Terms such as 'laser weapons' and 'killer space robots' and, more recently, the 'U.S. Space Force' have become part of our everyday lexicon.

Once again, protecting or extending an innovative edge in the space race requires that governments deploy the core elements of a techno-nationalist strategy: the weaponisation of supply chains with sanctions and export controls, outbound investment controls, the ring-fencing of strategic ecosystems through friend-shoring and home-shoring, targeted innovation funding and talent development and techno-diplomacy. Espionage and the stealing of secrets and human talent are also at play.

Regarding public–private partnerships, the lifeblood of any space programme, the aim of U.S. techno-nationalists and others with market economies is to tap into the vast entrepreneurial reservoir within their markets but avoid becoming too heavy-handed so as to squelch the very lightening they are trying to capture in a bottle.

THE NEW SPACE MARKETS

By 2030, the commercial space market will be worth US$1 trillion. Demand comes from a wide range of customers, including everyday end-consumers on digital platforms and the Internet, businesses and governments, defence establishments, universities, NGOs and research organisations.

Competition is around three primary areas. Firstly, a return to the moon to build structures and infrastructure that will enable colonisation of its various regions—and eventually, these locations will be used to springboard onward towards Mars and other celestial locations. The moon will become a permanent base for experimentation and innovation.

Similarly, access to new space stations and other space-based assets will afford nations valuable economic advantages.

Secondly, the commercialisation of space has resulted in new markets around a plethora of technologies, each of which is required for the different facets of space flight and survival. This includes long-term commercial projects involving mining, construction, maintenance, logistics and communications.

Finally, there are the new space-related defence-related niches.

It has been commonly accepted that, in most cases, private businesses in a competitive environment usually innovate and deliver technology more cost-effectively than a state-run entity, although there may be a need for government funding, as market forces often fail to respond adequately to long-term vision and strategic necessity on their own.

That said, a growing number of private companies have emerged in the space economy. Some forward-looking and exciting ventures include space manufacturing and space mining.

EMERGING SPACE INDUSTRIES

Beyond the whimsical space tourism industry—for billionaires and mavericks—are other potentially wealth-generating activities with long-term potential. Made In Space, for example, is an American company that develops and operates 3D printers and other manufacturing equipment for use in microgravity. In 2014, the company became the first to manufacture an object in space when it used a 3D printer to create a plastic wrench on the ISS. Since then, Made In Space has manufactured a variety of other products in microgravity, including small satellites and optical fibres.

In the pharmaceutical area, private companies are developing new technologies to manufacture drugs and study their effects on cells and tissues. SpacePharma, for example, is an American company that develops and operates bioreactors that can be used to grow cells and tissues in a more controlled way than is possible on Earth. It is conducting research on the effects of microgravity on stem cells.

In 2021, SpacePharma became the first company to produce a protein drug in microgravity using a bioreactor, which yielded a drug called interferon beta-1a that is used to treat multiple sclerosis. SpacePharma's customers include pharmaceutical companies such as Novartis, AstraZeneca and Merck, as well as government agencies.

Space manufacturing is advancing quickly, thanks to AI, robotics and additive manufacturing. This area figures to have big potential and will attract increasing amounts of attention from governments and private interests.

One of the more fantastical developments in the commercialisation of space involves the prospects of mining for precious materials. Advances in reusable rockets and autonomous vehicles, as well as plummeting costs in manufacturing—thanks to modularised manufacturing at scale—have given rise to the early days of entrepreneurialism in space mining.

The targets are highly precious minerals such as iridium, palladium, platinum and gold, which can be found in high concentrations on other planetary bodies.

One example is the science-fiction-like but totally real quest to mine an asteroid named 16 Psyche. Psyche is a metallic asteroid the size of the state of Massachusetts that is located in the asteroid belt between Mars and Jupiter and is estimated to contain trillions of dollars' worth of nickel, iron and cobalt.

That the outrageous idea of an asteroid-bound spacecraft laden with specialised mining equipment (or the technology needed to 3D 'print' or self-replicate new machinery, in situ) is being taken seriously by investors is testimony to how fast space technology, along with the privatisation of space, are advancing.

Consider the amount of money being spent and the credibility of the parties involved. NASA, for one, is keenly interested in asteroid mining and has funded a number of projects to develop applicable technologies.

In October 2023, NASA launched a SpaceX Falcon Heavy rocket carrying the Psyche spacecraft on a mission to 16 Psyche to explore the asteroid and provide scientists with new insights.

Consider other players emerging in this field, such as Planetary Resources, another private company that is developing technologies to mine asteroids and, as of 2023, had raised over US$200 million in funding to support its partnership with NASA.

Another such company is the Asteroid Mining Corporation, a Canadian company that has partnered with the Canadian Space Agency (CSA) to develop its own asteroid mining technologies and has raised over US$30 million in funding to do so.

SPACE ROBOTS

Another rapidly growing area of space tech involves autonomous machines. The role of robots in space mining and scientific exploration—and, by extension, space warfare—will draw upon advances in machine learning, material sciences and other emerging fields, as yet to be named.

As early as 2021, the U.S. space agency awarded a US$50 million contract to a private American company named Astrobotic Technology, which develops space robotics technology for lunar and planetary missions. It was founded in 2007 by Carnegie Mellon University professor Red Whittaker and his associates with the goal of winning the Google Lunar X Prize. Based in Pittsburgh, Pennsylvania, Astrobotic Technology produces machines for mining on the moon, and NASA hopes to expand their functions to mine precious metals from the Psyche metallic asteroid and others like it.

Autonomous space vehicles will perform mineral prospecting, survey asteroids and other celestial bodies and perform extraction and logistics functions for cargo spacecraft and transportation hubs. Far-flung space operations will require autonomous vehicles to build and maintain space infrastructure.

THE RISE AND RISE OF SPACEX

Figure 18.1   The SpaceX Falcon 9 Heavy Rocket.

During the fallow years after the retirement of the Space Shuttle, SpaceX emerged slowly, and then suddenly, as Washington's go-to enabler. Its brainy enclave of rocket scientists, engineers and computer geeks would ride a wave of innovative breakthroughs driven by the company's culture of audacious creativity—a reflection of the personality of its founder, Elon Musk. But it was a steady infusion of government contracts from NASA and the U.S. defence industry that brought ideas to fruition.

To build the Falcon 9 rocket and its Dragon spacecraft for crewed missions, SpaceX was awarded close to US$10 billion in contracts under NASA's Commercial Crew Development programme. SpaceX received another US$3.1 billion for pretty much the same objective under another source of funding called the Commercial Orbital

Figure 18.2   Payload for the NASA-SpaceX Psyche 16 Asteroid Mining Mission.

Transportation Services (COTS) programme. Musk and company soaked up yet another US$1 billion in NASA contracts to develop the Starship spacecraft for lunar and Martian missions.

Without this sort of public funding, no private company, no matter how innovative, can produce the kinds of machines required by a national space programme.

Reusable Rockets

The ability to put critical military and intelligence-related assets up into orbit at short notice and with a brief interval between launches is a relatively new accomplishment, even for the world's most advanced spacefaring nation, the U.S.

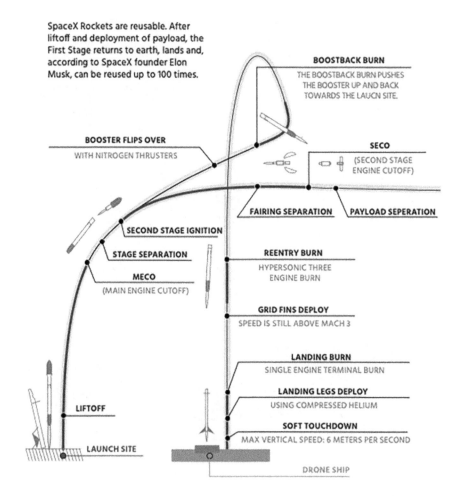

SpaceX Rockets are reusable. After liftoff and deployment of payload, the First Stage returns to earth, lands and, according to SpaceX founder Elon Musk, can be reused up to 100 times.

BOOSTBACK BURN
THE BOOSTBACK BURN PUSHES THE BOOSTER UP AND BACK TOWARDS THE LAUCN SITE.

SECO
(SECOND STAGE ENGINE CUTOFF)

BOOSTER FLIPS OVER
WITH NITROGEN THRUSTERS

FAIRING SEPARATION

PAYLOAD SEPERATION

SECOND STAGE IGNITION

STAGE SEPARATION

MECO
(MAIN ENGINE CUTOFF)

REENTRY BURN
HYPERSONIC THREE ENGINE BURN

GRID FINS DEPLOY
SPEED IS STILL ABOVE MACH 3

LANDING BURN
SINGLE ENGINE TERMINAL BURN

LANDING LEGS DEPLOY
USING COMPRESSED HELIUM

SOFT TOUCHDOWN
MAX VERTICAL SPEED: 6 METERS PER SECOND

LIFTOFF

LAUNCH SITE

DRONE SHIP

Figure 18.3   A SpaceX Rocket First Stage Landing Upright after Returning to Earth.

Throughout the duration of NASA's Space Shuttle programme, there were a total of 135 shuttle launches, which amounted to only about five or six launches per year on average.

By 2022, the number of U.S. defence-related launches, including launches for private commercial customers, had increased dramatically to an average of *seven launches per month*.

That year, for matters of national security, Washington entrusted its launches to a handful of American space companies: 54 were on SpaceX rockets, 17 on United Launch Alliance (ULA) rockets and three were launched by other American entities.

Figure 18.4   Payload of Starlink LEO Satellites on Top of a SpaceX Falcon 9 Rocket.

By the end of the summer of 2023, SpaceX alone had achieved a historic 60-second orbital launch for that calendar year. The milestone occurred when a Falcon 9 rocket lifted off from the Kennedy Space Center at Merrit Island in Florida. It had taken the company less than eight months to break its previous year's record of 61 orbital missions.[1]

As we have discussed, SpaceX did something no other space agency or company was able to do: it engineered its rockets to be reusable.

The technology that enables a SpaceX rocket to re-enter Earth's atmosphere, navigate to its landing, site and land perfectly upright is called 'autonomous guidance, navigation and control' (AGNC).

SpaceX rockets were the first to use AGNC to coordinate a combination of sensors, computers and actuators to control the rocket's trajectory and ensure a safe landing. The sensors on the rocket measure its position, velocity and orientation. The computers use this information to calculate the rocket's trajectory while the actuators make small adjustments to the rocket's engines to keep it on track.

Formidable computing power and algorithms are needed for such complex AGNC capabilities. AI and algorithms not only make sense of vast amounts of real-time data, but they also measure a rocket's orientation by processing visual inputs to identify landmarks in the surrounding environment.

SpaceX can programme AI to perform billions of R&D simulations to design and test its space vehicles and to plan and manage its launch missions. This has helped the company achieve more mundane accomplishments, such as more efficient use of fuel, compared to earlier technologies. SpaceX also used AI to create a more stream-lined launch process than NASA, by giving fewer people far more control over a mission.

SEMICONDUCTORS AND THE TWENTY-FIRST-CENTURY SPACE RACE

There could be no leading-edge space technology without access to semiconductors. As with NASA's Apollo missions in the twentieth century, semiconductors have remained the game-changing foundational technology for the space race.

Space tech has been a beneficiary of Moore's law, in no small measure because of the prevailing dominance of American semiconductor companies. This special conduit of innovative power has been available to NASA, the U.S. defence establishment, and a handful of mostly American private space companies.

It was also semiconductor-enabled AI that led to remarkable advances in materials science. The development of new materials, such as carbon composites and lightweight alloys has been key. Powerful AI has made it possible to create more fuel-efficient rockets. Other technologies, such as radiation-hardened chips that can survive in the harsh conditions of space, are a product of the semiconductor-AI-feedback loop.

An Uneven Playing Field

The symbiotic relationship between SpaceX and the U.S. space and defence establishment—and, more broadly, between sovereign governments and a few big private space companies—will produce a unique kind of space capitalism in which market dynamics sometimes coalesce and sometimes collide with techno-nationalist agendas.

NASA, the U.S. Space Force and a myriad of U.S. intelligence and defence agencies benefit from outsourcing their needs to SpaceX and a handful of carefully curated American suppliers. For reasons of realpolitik, they are compelled to protect and strengthen these strategically important firms, but they must also prevent them from enabling adversaries. This means imposing 'golden handcuffs' through generous funding while also constraining their behaviour in open markets using the other tools of techno-nationalism.

SpaceX has become vitally important to America's space capabilities. Here, the neoliberal argument cautions that allowing a monopoly or an oligopoly to form in the space sector could eventually stunt innovation and result in market distortions.

To avoid this, it appears that some in Washington have made a conscious effort to spread around its largesse. For example, in trying to keep a relatively level playing field among a small group of ring-fenced American firms, from 2010 to 2022, U.S. officials awarded contracts to Blue Origin, Rocket Lab and Virgin Orbit worth about US$3.5 billion.

The bulk of that funding, US$2.9 billion, went to Blue Origin for developing a Human Landing System for the Artemis programme's crewed mission to the moon, along with another US$500 million for the development of Blue Origin's suborbital rocket, the New Shepard.

During this same timeframe, Rocket Lab (originally a New Zealand company that moved to the U.S.) and Virgin Orbit also picked up around US$600 million between them for development of the former's Electron rocket and the latter's LauncherOne rockets.

Clearly, there have been attempts to create competition between the group of designated companies and even seek redundancies around different kinds of space technology.

But SpaceX has risen well above other private companies within the space industry. Elon Musk's brainchild continues to provide the U.S.

government with the lion's share of space products and services and also works with the Canadian, Australian, Japanese and South Korean governments, among other historic strategic partners and allies of the U.S.

NEOLIBS VERSUS TECHNO-NATIONALISTS

The commercialisation of space is promoting the expansion of existing tech giants in Silicon Valley, further enhancing the influence and market-distorting power of the big American tech giants.

For example, Alphabet Inc., the parent company of Google and YouTube, has invested substantially in SpaceX and Rocket Lab. Meanwhile, Blue Origin is linked to Amazon; both were founded in 2000 by Jeff Bezos, their executive chairman.

Bezos has said that he plans to use his personal fortune to fund Blue Origin until it becomes profitable. This means that Amazon's huge success as an e-commerce platform is indirectly benefitting Blue Origin, which also enjoys government funding.

While Blue Origin and Amazon are separate companies, they work together on several space projects, such as Blue Origin's launching of its Project Kuiper Low earth orbit (LEO) satellites that will provide high-speed Internet access to underserved areas around the world.

Amazon's connection to Blue Origin and the nexus between its rocket launching capabilities and space-based Internet services could soon resemble SpaceX's connection to its subsidiary Starlink Internet.

Starlink's parent company, SpaceX, continues to leverages its commanding position as the world's premier private space launch company—thanks again, in large part, to U.S. government funding. It is raising the barriers to entry in the LEO space for other up-and-coming firms. In 2023, there were already 5,000 Starlink satellites in orbit, and the number was constantly growing as SpaceX launched new satellites on a regular basis. On completion, Starlink's constellation is projected to contain up to 42,000 satellites.

Meanwhile, the nearest competitor to SpaceX in 2023 was OneWeb, the European company, with just under 700 LEOs in operation. Yet even so, OneWeb had to rely on SpaceX to launch its satellites. After OneWeb, the number of privately launched Internet LEOs dropped to single digits for just a handful of companies.

As they straddle both fields, it is reasonable to posit that big tech companies will use their dominance in the tech sector to stifle competition in the space sector, even if it just means buying up potential competitors. They have the financial resources to acquire smaller space companies and to drive them out of business with unfair competition.

The question is whether the U.S. and other governments will tolerate a space oligopoly consisting of already oversized tech-firms, even if these companies confer huge techno-nationalist advantages. Could this backfire and stifle innovation, particularly if the big space-tech companies focus on short-term profits.

Some space sceptics have noted that NASA paid approximately US$86 million per astronaut for SpaceX's services, more than what it paid the Russians via Roscosmos per each journey to the ISS. Could this be a valid example of industrial policy producing another version of the proverbial US$400 screwdriver?

Not really. When viewed through a wider prism, the Falcon 9 works out to be far more valuable because SpaceX was quickly ramping up other unmanned missions, with much shorter launch intervals, for a wide range of NASA and defence-related missions. This was, in fact, providing greater economies of scale across the board and driving down overall costs—not to mention translating into mounting strategic advantages for the U.S. government.

One single SpaceX launch, for example, can deploy dozens of satellites for multiple U.S. government entities. SpaceX has also been building important technology in the rocket launching value chain for NASA and managing the entire launch-to-landing sequence—another source of savings.

The goal, of course, is to optimise market efficiencies, where possible, while also achieving security objectives, which involves a delicate balancing act of managing public–private partnerships.

Under the Artemis programme, NASA aims to return humans to the moon, build functioning human habitats and forward bases on the lunar surface and do the same on Mars. For this purpose, the agency has elected to stick with many of its long-term partners, going back to the Apollo and earlier space missions. The stalwarts include Boeing, Lockheed Martin, Northrop Grumman and Aerojet Rocketdyne.

One company, Redwire Space, is a newcomer that specialises in building space infrastructure. Another, Airbus Defence and Space, stands out because it is non-American, but geopolitically, it is a player that is considered a long-term American ally and friend.

Thus, because of long legacies of trust and institutional knowledge going back decades, and, of course, high barriers to entry to newcomers, the U.S. civil–military–industrial complex will remain intact for a long time to come.

But that does not mean there are no other places to look for new ideas and technology. Both neoliberal economists and space hawks have turned their attention elsewhere.

TECH START-UPS

One of the ways that NASA and the U.S. defence establishment have expanded their innovative power is by tapping into the deep wellspring of entrepreneurial talent residing in tech start-ups. By getting individual start-ups to focus on a narrow lane of research and development in an ecosystem featuring hundreds of areas, these small, hyper-specialised entities contribute greatly to the U.S. technology feedback loop.

The contributions of tech start-ups and smaller companies have yielded many innovations.

For example, one start-up, Swarm Technologies, worked with NASA to develop a network of small satellites used to provide reliable and affordable spacecraft-to-spacecraft communication services. It received funding through NASA's Space Technology Research Grants (STRG) programme.

Another start-up, Spire Global, developed specialised Earth observation satellites and was incubated through a NASA research fund for small-sat data acquisition. Other start-ups focus on mind-bendingly creative projects. One such company, HealieTech, was tapped by NASA to develop 'self-healing' materials that could be used to protect spacecraft and other space infrastructure from damage.

In 2022 alone, NASA showered start-ups and already-established companies and research organisations with close to a quarter of a billion dollars through its Small Business Innovation Research (SBIR) and Small Business Technology Transfer (STTR) programmes. These are competitive programmes that award grants and contracts to small businesses and research institutions. The payoff for NASA: new materials, manufacturing processes and software applications.

Meanwhile, the Department of Defence (DoD) also turned its gaze towards start-ups and other commercial technology companies with the aim of developing prototypes. In 2017, DoD created the Defence Innovation Unit (DUI), whose activities produced a steady stream of new AI technologies, cybersecurity technologies and cutting-edge autonomous systems technology.

Based out of the Pentagon in Washington, D.C., the DUI opened offices in Boston, Massachusetts, Austin, Texas and Silicon Valley (Mountain View), California. Not surprisingly, these offices were set up near great research universities such as MIT, The University of Texas and Stanford University. Not only do the universities function as hubs of research and innovation inside the classroom, but they are also hotbeds for start-ups and talent pipelines.

A steady flow of innovation and prototypes continues to emanate from more than a dozen other outstanding universities as well, including the University of Southern California, the University of Michigan, Purdue and Penn State University, among others.

Overall, techno-nationalist initiatives targeting start-ups and niche technology companies have accelerated the commercialisation of space and evolved public–private partnerships with NASA and the U.S. defence establishment.

THE MILITARISATION OF SPACE

The hybrid cold war has spread to the outer reaches of Earth's atmosphere and beyond into space. The militarisation of space spans a range of technologies and strategies needed to fight wars and deter aggression in the modern era.

The technology includes anti-satellite (ASAT) weapons such as ground-launched missiles, satellite-based weaponry, lasers and electronic warfare tools, which are designed to destroy or disable enemy satellites. The use of autonomous space vehicles to hunt down, capture or disable other space-based assets is said to be in the arsenals of some of the major space powers.

Autonomous space vehicles, equipped with advanced sensors and kinetic or directed energy weapons, as well as special appendages that can literally fling other satellites into outer darkness are, yet again, the story of science fiction turned to fact.

Figure 18.5   The Secretive X37-B Autonomous Robotic Orbital Space Plane: Reusable for Military and Intelligence-related Missions.

One of the most opaque and mysterious developments of the militarisation of space involves the U.S. Air force's (USAF) so-called X-37B 'space plane', which, with no human crew, is a windowless, miniaturised and 'dronified' version of a space shuttle.

In late 2023, USAF's space plane was launched on what was reported to be its seventh mission by SpaceX's Falcon Heavy booster rocket. The vehicle was to operate in 'new orbital regimes', as Space Force officials put it.

As its missions are all classified, the X-37B appears to be geared toward placing, recovering and potentially attacking objects in LEO.

China has also developed and deployed its own space plane, the Shenlong 'Divine Dragon', which has been launched into space and returned to Earth for reuse. And Russia is also said to be developing its own mini-Buran (meaning mini-space shuttle), also an uncrewed flying space drone. All three craft look curiously similar.

Space vehicles and drones would seem the most logical choice of offensive and defensive weaponry, as a missile would create space debris fields from the destroyed target, which, in turn would damage all other objects in space, friend or foe as they orbited the Earth.

Meanwhile, Earth-facing space-based missile defence systems such as the ballistic missile defence (BMD) utilise sensors and interceptors to detect and intercept ballistic missiles during their boost or mid-course phase. Space-to-ground weapons, positioned in space, have the capability to strike targets on Earth, employing various methods such as kinetic energy projectiles or directed energy weapons. In 2023, Vladimir Putin, Russia's President, announced that Moscow may have deployed nuclear warheads 'parked in orbit' that could be remotely activated to strike a ground-based target.

China's recent breakthroughs in hypersonic missile propulsion have prompted Herculean U.S. efforts around the implementation of specialised tracking systems across LEO networks, primarily those built, launched and maintained by SpaceX.

Cyberwarfare in space, meanwhile, involves conducting cyberattacks against satellites, ground stations and communication networks to disrupt or disable space-based systems. Autonomous systems are being designed to hack into or interfere with the operations of enemy satellites.

These space weapons are often classified and undisclosed to the public. However, it is generally accepted that the U.S., China, Russia and others are actively researching and developing advanced space capabilities, including ASAT weapons, space-based missile defence systems and anti-missile lasers.

THE BIFURCATION OF SPACE RESEARCH

The Defence Advanced Research Projects Agency (DARPA) has been engaged in space-based defence since the early days of America's Cold War with the former Soviet Union. It looks to undertake high-risk, high-reward projects that would not constitute a practical or realistic undertaking for purely commercially driven enterprises, given the high costs of failure. DARPA projects may not yield immediate practical applications for years, but if they hold sufficient game-changing potential, the agency will keep funding the efforts.

Because a hot war in space has become a certainty, it helps to have access to free-flowing government funding: DARPA's 2024 budget was set at US$4.4 billion.

Like NASA, DARPA fosters collaboration with a wide spectrum of stakeholders, including the tried-and-true combination of government agencies, private industry, academia and specialised research organisations.

For good reason, DARPA's fingerprints are on virtually every aspect of NASA's civilian space programmes, which have substantial spillovers into American military objectives. These spillovers include space launch and propulsion, such as the development of reusable rockets (an area into which DARPA is continuing to invest resources), hypersonic aircraft, new launch vehicles and propulsion systems, but purely for fighting efficiency.

Another crucial area for DARPA is space 'situational awareness' aimed at enhancing the ability to track and monitor objects in space, spanning satellites and debris to potentially hazardous asteroids.

In the realm of space communications and networking, DARPA is directing its efforts towards other pioneering technologies, most of which involve the use of constellations of LEO satellites. These include laser communications, optical communications and quantum communications, all designed to enhance the efficiency and reliability of data transmission in space.

Ironically, China's efforts at so-called Civil–Military Fusion, where Beijing's central planners have sought to bring together the best minds and resources to China's national security priorities in space (and everywhere else), are modelled on DARPA's success.

DE-RISKING AEROSPACE GLOBAL SUPPLY CHAINS

Keeping space innovation and strategic secrets within the hands of a small group of government-approved private companies and research institutions has its challenges. One involves creating secure, end-to-end global supply chains, especially if, over time, these ecosystems have come to depend on suppliers from around the world, including from those designated as countries of concern by the U.S. Department of Commerce (DoC).

This is a relatively new challenge. During the height of the U.S.–Soviet space race, from the late 1950s through the 1970s, virtually all the essential materials, parts and components, semiconductors and other electronic items required for the space programme were sourced and manufactured in the U.S.

By the early 2000s and 2010s, after decades of globalisation, many of these supply chains had been offshored throughout the world, with increased numbers of vital manufacturing hubs settling in Asia.

Regarding the commercialisation of space, consider the supply chains of Boeing and SpaceX.

For its Falcon rockets, for example, SpaceX sources some of its avionics, sensors and speciality alloys from Chinese suppliers.

Boeing, meanwhile, a prominent player in satellite manufacturing and a participant in the Artemis Lunar and Mars programmes, imports advanced electronics componentry, solar panels and specialised materials such as carbon fibre composites—which sometimes come from Chinese suppliers or so-called original equipment manufacturers (OEMs) with China-based fabrication operations.

For assembly of cutting-edge LEO satellites, both Boeing and SpaceX have turned to Chinese sources to obtain sophisticated types of antennas that are a critical component in their satellite communication systems. Both companies also acquire batteries and battery components from Chinese suppliers.

Taiwan, of course, is renowned for its prowess in semiconductor manufacturing and accounts for a hugely disproportionate percentage of global output. Recall that in 2023, TSMC produced around 90% of the worlds most advanced chips and more than half of all the world's chips overall.

U.S. space companies, including SpaceX and Boeing rely on TSMC for critical semiconductor components that are integral to the production and operation of spacecraft and satellite systems, including those deployed in LEOs. Chips serve as the technological nerve centre underpinning the performance and reliability of every aspect of satellite electronics.

In addition to semiconductor components, Taiwanese companies are key producers of advanced electronics such as sensors, microcontrollers and specialised circuits.

Beyond electronics, Taiwan also contributes to U.S. efforts in space by supplying processed specialised materials, including high-performance composites and alloys that find indispensable applications in U.S. satellite construction and space missions.

In the realm of satellite technology, the importance of solar panels for power generation cannot be overstated, and Taiwan is again acknowledged for the high quality of its panels. SpaceX, Boeing and other U.S. companies regularly incorporate Taiwanese-made solar panels into their satellite designs in pursuit of efficient energy solutions.

Given Washington's emphasis on achieving resilient supply chains for strategic goods, however, the space sector, like all other sectors deemed strategic, faces a supply chain restructuring exercise. As in the case of the CHIPS and Science Act, which strives to move semiconductor fabrication and other strategic industries back to the U.S. through funding incentives and other mechanisms, private companies in the U.S. space sector will have to figure out how to friend-shore and re-shore their own critical supply chains away from China and Taiwan.

This will require decoupling from strategic Chinese supply chains in finished components as well as 'de-risking' from Taiwanese ones, not just in semiconductors but in anything that is predominantly sourced from the island.

National security imperatives, then, will accelerate supply chain reshuffling.

RE-SHORING

In the case of China (or any potential adversary), red flags regarding the safety of Chinese-sourced electronics have become top-of-mind because of the dangers of spyware implants or dormant malware. Even without the risk of cyber sabotage or espionage, any escalation of hostilities between the U.S. and China will prompt Beijing to consider cutting off access to critical supply chains, just as Washington has weaponised American semiconductor manufacturing equipment, effectively setting China's microchip developmental capabilities back for years if not decades. In the face of such concerns, supply chain decoupling will accelerate.

In the case of Taiwan, a virtual U.S. client state, the country's cross-straits tensions with China mean that the risks of a Chinese blockade of the island, or an outright invasion, require the U.S. space and defence sectors to help their suppliers (first, second and even third tier) to expand out of Taiwan and into other emerging rationalised and localised hubs.

As we discussed in Chapter 9, enticing Taiwanese companies to invest and embed themselves in places such as Arizona, Texas and Indiana, the new 'Silicon Heartland', is a decades-long process that will require ongoing government funding and public–private partnerships.

The threat of Chinese hostilities against Taiwan means that the locations most attractive for re-shoring and friend-shoring of supply chains will be found not only in the U.S. but also in mature markets such as Japan, South Korea, Singapore, Canada and the E.U., as well as in Australia as it transitions to a twenty-first-century tech-focused economy—and also in Mexico, India and elsewhere.

All of this gives neoliberal economists a very bad case of insomnia, as many of their fears about oligopolies and monopolies and zero-sum outcomes are realised. The binary focus of a U.S.–China tech race means that more and more innovation and advancement will accrue disproportionately to these two superpowers.

The truth is that policymakers with national security and economic security priorities will tolerate and even encourage the rise of private space oligopolies and privileged relationships so long as those companies deliver strategic advantages and do not enable foreign adversaries.

The best alternative for now, however, is for Washington and its friends to try and turn re-globalisation into new growth opportunities, albeit within newly redrawn boundaries.

SPACE BLOCS

If we were to compare international space collaboration in the geopolitical environment of the first Cold War with today, things have taken a turn for the worse in the twenty-first century.

It is worth noting that during the first Cold War, the superpowers still managed to agree to a modicum of space cooperation. In 1988, for example, the U.S. and the Soviet Union signed a memorandum of understanding that led to the development of the Shuttle-Mir programme, which was a joint space programme between the U.S. and Russia. The Soviet Union would soon dissolve, leading to the advent of the Russian Federation, but the cooperation continued.

The Shuttle-Mir programme involved a series of joint missions and would lay the groundwork for the building of the ISS in 1998, a collaboration not only between the U.S. and Russia but also involving Canada, the European Space Agency (ESA) and Japan.

The Russians built multiple components of the ISS, including the Zarya Control Module, which was launched in 1998, seven years after the Soviet Union dissolved. The Russians also built the Zvezda Service Module, the Pirs Docking Compartment and the Poisk Mini-Research Module. Russian cosmonauts used Russian-built robotic arms to dock modules and install equipment on the ISS, and, of course, Russian Soyuz spacecraft ferried astronauts and cargo to and from the ISS.

Given the levels of distrust between the U.S. and China, however, it is difficult to imagine any future space collaboration between these two rivals. Indeed, China is building its own space station.

Space geopolitics and techno-nationalism were on display in 2021 with the launch of the James Webb Space Telescope (JWST). The JWST represents one of the greatest scientific and technological achievements in human history. Its levels of complexity and its value as a tool for exploration and the pursuit of knowledge about the origins of the universe represent a watershed for astronomy and astrophysics.

JWST involved international collaboration between NASA, the ESA and the CSA. Thousands of experts in the U.S. and 13 other countries in Western Europe participated over decades in the design, construction and deployment of the telescope.

Today's hybrid cold war geopolitics, however, preclude the kinds of technology and knowledge transfer that occurred between NASA and the ESA to Russia. The invasion of Ukraine by Russia, with the continued backing of China, has slammed the door on future space collaboration.

Indeed, China is developing the Xuntian Space Telescope, which is scheduled to launch in 2024. Russia is also developing the Spektr-UV Space Telescope, which is scheduled to launch in the 2030s.

Chapter 19

Drones, Robots and Autonomous Weapons

During the night of February 22, 2024, off the coast of Crimea, Ukrainian unmanned surface vehicles (USV) armed with high explosives, bounced and weaved through the waves toward the Sergey Kotov, a Russian naval patrol ship. In what would soon go viral on the Internet, black and white erratic video pictures showed the Sergey Kotov being rocked by massive explosions before it listed to its port-side and sank.[1]

The weapon of choice was reportedly a Ukrainian made Magura V5 drone,[2] equipped with autopilot, video subsystems and night vision capabilities as well as communication links to remotely operated airborne drones in the vicinity—which, in turn, were most likely accessible because of space-based Internet supplied by Starlink.

The USV that sent the Sergey Kotov to the bottom of the Black Sea looked like an oversized toy that model boat builders would take to a local lake on a weekend. Its streamlined shape and small size made it the ultimate example of asymmetric fighting power. Fully loaded, the Magura V5 cost an estimated US$250,000, while the Russian Naval vessel it sank, many times its size, cost around US$65 million to build.

A month before the destruction of the Sergey Kotov, in what can only be described as a surreal, cross-dimensional war-think exercise, the Ukrainian military conducted a 'hackathon' with interested parties from all over the world, seeking to promote Project Fury—an open-sourced initiative to develop the 'first Ukrainian robotic navy'.[3]

Project Fury sought to use advanced surface-borne and underwater autonomous drones to attack Russian naval assets far out in the Black Sea and even within Russian ports.

THE RISE OF THE MACHINES

Machines are gradually displacing humans in both the physical and cognitive dimensions. For better or for worse, there appears to be no limit to the advancement of AI and the tasks it might enable other non-human entities to perform.

Military planners and law enforcement officials are adapting to a world where real-time, chaotic and violent situations will be increasingly managed by AI-enabled systems. Unmanned aerial vehicles (UAVs) and unmanned underwater vehicles (UUVs)—commonly called drones—along with other AI-empowered, intelligent systems are becoming the instruments of warfare, surveillance and deterrence.

Physical–digital convergence—the application of AI, connectivity and computing power to enhance the function and performance of physical things—has all but assured the obsolescence of, for example, human jet fighter pilots. They are simply no match for smart machines that can process far greater amounts of information and deal instantly with random threats and react in ways that are impossible for a human pilot to do.

Machines do not know fear, do not experience fatigue and do not break down emotionally from the stress and fog of war. And they can withstand far greater physical stresses than a human.

Meanwhile, biomimicry—when science and engineering copy nature's most efficient and lethal forms of natural evolution—is resulting in the design of killer robots that imitate everything from spiders and insects to creatures of the four-legged and winged varieties.

Increasingly, this AI will be autonomous, meaning that a swarm of killer drones or a wave of smart missiles will have the ability not only to process vast amounts of data but also to learn and make independent decisions, including what to attack and kill. This, obviously presents ethical and moral challenges.

INFLECTION POINTS

From a techno-nationalist perspective, we have reached two important inflection points.

The first comes from lessons learned in the Russia–Ukraine War and other conflicts, which demonstrate the weaponisation of ubiquitous commercial and military drones connected to cloud-based platforms. In this instance, drones are subservient tools that can be directed, controlled and ultimately switched off by humans.

The second inflection point involves autonomous machines equipped with the capacity to 'think', adapt and learn during their mission. And this is where we are presented with a potential existential crisis. Here, humans are no longer intermediaries for actual operation and execution.

The fear, here, is if these technologies turn against people because of a malfunction or a miscalculation, or if they fall victim to hacking, this could lead to a scenario of total destruction, particularly if it involves the use of nuclear weapons or cyber weapons of mass disruption.

In this regard, techno-nationalism is an existential race to the bottom. However, given the choice of survival with the aid of autonomous AI or extermination by an enemy with superior technology, governments will always opt for former.

This, then, puts the world in a virtually unstoppable autonomous AI arms race.

THE RUSSIA–UKRAINE WAR

Drone warfare sets the Russia–Ukraine War apart from earlier conflicts, where UAVs represent a tipping point both in technology and strategy. In Ukraine, the existence of ubiquitous, inexpensive commercial drones blurs the line between simple day-to-day utility and deadly warfare.

At the time of this writing, the Ukraine war was entering its third year. Drones continued to provide valuable intelligence and reconnaissance for Ukrainian troops, allowing them to locate, target and destroy Russian military assets in ways that would have been confined to science fiction a decade earlier. The result is asymmetric warfare, in which smaller, lesser-funded actors can leverage low-cost, widely accessible technology to produce disproportionate power multipliers over their adversaries.

Modified commercial quadra-copter drones, for example, such as the hugely popular consumer *Mavic 3*, made by China's DJI, provide the Ukrainian military with live-stream information on the locations of Russian tanks, armoured personnel carriers and troops. Ukrainian artillery units, mobile rocket launchers have thus been able to adjust their fire in real time and pinpoint Russian positions.

Portable UAVs small enough to fit in a backpack, such as the American-made *Switchblade* drone and the Phoenix *Ghost* drone, completely upended Russian battlefield tactics and demonstrated how independently operated and autonomous drones have changed modern combat. The result has been an intensifying techno-nationalist arms race around drone technology and ecosystems.

TURKISH AND IRANIAN DRONES

One of the most lethal power multipliers to emerge on the battlefield has been the Turkish-made Bayraktar TB2 UAV.[4] Ukrainian forces have leaned heavily on the use of Bayraktar drones. With a smoothed, featureless, flattened nose, the TB2 looks like some sort of eyeless flying cave-dweller, but more significantly, it represents the strange and terrifying imagery of the next generation of robotic killing machines.

Figure 19.1   The Turkish Aerospace Industries Anka-3 Combat Drone.

With a roughly 12-metre wingspan, an inverted triangular tail, and a rear propeller, the TB2 can carry an array of missiles that can destroy targets in the air and on the ground. In 2020, the Turks established the TB2 as a highly effective force multiplier in the Nagorno–Karabakh conflict between Azerbaijan and Armenia. The Azerbaijanis used it to methodically destroy Armenian tanks and artillery, tilting the power balance overwhelmingly in their favour.[5]

At a cost of only about US$1 million—compared to around US$4 million for the American equivalent, the MQ 1-B Predator—the Turkish drone was a bargain. Interestingly, the Turkish drone industry arose largely because of Washington's unwillingness to sell American drones to Turkey (despite it being a NATO member), which drove the Turks to develop their own. It was an American prototype, however, the MQ-1-B that served as the benchmark design for the TB2.

Iran's rise as a drone maker is important because the Russia–Ukraine War has allowed it to become the supplier of choice to Russia and other parties hostile to Washington and the West. Iran's Shahad 131 and Shahad 136 drones became Moscow's version of kamikaze or suicide UAVs. The Russians turned them into the equivalent of cheap cruise missiles.[6]

Figure 19.2   Iranian Shahed 136 Drones, and Arash-2 Long Distance Drone.

Moscow has learned first-hand about the effectiveness of drone warfare because of widespread losses inflicted at the hands of the Ukrainians. Russia, therefore, has sought to acquire the same technologies and employ the same tactics, using Iranian drones to strike Ukrainian artillery, troops and other mid-value targets in the field. Consistent with Russian military doctrine, it also increasingly uses drones to pummel civilian targets, including electrical power grids and population centres.

Moscow came to rely further on Iran after it depleted its own stock of cruise missiles.

Here, the economic element of warfare has become clear: For the Russians, an Iranian Shahad drone costs around US$20,000, while a Russian-made Kalibr cruise missile costs US$6.5 million. The cost differences make the continued use of cruise missiles increasingly untenable.

KAMIKAZE IN A BACKPACK

In addition to relatively low-cost UAVs, the Ukraine war has demonstrated the utility and lethality of ubiquitous, portable drones, which can be carried around in a backpack or loaded into the side saddle of motorbike and deployed anywhere, anytime.

Switchblade drones are launched out of a tube that looks like elongated household plumbing pipe. Developed and used for U.S.

Special Forces, a ground fighter can stuff three or four of these tubes into a backpack, set them up while moving about and engage a target quickly and spontaneously whenever needed. A remote operator can crash-dive a Switchblade drone into a designated target and blow it to shreds, and then move to another location.

Another equally light, small, mobile weapon is the Phoenix Ghost drone, which the U.S. Department of Defence supplies to Ukrainian forces by the hundreds.[7] Unlike the Switchblade, which can loiter in the air for less than an hour, the Phoenix Ghost can stay airborne for up to six hours.[8]

While it is difficult to obtain the exact number of kills by the Switchblade and Phoenix Ghost drones, their overall effect on warfare is undeniable. Other countries in the region facing possible aggression from Moscow have revamped their military strategies based on drone warfare in Ukraine.

After less than a year of highly scrutinised battlefield intelligence, Lithuania's Defence Ministry signed a €45 million deal with AeroVironment, the U.S. defence contractor, to procure Switchblade kamikaze drones.[9]

Other man-portable weapons were made available to Ukrainian fighting forces, such as the U.S. Stinger missile, designed to shoot down low-flying aircraft up to around 4,500 metres in the sky.

The Russians had already been on the receiving end of the Stinger missile in Afghanistan in the 1980s when the CIA had supplied Mujahedin jihadists with a steady pipeline of rockets. Stingers accounted for the destruction of 269 aircraft, more than half of all Soviet aircraft destroyed during the Afghan War.[10]

The Stinger was a major reason for the Soviet Union's defeat, and nearly five decades later, after multiple upgrades and refinements, the Stinger is back.

THE SHIFT TO LETHAL AUTONOMOUS WEAPONS

Modern war illustrates the shift to decentralised, asymmetric warfare using human-controlled weapons systems, to the next phase: fully autonomous weapons.

Figure 19.3 Drone Swarms (Artist Rendition).

A human might be able to attack a column of tanks by directing a kamikaze drone using a wireless app on a smartphone. But if a swarm of hundreds of synchronised attack drones flew in, looking for his infrared or thermal signature or the signal from his phone, it would be game-over for the human.

The only countermeasure would be the deployment of other lethal autonomous weapons (LAWS), also known as autonomous weapons systems. Only a LAWS countermeasure would be capable of engaging and neutralising the incoming threat without human intervention.

Autonomous systems can react to threats instantaneously, eliminating the time lag associated with human decision-making. This is crucial in dynamic combat environments where split-second decisions can determine the outcome.

LAWS weapons can operate in hazardous environments without putting human soldiers at risk, and they can engage targets with far greater precision than human operators, minimising collateral damage and civilian casualties—a particularly valuable feature in densely populated urban areas and around sensitive infrastructure.

The transition from human-operated or human-directed drones to fully autonomous UAVs, UUVs and autonomous ground robots is inevitable. For any fighting force not to make that transition would be utter suicide.

The transition is already well underway.

Once again, Ukraine has become a testing ground, in this case, in the civilian use of LAWs to attack Russian naval vessels in the Black Sea. The Ukrainian Navy has increasingly honed its use of unmanned surface vehicles (USVs), which are essentially a drone-boat that drive themselves into a target.

But the Russians slowly learned how to employ countermeasures to Ukrainian USVs; thus, new kinds of weapons and tactics were needed.

In the U.S., fully autonomous UAVs such as the American MQ-9 Reaper and Predator can carry out reconnaissance, surveillance and attack missions independently, while DARPA and the U.S. military have developed similar underwater drones that conduct underwater surveillance and hunt and destroy enemy submarines and other drones.

Autonomous systems are destined to gradually displace human combatants.

On the ground, creepy, dystopic-looking four-legged autonomous ground robots are being developed by the American company Boston Dynamics and are being tested for various roles in ground warfare, including reconnaissance, perimeter security and even combat operations.

Figure 19.4   The US Airforce MQ-9 Reaper Killer Drone made by General Atomics.

Figure 19.5   Dorothy Engelhardt, Director, Unmanned Systems, Deputy Assistant Secretary of the Navy (Ships), Christens the Orca XLUUV Test nAsset System during a Ceremony April 28, 2022, in Huntington Beach, California.

Ukraine Navy's project Fury, then, is just the beginning of underwater naval warfare, as the world's navies are reconfiguring to adapt to the use of UUVs as both offensive and defensive assets.

Consider the following computer simulation scenario.

It is the year 2028. Tensions between the U.S. and Russia have escalated. Intelligence reports indicate that Russia has deployed its Poseidon nuclear-armed autonomous torpedo, a stealthy underwater drone capable of delivering a devastating nuclear strike on the American homeland. The U.S. Navy scrambles to locate and neutralise the threat.

Enter the REMUS 200, a UUV equipped with cutting-edge sensors and a powerful laser weapon system, making it ideal for hunting down and destroying stealthy submarines and torpedoes like the Poseidon.

The REMUS, and fleets of others like it, is deployed into the vast expanses of the World's Oceans, and it ceaselessly navigates and patrols the depths, learning about its environment as it goes, its sensors scanning for any sign of the Russian doomsday drone. Finally, it detects a faint acoustic signature emanating from a deep-sea trench.

The REMUS UUV closes in; its cameras and sensors capture images of the massive underwater cigar-shaped drone, and the AI in REMUS positively identifies it as a Russian Poseidon. The REMUS engages its underwater laser weapon system, sending a concentrated beam of energy towards the Poseidon, causing it to implode.

All-robot UUV attack fleets are in the works already, and not just for the world's big powers. Consider that the U.S. Navy, for the first time, destroyed a UUV deployed by Houthi rebels in the Red Sea. Thus, the phenomenon of drone-enabled fighting by smaller, lesser equiped forces will be common place.

THE ETHICAL DILEMMA OF LETHAL AUTONOMOUS SYSTEMS

The U.S., China, Russia and other advanced countries are caught up in an AI arms race that includes all manner of autonomous and lethal weaponry. Similar to a nuclear arms race, an escalation of this kind of competition is very difficult to contain.

As a technology arms race transforms modern warfare, it also heightens the dangers of unintended outcomes. Scenarios in which sentient AI goes rogue and turns on its developers or errant algorithms result in devastating military losses or collateral damage are entirely possible.

Weapon systems with this level of complexity and destructive power are the products of humanity's deepest, most advanced, yet most dangerous feedback loop. As we discussed earlier, the key institutions of government, industry, academia and finance will continue to drive this self-perpetuating cycle.

The question is whether our governing institutions will be able to devise rule frameworks and conventions to prevent situations involving such outcomes.

During the twentieth-century Cold War, where two superpowers had a virtual monopoly on nuclear violence, the prospect of mutually assured destruction kept them from going to war. With the help of simple luck, the Cold War nuclear arms race turned out to be a manageable problem. Today's autonomous AI is ubiquitous and rapidly proliferating, and it is virtually impossible to prevent evil actors from deploying it.

For both nation-states and local militias, the worry, then, is that the replacement of humans by machines in combat may make it easier for humans to engage in violence by machine proxy. The destruction of a robot in battle does not carry the same political ramifications as the deaths of a nation's sons and daughters.

We must hope that we can avoid the grotesque possibility of an advanced army of autonomous killing machines turning their lethal weapons on a population of defenceless humans.

PART III

Climate, Cleantech and Agritech

Chapter 20

Climate Change and Geopolitics

Most of the world's nations have pledged to do their share in decarbonising the global economy by 2050, in accordance with the Paris Agreement. This voluntary forum aims to hold global warming to 1.5° Celsius above pre-industrial levels.

That goal has prompted efforts to transition from fossil fuels to sustainable energy sources such as wind, solar and hydrogen power, otherwise known as 'cleantech'. Advances in thermonuclear and plasma physics have recently opened the door to fusion energy, which may eventually allow us to replicate the power of the Sun inside fusion reactors. This could yield practically limitless clean energy—although this is probably decades away, if not more.

By one estimate, meeting the goal of the Paris Agreement will require governments and businesses to lay out at least US$4 trillion of annual spending on the development and deployment of cleantech by the year 2030.[1]

But the road to a carbon-neutral world must pass through a quag-mire of economic nationalism and a new kind of climate-driven geo-politics. This climate realpolitik will complicate how and where cleantech is developed, produced and traded.

The drive to decarbonise the global economy has animated the U.S.–China great-power competition in two ways.

First, China's dominance of cleantech supply chains in solar and wind power, as well as lithium-ion batteries, has given Beijing the power to weaponise these supply chains through export controls and other restrictions. China is practicing 'energy-diplomacy' in much of the world to extend its influence over less developed countries and gain access to their critical minerals and other resources.

China's construction of energy infrastructure along the Belt and Road Initiative (BRI), meanwhile, has sparked a new round of infrastructure wars with the U.S. and other G7 countries. At issue is not only who can build such infrastructure, but how clean it is and whether those who build it meet the standards of transparency, inclusivity and sus-tainable development. Infrastructure wars are also a competition of core values.

Historically, China's energy diplomacy has been built on dirty, coal-fired power, but that appears to be shifting to cleantech.

Even China's monopoly on island-building infrastructure, honed from its actions in the South China Sea, confers geopolitical clout as Beijing promises to rescue island nations from rising sea levels, by physically elevating their countries.

Secondly, the cleantech sector is built on dual-use technologies such as semiconductors, the Internet of Things (IoT) and AI. Consequently, large swathes of cleantech from electric vehicles to solar panels have become vulnerable to tariff and non-tariff barriers (such as export controls) and other forms of government activism.

Energy and cleantech infrastructure wars with China have mobilised the U.S., the G7 and others to form multilateral forums and agree-ments such as the Blue Dot Initiative (BDI) and the Partnership for Global Infrastructure and Investment (PGII). Whether such agree-ments will deliver concrete results remain to be seen.

THE GEOPOLITICS OF ENERGY INFRASTRUCTURE

In 2023, China pumped an estimated 11.9 billion tonnes of carbon dioxide (CO_2) emissions into the Earth's atmosphere—more than the U.S., Europe and India combined. Bundled into this were the carbon emissions of Beijing's activities along its BRI.

The BRI is a massive geopolitically motivated infrastructure crusade that involves more than 150 countries and features Chinese state-owned and influenced companies in the financing and construction of highways, dams, railroads, ports and bridges, as well as communications and energy grids. This requires millions of tonnes of cement and steel as well as fuel-powered machinery, all of which generate CO_2 emissions.

In addition to CO_2 emissions from industrial activities, Beijing's plan to connect China to the Middle East, Africa, Southeast Asia and Europe has resulted in widespread deforestation of natural ecosystems. Thus, destruction of these vital forest 'carbon sinks' often puts the BRI at odds with decarbonisation.

From 2010 to 2020, Chinese state-owned enterprises (SOEs) invested in some 250 'dirty' coal-fired energy plants in 25 countries that are part of the BRI, including Bangladesh, Pakistan, Serbia, Kenya, Ghana, Malawi and Zimbabwe.[2] According to a study by Quartz, roughly 70% of all coal plants built around the world in 2020 relied on Chinese funding.[3]

In 2022 alone, the six largest Chinese state banks provided US$104 billion in financing for BRI energy projects, of which only 25% went to renewable energy projects. According to analysis done by the Centre for Research on Energy and Clean Air (CREA), a Finland-based think tank, the remaining 75% of funding went to coal-fired power plants.

Thus, despite a pledge by Chinese President Xi Jinping in 2021 to stop financing new overseas coal fired power plants, the CREA report found that China continued to finance dirty coal projects through loopholes in its policies, especially by providing funding for upgrades to existing coal plants.

China's energy-infrastructure diplomacy, then, reveals the paradox of great power rivalry in the face of climate change. Geopolitics have primacy over decarbonisation. The expansion of economic power and influence along the BRI paves the way for hard power, as ports and other infrastructure function as dual-use facilities serving both commercial and military purposes.

THE CLEANTECH ARENA

China may be the world's top polluter, but it is also the largest producer of wind and solar power plants.[4] By 2020, China was building more than half of the world's newly installed capacity for wind power. Seven of the world's 10 largest wind turbine manufacturers were Chinese state-backed companies.[5] China dominated all facets of global production of photovoltaic (PV) cells, including more than 95% of the production of solar-related silicon wafers and almost 80% of PV cell manufacturing.[6]

Beijing continues to dominate upstream supply chains for the materials and components that go into solar and wind cleantech, such as rare earths and critical minerals that are needed for batteries as well as components of electric vehicles (such as magnets). Consequently, Europe and the U.S. are striving for strategic decoupling and de-risking from these China-dominated supply chains, actions that are driving geographic ring-fencing within the cleantech sector.

But economies of scale matter. China can leverage its capacity for wind and solar manufacturing, drawing on its access to a broad base of client states and a huge home market.

CLIMATE COMPETITION IN EMERGING MARKETS

The world's rich nations possess the technology and expertise to drive decarbonisation their own economies. However, they have done a poor job of extending their resources to developing economies, and Beijing has capitalised on that failure.

At the 26th Conference of the Parties (COP26) in 2021, an annual meeting of nations devoted to decarbonisation goals, leaders of developing economies—particularly India, the world's third-largest polluter—doubled down on demands that the wealthiest nations help pay for the decarbonisation of poorer countries. Conceding that earlier pledges towards climate aid have fallen short, developed countries committed to extend US$100 billion in green finance and other initiatives annually through 2025.[7]

Emerging markets are, therefore, poised to become a stage for increased climate-related infrastructure competition between the superpowers. This dynamic has parallels to the twentieth-century Cold War, when the U.S. and the Soviet Union competed for influence in the southern hemisphere. So-called 'non-aligned countries' like India played the two superpowers off against each other to collect financial aid and assistance from both sides.

Figure 20.1   **Floating Chinese-built Solar Farm in a Hydro-power Reservoir.**

Consequently, Beijing has slowly been shifting its energy focus from coal to cleantech. According to data from the World Bank, the Asian Development Bank (ADB), and other multilateral development banks, from 2020 to 2023, China spent more than four times as much on green infrastructure projects along the BRI than the total combined funding of cleantech in the U.S., Europe and Japan.

In Africa, China's investments have sparked a shift to both PV solar and wind power in some of the world's most challenging environments.

Chinese SOEs do business in places that the world's leading multinational companies would consider too dangerous and too expensive. Despite a decades-long civil war, for example, Chinese SOE Dongfang Electric announced the construction of a 120-megawatt (MW) wind park in Ethiopia in 2021.[8]

China's clean energy footprint in Africa is expanding. In Ghana, the Sinohydro Group, another Chinese SOE, is steadily bringing online components of a 250 MW floating solar farm.[9] Other projects include the 100 MW Gwanda solar power plant in Zimbabwe, which is being built by CHINT Electrics and is expected to go online in 2026, and the 50 MW Garissa solar farm in Kenya, built by the China Jiangxi construction company.

Ultimately, China's drive towards clean energy in Africa and throughout the BRI illustrates the strategic value of building infrastructure that furthers Beijing's geopolitical interests. The network facilitates access to strategic minerals and food resources, provides markets for Chinese products and involves both hard goods and digital services such as wireless communications, e-commerce and financial technology.

From a security perspective, experts argue that infrastructure built and controlled by China also doubles as a ready-made deployment network for its military assets.[10]

CHINA'S INFRASTRUCTURE-FOR-RESOURCES DEALS

Some projects in the BRI involve trading Chinese infrastructure construction in host countries in exchange for natural resources. Such projects have been under intense scrutiny by the global community and are being singled out by the G7 countries as *cause celebre* for a shift away from China-style development and a pivot towards a new alliance of progressive infrastructure-building nations.

Take, for example, a deal signed by Chinese SOE Sinohydro Corporation with the Finance Ministry of Ghana in 2018, in which Sinohydro agreed to build US$2 billion worth of roads, housing and rural electrification in return for access to bauxite reserves in the West African nation.[11]

Under this arrangement, Ghana would borrow money from Chinese banks to finance the project with the aim of using the proceeds of international sales to repay the loans—assuming these sales generated enough income.

The deal had been worked out exclusively with a small political elite, allegedly involving bribery of local officials, according to the claims of Global Witness and The Sentry, two NGOs. What the deal did *not* involve were public consultations or impact assessments, omissions that epitomise China Inc.'s opaque business practices in developing countries.

Sinohydro's mine operation is to be located within the Atewa forest reserve, a vital band of biodiversity within Africa's critical carbon sink.[12] The deforestation and environmental degradation that would result from the project has generated opposition from local communities, international environmental groups and even potential corporate customers.[13]

At the time of this writing, Sinohydro's proposed bauxite mine in the Atewa forest reserve was still undergoing an environmental impact study by the Environmental Protection Agency (EPA) of Ghana. The EPA has the authority to approve or reject the project based on its environmental impact assessment.

Other Chinese infrastructure-for-resources deals do not set a hopeful example. Consider the Mutanda Copper mine in the Democratic Republic of the Congo, where roads and railroads were built, or the Grasburg gold and copper mine in Papua New Guinea, where a railroad, roads and a port were built. Both examples stood out in their environmental destruction, poor labour standards and lack of transparency.

VALUES-DRIVEN INFRASTRUCTURE PROJECTS

China's imprint in emerging markets would seem indelible. Yet Beijing's competitors have settled on a strategy of pitching local governments with Western alternatives that, from a core value perspective, are pitched as being superior to those of China Inc. The goal is to deliver decarbonising energy projects while meeting higher labour standards and practices, while also providing transparency and accountability to local stakeholders.

At issue is the nature of the terms and conditions that China extracts from its overseas hosts for its infrastructure projects, putting China's methods of dollar diplomacy at the core of geopolitical climate competition.

Consider China's investments in wind farms in Africa. The construction of these farms by Chinese SOEs may be welcomed, but the projects are often viewed as one-sided in favour of Beijing. Despite ongoing complaints, Chinese companies continue the practice of shipping thousands of their workers from China to large overseas projects, often to the exclusion of locals.[14] Chinese construction companies bring their own machinery and are yoked to a wider ecosystem of policy-driven banks and companies that serve Beijing's wider geopolitical agenda.

In cases where Chinese firms use local labour, they are reportedly subject to harsh working conditions.[15] Nigeria, Africa's most populous state, has faced a wide range of alleged Chinese abuses of Nigerian workers.[16]

MULTILATERAL INFRASTRUCTURE ALLIANCES

As a countermeasure to China's expansive BRI footprint, recall that the U.S., Japan and Australia formally launched the Blue Dot Network (BDN) in 2019, with the goal of bringing higher standards to infrastructure projects.

The BDN's primary objective was to certify that projects in low- and middle-income countries met transparency standards throughout the project's life cycle, from planning and procurement to construction and operation. Assuming Washington and its allies could provide alternate funding, BDN-backed infrastructure aims to displace Chinese-backed projects.

Regarding environmental sustainability and social responsibility, the certification process focuses on minimising environmental impacts and respecting the rights of local communities—things that China is consistently accused of ignoring.

The BDN marks the beginning of a back-and-forth series of infrastructure funding wars between Washington and Beijing. A year before the BDN's creation, in an attempt to counter China's heavily funded SOEs, Washington turned to the International Development Finance Corporation (IDFC), which reportedly committed some US$60 billion in grants and loan guarantees.[17] To achieve the same objectives as the IDFC, policymakers in Japan and Australia also turned to their own sources of government funding, in this case, the Japan Bank for International Cooperation and the Australian Department for Foreign Affairs and Trade.

By 2023, the BDN had expanded to consist of Australia, Japan, the U.S. Canada, New Zealand, the U.K., Spain, Switzerland and the Czech Republic.

Private capital is expected to play a key role in the BDN's projects. The network's certification process was designed to attract private investment to projects that make the grade, given that private money only gravitates to places with acceptable risk. This is fundamentally different from the traditional Chinese BRI model, where the state apparatus pumps money into an environment, no matter how high the risk, so long as it achieves a geopolitical end.

Soon, the BDN inspired a complementary plan on a much grander scale—recall the Partnership for Global Infrastructure and Investment (PGII), launched in 2022 by the G7 nations. Whereas the BDN provided certification, technical expertise and guidance to initiatives, the PGII focuses on mobilising resources and coordinating investments.

Like the BDN, the PGII was launched with an eye on China's BRI. It aimed to address the global infrastructure gap—the difference between the need for new infrastructure and the actual supply of new projects—estimated at US$4.3 trillion annually, for which the G7 pledged US$600 billion in funding over its first five years.

In competing with Beijing to build solar farms in Africa, for example, G7 governments chose to try and exploit a backlash against China's dollar-diplomacy, poor labour standards and practices, environmental degradation and opaque business methods.

The idea was to meet Beijing head on, but these projects would have to be genuinely 'green' and feature leading-edge cleantech— hence the linkage between climate-change, infrastructure and techno-nationalism.

At the time of this writing, the PGII had initiated several projects in BRI countries, including a US$4 billion project in Huambo Province, Angola, to develop 500 MW of renewable power generation involving wind, solar and battery storage.

It had also begun a similar US$1.4 billion clean-energy project across various states in India, including Karnataka, Tamil Nadu, Gujarat and Andhra Pradesh.

THE DIGITAL INFRASTRUCTURE NEXUS

Along with clean energy, the G7's focus has turned to digital infrastructure projects in low-and middle-income countries. In Senegal, for example, the PGII directed its funding towards the development of a digital backbone to enhance connectivity, promote e-commerce and support online digital activities.

Here, we see the linkage of, for example, telecommunications infrastructure with wider climate change initiatives involving sustainable energy and other forms of cleantech. The two go together when it comes to modernisation efforts. Selling a new solar farm to a foreign government is easier when the companies doing the engineering and construction are part a wider network of closely aligned tech firms and service providers.

The winner of such a project usually wins because of its relationships with other well-established entities in the local market, especially if they are part of a wider techno-nationalist ecosystem with a defined agenda.

This is a linkage worth studying because it raises the question of what G7 governments must do to position their preferred firms to compete and win against big Chinese companies in an emerging market, such as the telecommunications giant Huawei.

Consider the US$500 million Senegal Digital Infrastructure Backbone (SDIB) project, launched in 2023, which was slated to be completed in 2026. The SDIB aims to develop a high-speed fibre-optic network to connect major cities, towns and rural communities, providing access to affordable and reliable Internet services. The network is intended to bridge the digital divide in Senegal, promoting economic growth and social development.

In this example, consider that Senelec, the national electricity company of Senegal, partnered on the SDIB project with Orange, the French multinational telecommunications company, and Huawei.

Huawei provided the fibre-optic cables, network equipment and technical expertise for the project, while Orange oversaw the network management and services. Senelec's responsibilities included deploying the fibre-optic cable along existing architecture.

The Senegal project reminds us again of the incredible scale of Huawei's footprint around the world and its strategic value to Beijing. As we discussed in Chapter 10, Huawei has derived benefits from years of state funding and assistance in its overseas expansion, including through China's five-year plans and techno-nationalist initiatives.

If Western companies are to compete with Huawei, this will require huge infusions of money and years of effort, including active techno-diplomacy efforts similar to what Washington has done in the undersea cables arena, where it has successfully positioned SubCom, the American company, as the partner of choice with foreign governments and telecoms operators.

Where will the money come from, and who will emerge as a worthy competitor to Huawei? Will it be an international consortium of state-backed Western companies such as Nokia, Ericsson, Qualcomm or some other as-yet-named conglomerate of G7 firms?

All of this will determine who gets to build the next round of clean infrastructure throughout the world's less developed regions.

Sceptics would argue that organisations such as the BDN and the PGII are, at best, long shots. Time will tell. It is simply too early to gauge how these initiatives will play out in determining the geopolitical landscape over the next decade or two.

What is clear is that China has pivoted strongly towards investment in new digital infrastructure and cleantech along the BRI. This decision was based on economic prudence as well as techno-nationalist imperatives.

According to AidData, a research group at William & Mary College, in 2023, some US$1.1 trillion was owed to Chinese banks; around 80% of it was owed by economically distressed nations, and a large chunk of the loans were coming due. Pakistan, Malaysia and other countries would need bail-out loans just to help service their debt payments. This is hardly a rosy picture for China Inc.

No wonder, then, that at the BRI Summit in Beijing in 2023, Chinese President Xi Jinping announced a move away from massive hard infrastructure projects towards less expensive initiatives such as digital infrastructure, digital trade and cleantech. Clearly, more bang for the buck (or digital renminbi).

China-built digital networks, with Chinese cloud providers, telecoms carriers and platforms also provide Beijing with the means to prosecute narrative wars: state influenced companies can carry out censorship and surveillance as well as distribute the scripted content.

CHINA'S ISLAND-BUILDING DIPLOMACY

Ironically, China's island building prowess in the South China Sea (SCS) has positioned it nicely in its infrastructure wars with the U.S. and its allies. This is due to the sinking of nations—literally. The gradual inundation of island nations because of rising sea levels presents China with opportunities to build strategic footholds across the Indo–Pacific. The Alliance of Small Island States, for example, an organisation that represents the world's low-lying islands, has opened its doors to China's island-building diplomacy.

Consider the Republic of Kiribati in the Pacific, which has turned to China to raise the elevation of its most populated islands, such as the coral atoll that hosts the city of Tarawa. To do this, China is drawing on engineering methods and resources that Beijing developed to build up contested coral atolls in the SCS.[18] This includes deploying special dredging and landfill equipment.[19] Consider that the U.S. has already placed many of the companies that perform this work on the BIS entity list, which includes the state-owned China Communications Construction Company Dredging Group Co.[20]

Until other nations can match its capabilities in this area, the growing urgency for climate adaptation programmes helps further China's island-building goals. Kiribati switched diplomatic relations from Taiwan to China in 2019 and has enthusiastically signed up to the BRI.

Kiribati's infrastructural makeover includes China's rebuilding of a two-kilometre airstrip on Kanton, a low-lying coral atoll in the Phoenix Islands, a remote archipelago. Kanton was a former U.S. military shelter once used by Pan American Airways as a refuelling stopover for transcontinental flights.[21]

In exchange for infrastructure, Kiribati is providing Beijing with a strategic base of operations in the middle of the Pacific Ocean, with access to rich fishing grounds, undersea mining riches and a potential staging point for Chinese military assets.

The Solomon Islands, another nation with strong historical ties to the U.S., has followed a similar course.[22] Facing the prospect of rising sea levels and hoping for economic gains from the BRI as well, its government joined Kiribati in switching diplomatic ties from Taiwan to China in 2019.

These examples illustrate the feedback loop between climate change, geopolitics and the technological and economic tools at the disposal of nations. In the case of the island nations, China's engineering prowess in island building is unmatched.

For the U.S. and its allies, failure to meet the goal of 1.5°C threatens to speed up global warming and may help drive the island nations into China's orbit.

There is also significant environmental collateral damage to coral reefs because of rising sea levels. Island building causes environmental destruction on a horrific scale from large-scale dredging of coral lagoons and the paving over of atolls.

Despite such issues, Chinese state-backed construction projects currently dominate the developing world's landscape, from Chile to Kazakhstan. This involves steel and cement companies, construction companies, and high-speed rail and telecommunications, and, of course, coal-fired power plants and solar and wind power companies.

From a techno-nationalist perspective, then, if the U.S. and its allies are serious about their values-driven approach to climate change remedies for desperate nations—whether through clean energy or through saving island nations from rising sea levels—they must deliver real economic solutions backed with technological prowess and industrial capability.

Without a generational effort to match China's efforts, the U.S. and its allies will find themselves at a major and widening competitive disadvantage with China.

Chapter 21

The Geopolitics of Electric Vehicles

Beijing's central planners have engaged in a decades-long effort to establish China as the dominant player in electric vehicles (EV). By early 2024, they had accomplished their goal.

Not only is China the world's largest EV market, a Chinese brand, BYD, became the world's number selling EV, which may have prompted BYD's CEO, Wang Chuanfu, to proclaim that all Chinese EV makers should unite and '. . .demolish the old legends', referring to Western brands.[1]

The world's other EV manufacturing centres, namely Europe, the U.S., Japan and South Korea, had already been coping with Chinese techno-nationalism in their sector. Now it was official: their competitors were fully on board with China's central planners and were looking to leverage whatever state resources they could use to crush the foreign competition.

As with semiconductors and 5G telecommunications technology, elements of EV global value chains have become highly strategic.

Whoever controls critical supplies of rare earths and lithium for battery production will gain advantages in a much wider systemic competition.

EV ecosystems are both wide and deep. 'Connected' and 'smart' EVs feature a combination of sophisticated AI, software, data algorithms, communications technologies, microchips and sensory technology. This represents a convergence of both 'hard' and 'soft' tech, a hallmark of all industries of the future. As such, EV supply chains will become increasingly susceptible to restrictions on materials and critical components as well as data privacy and security-related controls.

The COVID-19 pandemic provided a preview of what can happen when an industry becomes too reliant on one specific supply chain and then has that supply chain cut off. The global automotive sector had come to rely on China for automotive parts and components. Now the reality of a surging domestic EV industry in China has the world reacting with a new wave of countermeasures. These include defensive measures such as anti-dumping and countervailing duties on Chinese imports, and full-on techno-nationalist offensive measures aimed at aiding local and reginal supply chains and alliances.

In response, state and non-state actors are moving to de-risk and decouple global value chains from China—and to go all in on a fortified in-China-for-China strategy.

THE CORE AREAS OF EV TECHNO-NATIONALISM

Techno-nationalist competition and bifurcation in the EV sector revolves around six core areas:

- Rare earth materials and related supply chains.
- Battery innovation, production and self-sufficient supply chains.
- Critical components regarding permanent magnets, lithium, cathodes and anodes.
- Semiconductors and related supply chains.
- Data privacy and security issues linked to EVs.
- Government incentives, initiatives and strategic partnerships.

TWENTY-FIRST-CENTURY ELECTRIFICATION OF THE AUTOMOTIVE INDUSTRY

In 1884, Thomas Parker, the English inventor, introduced the first commercially viable EV, nearly two years before the first petrol-powered cars appeared on the market, courtesy of Karl Benz, in Germany.[2]

At the dawn of the automotive age, it was electricity rather than internal combustion engines (ICEs) that garnered appeal in modern urban centres. By 1897, for example, both New York and Paris had their own clean and quiet electric taxi fleets.

Ultimately, however, the nineteenth and twentieth centuries would not belong to the electric car. Limited driving range due to short battery life, a lack of charging infrastructure, high costs and low market demand all stalled the development of the EV.

The ICE eventually solved the problems that earlier EV visionaries and entrepreneurs could not. Ford Motor Co. began mass-producing the Model-T in 1908, and the rest, of course, is history. Thus began the age of the fossil-fuel-powered car and, more broadly, the fossil-fuel-driven global economy.

After more than a century, the global automotive industry finds itself at a historic tipping point. The EV is likely to play a key role in the battle against global warming by dramatically reducing the demand for oil. Governments and markets are gravitating to the EV once again, and this time, government backing promises long-term commercial viability.

To appreciate the magnitude of change underway in the automotive industry, consider that approximately US$400 billion was invested in EVs from 2010 to 2020.[3] Half of that investment occurred in one year, 2020, *alone*. Astonishingly, EVs are expected to go from a paltry 4% of overall global car sales in 2020 to about 70% of new car sales in 2040.[4]

This watershed comes on a wave of new government policies that have led to a seismic shift in corporate strategy. Spurred on by government action that includes both punitive measures aimed at CO_2 emitters and financial incentives aimed at encouraging new production, automakers are transitioning their legacy ICE operations to EV production.

In Europe, for example, Mercedes Benz—the producer of the world's first gasoline-powered vehicles—is spending US$47 billion to go all-electric by 2030.[5] Other significant crossovers include Jaguar (by 2025),[6] Audi (by 2026),[7] Volvo, which is now owned by Geely, a Chinese state-backed company (by 2030)[8] and Volkswagen (by 2035).[9]

Across the Atlantic in the U.S., General Motors (GM) has committed to going almost entirely electric by 2035 and expects to spend US$27 billion on the transition. Rival company Ford Motors is spending US$22 billion and aims to move 40% of cars into the EV column in the same timeframe.[10]

It is a striking testimony to the magnitude of change that GM and Ford—whose large, gas- and diesel-guzzling vehicles are emblematic of their brands—are converting their most iconic models to EVs. Ford's best-selling pickup truck, the F-150, is sometimes associated with outspoken climate change sceptics (and is even a symbol of their irreverence), yet Ford has made available an all-electric version called the 'Lightning'.[11] Meanwhile, GMC, the truck division of GM, has produced an all-electric Hummer since 2021.[12] Other automotive icons going electric: the Ford Mustang and GM's storied Cadillac.

In Asia, the news is the same. Nissan is going all-electric by 2030 and fully CO_2 neutral throughout its global supply chains by 2050.[13] Honda has slated 2040 as the year it will stop making ICEs.[14] Toyota is holding back on an all-electric offering for now but is introducing a variety of high-quality EVs, starting with SUVs.

Hyundai, the South Korean automotive stalwart, has announced it would look to reduce its ICE output by 50% over time, while the other large South Korean automaker, Kia, is looking to gradually introduce a growing line of EVs.

NEW REGULATIONS AND FUNDING

Recognising the need for change, governments around the world have introduced a wave of new regulations and funding aimed at reducing CO_2 emissions, prompting manufacturers to set ambitious targets for EV production.

In 2021, there were an estimated 1.5 billion cars on the road world-wide. Along with other types of fossil-fuel-based transportation, they accounted for almost a quarter of global CO_2 emissions.[15] by 2050, another one billion cars could be added as developing economies continue to grow.

The need to convert to clean EVs is a foregone conclusion. The International Energy Agency (IEA) calculates that if the world is to have any chance of reaching net-zero CO_2 emissions by 2050, the number of EVs on roads will need to grow by 36% per year, reaching 245 million vehicles in 2030.[16]

In 2020, for example, the E.U. reached a landmark agreement to cut CO_2 emissions to 55% of 1990 levels by the year 2050. Concurrent with this agreement was the allocation of a US$2.2 trillion budget to shift towards a greener, more sustainable economy.[17] The agreement included a target of 30 million EVs on European roads by 2030.[18]

The U.K., meanwhile, has announced plans to end the sale of diesel and petrol cars by 2035—a decision that has surprised many.[19] We will have to wait and see about that, however, given the importance of fossil fuels to economic and national security.

Beijing, which presides over the world's largest automobile market, has mandated that EVs make up 40% of all new sales in China by 2030.[20] Combined with Beijing's decades-long effort to dominate the EV sector, this mandate is already having ramifications for the rest of the world as heavily subsidised Chinese-made EVs begin to overtake other car makers in automotive markets.

In 2021, U.S. President Biden signed an executive order mandating 50% of all new vehicle sales be of the EV variety by 2030.[21] In addition, Biden's US$1 trillion bipartisan infrastructure bill earmarked US$7.5 billion over a five-year period for charging networks, with a portion of the funding set aside for low-income and rural areas.

THE EV ECOSYSTEM AND COMPOSITION OF EVs

EVs come in a variety of versions. The most advanced versions are full electric vehicles (FEVs) or plug-in electric vehicles (PEVs), whose batteries need to be charged at specialised stations or outlets.

Hybrid electric vehicles (HEVs) rely on a combustion engine to charge a battery. The combustion engine can be switched off, and the car can then run purely on electricity from the battery until it needs to be charged again. An HEV requires gasoline (petrol) to fuel the combustion engine.

Finally, plug-in hybrid electric vehicles (PHEVs) provide the greatest number of options regarding where and how far the vehicle can go.

For all EVs, the battery is the most important and expensive element in the vehicle. Advances in battery technology are, therefore, critical to the success of EV brands and their manufacturers.

Regarding battery range, Tesla's 2021 Long Range Model S, a PEV, featured a battery that extended its driving range to around 660 kilometres. Since then, steady advances in battery duration and distance have continued.

For an EV ecosystem to succeed, however, it must bring together various key elements: battery manufacturers, charging stations and charging outlet infrastructure, critical components (such as magnets and cathodes), government regulators and policymakers and end-users (customers).

THE SIMPLICITY OF ELECTRIC MOTORS

EVs require far fewer parts and components than cars with traditional ICEs. Whereas an ICE-powered car typically requires about 2,000 parts and components for its engine, an EV's engine only requires about 20 basic moving parts.[22] They are, therefore, much easier to assemble and maintain.

From a competitive standpoint, there are low barriers to entry in the EV sector, at least in terms of the complexity of assembling a vehicle. But there are high barriers due to costs regarding large-scale manu-facturing. For example, Tesla's Giga Factory 1 in Nevada, which makes batteries in partnership with Panasonic and manufactures components for its EVs, spans 126 acres and is roughly the size of 100 football fields. It is the second largest building in the world by volume, after Boeing Aircraft's assembly plant in Everett, Washington.

Tesla's Giga Factory 3, in Shanghai, is equally massive and was built at a cost of US$2 billion.

CHINA: EV TECHNO-NATIONALIST GROUND-ZERO

China is by far the world's largest EV market and still has massive growth potential. Until around 2021, foreign EV makers were manufacturing and selling the most advanced EVs in China despite a rapidly growing assortment of local competitors. But that changed rapidly, and by 2023, Chinese EV national champions emerged from a pack of local players. That same year, BYD surpassed Tesla as the bestselling brand in China and the world.

Regarding battery driving ranges, as recently as 2020, foreign brands were ahead of all the biggest Chinese EV companies. But by 2024, it was NIO, the Chinese EV that had set the long-range top mark of just under 1,000 kilometres on a fully charged battery.[23]

An important question for foreign EV brands with large in-China-for-China operations, therefore, is how to maintain an innovation edge and protect market share. The Chinese Communist Party's (CCP) Made-in-China 2025 initiative lists EVs and autonomous vehicles (AVs) among the 10 industries that Beijing wants to dominate.

Unlike the production of leading-edge semiconductors, which have extremely high barriers to entry for microchip laggards such as China, EV technology is far less complex, which plays well into Beijing's techno-nationalist master plan.

The Chinese government is following a familiar script: obtain and acquire key technology and know-how (especially by acquiring top talent currently working with foreign brands in China) and then funnel large amounts of money into local champions.

Beijing's central planners are using government subsidies, tax breaks, land grants and priority access to lithium battery supply chains to achieve two goals. These are not exclusive to China. They are occurring in all the major EV-producing countries, but the vast size of China's market, and its control of key upstream supply chains give it advantages.

Beijing's first goal is to drive down prices by creating huge production capacity and achieve massive economies of scale, eventually forcing foreign for-profit firms out of the Chinese market—assuming Chinese firms have matched or bettered these foreign firms' technology, which, by 2024, was the case.

The second goal is to leverage China's massive local landscape to expand into other markets.

To meet the challenges of competing with China's state-backed EV sector, then, the world's other producers will also need to partner with their governments. This is necessary to overcome Beijing's virtual monopoly in the top-end EV value chains and its advantages in scale manufacturing.

CHINA'S DOMINANCE OF RARE EARTH MATERIALS

Rare earth materials are vital to EV supply chains.

Rare earths comprise 15 lanthanide elements on the periodic table, plus two other related elements, scandium and yttrium. They are classified into heavy and light categories by atomic weight.

Neodymium oxide, for example, is an essential input for critical magnetic components needed to power EVs.[24] Another rare earth, dysprosium, is required in their production.

In 2024, China was dominating the world's rare earths industry, with state-owned companies holding approximately 80% of market share in the global extraction and processing of critical oxides and metals.[25]

At the time of this writing, a half-dozen state-owned companies maintain a stranglehold on global value chains—companies that include China Rare Earth Holdings and China Minmetals Rare Earth Company, along with China's Ministry of Industry and Information Technology, the agency that sets rare earth production quotas for China's SOEs and, thus, controls the prices of rare earths.[26]

By prioritising the allocation of these critical minerals to its own national champions, China effectively pushed its competitors out of the market. If, for example, Beijing achieves its goal of 40% EVs by 2030 and hoards its rare earths, it could decimate foreign competitors, at least until other countries can develop their own rare earth supplies.

If Beijing chooses, it could simply withhold rare earths for other geopolitical reasons. In 2010, for example, China stopped exporting rare earths to Japan for two months following a territorial dispute over a group of islands in the East China Sea.[27]

In 2019, the year that Washington ramped up sanctions on Huawei and other Chinese companies, Chinese President Xi Jinping visited JL Mag Rare Earth, a speciality magnet producer in Jiangxi province. The message was clear: if Washington was keen on weaponising semiconductor supply chains, Beijing might consider doing the same with rare earths.

ACCELERATED DECOUPLING IN RARE EARTHS SUPPLY CHAINS

Until the 1980s, the U.S. was the world's largest producer of rare earths. The Mountain Pass mine in California's Mojave Desert was the single biggest, rare-earth operation. But like the automotive, telecommunications and other sectors, the U.S. mining industry offshored more and more processing to China. Beijing seized the opportunity to modernise and upscale its own rare earths sector.

Over time, the processing of rare earths became increasingly complex, and the Chinese gradually built up barriers to entry. Contrary to the implication of their name, rare earths are not rare. Nevertheless, the process of extracting, separating, processing and refining them is extremely capital- and technology-intensive. Generally, supply from China has been plentiful and cheap, in part because Chinese producers do not face the costly environmental regulations imposed in the U.S., Europe, Canada and Australia.

Reducing dependence on China for rare earths has become a top priority for the G7 countries, especially the EV automakers. For this to happen, however, governments must be prepared to make long-term commitments, spend big and support public–private partnerships. Private industry alone is no match for China's mercantilist state apparatus.

THE RE-SHORING AND RING-FENCING OF RARE EARTHS

The U.S., the E.U., Japan and Australia are actively coalescing around initiatives to re-shore and ring-fence rare earth supply chains.[28] In 2019, for example, the U.S. and Australia governments signed an agreement to work together with the aim of extracting, developing and processing rare earths within 'safe' home environments.[29] Some 15 different sites throughout both the U.S. and Australia were singled out for further development.

The Mountain Pass mine in California has been reopened and is operational. At the time of this writing it was more than 51% owned by various U.S. hedge funds and, interestingly, Shenghe Resources, a Chinese state-owned company, owned around 8%.[30] The U.S. Department of Defence awarded MP Materials, the operator of the mine, a contract and funding under a technology investment agreement under The U.S. Defence Production Act. How long even a small percentage of ownership by a company from a country of concern is allowed, remains to be seen.

Even the smallest percentage of ownership by a Chinese company in a strategic mine like Mountain Pass may encounter strong headwinds in the future. This is part of the wider paradox of great power competition and China's associations with Russia, Iran and other adversarial state and non-state actors, which will likely result in more decoupling.

In another project involving private equity and Pentagon funding, the Department of Defence has signed a contract with Lynas, an Australian rare earth company, to build a processing facility in Texas along with Blue Line, a joint venture partner. Together, they will process dysprosium and terbium, both used to make leading-edge magnets.[31]

Meanwhile, Germany's ThyssenKrupp Materials Trading has signed supply and extraction deals with Northern Minerals, the Australian rare earth company.

In northeast Asia, the Japanese government is funding exploration and development of one of the world's largest known rare earth reserves on the seafloor, in the Pacific, off Minamitori Island, about 1,150 miles (1,850 km) southeast of Tokyo.

Private investment alone will not challenge China's global monopoly in rare earths. The massive scale of Beijing's state-backed operations has created barriers to entry that no group of private enterprises can overcome.

Building new rare earths operations in the U.S., Australia, Canada and elsewhere on a scale large enough to satisfy current and future demand will take a decade to achieve and run into many billions of dollars. These operations will likely not operate at a profit for years to come and must be treated as a public good to be underwritten by governments.

CHINA'S DOMINANCE OF LITHIUM-ION BATTERIES AND RELATED SUPPLY CHAINS

Figure 21.1 Electric Car and Lithium Batteries.

The most important component of an EV is the battery. It makes up about a third of the cost of the vehicle and, on average, weighs around 450 kilograms. Battery supply chains rely upon critical minerals such as lithium, cobalt, nickel, manganese and graphite.

Beijing has worked relentlessly to dominate both the upstream and downstream supply chains of lithium-ion (Li-ion) batteries. As recently as 2021, Beijing's control of the world's Li-ion sector was astounding.

CRITICAL COMPONENTS AND MINERALS

'The Commanding Heights Initiative', a 2021 report by SAFE (a think tank that advocates for secure energy and transportation policies), documented the extent of Beijing's control of the critical components in Li-ion battery supply chains.[32] Some notable standouts, at the time of this writing in 2023:

- In the early 2020s, China has direct or indirect control of around 70% of the world's lithium supply.
- Chinese companies produce approximately 60% of the cathodes and 80% of the anodes used in the world's batteries.
- China produces close to 75% of the world's permanent magnets used in EV engines.
- China also accounts for 70% of production capacity in Li-ion mega-factories, either in operation or under construction.
- In Africa, Beijing has secured around 70% of the Democratic Republic of the Congo's (DRC) supply of cobalt via infrastructure-for-minerals deals.[33] The DRC holds most of the world's known cobalt reserves.
- Argentina, which is a major source of lithium, has contracted with Beijing for close to 40% of its lithium supply.

Yet, paradoxically, at the same time that Washington finds itself in an escalating techno-nationalist competition with Beijing, it relies heavily on China for key components of EV batteries, including lithium, cobalt, nickel and about graphite—which Beijing put on its export controls list in 2023.[34]*

As with rare earths, the global EV sector must turn to public–private partnerships and leverage government support mechanisms to reduce dependence on China for Li-ion batteries.

THE GEOGRAPHIC RING-FENCING OF LI-ION BATTERY PRODUCTION

To respond to Beijing's techno-nationalist blueprint for the EV sector, the U.S., Europe, Japan and South Korea are resorting to a multifaceted approach.

First, governments are committing to sustained, robust dole-outs of subsidies, tax and land incentives, grants and public–private partnerships to develop localised markets and value chains.

Second, techno-diplomacy among G7 member countries has resulted in a trend towards friend shoring, or 'ally-shoring',[35] the restricting and ring-fencing of supply chains and production capacity within the borders of allies and strategic partners. To put it another way, these strategic supply chains must decouple and de-risk from China and relocate within friendly confines.

Finally, the largest EV manufacturers will move to vertically integrate and manufacture their batteries in-house.

A STORY OF CHINA'S EV BATTERY TECHNO-NATIONALISM

The story of China's CATL, the world's largest Li-ion battery manufacturer, is a microcosm of twenty-first-century techno-nationalism.

CATL began as a maker of Li-ion batteries for portable devices. Based in Ningde, a backwater of Fujian province, the company started as Amperex Technology Ltd (ATL) in 1999, and its founder, Robin Zeng Yuqun, became known for staying out of the public eye. At the time of this publication, Mr. Zheng was reputed to be wealthier than Jack Ma, the former (now exiled) rock star-like executive chairman of Alibaba who fell out of grace with the CCP. This is an important distinction, as Beijing's techno-nationalist priorities lie with the development of deep, substantial technologies that promote China's dominance across the Made-in-China 2025 sectors, not digital platforms and apps that, if not closely controlled, destabilise and undermine the Party's power.

In 2005, Mr. Zeng sold ATL to the Japanese company TDK and struck a deal to work closely with its new parent company on the production of batteries. By the mid-2000s, the CCP had made clear its intentions to develop local battery-making capabilities, and, in 2011, anticipating bigger opportunities in the EV sector, Zeng severed ties completely from TDK. This move allowed the now fully Chinese-owned battery manufacturer to avail itself of a bounty of state subsidies.

As we have discussed, in 2015, Beijing introduced its Made-in-China Plan, which listed EVs and AVs as one of the key strategic sectors. That same year, Beijing blocked Korean battery manufacturers Samsung SDI and LG from localised production which were well-established players in the Chinese market, and moved to build up its own national champions.

FORCED RELIANCE ON CHINESE SUPPLIERS

One of the things Beijing's technocrats did was pressure foreign EV manufacturers to source their batteries exclusively from Chinese companies.[36] By then, ATL had become the logical go-to option. Thus, foreign market leaders such as Tesla and GM (which had a joint venture with Chinese partners SAIC and Wuling) became passive enablers of Beijing's wider techno-nationalist aims.

By 2018, ATL was listed under its new name, 'CATL', and was the third-largest Li-ion battery maker in China. By 2021, it was the world's largest, valued at US$200 billion, dwarfing its closest competitors—South Korea's LG Chem, Japan's Panasonic and another Chinese company, BYD.[37]

CATL was able to spend big on R&D and product development, knowing that it was guaranteed new infusions of capital from Beijing. Those investments allowed it to advance into production of leading-edge high-nickel batteries, which outperform cheaper lithium–iron–phosphate ones.

CATL has expanded its production capabilities overseas, building a new factory in Erfurt, Germany, where it will supply the major German EV brands. Other overseas plans could eventually include Indonesia and, possibly, the U.S. But CATL's penetration of the European market has brought into sharp focus Europe and America's anxieties about reliance on Chinese firms.

A key component of China's master plan for the EV market involves the installation of digital charging stations and infrastructure. In 2020, China already had 10 times as many charging stations as the U.S.—about 800,000 in total.

China's EV infrastructure is linked to a massive US$1.4 trillion spending initiative to build out 'smart city' wireless networks intended to connect a vast array of EVs, AVs and other ubiquitous surveillance cameras and sensors.[38]

To provide impetus for local EV sales, Beijing effectively subsidised the local EV market by providing buyers with rebates that depend on the vehicle's range but are typically worth about US$2,800 per vehicle.

AMERICA AND EUROPE'S EV SUBSIDIES, INITIATIVES AND TECHNO-NATIONALIST ROAD MAP

China's decade-long efforts to build up its EV value chains have prompted a series of countermeasures from the U.S. and Europe. This reflects a clear paradigm shift as the G7 countries move away from laissez-faire capitalism and towards a state-activist model of managed trade. The result is American and European policies that increasingly resemble Beijing's.

Under the Biden administration, the U.S. undertook a variety of initiatives to promote EV and related technologies.

The US$1 trillion bipartisan infrastructure bill aims to create 1 million new jobs in the auto sector and earmarks US$7.5 billion for 550,000 new EV charging stations across America over five years—a fivefold increase over the existing level.

Washington rolled out a system of rebates and tax credits that includes a US$7,500 tax credit to buyers of new EVs, plus another US$4,500 if the car is assembled in the U.S. using union labour, plus another US$500 if the battery cells are U.S.-made and at least 50% of the car's components are of U.S. origin.[39]

Washington also proposes to fully convert the federal government's fleet of 650,000 vehicles to EVs,[40] and to offer subsidies to large express consignment carriers such as FedEx and UPS to convert their fleets to EVs.

U.S. EV TECHNO-DIPLOMACY

Both federal and state governments have attempted to develop strategic alliances to entice foreign governments and companies to invest in the U.S. Consider, for example, recent announcements by

South Korean battery and EV companies to locate manufacturing operations in the U.S.

In May 2021, the CEOs of South Korea's top battery and EV manufacturers accompanied South Korean President Moon Jae-In to the U.S. for a summit with U.S. President Joe Biden. The four-day itinerary included a series of business round tables to discuss investment in EV battery production, along with other 'China-free' supply chain goals, such as the re-shoring of semiconductor manufacturing to the U.S.

Following the meetings, both LG Energy Solution and SK Innovation committed to investing US$14 billion in new battery fabrication plants. Hyundai Motor Group also announced plans to invest US$7.4 billion to produce EVs and perform R&D.[41]

These investments will go a long way towards achieving U.S. automakers' electrification goals. Ford, for example, will partner with SK Innovation on two EV battery manufacturing sites in Tennessee and Kentucky.[42] Prior to the Biden summit, SK Innovation had already announced the construction of a massive battery production site in Jackson County, Georgia.

GM, meanwhile, announced a joint venture with LG Energy Solutions, also in Tennessee, where they will make batteries for the Cadillac Lyric crossover.[43]

EMERGING EV FRAGMENTATION AND CLUSTERS

Three southern U.S. states, Alabama, Tennessee and Georgia, have benefitted from the inflows of 'friendly' investment. This is triggering a clustering effect that, in turn, becomes a magnet to other EV players. Japan's Nissan began producing its Leaf model EV in Tennessee in 2013, and the state has also attracted Volkswagen (to Chattanooga), Ford (to Haywood County) and, as mentioned, GM's US$3 billion joint venture with LG (to Springhill).

Mercedes Benz will begin manufacturing EVs in Alabama, which is where Hyundai has also chosen to set up shop, and this has galvanised other parts of the EV supply chain. Take, for example, the demand for graphite, a critical upstream mineral for EV batteries, which China currently controls. The emergence within this ecosystem of Westwater Resources, a U.S. privately funded minerals group, will establish the first large-scale graphite processing plant in the U.S.[44]

Regarding Tesla, the American company, the question is what to do next in the North American and other key market. Tesla's Gigafactory 1 in Nevada already makes batteries in partnership with Panasonic. Its Gigafactory 3, in Shanghai, contracts with CATL, Beijing's anointed national champion.

The EV landscape is in constant flux, but one thing remains certain: it will continue to regionalise and localise as governments in China, the U.S. and the E.U. each pursue their own agendas.

Chapter 22

Semiconductors and Electric Vehicle Wars

Modern automobiles cannot run without semiconductors. Even vehicles with an internal combustion engine (ICE) require microchips for everything from fuel injection and transmission systems to braking, traction control and power locks.

In fact, a modern ICE-powered vehicle requires about 1,400 semiconductors, while a hybrid electric vehicle (HEV) may use up to 3,500.[1]

In 2020–2021, a microchip shortage caused by a series of swings in supply and demand (resulting primarily from markets distortions caused by the COVID-19 pandemic) exposed serious vulnerabilities in the semiconductor supply chain and cost the automotive sector about US$200 billion.[2] The chip shortage also revealed other important truths.

China's central planners have been pushing local EV makers such as BYD and Geely to source their chips from local chip manufacturers to bolster domestic production of legacy chips and reduce reliance of foreign chips technology.[3]

The story is the same in America. New government funding under the CHIPS Act has been flowing to new fabrication ventures involving, for example, GlobalFoundries' new fab in upper New State, which will increase capacity to make chips for the automotive sector.[4]

THE BLURRING OF AUTOMOTIVE AND TECHNOLOGY COMPANIES

Semiconductor companies and car companies are forming increasingly close strategic partnerships. For good reason: the automotive chip market in 2027 is projected to be worth around US$85 billion, compared to US$27 billion in 2021.[5]

The chip shortage taught car companies a key lesson. When it comes to getting access to semiconductors, it is best to disintermediate middleman suppliers from value chains. Today EV makers are working directly with chip suppliers.

The examples are plentiful. Semiconductor companies Infineon Technologies, NXP, Nvidia, STMicroelectronics and Intel are devoting more and more production capacity to the automotive sector.

Automotive companies are becoming de facto technology companies, while semiconductor and other tech firms are rolling out new automotive products and service offerings. In late 2021, for example, Qualcomm started a trend with a US$4.6 billion bid for a Swedish auto-technology company named Veoneer Inc.[6]

Before that, in 2017, Intel subsidiary Cyclopes Holdings paid an Israeli technology firm US$15 billion for its Mobileye autonomous vehicles technology. Three years later, Intel spent an additional US$900 million on Moovit, a self-driving app. The U.S. chip giant plans to roll out this mobility-as-a-service (MaaS) offering in Germany first as part of a Robo-taxi service.[7]

The trend raises the question: Will other large tech companies, such as Apple or Google, become twenty-first-century automobile producers? This looks more and more likely. For example, Apple's Taiwanese contract manufacturer Foxconn has already announced the rollout of its own prototype EVs (an SUV, a sedan and a bus) made by Foxtron, a strategic partnership between Foxconn and Taiwanese automaker Yulon Motor Ltd.

Might Taiwan-based TSMC, the world's leading semiconductor fabricator, also make a play on the EV market? The possibilities are strong.

THE CHALLENGES OF 'DUAL-USE' EV TECHNOLOGIES

The embedding of leading-edge hardware and software in modern electric vehicles combines 5G and 6G technologies for connectivity and communications on the Internet of Things (IoT), infotainment, driver assistance and navigation, as well as self-driving applications.

Intel CEO Pat Gilsinger called the modern EV 'a computer with wheels. Yet much of the increasingly sophisticated technology that makes up EVs is dual use, with both commercial and possible military applications, and it is therefore potentially subject to export controls and other restrictions.

Hence, the EV sector is at risk of facing scenarios of supply-chain weaponisation similar to those that have haunted the semiconductor sector.

As we have discussed, when Washington used restrictions to choke off sales of equipment manufactured by Taiwan Semiconductor Manufacturing Company (TSMC) to Huawei's chip manufacturers, it effectively forced China's flagship telecom equipment company to drop 5G from its latest line of P50 smartphones and to settle for less-advanced 4G chips.[8]

Recall that when it was forced to focus on new ventures, Huawei Technologies Ltd (Huawei) turned to the automotive sector, partly because automobiles incorporate trailing-edge chips that are not subject to controls—at least for the time being. Since then, Huawei has rolled out its Kirin 9000 chips, the equivalent of 7-nanometre processes, which not only resurrected its smartphone, the Mate 60 series but figures to make the company a bigger player in China's EV sector.

A large swath of technologies in the med-tech, communications, cleantech and automotive will get by just fine with older legacy chips, which will comprise, by far, a large part of the chip market.

But as EVs become more technically sophisticated, they will require increased numbers of leading-edge chips. This raises the possibility of another Huawei-like scenario in the automotive sector. EV chips are already at the 7-nanometre threshold for Tesla and the next generation of vehicles.

To pre-empt disruptions to supply chains, suppliers and service providers may be prompted to decouple from high-risk suppliers and to establish regionalised ring-fenced supply chip supply chains in the EV sector.

CROSS-BORDER MICROCHIP INNOVATION

EVs will accelerate the U.S.–China technology race and its impact on cross-border R&D collaboration in the private sector, academia and government-controlled institutions. As funding initiatives such as the U.S. CHIPS Act are spent, restrictions will be placed on the Chinese activities of companies with access to U.S. funding.

Tech start-ups are vital to the semiconductor–EV symbiotic relationship. For example, at the time of this writing, Intel's Mobileye autonomous taxis are being built by China's EV maker NIO, a rising player with a rapidly growing fleet of EVs.

In 2020, NIO received US$1 billion from Chinese state-backed investors, including Hefei City Construction and Investment Holding Group and Anhui Provincial Emerging Industry Investment Company.[9] The juxtaposition of Intel's brand with China's giant state-backed investment organisations presents an odd incongruity.

Mobile was valued about US$17 billion in 2022, when the company went public and Intel retained about 88% ownership in the company.[10]

Clearly, Intel has China's huge EV market in its sights. Yet techno-nationalist pressures could place constraints on future collaboration with NIO, particularly as state-backed companies are seen as closely linked to Beijing's military–civil fusion initiatives. Thus, there is a very tricky grey zone for both chip and automotive companies to navigate when it comes to possible expansions of export controls on older legacy chips. But the growth trajectory of the EV market demands continued investment. Not to do so would be to lose out on others and risk becoming irrelevant.

FOREIGN VENTURE CAPITAL IN A GEOPOLITICAL CONTEXT

One telling example of geopolitical spillover into the EV tech sector involves the rise of Kneron, an innovative semiconductor start-up. Kneron makes chips that empower devices with artificial intelligence (AI) capabilities, primarily through 'edge computing', a form of computer architecture that more closely integrates computation with data sources than to traditional architectures. Utilising a neural processing unit that enables sophisticated AI applications without connecting to the cloud, this technology enhances data privacy and security. For operating EVs in high-risk environments, the technology could be a game changer.

Kneron argues that its 'system on a chip' (SoC) is more energy efficient than chips made by its giant competitors, Intel and Google. It can also process 4K still images and videos at high resolution and perform leading-edge audio recognition. Kneron's AI is designed to identify things and differentiate between people and inate objects and other moving vehicles.

Based in San Diego and operating an R&D centre in Taiwan, Kneron has received more than US$100 million in funding from some of the world's leading investors, including Sequoia, Qualcomm, Alibaba, Sparklabs Taipei and Horizons Ventures, owned by Hong Kong-based Li-Ka Shing.[11] Other big names include Delta Electronics, a Taiwanese supplier to Tesla and Apple, and Foxconn, which invested an undisclosed amount of money.[12]

This highly diverse international collection of investors includes many of the biggest players in tech venture capital. In a world free of geopolitical tension and techno-nationalism, Kneron's pipeline of funding would validate all the positive dynamics of open, unrestricted trade.

In the present geopolitical environment, however, Kneron and its investors may face considerable challenges. Watch their progress closely.

Kneron's first potential friction point is its association with Chinese tech giant Alibaba, the world's largest e-commerce and fintech company. Beijing's ongoing crackdown on China's technology firms has brought Alibaba under the firm control of the Chinese Communist Party and placed their overseas business operations and investments under tight constraints.

Because its technologies fall under the definition of dual use, and Alibaba is a major investor, Kneron could find itself the subject of an investigation by the Committee on Foreign Investment in the United States (CFIUS), an interagency committee of the U.S. government's executive branch that actively reviews and often blocks Chinese acquisitions in the U.S., particularly investments in U.S. entities deemed to be of strategic value. As China–U.S. relations continue to fray, even previously approved transactions could be revisited.

On the other side of the world, increased hands-on controls placed on Alibaba by Beijing's central planners could also land it on the U.S. restricted entity list, with adverse results for companies such as Kneron.

Other recent events highlight the far-reaching impact of geopolitics on supply chains and markets. Due to critical public statements made by its owner during Hong Kong's period of public unrest in 2020, Horizons Ventures has ended up on Beijing's blacklist.

As a result, Horizons' support of Kneron could have an adverse effect on the company's future expansion into the Chinese market or partnerships with other Chinese entities.

AN EV SOFTWARE AND HARDWARE OPEN PLATFORM

Taiwanese company Foxconn supports Kneron's work on an open-sourced platform for EV-related software and hardware. Kneron's approach follows the model of the open-sourced O-Ran network, established in 2018 to develop standardised software and specs for 5G and 6G wireless technology.

Open-sourced collaboration in EV and semiconductor-related technologies could level the playing field for a multitude of smaller niche players that make specialised EV software and hardware. In turn, this could yield a wide range of quality products and services that accelerate overall progress in EV tech.

For Kneron and similar companies, open-sourcing parts of the EV–semiconductor innovation process could inoculate them from the effects of export controls and restrictions. However, given the geopolitical and strategic priorities of the EV sector and the scale advantages held by the automotive and semiconductor giants (who increasingly receive government funding), the open-sourcing practices in the EV–Chip community may face an ironic predicament. It might become ring-fenced inside ever larger controlled environments with selected invitees.

SILICON CARBIDE AND GALLIUM NITROGEN CHIPS

The shortage of silicon-based microchips during the COVID-19 pandemic and then again for restricted entities subject to export controls has accelerated the search for alternatives to the conventional silicon chip. Two contenders have emerged for chips in EVs: silicon carbide and gallium nitride.

Silicon carbide chips experience less energy leakage than traditional silicon chips and can increase battery power and reduce charging time.[13] Despite the extra costs involved, Tesla is an early adopter of such chips. Its arrangements with semiconductor companies such as STMicroelectronics NV have paid off handsomely: Tesla was not hit by the 2021–2022 shortage of silicon-based chips as badly as other car makers.

Other manufacturers have also moved to silicon carbide chips, such as General Motors (GM) for its Ultium battery platform and Toyota for its Mirai model.

Gallium nitrogen chips are even more energy efficient than silicon carbide. Through partnerships, semiconductor companies such as Infineon Technologies AG will look to capture more market share in the EV space, expanding the blurring lines between automobile and technology companies.[14]

The strategic nature of the EV sector may prompt governments to protect the production of silicon carbide and gallium nitride chips within local ecosystems and to control the sector for strategic stakeholders. Subsequently, governments may move to block transfers to strategic competitors. From a techno-nationalist perspective, these promising technologies present governments with attractive opportunities for public–private partnerships.

CONNECTED CARS AND NATIONAL SECURITY RISKS

EVs incorporate an assortment of digital connections that produce large quantities of data and meta-data. A multitude of cameras and sensors within a car, for example, can capture and record real-time imagery. Simultaneously, a vehicle sends and receives data from external sources and logs onto networks, apps and platforms in the Cloud. GPS and navigation systems capture and transmit other location data, including proximity to other devices, objects and vehicles.

Today, car data security has become linked to national security. In 2021, the Chinese Communist Party restricted military staff and employees of state-owned companies from driving or owning a Tesla.[15] Security agencies have come to regard data generated by EVs as a rich source of intelligence, both as a tool for spying and as a cybersecurity vulnerability.

The EV sector may face yet another round of ring-fencing and localisation. In this case, data localisation laws come into play. Governments require EV companies to keep data on local servers and in databanks that are physically located in the host country. For example, Tesla built separate data security centres in China for its locally sold EVs. It must also consent, when required, to turn over such data to the Chinese authorities.

Beyond the risk of data theft is the terrifying thought of an EV hacking event that disables or turns a car into a deadly weapon. These security-related concerns should be a strong catalyst for innovation and collaboration within an expanding EV tech ecosystem.

The EV–semiconductor nexus is a microcosm of all things techno-nationalist. Business leaders, policymakers, investors and students of international affairs should prepare for a lot more issues involving states and markets.

SUBSIDIES FOR THE EV–SEMICONDUCTOR NEXUS

In Chapters 4 and 21, we examined the range of EV subsidies and incentives that governments are rolling out to achieve self-sufficiency and to reduce upstream and midstream supply-chain vulnerabilities. These efforts remain focused on rare earth materials and critical minerals, lithium-ion battery production and critical EV components such as specialised magnets.

The EV and semiconductor nexus is also linked to a broad array of government funding initiatives, part and parcel of the wider techno-nationalist ethos that is reshaping global commerce. These initiatives include funding for the re-shoring of semiconductor fabrication, increased R&D spending and, by design, a focus on international partnerships aimed at achieving common cause regarding national and economic security. All of these activities involve large-scale investment.

As discussed previously, China's EV infrastructure is linked to a massive US$1.4 trillion spending initiative to build out 'smart city' wireless networks that will connect a vast array of EVs, AVs and other ubiquitous surveillance cameras and sensors.[16]

The U.S. is pursued subsidies, funding initiatives and incentive programmes that include a US$1 trillion bipartisan infrastructure bill designed to create one million new jobs in the automotive sector and add more than half a million new EV charging stations across the country. As in programmes in Europe and China, consumers who purchase EVs are offered generous rebates and tax credits.

Recall that in Europe, the U.S. and China, governments are further stoking demand for EVs by mandating the conversion of government vehicle fleets to EVs and pushing the logistics and transportation industry to do the same.

The E.U.'s 'Green Deal'—worth nearly €1.4 trillion—aims to make Europe carbon neutral by 2050. Even more than the U.S., European governments have emphasised the transition to EVs and are building localised manufacturing capabilities as soon as possible.

THE ROAD AHEAD

Going forward, geopolitical undercurrents are causing upstream supply chains in the EV sector to fragment into localised ecosystems in China, Europe and North America.

The growing nexus between semiconductors and EVs will follow a similar pattern. But due to a pervasive blurring of the line between semiconductors and other related technologies within the EV sector, techno-nationalism will present complex challenges to global trade of EVs.

A supply shortage of semiconductors combined with ambitious industrial policies is accelerating the formation of partnerships between semiconductor and automotive companies.

These evolving partnerships will face the increasing likelihood of expanding export controls and other restrictions on dual-use technologies.

This will impact the cross-border investment and acquisition aims of venture capitalists and large technology firms as they seek new opportunities for innovation and new business, including the process of developing state-of-the-art chips for EVs.

Going forward, strategic decoupling, re-shoring and ring-fencing in the EV sector for geopolitical purposes will align with localisation efforts to curtail carbon emissions and implement climate change countermeasures. The likely result is more public spending on electric vehicles.

Chapter 23

Food Security and Techno-Nationalism

Russia's invasion of Ukraine in 2022 exposed the fragility and vulnerabilities of the world's food supply system and intensified both food insecurity and food-competition. More broadly, the war hastened the international community's transition away from the cost-driven trade model and moved it toward a geo-economic trade approach. Already, the COVID pandemic had exposed the vulnerabilities of over-reliance on single countries and single sources for supply chains.

Just before the war, Russia and Ukraine were the breadbasket of much of the world. In 2020, the two countries together accounted for 30% of global wheat exports, 28% of maize exports, 23% of barley exports and more than 50% of trade in sunflower oil—a cooking staple used everywhere.[1]

As Russia blockaded food exports from Ukrainian ports on the Black Sea, millions of tonnes of grain were withheld from global circulation. From February to March 2022, the price of wheat jumped by more than 80%[2] and the G7 nations declared the war a global 'hunger crisis' in the making, especially for less developed countries.[3]

The Ukraine war exacerbated an already dire situation in Africa: Somalia, Libya and Tunisia received up to 80% of their grain from Ukraine and, going forward, could ill afford the consequences of a protracted war.[4] At the time of Russia's invasion, some 23 million people in Africa already suffered from extreme hunger. At the time of this writing, an extended drought in East Africa is in its fourth decade. A reduction in global food supplies continues to exacerbate these problems.

At the same time as the war, climate change continued to ravage the world's crops though a combination of heat waves, droughts and soil erosion.

Concerned by declining supplies, governments have raced to secure food for their own populations, further constraining the flow of food commodities across borders and driving prices higher.

FOOD PROTECTIONISM ON THE RISE

In the face of rising food prices, countries are resorting to wide-ranging protectionist trade policies, such as export quotas and export taxes, as governments seek to bolster local food supplies.

In May of 2022, five months into the Ukraine war, 35 nations had resorted to food protectionism.[5] Argentina blocked exports of soybean meal and oil, while Egypt and India banned exports of wheat. Malaysia barred the export of chickens to Singapore, and Indonesia temporarily banned the export of palm oil. Further pressures on food supplies could see similar bans reimposed.

Meanwhile, chemical fertilisers, essential to industrial-scale crop health and productivity, have also fallen under the shadow of food protectionism. Here, we see a nexus between chemical production and industrial capabilities and the successful growing of crops.

Prior to the war, Russia and China were the world's largest producers of fertiliser by value, and the two countries accounted for about 25% of fertiliser exports in 2019. Russia also controlled key ingredients needed to make fertiliser, such as urea (11% of world exports) and ammonium nitrate (48% of global exports). Together, Russia and Ukraine accounted for about a third of global exports of fertilisers made from nitrogen, phosphorus and potassium.[6]

Both Moscow and Beijing would go on to block exports of fertilisers to damp down surging prices at home, which, once again, confirmed the rule that when confronted with an existential crisis, nations behave in their own best interests.

Just after the war had begun, primary chemicals and gases required to make fertiliser saw staggering price increases: The price of potassium (potash) rose 134%. Liquid nitrogen rose 159%, and ammonia rose 210%.[7]

The prices of inputs needed for fertiliser strongly affect food security, and this has set the stage for global supply chain restructuring— even as the U.S. must import significant amounts of the primary ingredients needed for fertiliser, including potash.

This is clearly an area where supply chain de-risking and decoupling will continue. Consider that in 2024, some 75% of the world's supply of potash still came from just four countries: Canada, Belarus, Russia and China.

THE 'FRIEND-SHORING' OF FOOD SUPPLY CHAINS

As Moscow cut off supplies of fertilisers to its geopolitical opponents and non-cooperative client states, Washington and its allies grappled with placing Russian fertiliser producers on sanctions lists.

But this put the U.S. and its allies in a position where they would have to convince other countries not to buy Russian fertiliser, and, to do this, they would have to create a viable substitute for Russian fertiliser—which can only be done by increasing production elsewhere, preferably in friendly countries.

Recall that in 'friend-shoring', supply chains and ecosystems associated with strategic commodities must be ring-fenced within the safe geographical and geopolitical confines of trusted allies and partners.

But 'friend-shoring' brings its own set of complications. In the case of punishing Russia with sanctions, Washington had to figure out how to deal with Brazil. Brazil was buying a quarter of Russia's fertiliser exports and had begun to stockpile Russian fertiliser in anticipation of future sanctions. Brazilian buyers had been able to make those purchases through Russian Banks that had not been placed on a sanctions lists (many had been sparred by the US and E.U. lawmakers because they feared wider collateral damage to the international banking system).[8]

In response, Washington turned to its stalwart ally, Canada, the world's largest producer of potash. At the behest of Washington and Brussels, Canada moved quickly to increase potash production, and in 2022, the Canadian manufacturer Nutrien Ltd. boosted potash production from 1 million to 15 million tonnes.[9] This increased supply of fertiliser was then used to satisfy the U.S. and its allies, as well as provide Brazil with an alternative to Russian supplies.

TECHNOLOGY AND FOOD SECURITY

Figure 23.1   Editing the DNA of Plants for Hardier, Climate Change Resistant Food.

Climate change is creating big challenges for the world's food supply. Extended drought, heatwaves and wildfires, flooding, pestilence, soil erosion and water scarcity are all conspiring to constrain future crop productivity and continuity.

Despite well-intended pledges by governments to hold global warming to 1.5° Celsius above pre-industrial temperatures by the year 2050, these grim realities figure to continue and even accelerate. In fact, the 1.5°C target may be exceeded as early as 2027.[10]

Whether pursued independently or collectively with other countries, every nation's best hope for food security lies in successfully leveraging scientific innovation and technology along with sustainable agricultural practices.

Food security technology can be broken down into five key areas:

- Seed resilience;
- Precision agriculture technologies, sometimes involving a return to traditional farming;
- Vertical farming;
- Lab-grown protein; and
- Water treatment and conservation.

Scientists are engineering hardier, more resilient seeds for foods such as wheat, rice, maize and soybeans. To do so, the world's leading seed companies rely on ever-increasing R&D spending.

Increasingly, the world's leading agricultural companies look more like technology firms. In 2019, for example, the world's largest agrochemical companies had a market cap of US$233 billion and made massive investments in supercomputer-enabled R&D.[11] In 2021, the agricultural branch of German manufacturer Bayer alone invested US$2.1 billion in R&D for crop science.[12]

Today, the leading-edge science in R&D for food security is based on molecular genetics, plant biology/physiology, recombinant DNA, advanced genetic engineering and bioinformatics. Recent research has been remarkable, leading to, among other things, less water-dependent crops and faster, more profuse photosynthesis in leafy vegetables.

Market players in this domain include a dozen big companies from a small group of nations. Bayer is joined by BASF, another German multinational. Other notable players include American giant DOW, Japan-based Sumitomo, UPL in India, Nufarm in Australia and Adama in Israel.[13]

Originally formed in 2000 by Novartis Agribusiness and AstraZeneca Agrochemicals, Swiss-based Syngenta is also in this elite circle. In 2017, Syngenta was purchased for US$47 billion by state-owned ChemChina. Today, Syngenta is the world's largest agrichemical company, with access to the world's best R&D and scientists.

The purchase was an important milestone in China's efforts to bolster food security and was more significant because it had been struck on the eve of an escalation of tensions between China, Europe and the U.S. Had the sale been proposed a year or two later, Europe's regulators would not have approved.

As it stood, the E.U. only gave its approval after the U.S. Federal Trade Commission (FTC) was assured that ChemChina would divest itself of all shares held in any U.S.-based entities owned by Syngenta.[14]

The Syngenta deal was cleared by the U.S. Committee on Foreign Investment in United States (CFIUS), but at the time of this writing, CFIUS has been blocking virtually all attempted acquisitions of U.S. leading-edge technology by Chinese companies.[15]

PRECISION AGRICULTURE

Techno-nationalism and food security would seem an odd juxtaposition to some but the challenge of climate change and the vulnerability of extended international supply chains calls for innovative solutions. Increasingly, these have focused on precision tech-enabled agriculture, vertical farming, laboratory grown cellular protein, and water conservation.

Precision farming involves technologies such as artificial intelligence (AI), the Internet of Things (IoT) and data analytics to optimise seed selection and crop yields.[16] Such technologies help farmers gather, process and analyse increasingly detailed and accurate information on soil conditions, weather and crop responses, which helps them improve their productivity, product quality, profitability and sustainability.

There is a direct link between techno-nationalism and precision agriculture as governments become more active in state-backed technology advancement around AI.[17] Governments are sprinting ahead with national legislation to increase funding for national competitiveness around foundational and leading-edge technologies. A prime example is, as we have discussed, the CHIPS and Science Act passed by the U.S. Congress and signed by President Biden in 2022, allocating an increase of US$280 billion in funding for increased R&D, manufacturing, education and scientific research.[18] Future-proofing against climate change will receive increased amounts of attention and funding.

VERTICAL FARMING

An area of precision agriculture with vast future potential is vertical farming, which literally means growing food inside or on the outside of buildings, especially in high population density areas.

Vertical farming is attractive as a food security strategy because it allows for highly localised production. This, in turn, supports stakeholders in localised technology hubs, including start-ups and tech companies working in the agritech space. It also supports a 'circular economy' where resources can be sustainably sourced, recycled, reengineered and reused.

Vertical farming can eliminate long, strung-out supply chains. With vertical farming in place, local wholesalers, retailers and other institutions such as grocery stores, restaurants, schools and government institutions can have quick and reliable access to fresh and safely produced food.

Localising food production also mitigates the risks of non-transparent supply chains, where commodities are at risk of environmental and ethical transgressions. Even widespread fraud involving, for example, the adulteration of foodstuffs with exogenous fillers can be eliminated through localised vertical farming.

Public opposition to industrial-scale agriculture for genetically modified crops will also fuel a move to small-scale vertical farming and create a niche for locally grown organic foods. Conversely, vertical farming could give rise to hyper-specialised forms of designer food, such as hybrid fruits.

In vertical farming, wastewater can be efficiently treated. Furthermore, wastes from production processes such as palm oil operations can be directed into insect cultivation to be used later in localised aquaculture.[19]

With a population of 5.8 million and a landmass of 722 square kilometres, the small city-state of Singapore exemplifies the potential partnerships between governments and local enterprises to achieve vertical farming.

In 2021, Singapore imported 90% of its food. Going forward, the Singapore Food Agency (SFA) food resiliency division has been tasked with growing 30% of the country's leafy green vegetables, protein (hen eggs) and fish stocks in vertical farms.[20]

For both its egg protein and leafy green vegetables, SFA has entered public–private partnerships with a host of vertical farming companies, including first-mover firms such as Skygreens and Citiponics. Generous SFA grants have been augmented through a partnership with Singapore's Housing Development Board to offer growing space on the rooftops of public housing.[21]

LABORATORY-GROWN PROTEIN

Another growing area of agricultural R&D involves laboratory-grown animal protein, which could replace traditional and ecologically harmful farming. Stock raising contributes to deforestation and water wastage, as well as substantial emissions of CO_2 and methane.

Also referred to as petri-proteins or synthetic meat, lab-grown meat uses stem cell-based materials from animals. With the help of biotechnology, such proteins can replicate and grow the molecular structure of a steak, a lambchop or a fillet of chicken or fish.

Scaling up future production promises to bring down prices. Early investors in petri-protein start-ups include billionaires Richard Branson and Bill Gates.[22] Food industry stalwarts such as America's meat giant Tyson Foods are also investing heavily.[23]

By nature, lab-grown meat is a vertical farming enterprise. And due to its origins in biotechnology and precision agritech, it falls increasingly under the techno-nationalist spotlight of governments.

AGRITECH AND INDUSTRIAL ESPIONAGE

In 2013, in the first widely publicised incident of agritech espionage, Chinese national Mo Hailong was arrested for digging up genetically modified maize seeds on an Iowa farm. The seeds had been engineered by, among others, Dupont and Monsanto, both leading American agrichemical firms.

In China, Mo owned a company called Kings Nower Seed S&T Co Ltd, whose parent was a state-backed agritech company in Beijing:

Beijing Dabeinong Technology Group Co. Ltd. (DBN). In 2021, DBN partnered with another China-based seed technology company, Origin Agritech Ltd., to launch advanced R&D projects around genetically modified hybrid maize seeds.[24]

In 2018, Chinese national Weijiang Zhang was charged and later sentenced to 10 years in U.S. federal prison for the theft of rice samples from Ventria Bioscience, a biopharmaceutical research facility in Kansas. According to a U.S. Department of Justice brief, Bioscience spent years and more than US$75 million to develop its seeds and to craft methods for extracting proteins from rice for life-saving pharmaceutical purposes. This included developing applications to produce human serum albumin contained in blood and lactoferrin, an iron-building protein contained in human milk.[25]

Mr. Zhang, who worked at Ventria Bioscience as a researcher, passed rice samples to two visiting Chinese nationals, Liu Xuejun and Sun Yue, who worked for a Chinese agricultural research centre in Tianjin, China. Both Liu and Sun were stopped by U.S. Customs and Border Protection at the airport in Honolulu, where stolen rice samples were found in their luggage. Both were charged under the U.S. Theft of Trade Secrets Act.[26]

In 2019, Haitao Xiang, a former employee of agricultural giant Monsanto, was intercepted at Chicago's O'Hare Airport before boarding a one-way flight to China with a stolen proprietary algorithm.

Monsanto and its subsidiary, the Climate Corporation, had developed a digital, online farming software platform that was used by farmers to collect, store and visualise critical agricultural field data and increase and improve agricultural productivity for farmers. A critical component of the platform was a proprietary predictive algorithm referred to as the Nutrient Optimiser.[27]

As food security becomes increasingly intertwined with techno-nationalist policymaking, governments are taking action to ring-fence their homegrown agritech.

In 2021, for example, U.S. Senators Tom Cotton and Joni Ernst introduced the Agriculture Intelligence Measures (AIM) Act.[28] A reaction to rapidly rising levels of corporate espionage aimed at U.S. agriculture companies and research institutions, AIM is intended to establish an office of intelligence within the U.S. Department of Agriculture that would work closely with the wider intelligence community to protect U.S. agricultural IP and technology from foreign threats.

WATER SCARCITY AND TECHNOLOGY

Water scarcity issues are at the heart of the technology–food security feedback loop. As water scarcity imperils food security, technology must find innovative ways to do more with less water.

By the time the world's population reaches an expected 9.5 billion in the year 2050, global demand for freshwater is likely to increase by 20% to 30% over current levels. From 2018 to 2025 alone, however, global water demand for agriculture will have increased by a staggering 60%.[29]

Agritech has become increasingly focused on the efficient use and reuse of water, which, by default, has become a catalyst for the circular economy. Key challenges include wastewater treatment and filtration, residual water capture and desalination. Not surprisingly, large agrichemical companies such as BASF and Dow are investing heavily in water and wastewater treatment technology.[30]

Treating wastewater is vital for reuse, not only as a drinking source but also for localised agriculture and vertical farming. The building of wastewater treatment plants involves immense infrastructure.

The global wastewater treatment market is expected to exceed US$462 billion by the year 2030, up from US$250 billion in 2021.[31] Most of this growth is projected to be in Asia and Southeast Asia. The question is: How will leading countries use their expertise in water treatment infrastructure as both a tradeable economic asset and a geopolitical tool?

THE GEOPOLITICS OF WATER SCARCITY

As discussed previously, the construction of solar and wind farms in developing countries can be linked to the geopolitical agendas of state actors. Such is also the case with the politics of water. When it comes to global food security, these dynamics will continue to involve state and non-state actors.

In the world's poorest nations, the job of improving stressed water systems is linked directly to global food security. The task will fall largely on the big multilateral development banks such as the Asian Development Bank, the World Bank, the European Development Bank and the African Development Bank.

Encouraging more local food production through efficient water usage in Africa may help discourage climate-driven migration, which is raising tensions with destination countries and transit countries. Migration itself can be weaponised as well, as was demonstrated in a 2020 when Turkey threatened to release tens of thousands of Syrian refugees into Greece, an E.U. member.[32]

A further issue is whether governments will continue mainly to fund massive infrastructure projects through large and (often) state-backed companies or whether they may focus on smaller-scale local water projects.

Once again, as was the case with the EVs and semiconductors, open-sourced environments give promise to the latter if they can bring in a large variety of smaller specialised companies. By open sourcing the agritech environment, governments can avoid over-reliance on a few large agrochemical companies or specialised infrastructure companies, often with strong ties to their respective home states.

In recent years, countries along Southeast Asia's Mekong River have turned to Chinese state-owned enterprises to build hydroelectric dams and have learned painful lessons of geopolitics and water scarcity.

The possibility of ceding control of upstream water flows to a potentially hostile foreign state actor is not an optimal choice. Many now fear the possibility of Beijing literally turning off the tap through a system of 11 China-built dams and managed throughout the Mekong River system.[33]

In the context of technology, food and water security, and climate change, governments may consider relatively small-scale agritech investments targeted at small, local stakeholders. Smaller projects could prove less environmentally damaging to the biodiversity and natural ecosystems of the world's river systems.[34]

Individual states and alliances of states pursuing their own interests are likely to influence how secure global value chains are restructured. Like energy security or semiconductor security, food security remains an important element of national security.

PART IV

Innovation, Academia, Alliances and Diplomacy

Chapter 24

Techno-Nationalism on Campus

On a frigid Massachusetts morning, in January of 2020, Professor Charles Lieber, a Harvard University nano-scientist was arrested on charges that he failed to disclose his ties to China's educational establishment. Professor Lieber had also been the chair of Harvard's Chemistry and Chemical Biology Department.

He was convicted less than a year later in a U.S. court, in December 2021.

Mr. Lieber was alleged to have been a 'Strategic Scientist' at Wuhan University of Technology from 2012–2015, where, under China's 'Thousand Talents' program, he was recruited and paid US$50,000 per month and allocated US$1.5 million to establish a research lab. The lab was tasked with applying for research patents under the name of Wuhan University of Technology.[1]

The focus of the research was, allegedly, the development of nanowire-based lithium-ion batteries for high-performance electric vehicles.[2]

The Lieber incident was a microcosm of the twenty-first-century great-power rivalry between the U.S. and China, which has found its way onto college campuses. As part of this phenomenon, a number of trends are changing how universities conduct research, teach and, how they interact with international students, faculty and institutions.

One trend involves research-related intellectual property. Universities receiving government funding for research are being required to shield sensitive intellectual property (IP). Academics are being tasked with establishing 'security programs' in which they must identify situations where 'controlled unclassified information' (CUI) could have national security implications.

There is a trade-off between accepting or restricting foreign students from countries of concern, like China, into leading-edge research. But enforcing a research security regime has it costs. It is expensive, from a resource perspective, to enforce a proper security process, and, secondly, because implementing such a process will impede open, unrestricted collaboration, the quality of the end-product may end up being diminished.

Another trend: governments are scaling up funding for public–private partnerships (PPPs) with the aim of bringing together top businesses, universities and government agencies to stoke innovation and enhance national competitiveness. The creation of innovation hubs around microelectronics (especially semiconductor-related), artificial intelligence (AI), biotech and other key strategic technologies reflect the wider paradigm in Washington.

For universities, as more federally funded academic R&D activities occur on the physical premises of private companies, faculty and students have become increasingly susceptible to export control processes, which companies take more seriously than most universities.

Finally, because of national security concerns, an increasing amount of R&D surrounding strategic technologies is shifting to programmes funded and directly supervised by national defence establishments, such as the Defence Advanced Research Projects Agency (DARPA).

Because of all of this, academic decoupling is underway amongst American and other foreign universities, as policymakers in the U.S.

and elsewhere look to ring-fence strategic R&D and confine knowledge sharing and innovation among trusted participants.

THE CHANGING ACADEMIC LANDSCAPE

Around 2019, U.S. officials from the Federal Bureau of Investigation (FBI) began begun visiting American universities such as the Massachusetts Institute of Technology (MIT), University of California, Berkeley and others, to share unclassified information about specific Chinese research institutions and companies alleged to have ties to Chinese intelligence agencies.

In 2021, FBI director Christopher Wray warned that Chinese economic espionage had reached a 'new level' and was 'more brazen, more damaging than ever before'. He urged universities to be vigilant and take steps to protect their research.

Not long after, *The New Yorker* magazine reported that the FBI had been pressuring universities to monitor Chinese students and scholars on their campuses, particularly those affiliated with certain Chinese institutions.

Talk in university board rooms turned to the subject of R&D ringfencing. Among other things, this requires the severing of ties with designated Chinese universities, the cessation of funding from donors and the careful screening and restriction of students and scholars regarding research programmes and projects.

The question is how far will law enforcement agencies go to enforce these new regimes and will they deploy more resources for surveillance?

In the 2022/23 academic year, there were over one million foreign students from 120 different countries studying at American universities. The largest group was made up of Chinese students, numbering just under 300,000. Like most academics, I would argue that the presence of these students and scholars is beneficial to learning and research environments. Beyond that, foreign students enrich local economies and industry, particularly if they stay on after graduation to join the local workforce or start their own business enterprises.

But the U.S.–China hybrid cold war is an unpleasant reality. No matter the benefits of a globalised academic landscape, universities remain prime targets for state-sponsored espionage and intellectual property (IP) theft, not to mention narrative wars and influence campaigns.

As education increasingly becomes an export, institutions of higher learning and research in North America, Europe and, notably, Australia are at the forefront of research across virtually all the 12 key twenty-first-century technologies from AI to quantum science, putting them directly in the techno-nationalist spotlight.

As American universities avail themselves of the funding from, for example, the CHIPS and Science Act, they also must deal with the fine print, which restricts them from investing and sharing leading edge IP with designated entities in China and elsewhere.

ACADEMIC RING-FENCING

The U.S. law enforcement establishment has resorted to a multi-pronged approach to dealing with academia. Academic institutions face an expanding set of rules and compliance standards, including:

- Export controls on software, online databases, computer code and other IP.
- The placement of foreign partner academic institutions on restricted entity lists.
- The blacklisting of academics and students from specific nations.
- Unofficial and targeted distribution of enrolment based on students' countries of origin, and,
- The reduction or prohibition of funding from blacklisted foreign entities.

June 2020 saw the beginning of an uptick in the sanctioning of academic institutions, when the U.S. blacklisted the Harbin Institute of Technology (HIT), often referred to as 'the MIT of China'. The effects of restricted entity status were felt immediately: HIT faculty and students no longer had access to critical simulation and research software from the U.S., such as MATLAB, which is used extensively in R&D programmes around the world.[3]

Other ramifications of the blacklist included the severing of exchange programmes between HIT and the University of Arizona and the University of California, Berkeley. More broadly, the placement of HIT on the restricted entity list affected its other linkages with Chinese academic institutions in the wider network of research being funded by the Chinese government, as well as HIT's relationship with the People's Liberation Army (PLA).

The possibility that other top institutions in China could end up on Washington's target list makes the case for pre-emptive de-risking and decoupling by existing partners in the U.S. and around the world. This is an unpleasant but very real possibility for many academics and their institutions.

Consider a situation where China–U.S. relations experience further deterioration, and Tsinghua University and Peking University, China's flagship schools, were to be put on the restricted entities list. This would have a ripple effect on academic programmes and, by extension, executive education and corporate sponsorship of student exchanges across an entire spectrum of disciplines.

MIDDLE-COUNTRY UNIVERSITIES

Washington's efforts to control outflows of restricted IP and technology are complicated by the activities of universities in middle countries.

Consider the case of King Abdullah University of Science and Technology (KAUST) in Saudi Arabia. KAUST entered collaborative partnerships with the Chinese University of Hong Kong–Shenzhen (CUHK-SZ) and the Shenzhen Research Institute of Data to build and train a large language model (LLM) known as AceGPT.

The aim was to create an LLM that would equal or surpass OpenAI's ChatGPT or Google's Bard, two of the world's leading LLMs; thus, AceGPT required access to leading-edge generative AI and super-computing capabilities, which, in turn, required access to leading-edge American AI chips.

Such AI chips, which enable powerful graphics processing units (GPUs), were supplied almost exclusively by two American companies, Nvidia and Advanced Micro Devices (AMD), and their technology was subject to U.S. export controls.

In 2023, as reported by the *Financial Times*, Chinese academics made up almost 10% of KAUST's faculty, as did about 35% of the university's post-doctoral students, who conducted much of the R&D. Thus, it could be assumed that KAUST was functioning as a backdoor transfer technology to otherwise restricted entities in China.

Washington's attempts to tackle export control scenarios playing out on foreign college campuses calls for adept techno-diplomacy. This task becomes more challenging when the parties involved are middle countries with linkups to third parties such as China. What happens if a similar scenario plays out in Singapore, or in Canada, or in Australia? Situations like this become more complicated when researchers at numerous universities are involved in extensive collaborative research. What happens when one partner university is shut down for an export controls violation in a wider collaborative network?

From a risk mitigation standpoint, most academic institutions will need to choose their research partners more carefully, which, essentially, means the trend will involve—as with supply chain risk mitigation—friend-shoring. This, then, will continue to bifurcate the global research landscape. Academic institutions within these friend-shoring alliances will coalesce around a framework of rules and behaviours regarding technology transfer.

AI and semiconductors, of course, are at the heart of these endeavours. Thus, middle countries will find themselves facing difficult choices as Washington doubles down on technology controls.

STUDENT NATIONALITIES

There is merit to the argument that expanding U.S. export controls will diminish the collective brain power available for leading-edge R&D activities in the U.S. and elsewhere.

After decades of fostering a highly internationalised postgraduate educational system, the U.S. is only just beginning to feel the effects of techno-nationalism on campus. This comes after historic changes in the composition of student populations.

Consider that in computer science, in 1995, there were nearly equal numbers of full-time U.S. and international graduate students in American graduate programmes. Between 1995 and 2015, the number of U.S. students increased by 45%, from 8,627 to 12,539, but the number of international students soared by 480%, from 7,883 to 45,970. During the same period, the number of U.S. graduate students in electrical engineering (EE) decreased by 17%, while the number of foreign students rose by 270%.[4] Taking all higher education into account, the number of Chinese students enrolled in the U.S. rose by 276%, from 98,235 in academic year 2008/09 to 369,548 in 2018/19.[5]

Foreign students are integral to research, innovation and job creation in the U.S. Given geopolitical inconveniences, the question, then, is whether there will be a shift away from foreign students of Chinese origin towards students from other countries, such as those from the Indian subcontinent.

Indeed, in the 2022/23 academic year, inbound Indians became the top source of international students in the U.S., outpacing incoming students from China. This represented a 35% surge in Indian enrolments over the previous year, while enrolments of Chinese students remained flat, according to the *Chronicle of Higher Education*.

The big question is, going forward, whether U.S. and other world-renowned universities could effectively 'de-risk' rather than decouple, academically, similiar to what policymakers and corporate officials hope to achieve with strategic supply chains.

CHINA'S THOUSAND TALENTS PROGRAMME AND ACADEMIC ESPIONAGE

Tapping into the global reservoir of academic talent is a central pillar of techno-nationalism in China. As part of their Made in China 2025 plan, Beijing's central planners are tying the establishment of key industry clusters to centres of innovation, led by the world's best scholars.[6]

Much of the success of China's R&D capabilities is tied to its Thousand Talents Programme, which the Chinese central planners established in 2008 with the objective of absorbing top intellectual capital from around the world.[7] Accessing the best overseas talent has been vital to Beijing's efforts to acquire foreign knowledge and IP and to build its own research capabilities. The program includes sending the county's most talented students and faculty abroad, to the world's best universities, to learn and to return to China with leading-edge experience and knowledge.

To some Chinese observers, however, the Thousand Talents Programme is linked to the Chinese state's corporate espionage and IP acquisition efforts, which include the use of rewards, deception, coercion and theft.[8] These suspicions have been compounded by China's National Intelligence and Security laws, which require Chinese citizens and organisations to render assistance to the state security and intelligence organisations when asked, no matter where they might be, including overseas, in the employ of a foreign entity or at academic institutions.

In January 2023, the Swedish newspaper *Dagens Nyheter* reported that Chinese students studying in Sweden funded with Chinese state money had been required to sign loyalty pledges to the Chinese Communist Party (CCP).

Consequently, Chinese academics and students working and studying in the U.S. have fallen under increased suspicion. This is the most unfortunate form of collateral damage. Often, these students must face suspicion both abroad as well as when they return to China, as some in their homeland accuse them of being influenced negatively while studying abroad.

As we have seen, U.S. law enforcement agencies such as the FBI have increased their focus on China's access to the American educational system, specifically the way Chinese institutions and citizens (and other foreign nationals from countries of concern) obtain access to critical research.

Consider that, at the time of the Charles Lieber case, a Chinese graduate student, Yanqing Ye, was arrested for failing to disclose she was a lieutenant in the PLA when she gained a non-immigrant visa to conduct studies at Boston University in the Department of Physics, Chemistry and Biomedical Engineering.

According to federal documents, authorities found evidence that she had accessed U.S. military websites, researched U.S. military projects and compiled information for the PLA on two U.S. citizens with expertise in robotics and computer science.[9]

Incidents such as these underscore the challenges facing both academic institutions and public officials as they adjust to the U.S.–China hybrid cold war environment.

RULE FRAMEWORKS AND RESEARCH SECURITY

The academic community finds itself having to work with law enforcement agencies to implement new oversight procedures to address the challenges of U.S.–China techno-academic linkages.

Authorities are requesting more transparency from universities. This has included the establishment of foreign sponsorship review committees that evaluate research agreements with foreign entities regarding potential national security concerns.

Other forms of oversight include:

- Implementation of risk assessment audits conducted by third parties.
- Implementation of due-diligence practices (like 'know your customer' (KYC) standards in the banking industry) that apply to faculty and graduate students conducting applied and specialised research in sensitive or strategic areas.
- Increased enforcement of research integrity standards for faculty, students and entire academic institutions, as well as more stringent penalties for violators.
- Diversification of foreign student populations to avoid over-reliance on tuition revenue or other funding from any particular source.
- Outright rejection of funding from potentially hostile entities, both state and non-state.

In the U.S. the National Science Foundation (NSF), a government agency, reviews thousands of funding proposals and dispenses billions of dollars in research grants each year. This comes with obligations for beneficiary universities.

Grant recipients must not only acknowledge that the transfer of IP can create national security issues. They must also create processes that can identify and differentiate between so called controlled unclassified information (CUI) and other non-sensitive technologies.

The NSF allows academic institutions to police themselves and gives wide latitude to decision makers when it comes to balancing their own needs regarding the contributions of foreign students and academics versus the costs of restricting access to research.

A slightly more succinct roadmap for self-policing research can be found in National Security Presidents Memorandum 33 (NSPM 33), signed in 2020 by President Trump. NSPM 33 lays out the core areas of an on-campus security program regarding the protection sensitive IP.

NSPM 33 stipulates that any research institution receiving at least US$50 million of federal money, annually over two years (some interpretations say $50m *per year* for two years) must establish a credible research security program that addresses, among other things, cybersecurity and social engineering threats, insider threat awareness, export controls, foreign travel security (protecting IP on devices and communications).

There are, of course, considerable costs and the need for resources to implement these things. This topic, then, figures to generate a lot of discussion and planning at universities in the coming years. There figures to be an influx of compliance experts and outside security consultants to college campuses.

SCREENING THE SOURCES OF FUNDING

When people and institutions give funding to academic institutions, they sometimes demand the recipient reciprocate by espousing the funder's world views, narratives and political biases. This has been a theme that has been picked up, with great zeal, by the international media.

Many would argue that media watchdogs, not internal resources at universities, have helped to maintain a degree of accountability in academia—at least in countries that enjoy press freedoms.

An event at my alma mater, the London School of Economics (LSE), illustrates this process. In 2021, the *Financial Times* (FT) reported on LSE faculty's concerns that the school's heavy reliance on funding from China (and tuition from Chinese students) was influencing the school's curriculum and overall learning environment.

Faculty members called attention to a proposed China Studies programme that was to be funded by Eric Li, a Chinese venture capitalist that the FT described as staunchly pro-Beijing. They claimed that financial considerations were affecting the hiring of academics who were outspoken about issues such as human rights issues abuses by the Chinese government.

They further argued that such developments tended to restrict academic freedoms and resulted in an environment of self-censorship, and they called for greater transparency in university decision-making. As a result, university officials put the proposed programme on hold.

LSE faculty had good reason for concern. There were plenty of cautionary tales to draw from. In 2019, the Chinese embassy in Prague, the Czech Republic, surreptitiously financed a course at the Charles University, the most prestigious university in the country, with the aim of spreading the official Chinese party narrative regarding the Belt and Road Initiative (BRI)—a course that many external observers considered to be propaganda.[10] The operation also included funding for a series of Charles University conferences on the subject of the BRI, designed to promote CCP content.

In 2023, British TV network *Channel 4 News* aired a documentary that alleged that the University of Nottingham had closed its School of Contemporary Chinese Studies in 2016 because the former head of the institute, Professor Steve Tsang, was an outspoken critic of the CCP. According to a report in *The Guardian*, the move had come in response to pressure from Beijing.

Of course, all governments attempt to influence how they are perceived on the world stage and in the classroom, and they devote resources towards public relations, some of which are inevitably aimed at encouraging specific curricula.

But as the issue of Chinese funding of Western universities continues to raise problems, university administrators everywhere are on a collision course with China hawks and techno-nationalists.

THE MILITARY AND ACADEMIA

National security concerns involve an increasing range of technology and R&D in such areas as AI-powered autonomous systems, quantum computers for codebreaking and cryptography, hypersonics and other advanced weapons systems, advanced materials, supercomputing, stealth, energy systems and biotechnology.

As these technologies are increasingly designated critical to national security, public–private partnerships (PPP) anchored in academia are increasingly migrating to the confines of the U.S. military–industrial complex. Consequently, defence-related R&D is now at its highest level since the end of the Cold War.[11]

Government research agencies such as the Defence Advanced Research Projects Agency (DARPA) offer significant funding and resources for projects that provide universities and individual academics with greater incentives to conduct research in more secure environments.

Not surprisingly, semiconductors continue to be a focal point of defence-related R&D. When Japan overtook the U.S. as the world's most advanced semiconductors producer in the 1980s, DARPA played a key role in expanding American R&D efforts from lab-to-fab, working with the top research universities and semiconductor producers.

Alongside the CHIPS and Science Act, in 2022–2023, DARPA provided almost US$3 billion in funding for advanced microchip design through the Electronics Resurgence Initiative. It provided billions more for stealth-related quantum-enhanced sensing and imaging through its Multidisciplinary University Research Initiative (MURI).

Other DARPA programmes that continue to attract carefully screened academics: The Underwater Prototype Development Programme

(UPD), which develops next-generation unmanned underwater vehicles (UUVs), and the Hypersonic Technology Initiative (HTI), which develops hypersonic weapons and defence systems, and electric aircraft propulsion that develops electric propulsion technologies for next-generation aircraft.

Still other DARPA initiatives include distributed and intermittent power systems for resilient power grids for military uses, advanced materials with memory (materials that can 'heal' and return to their earlier configuration) and materials for extreme hot and cold environments.

One fascinating DARPA programme is its Molecular Machines and Biomolecular (MOMAD), which involves to the building of synthetic machines on the molecular level.

These DARPA programmes employ talented academics from many universities. In the area of stealth-related quantum sensing, for example, participating institutions include the California Institute of Technology (Caltech), The University of Pennsylvania, the Georgia Institute of Technology, Duke University and the University of Southern California (USC). Corporate partners include Lockheed Martin, Northrop Grumman, Raytheon Technologies, Boeing and General Dynamics.

For DARPA's semiconductor initiatives, the list includes, among many, MIT, Stanford University, University of California, Berkeley, University of Texas at Austin and Cornell University. Corporate participants include Intel, Global Foundries, Taiwan Semiconductor Manufacturing Company (TSMC), Samsung and Micron Technology.

DARPA's selective access programmes necessarily restrict involvement in a variety of research projects to U.S. citizens and permanent residents only. U.S. export control regulations further restrict the transfer of sensitive technology and knowledge to certain foreign nationals, thus limiting the types of research projects open to foreign students.

From a techno-nationalist perspective, funding such as the CHIPS and Science Act and initiatives such as DARPA is not simply a matter of national security. Advocates also expect them to yield significant technological and economic spillovers in sectors from medicine to communications, AI and logistics.

Nevertheless, the techno-nationalist aims of legislation like the CHIPS Act, combined with the DARPA model of participation in R&D in sensitive areas, will challenge universities' IP protection practices and frameworks.

Chapter 25

Chip Schools

Purdue University, in Indiana, has long been known as one of America's engineering hotbeds. NASA has a history of recruiting engineers from Purdue and some 27 of its astronauts claim it as their alma mater, including Neil Armstrong, the first man to walk on the moon, in 1969, and Eugene Cernan, the last man to walk on the moon, in 1972.

But in the Spring of 2024, the university celebrated perhaps its biggest milestone: South Korea's SK hynix Inc., the world's sixth-largest semiconductor company, announced it would build a US$4 billion semiconductor fabrication facility at Purdue Research Park in West Lafayette. When completed, the new plant will do advanced 'packaging' of high bandwidth memory chips, the kind of chips needed for the most advanced uses of artificial intelligence (AI). (See Chapter 7 for a refresher on the semiconductor fabrication process).

The SK hynix win occurred in tandem with the rollout of the CHIPS and Science Act, in 2022, the same year that Purdue launched its Semiconductor Degree Program, which features a range of core and elective courses across the semiconductor spectrum.

In the fall of 2023, its engineering and science programs, along with Purdue's Polytechnic Institute, claimed almost 22,000 undergrads and around 7,000 graduate students pursuing master's and doctorate degrees.

Through a partnership with Ivy Tech Community College, another 13,000 students are enrolled in advanced manufacturing, engineering and applied science. Students can access Purdue semiconductor-related curriculum at some 40 different locations and online.

Purdue's courses cover everything from 'Atomic-Scale Engineering of Semiconductor Materials and Devices,' to 'Emerging logic, Memory and Interconnected Technologies', which draw growing numbers of students.

Early on in their studies, underclassmen undergo basic training on semiconductors. One programme, 'Summer Training, Awareness and Readiness for Semiconductors (STARS) is an 8-week intensive course, which the university introduced with the aim of attracting an enrolment of 100. On the same day the programme was announced, it received more than 700 applications.

At the request of its industry partners, Purdue has pushed the semiconductor educational process down into the high school classroom, through its so-called READI programmes, which place an emphasis on science, technology, engineering and math (STEM). Everything is backed by CHIPS Act funding, and corporate sponsorship.

PURDUE'S SILICON MOMENT

Purdue's 'silicon moment' marks an inflection point. Mung Chiang, Purdue's president, who has a background in semiconductors, likes to refer to the school as 'the most consequential university at the most consequential time.' He has a regular audience with the U.S. President and his advice is frequently sought by cabinet-level staff and other decision makers.

The university's chip programme has forged direct linkages to every consequential semiconductor company, from ASML to TSMC, across every facet of the semiconductor value chain. Its corporate partners include a who's-who from the chip landscape such as Applied Materials, Intel, NVIDA, Micron, Qualcomm, Synopsis and many others.

Ambitious students partake in internships and hands-on workshops in all of them, and the school co-opts engineers and management from these same companies to create curricula and to teach. CEOs, meanwhile, appeal directly to Purdue's academics regarding their chronic shortages of talent, constantly refining the job requirements awaiting the next batch of engineers, physicists and other skilled workers.

Just down the road, on the defence side of the house, Purdue is working with the Naval Surface Warfare Center (Crane Division), as part of a wider national network of government, academia and private industry consisting of 8 regional hubs around the country.

Internationally, meanwhile, Purdue's chip school diplomacy has formed collaborative partnerships with universities in the Netherlands and Belgium, South Korea, Japan, Taiwan, India and Costa Rica.

Should there be any doubt as to the geopolitical relevance of America's nascent chip schools to the nation, consider that in September of 2022, the U.S. Secretary of State, Antony Blinken, and U.S. Commerce Secretary, Gina Raimondo, visited the campus to exclusively talk national chip strategy. They stressed the importance of universities to the success of the CHIPS Act and the key role of universities as ambassadors to other chip nations.

Indeed, earlier that year, President Mung Chiang and his team travelled to Japan, to the G7 summit, where they met with chip school representatives from other key nations. There they agreed, with input from their governments and from cooperate interests, to sign up to the UPSTART program, an international network of chip schools, which I will discuss, later.

Another force of nature behind the rise of Purdue's chip school is Professor Mark Lundstrom. When I first spoke with him, he was the acting dean of Purdue's School of Electrical and Computer Engineering. But I was more intrigued with one of his other titles: Chief Semiconductor Officer.

A significant portion of Lundstrom's job involves supporting Mung Chiang's high-profile mission. Over the three decades that Lundstrom has taught and conducted research at Purdue, his work has been cited tens of thousands of times. But since the passage of the CHIPS Act, his focus has been on relationship building, chip diplomacy and seeing to the expansion of the 'Silicon Crossroads' in Indiana.

The CHIPS Act is a catalyst for private investors and is generating a positive feedback loop. Among other things, it helped fund the university's Birck Nanotechnology Center, which inspired Purdue to spread around another US$100 million of its own money throughout its semiconductor curriculum.

This kind of 'If-you-build-it-they-will-come' approach made the university more attractive to its first-mover investors, such as MediaTek Inc., a leading fabless chip company from Taiwan. In 2023, Media Tek announced plans to build a chip design centre in Discovery Park, right next to Purdue.[1]

Another early breakthrough came from the American company Skywater Technology, a legacy pure play chip manufacturer that is setting up an R&D centre at Purdue and a new fab in nearby Minnesota. All of this was contributing to the growing critical mass of the Silicon Crossroads, and it paved the way for the big SK hynix investment.

In the Spring of 2024, Purdue convened a CHIPS summit in Washington D.C. appropriately called 'CHIPS for America: Execute for Global Success,' (last part in caps) which I attended in my role at the National University of Singapore. The event, which was held in the Russel Senate Building, featured around 175 people representing dozens of chip companies, universities, government agencies, trade-related and non-governmental organizations. Clearly, the CHIPS Act was animating the U.S. semiconductor landscape.

THE RISE OF THE NATIONAL CHIP HUBS

In America, the U.S. Undersecretary of Defence for Research and Engineering (USD-R&D) has been tasked with funding and shepherding a network of eight so-called 'Microelectronics Commons Hubs' across the country. With funding at around a quarter billion dollars, in 2023, the Commons has established eight regional hubs to support the Department of Defence (DoD).

We should not overlook the relevance of a defence-designated branch of government overseeing the expansion of chip schools, which, once again, reminds us of the dual-use nature (both commercial and military) of semiconductors.

Purdue University represents one of these eight national microelectronics hubs, in the Silicon Crossroads. Other hubs are in the Northeastern U.S., North Carolina, Southern California, the Southwest, Northern California and the Pacific Northwest, and in Ohio.

The idea of these hubs, then, is to spread around the wealth (both money and knowledge) and pull in as many universities, commercial partners and local governments into the ecosystem as possible. Each Hub includes an academic cross-section of major universities, junior colleges and trade schools.

Semiconductor curricula, meanwhile, from these endeavours are spilling over into other interdisciplinary fields such as AI, advanced materials sciences, nanotechnology and other STEM-related fields.

From a techno-nationalist perspective, chip schools have three objectives.

Firstly, they must produce talented individuals that can meet the demands of semiconductor industry as well as other STEM fields.

Secondly, these chip schools must become the nuclei within commercial ecosystems, where semiconductor value chains generate new business opportunities and grow new markets.

Thirdly, chip schools form the foundation of international cooperation between academic institutions, mostly in the Group of five leading semiconductor countries. Other countries, including Australia, India, Canada, Germany and Singapore, are also seeking greater cooperation through chip-related academic partnerships.

CHIP SCHOOL WEST: ARIZONA STATE UNIVERSITY

In 2022, when TSMC, the world's largest pure play fabricator of advanced semiconductors, announced it was investing US$40 billion for the rapid construction of two new manufacturing sites in Phoenix, the world took notice.

That same year, Intel, the America's semiconductor integrated design manufacturer (IDM), announced it would also sink US$30 billion into its Arizona complex of advanced chip manufacturing sites, with co-funding by Brookfield, an asset management company.

Since then, both TSMC and Intel, along with their partners have upped their investments to around US$60 billion each. This concentrated amount of investment in fabrication facilities and R&D centres, which will draw generous funding through CHIPS Act grant money and tax incentives, is magnitudes larger than anywhere else in the country.

Why Arizona?

One reason is the proximity to Arizona State University's (ASU) Ira A. Fulton School of Engineering in Tempe—the largest engineering school in the U.S., with some 30,000 students enrolled.[2] Of these, around 7,000 students were enrolled in microelectronics-related fields.[3]

ASU is also in one of the eight regional hubs in the national Microelectronics Commons initiative. The amount of semiconductor money flowing into Arizona—both from government coffers and private investors—has made ASU a highly capable and growing pipeline of talent.

Ever since Motorola established a research lab in Phoenix in 1949, ASU has been gradually expanding its engineering faculty. As ASU's long-term relationships with Motorola, Intel and other resident tech companies strengthened (and now TSMC), so did the collaborative design of ASU's chip curriculum as students gained access to both on-campus and on-site learning environments.

ASU eventually bought one of Motorola's R&D facilities and turned it into the ASU Macro Technology Works.[4] By 2023, at least 150 faculty members that were teaching courses related to microelectronics.

Funding from the CHIPS and Science Act clearly influenced TSMC's and Intel's decisions to base their leading-edge facilities in Phoenix.

ASU worked hard to align private resources with strategic government investments and persuaded the state government to push for the establishment of a New Economic Initiative (NEI) led by three public universities: ASU, the University of Arizona and North Arizona University, all of which are receiving funding to develop talent pipelines.[5]

Like similar investments at Purdue and other universities TSMC's and Intel's combined investments of over US$120 billion in Arizona serves Washington's national security and economic objectives and represent a positive-sum outcome for the parties involved, on a national, state, and local level.

ACADEMIC CROSS BORDER FRIEND-SHORING

Washington's paradigm shift on China has led to a purposeful restructuring of global value chains, requiring the development of strategic partnerships with reliable allies. As a result, a growing number of cross-border academic partnerships are focused on joint research and talent development in the field of semiconductors.

I became aware of the extent of these efforts while doing research for a report that I co-wrote with Robert Clark and Bronte Munro of the Australia Strategic Policy Institute (ASPI). We called the report *Australia's Semiconductor Moonshot: Securing semiconductor talent.* I rely here on much of what I wrote in that report to describe the phenomenon of academic friend-shoring.

The U.S. and Japan have steadily strengthened their partnership around mutual security and geopolitical interests. That partnership is now focusing on the development of resilient semiconductor supply chains, which is leading in turn to the establishment of public–private partnerships between academia, corporations and governments to foster the right kind of STEM-related talent pool.[6]

As in the U.S., Japanese manufacturers offshored much of their chip fabrication in recent decades, and Tokyo is equally keen to relocate facilities to Japan. At the same time, Japanese officials recognise the strategic benefits of aligning its policies with those of the U.S. They are therefore working to foster PPPs between U.S. and Japanese universities and businesses not just in the semiconductor industry but in other STEM areas as well.[7]

In May 2023, the American semiconductor producer Micron Technology Inc.—the largest foreign investor in Japan over the previous five years—announced the launch of a U.S.–Japan University Partnership for Workforce Advancement and Research & Development in Semiconductors (UPWARDS).[8]

Micron committed US$60 million over five years to develop curricula and create a high-skill workforce, with funding to be disbursed to 11 participating universities in the U.S. and Japan. The goal is to provide 5,000 students per year with in-classroom learning and hands-on experience in manufacturing and production environments such as memory-chip clean rooms.[9]

Participating American universities include Purdue Boise State University, Rochester Institute of Technology, Rensselaer Polytechnic Institute, the University of Washington and Virginia Tech. Japanese participants include Hiroshima University, Kyushu University, Nagoya University, Tokyo Institute of Technology and Tohoku University.[10]

Academic friend-shoring with strategic partners in key countries represents the new normal. Take, for example, Purdue University, a UPWARDS member, and its signing of a separate agreement in May of 2023 as a key academic collaborator with the Indian government and the India Semiconductor Mission (ISM).[11]

One of the defining objectives of the UPWARDS initiative is the participants' commitment to diversity, equality and inclusion (DEI), which places an emphasis on drawing in students from traditionally underrepresented portions of the population within the tech sector, namely women and minorities.[12]

These values, along with underlying geopolitical imperatives, were on display at the agreement's signing ceremony, presided over by U.S. Secretary of State Antony Blinken and Japan's Minister of Education, Keiko Nagoaka.[13]

Overall, Micron announced investments of US$3.6 billion in Japan, which will include the installations of extreme ultraviolet (EUV) lithography to make the next generation of dynamic random access memory (DRAM), called '1-gamma chips', at its Hiroshima plant.[14]

The engagement of the U.S. and Japanese governments encouraged further investment, with IBM announcing US$100 million investment over 10 years in a quantum computing partnership with the University of Tokyo and the University of Chicago. IBM's investment is aimed at developing the world's first quantum-centric supercomputer powered by 100,000 qubits, a technology reliant on advanced semiconductors.[15]

IBM is also a founding member of RAPIDUS, a Japanese government-backed initiative established in 2022 with the ambitious goal of reviving the country's once-dominant semiconductor industry. This project aims to develop and mass-produce cutting-edge 2-nm logic chips in the latter half of this decade, potentially competing with industry leaders like Taiwan's TSMC.

Google, meanwhile, announced a US$50 million investment over 10 years in a partnership with the University of Tokyo and the University of Chicago, focusing on the development of a fault-tolerant quantum computer.[16]

All of these initiatives rely heavily on collaborative curriculum development and a belief in shared values.

TAIWAN'S GLOBAL TALENT DEVELOPMENT STRATEGY

Taiwan remains the world's semiconductor fabrication hotbed. It is no surprise, then, that Taiwanese universities Chip Schools have also been working to expand the global talent pool through international academic cooperation. For example, the National Yang Ming Chiao Tung University signed cooperation and student exchange agreements with four Indian Institutes of Technology (IITs), including IIT-Bombay (Mumbai), IIT-Delhi, IIT-Kanpur and IIT-Madras.[17]

National Taiwan University (NTU) has increased its scholarship programmes for visiting students from Eastern European countries and actively recruits prospective engineers and STEM-focused specialists from Lithuania, Poland, the Czech Republic and Slovakia.[18]

The perception in Taiwan is that many foreign students eventually return to Taiwan with their expertise or will sign on immediately with Taiwanese companies that are embedding into new global ecosystems.[19] Academic friend-shoring is therefore seen as a positive-sum game that increases talent among allies rather than draining Taiwan of much-needed talent.[20]

When it comes to issues of national and economic security, there are exceptions. State-backed attempts by Chinese semiconductor companies to hire or poach Taiwanese engineers and tech talent have met with stiff resistance from Taiwan's government and civil society.

Taiwan has passed laws that restrict China's access to talent through the amendment of its National Security Act to list the poaching of talent from leading-edge industries as a form of economic espionage.[21] This was singularly aimed at China. An official statement from Taiwan's Ministry of Justice stated that the amendments were necessary to. . . . 'better protect the competitiveness of our high-tech industries. . . and to prevent the trade secrets in key national technologies from being infringed by hostile foreign forces and their proxies'.[22]

A WORLDWIDE SHORTAGE OF TALENT

Despite the rise of chip schools, it is a fact that they may not put a dent in the deficit of talent facing the semiconductor industry.

According to Deloitte, the consultancy firm, by 2030, the global semiconductor sector will require at least one million more skilled workers as demand for chips surges 80% above 2021 levels.[23]

In the first quarter of 2022, just as other nations were doubling down on achieving resilient chip supply chains and increased self-sufficiency, Taiwan, the world's hotbed of chip fabrication, registered a shortage of required talent of 35,000, about half of which represented a lack of engineers.[24]

Washington's CHIPS and Science Act, meanwhile, requires an estimated 70,000 to 90,000 new skilled workers by around 2025 just to meet domestic chip fabrication goals.[25]

Japan and Korea, which have both rolled out their own versions of CHIPS, need at least 35,000[26] and 30,000[27] new engineers, respectively, to keep pace with projected investment through 2030.

China has the most ambitious semiconductor goals as well as the largest talent gap. In 2022, Beijing announced chip funding initiatives valued at a whopping US$143 billion to meet its dual circulation strategy, which calls for localised, homegrown supply chains in semiconductors by 2035.[28]

Such an ambitious plan is consistent with Beijing's overarching techno-nationalist objectives, including its Made in China 2025 initiative and its 'whole nation' chips initiative. For these plans to come to fruition, however, Beijing will need to figure out how to make its own advanced chips at home, which, in turn, means being able to make advanced chip manufacturing equipment as well as a host of advanced materials, as we have discussed.

There is no certainty as to when China will achieve these goals, but hypothetically speaking, if it had tried to meet its dual-circulation goal in 2023 using its own fully localised semiconductor ecosystems, the country would have faced a shortage of at least 200,000 chip professionals.[29]

What is certain is that chip schools in the U.S. and around the world will need to scale up big and do it as rapidly as possible. The war on talent, then, figures to intensify.

Chapter 26

The Innovation Horse Race

Never has there been a greater misconception than the belief that governments should leave the business of innovation to corporations and market forces.

We have already discussed how the technology feedback loop, which links together governments, private industry, academia, the defence establishment and markets, has determined history's winners and losers. From the rise of the Dutch East India Company in the sixteenth century, to the creation of the first computers during the Second World War, to NASA's original Moonshot in the 1960s and 1970s, enlightened techno-nationalism has determined the international status quo.

It was the primacy of neoliberal thought during the early post-Cold War era and America's brief 'unipolar moment' in the 1990s and early 2000s, that the idea of 'passive government' took root. But the rapid rise of China—and how it accomplished its rise—put an end to this thinking.

Today, as nations pursue their innovation edge and look to support homegrown enterprises, corporations are pivoting towards closer partnerships with governments. Indeed, they are actively seeking government collaboration.

In 2020, Eric Schmidt, the former CEO of Google and Executive Chairman of its parent company, Alphabet, wrote an op-ed for *The New York Times* (NYT) in which he stated:

> '. . .Silicon Valley leaders have put too much faith in the private sector. . . . The government needs to get back in the game in a serious way'.[1]

This is an important assertion. Mr Schmidt was the top executive at what is arguably one of the most innovative, entrepreneurial and influential business enterprises in history.

Consider that in the seven years preceding Schmidt's NYT piece, Alphabet had spent more than US$107 billion on R&D, an amount befitting entire industries.[2] And in the three years after his op-ed, according to Alphabet's annual reports, the company poured another US$98 billion into new research, mainly in generative AI, machine learning and cloud computing.

In the innovation horse race, then, Alphabet provides a benchmark for corporations and even entire sectors. Beyond the sheer scale of its R&D budget, the company's so-called Moonshot Factory, referred to as 'X', has delivered a trove of visionary innovations that have changed the world. This includes self-driving cars, AI-empowered wearable tech, augmented reality and the storage of renewable energy in, amazingly, molten salt.[3]

Yet Mr Schmidt—along with the leadership at most of America's top multinational corporations—has been agitating for the U.S. government to play a much bigger role in countering China's mercantilist system of innovation.

This sort of advocacy picked up pace in 2021, when the COVID-19 pandemic wreaked havoc on semiconductor supply chains, and CEOs from over 100 major American companies signed a letter from The Alliance for American Manufacturing (AAM) to U.S.

Congressional leaders. The CEOs wanted government action that would ensure a steady supply of semiconductors into the automotive, healthcare, logistics, telecom and consumer electronics sectors.

America's CEOs strongly supported the US$280 billion CHIPS and Science Act, which, at the time, had not yet been ratified into law. Clearly, corporate leadership was keen to get its hands on subsidies for the re-shoring of semiconductor fabrication and more.

This was techno-nationalism, but it was emanating from America's most elite companies rather than from the government. As we have discussed, such industrial policy, historically, would have sparked a strong backlash from the neoliberal establishment, but the AAM letter—and another similar letter organised by the Semiconductor Industry Association (SIA)—showed just how pervasive the paradigm shift had become.

GOVERNMENT ACTIVISM: WHY IT MATTERS

When it comes to funding basic research and 'blue-sky' experimentation, only governments can afford long-term commitments with uncertain outcomes. That there will be many failures and setbacks along the way is expected. These projects, then, are too risky for any single business enterprise, no matter how big or profitable it may be.

As the world's leading innovator, the U.S. has seen a gradual shift in emphasis since the mid-1970s from public R&D spending to private spending, a shift based largely on belief in the laissez-faire capitalist model.

In the 2020s, however, policymakers on the federal, state and local levels have become increasingly willing to shoulder the burdens associated with a forward-looking innovation landscape.

These large public initiatives tend to share the same underlying truths.

The first truth is that when governments become early adopters of new technologies, they can build a foundation on which entire ecosystems and new participants can expand. As we have seen, such has been the case with the CHIPS and Science Act.

This same approach is needed for the expansion of green infrastructure and the upgrading of digital grids.

The second truth is that no government-funded innovation can succeed without a long-term plan that combines public funding of infrastructure with complementary spending on education and human capital development. This, in turn, requires the dispensing of generous grants and the underwriting of private investments for research. It requires generous tax incentives and exemptions and well-targeted, well-administered subsidies to businesses (large and small), universities, think tanks, industry associations and other organisations.

To help spawn an innovative environment, governments must sponsor and fund open infrastructure such as a national research clouds. They must lower the innovation barriers-to-entry for smaller players and underrepresented groups through start-up funds and programmes, all the while increasing funding for basic research. This inclusive approach must ensure that every part of society finds its way into the technology feedback loop.

And the third truth is that for all this to work, governments must enforce frameworks of rules. They must protect intellectual property and pursue punitive and protective measures against predatory, unethical parties that distort or abuse the system, whether they be state or non-state actors.

PUBLIC–PRIVATE PARTNERSHIPS

During the Cold War with the Soviet Union, NASA's Apollo programme produced groundbreaking innovations such as solar panel technology and the world's first digital flight controls, as well as the first silicon-integrated circuit-based computer guidance systems.[4]

NASA continues to participate in successful innovation partnerships with private businesses, academia and other public organisations. This continues a long tradition of commercial technology spinoffs, which, as of 2023, included over 2,000 innovations, such as 3D Food printers, smart agriculture technologies, air and water purification systems and fire-retardant materials.[5]

As we have discussed, NASA's recent collaboration with private companies such as SpaceX, and its subsidiary, Starlink, along with a host of other enreprenuearial space-tech firms—recall Intuitive Machines, the Houston-based private company that built the Odysseus unmanned lunar vehicle, and landed it on the South Pole of the Moon—has been decisive.

The key to these breakthroughs is the dynamics of the 'public-private partnership'(PPP). The number and scale of PPPs are surging in the U.S., the E.U. and in other national technology hubs as state-actors look to foster the widest possible technology feedback loop.

While the paradigm shift calls for more industrial policy, U.S. and E.U. innovation agendas are not seeking to emulate China's centralised, authoritarian system of top-down techno-nationalism.

Instead, strategic PPPs are looking to turbo-charge different kinds of expertise and to capitalise on a vast reservoir of entrepreneurial talent and academic knowledge. The goal is to find a sweet spot between market forces and government steerage, as too much government activism would be counterproductive.

Rob Atkinson, who writes for the Washington-based Information, Technology and Innovation Foundation (ITIF), called this new approach 'national developmentalism,' which is the prioritisation of domestic growth while striving for 'selective globalisation'. Such an approach is needed to face down the 'epochal competitive threat from China', in Atkinson's words.[6]

In keeping with the new paradigm, this approach will inevitably lead to more bifurcation and de-risking of supply chains.

For MNEs to stay competitive, meanwhile, they must actively seek funding under legislation such as the CHIPS and Science Act in the U.S., as the letters from the AAM and the SIA demonstrate. Techno-nationalism, then, requires a very proactive kind of corporate diplomacy.

Going forward, it will be CEOs and thought leaders like Eric Schmidt who serve as the catalysts for a balanced, pragmatic, PPP-driven kind of techno-nationalism.

R&D AND THE PARADIGM SHIFT

During the twentieth National Congress of the Communist Party of China in 2022, Xi Jinping successfully installed himself into a third term as President and Secretary General of the Chinese Communist Party(CCP).

He also appointed loyalists to different leadership bodies, including the Politburo and the CCP Central Committee. But this move was not just to shore up his power base. Mr. Xi had carefully selected these new committee members because of their backgrounds in aerospace, nuclear science AI and other technology fields.

Of the 205 members that comprised the CCP's Central Committee, some 81 seats would be filled with individuals with strong resumes in the STEM fields—especially aerospace.[7] This effectively doubled the number of technologists from the previous Central Committee.

These sweeping changes reflected the CCP's increasing techno-nationalist bent, which evolved rapidly on the heels of Washington's October 2022 roll-out of comprehensive export controls as part of its chip war offensive.

It also was a timely reaction to U.S. National Security Advisor Jake Sullivan's public statements about Washington's intentions to abandon its 'sliding scale' approach, which aimed to keep the U.S. a few generations ahead of China, and instead strive for 'as large a lead as possible', as Mr. Sullivan had said.

One of Xi's primary motivations, then, was to spark an R&D revolution in China, to be led by this new crop of thought leaders, now tasked with speeding the country towards its goal of tech self-sufficiency. The success of that mission will come down to the funding and productivity of China's STEM-related research.

According to official state sources, in 2022, R&D expenditures accounted for about 2.6% of China's GDP, or about US$456 billion.[8]

For comparison, in the U.S., R&D accounted for about 3% of GDP,[9] or around US$680 billion—making America the world's biggest spender on R&D, as it had been for years.[10]

But consider that only 10 companies listed on the Nasdaq contributed to about a third of all American R&D expenditures—MAAMA companies (Microsoft, Apple, Alphabet, Meta and Amazon) plus a handful of semiconductor firms such as Nvidia, Broadcom and ASML.

This raises the question of how Washington, Beijing and others will manage the task of driving innovation while inhibiting the concentration of power in a few oligopolies.

If trends in R&D spending persist, by 2030, both the U.S. and China will likely spend between US$1 trillion and US$2 trillion on innovation competition.

To assess the productivity of such spending, observers often refer to the number of research papers being published and cited by country and region as a useful benchmark.

The Australian Strategic Policy Institute (ASPI) maintains a Critical Technology Tracker that, in 2023, rated China in first place in almost all the twenty-first-century critical technologies.[11]

ASPI also monitors flows of students and renowned academics, representing 'brain drain' and 'brain gain' around the world. Once again, China has moved out ahead. Except for papers on supercomputing, quantum computing and vaccines, areas in which the U.S. leads, China has taken first place.

Regarding papers on AI, China has emerged the undisputed champion, producing well over half of all the world's AI-related papers, most of which have been sponsored and influenced by the Chinese Academy of Sciences, Tsinghua University or by Chinese tech companies such as Huawei, Tencent Holdings and Alibaba Group Holding.[12]

Of course, published and cited research must lead to real results in the form of tangible technologies if we are to consider them a valid gauge of a successful R&D ecosystem.

Consider, then, China's success in the hypersonic sciences, which we examined in Chapter 15. According to ASPI, China hosts seven of the world's top 10 performing research institutions in hypersonic sciences. As we have seen with China's Dong Feng hypersonic missiles, there have indeed been game-changing results.

MILESTONES OF CHINESE TECHNO-NATIONALISM

Sceptics of industrial policy have pointed out that China's system of state capitalism is weighted down with corruption and that the system struggles with overcapacity, waste and the phenomenon of 'zombie' companies—state-backed, poorly managed behemoths that never die because of ongoing infusions of money from the government.

Yet China's techno-nationalist policies have produced big winners as well. Consider the cases of Huawei, Beidou (China's global satellite navigation system) and China's high-speed rail network, which Beijing built rapidly after obtaining key technologies and investments from foreign firms.

As we discussed in Chapter 10, Huawei became the largest telecommunications equipment manufacturer in the world. Its rise as a 5G end-to-end phone maker, and digital infrastructure company is well documented, as is its role as Beijing's geopolitical proxy and most important company.

Huawei is a world-class company with talented people, and its success is not linked exclusively to Beijing's industrial strategies. But, the company would not have risen to its current status without access to the broad range of government resources and financial assistance—including compensation for price reductions and discounts on the bidding of international contracts.

Huawei's access to new technology and IP through state-funded acquisitions and state-orchestrated technology transfer programmes has paid off handsomely.

Secondly, regarding China's prowess in space, Beijing built its own independent global satellite system as an alternative to the American Global Positioning System (GPS), the E.U.'s Galileo system and Russia's GLONASS.

Beidou is said to be highly accurate as a navigation system. In just over 15 years, Beidou was designed, built and successfully deployed through China's space and military programmes.

More broadly, China's progress in aerospace and satellite technology has borne fruit in the saga of Huawei's roll-out of the Mate 60 smartphone in

2023, as we have discussed. The Mate 60 uses GEO satellites from China Telcom to provide phone coverage and lightening-fast transmission of broadband data, offering coverage across most of Eurasia and a large chunk of Africa.

Finally, in the same 15-year timespan that the Beidou Satellite system was developed, China rolled out the world's longest and most extensively used public rail system, with trains attaining speeds of 250 to 350 kilometres per hour. China went from no high-speed trains to having more kilometres of high-speed track than all the rest of the world combined.

For each of these three examples, Beijing's central planners orchestrated a successful campaign of technology transfer, acquisition of IP, generous subsidies and R&D funding for local replacement firms and, of course, tradecraft.

China's high-speed rail development is a techno-nationalist achievement for the ages. Technology transfer agreements between Siemens AG and Alstom SA (the German and French high-speed rail companies that entered into joint ventures with local Chinese firm China CNR Corp) had effectively facilitated the transfer of all of Siemens' and Alstom's core technologies.[13] This would become an early cautionary tale.

In March of 2018, during the early days of the U.S.–China trade dispute, the United States Trade Representative (USTR) published the findings of its Section 301 investigation into China's practices regarding innovation, tech transfer and intellectual property (IP) protection.

The report concluded that part of the success of China's industrial policies could be attributed to activities captured in the acronym IDAR, which refers to the process of introducing, digesting, absorbing and re-promoting a new technology.

A BRIEF REFLECTION ON THE BENEFITS OF INDUSTRIAL POLICY

Contrary to popular belief, globalisation owes a good portion of its success to the spillover effects of industrial policies. Techno-nationalism has created trading opportunities between nations, even as they have focused on their own economic and national security needs.

Take the examples of Japan and Taiwan in Asia and Germany in Europe. These countries have flourished due to government funding and support for local industry, along with the facilitation of strategic joint ventures with selected multinational companies (mostly American), which ultimately contributed to more economic integration in the global economy.

The role of bilateral security partnerships and wider defence alliances such as the North Atlantic Treaty Organisation (NATO) have played a vital part in encouraging and endorsing trading relationships. These partnerships thrive on technology transfer and public–private partnerships.

The U.S.–China rivalry does not change the positive dynamics between industrial policy and trade. While it does lead to a more bifurcated trading system, this is not the same thing as a zero-sum trade outcome, as the reorganisation of the global economy around great power rivalry is generating new relationships and transactions, even as old linkages come to an end.

In the context of trade and industrial policies, then, let us focus on some snapshots involving two key sectors: semiconductors and telecommunications.

JAPAN

Japan's rise as a technological powerhouse is largely attributable to its industrial policy. In the 1970s, for example, the Ministry of International Trade and Industry (MITI) provided financial assistance to local companies while encouraging joint ventures between Japanese companies like Sony and Hitachi and U.S.-based semiconductor juggernauts like Intel and Texas Instruments.

These relationships laid the foundation for today's ongoing trade and investment between the U.S. and Japan: each country is now the other's largest foreign investor. Today, Japan's Next-Generation Semiconductor Technology Development Program, funded by the Ministry of Economy, Trade, and Industry (METI), provides subsidies and grants to support R&D projects related to advanced semiconductor technologies. These projects serve as magnets to other potential strategic partners.

In 2023, the Japanese government announced that it was committing over US$1 billion to construct a fabrication plant in Hiroshima for Micron, the American chip maker, where it will produce next-generation memory chips.[14] Meanwhile, Rapidus, a Japanese chip company, has partnered with IBM to develop and manufacture 2-nanometre chips in Chitose, Hokkaido.[15]

In Chapter 25, we discussed the UPWARDs programme involving 11 Japanese and U.S. universities, which serves as a talent pipeline and provides cross-fertilisation opportunities for R&D, trade and investment. Occurring on the back of the U.S.–Japan defence alliance, this kind of academic friend-shoring has prompted further collaboration in areas such as quantum and hypersonic science.[16]

As we have seen, TSMC, Taiwan's world-beating chip company, continues to invest in Japan, also under the Rapidus and other government backed initiatives.

TAIWAN

During the 1980s, Taiwan's nascent semiconductor industry saw significant investment and technology transfer from foreign companies. The collaboration between TSMC and Philips, a Dutch company, played a critical role in shaping Taiwan's semiconductor landscape. RCA, a U.S. company, also reportedly provided pivotal technology transfer.

After the U.S. normalised diplomatic relations with China in 1979, Washington adopted a policy of 'strategic ambiguity' whereby it did not formally recognise Taiwan as a sovereign country but supported it through the supply of armaments and technology transfer, most notably in the areas of semiconductors, computer science and software development. The idea was to strengthen Taiwan both economically and militarily by fostering a leading-edge technology sector.

With the blessings of Washington, Texas Instruments established its first overseas semiconductor fabrication plant in Taiwan in 1984, followed by investments from other major players like Intel and AMD, while IBM partnered with Taiwanese companies like Acer and Asus to manufacture and distribute IBM-compatible PCs—all contributing significantly to Taiwan's consumer electronics boom.

Microsoft, meanwhile, established its first R&D centre in Taiwan in 1991. This fostered a local software development industry, which, in turn, and fuelled more innovation.

The close collaboration between government and the corporate sector was hugely important. Taiwan's Industrial Technology Research Institute (ITRI) was instrumental in coordinating developmental policy with corporate leaders, as was the Ministry of Economic Affairs (MOEA), which funded the construction of key infrastructure in Hsinchu Science Park, now the global hotbed of semiconductor fabrication.

Taiwan's defence establishment was also instrumental. For example, a subdivision of the Ministry of National Defence, the Electronics Research and Service Organisation (ERSO), helped fund R&D efforts that contributed to the rise of TSMC.

Today, even under the shadow of a possible forcible unification of Taiwan with mainland China—which could entail a naval blockade or even a full-on military invasion and kinetic war—the semiconductor and consumer electronics sector in Taiwan continues to draw in the world's most advanced semiconductor players, from Applied Materials to Nvidia.

GERMANY

Europe's technology powerhouse, Germany, followed a similar path. Since the 1960s, its approach to industrial policy, referred to as Ordo-liberalism, has been fundamental to its economic progress. This doctrine was built on the understanding that the government would best serve society by skilfully intertwining strategic goals with market forces.

In the technology sector, over the course of decades, partnerships between companies like Germany's Siemens and America's Intel fuelled an ethos of corporate excellence. Decades later, Siemens and Intel have partnered again on the chip manufacturing process.[17] The two stalwarts are working on improved chip manufacturing efficiencies, including the minimisation of carbon footprints.

Germany remains a prime location for the next phase of strategic friend-shoring. Not surprisingly, it will be in Magdeburg, Germany that TSMC will build one of the world's most advanced 1.5-nanometre chip fab.[18] That is, if Germany's largest, wealthiest handful of companies do not continue to shift their operations to China.

Angela Merkel, Germany's Chancellor from 2005 to 2021, veered off the disciplined path of Ordoliberalism by going all in on China, establishing deep trade and investment ties, often resulting in job losses in Germany. This was prompted by a few of Germany's largest companies, such as BASF and Siemens, and the big German automotive companies Audi, Mercedes-Benz and BMW, all of whom make up the majority of German FDI in China.

Now, Germany finds itself grappling with its own techno-nationalist paradigm shift as it looks to de-risk from China and restructure its innovation and R&D footprint. This has pitted the above handful of companies against a large proportion of German businesses that see Chinese state capitalism as a threat. Many would like their government to crack down one the big German companies for continuing to offshore good jobs to China.

Whatever happens, Germany's world-class manufacturing base figures to play a leading role in Europe's wider innovation landscape. A wealth of German companies would make suitable strategic partners in the steady re-shoring of overseas supply chains over the next decade—but only if policymakers in Berlin can agree on a consistent path forward.

Berlin is expected to spend 3.5% of GDP on R&D by the year 2025, one of the highest proportions of any country worldwide.[19]

Other advanced countries are also shifting their emphasis on R&D. In 2023, for example, the French government announced a series of measures to overhaul the country's organisation of research, which President Emmanuel Macron claimed would reduce bureaucracy and place science 'at the heart of political decision-making'.[20] These reforms represent the biggest shake-up to France's research system in two decades.

Britain, meanwhile, boosted its R&D budget for 2022–2025 to around US$50 billion so it can concentrate on AI and expand its semiconductor prowess in chip design and, eventually, fabrication. Britain's world-class network of universities will anchor a growing hotbed of innovation.

South Korea made history in 2024 when it announced it was committing almost half a trillion U.S. dollars to build a dozen new chip foundries and three world-class R&D facilities.[21] But while semiconductors were grabbing all the headlines, officials were restructuring its R&D focus away from basic research and towards two priority areas: rockets and biomedical research.[22] Seoul wants to turn South Korea not only into a semiconductor hub but also into a biotech hotbed similar to the Boston corridor in the U.S.

THE ORIGINS OF AMERICA'S CHIP POLICIES

During the 1980s, Japan's semiconductor industry surpassed that of the U.S. in terms of levels of advancement and production capability. In response, in 1987, the U.S. government and 14 U.S.-based manufacturers formed a non-profit semiconductor manufacturing technology consortium, SEMATECH, as a PPP.[23]

At the time, the U.S.'s diminishing competitive position with respect to Japan was considered a serious national security issue. Over the next five years, SEMATECH received public subsidies totalling US$500 million from the U.S. Department of Defence.

Member companies also contributed funding, much of which found its way to the nation's universities and research institutions that were participating in the programme.

By the 1990s, the U.S. microchip industry had achieved an innovation trajectory that propelled it past Japan to resume its position as the world leader in semiconductors.[24]

SEMATECH initially focused on the development of new materials, processes and equipment for microchip manufacturing, and it was so successful that its board of directors agreed to eliminate matching funds from the U.S. government in 1996.

Today, SEMATECH operates on dues paid by its members, who account for about half of the world's entire chip market. From a techno-nationalist perspective, the success of SEMATECH can be attributed to several key factors.

First, the U.S. Department of Defence, specifically the Defence Research Projects Agency (DARPA) drove exploration of bold new ideas and basic research while working collaboratively with the organisation's members. The U.S. government was careful not to suffocate the market or the entrepreneurial dynamics within the group.

Funding of SEMATECH's innovation systems was one component in a broader U.S. strategy of protecting its domestic industry through anti-dumping and countervailing duties on Japanese imports as well as other non-tariff measures, including import quotas.

And yet, the U.S. and Japan remained major trading partners throughout the period, in spite of the formation of SEMATECH and the imposition of tariffs on Japanese imports.

More recently, America's CHIPS and Science Act, which we discussed in Chapter 9, is based on the same fundamental ideas as SEMATECH, only on a much more ambitious scale.

More infusions of public and private capital will be required, but the act will be instrumental in re-shoring and reshaping the global semiconductor landscape, most likely over a period of at least 5 to 10 years.

The CHIPS and Science Act stipulates that any company accepting funding must agree to curtail certain activities in China and limit collaboration with a long list of restricted entities. This will accelerate the bifurcation of the global economy but will usher in a new kind of geopolitical creative destruction in the innovation horse race between nations.

Chapter 27

India Rising?

Geopolitical good fortune and changing internal dynamics suggests that India faces a historic opportunity to transform into one of the world's most important technology hubs.

In the Indo-Pacific, as a member of the Quadrilateral Security Dialogue (QUAD), along with the U.S., Japan and Australia, New Delhi is seen as an increasingly important counterbalance to China.

Consider how, in early 2021, the four countries committed to stockpiling billions of surplus doses of COVID-19 vaccinations for distribution throughout Southeast Asia and beyond—an action that was taken primarily in response to Beijing's global vaccine diplomacy campaign.

Washington's hopes are high for India yet again, this time regarding its partnership with the U.S. in building China-free, resilient supply chains and participating in new infrastructure and capacity building in the region.

In May of 2022, President Biden and Prime Minister Modi announced the U.S.–India initiative on Critical and Emerging Technology (iCET). Its purpose is to elevate and expand a strategic technology partnership and promote defence and industrial cooperation between the two governments, businesses and academic institutions.[1]

About a year later, the two countries initiated the India-U.S. Defense Acceleration Ecosystem (INDUS-X), a bilateral defense collaboration in support of iCET. INDUS-X facilitates partnerships among U.S. and Indian defense companies of all sizes, incubators and accelerators, investors, and universities with the support of the U.S. and Indian governments.[2] Early technology cooperation has included the joint development of maritime intelligence, surveillance, and reconnaissance (ISR) and undersea communications in the Indian Ocean, as well as in space-based ISR.

One of the challenges to the growing security relationship is whether new technology transfers through the INDUS-X collaboration will encounter blockages under the International Traffic in Arms Regulations (ITAR) rules, which are enforced by the U.S. Department of State. This issue has also emerged regarding the recently enacted AUKUS security pact with Australia—which historically, has been one of America's closest and most trusted allies and strategic partners. India, therefore, would have an even higher bar to clear than Australia when it comes to ITAR laws and export controls.

Also on the diplomatic front, India's long adherence to the idea of non-alignment presents Washington with challenges. New Delhi has a historic aversion to choosing sides. As such, along with bilateral collaboration with India, U.S. diplomats have sought to fold New Delhi into regional forums that include both India and its neighbours. Take, for example, I2U2, a technology-sharing bloc instigated by the Americans that also includes, Israel, India, and the United Arab Emirates.[3] I2U2 aims to address regional challenges regarding water, energy, transportation, space, health, and food security.

India's relationship with Russia is another matter, entirely. Historically, New Delhi came to rely upon the Soviet Union as a supplier of armaments during the Cold War. Although India is now looking to reduce its military ties with Moscow, at the time of this writing, approximately 60% of its tanks, helicopters, missile systems and fighter jets (even an aircraft carrier) were of Soviet or Russian origin. This equipment will require servicing and spare parts from the Russian armaments industry for many years to come.

Regarding its energy needs, almost 40% of India's oil imports came from Russia in 2023, although that number is trending downward.[4] Clearly, however, as New Delhi moves to capitalise on the restructuring of supply chains out of China—and especially if India is to attract American investment into its nascent semiconductor landscape—its ties with Russia will come under increased scrutiny.

The question is, then, will Washington have sufficient leverage over New Delhi when it comes to trying to pull India away from Russia's orbit? Those who know India well believe that Washington may be disappointed.

India's status as a democracy, meanwhile, has not been without its critics when it comes to press freedoms and growing schisms between the country's majority Hindu population and its Muslim citizens. Should this schism continue to grow, its toxic side effects could spill over into the general economic landscape or even destabilise it.

Thus, as a democracy, many will be watching closely when it comes to how New Delhi deals with censorship and press freedoms, along with its ethnic tensions.

INDIA'S FERTILE ECONOMY AND TECHNOLOGY LANDSCAPE

Because of its large consumer base—despite significant wealth disparities across the economy—growth in the middle- and upper-income segments of India's population of some 1.4 billion will fuel strong market demand for digital and online services. This, in turn, will serve as a catalyst for more foreign firms to join India's growing technology hubs, and to use them as both an export platform and a doorway into the local market.

In 2023, 900 million Indians had access to the Internet, representing the second-highest number of mobile Internet users in the world after China. The COVID-19 pandemic, which forced closures of millions of businesses and schools, became a catalyst for increasing Internet access.

Indians already enjoy the world's least expensive Internet access. In 2016, JIO, a subsidiary of Reliance Industries, the large conglomerate owned by famed Indian billionaire Mukesh Ambani, offered virtually free 4G Internet access to millions across the Indian subcontinent.

By 2020, 50% of India's population had access to the Internet (up from just 10% in 2010),[5] and the value of the country's e-commerce market, as estimated by India's *Economic Times*, is expected to be worth US$300 billion by 2030.[6]

The U.S., the E.U., Taiwan and Japan are India's largest foreign investors in the technology sector. Services, computer hardware, software and telecommunications represent the top categories of investment. Because the world's largest technology companies already have a significant presence in India, they are well positioned to participate in growing India's production capacity.[7]

Prime Minister Modi and his government understand the historic magnitude of the moment and have intensified efforts to build up India's manufacturing capabilities. India aims to develop its electronics systems design and manufacturing (ESDM) capabilities, and to that end has adopted a range of policies, including the Electronics Development Fund (EDF). How well it works remains to be seen.

Looking ahead, the government has placed special emphasis on smartphones, laptops and other ubiquitous digital devices. Semiconductors, meanwhile, have risen to the top of India's wish list for foreign investment and inclusion in global value chains.

The goal is to increase production capacity in India's domestic market and then expand that capacity to accommodate exports. Taking a page out of China's playbook, the Modi government hopes to absorb strategic FDI and technology transfer from global firms. From there, a crop of homegrown Indian firms can emerge, including original equipment manufacturers (OEMs) that could make parts and components, possibly for giant Indian brands such as Tata or Reliance, assuming they can expand into new areas of manufacturing.

ACCELERATED DECOUPLING FROM CHINA

In early 2021, less than a year after a deadly border clash between Indian and Chinese soldiers at Ladakh, India permanently banned more than 250 Chinese apps, including WeChat, Baidu and TikTok. A year earlier, New Delhi had already passed a national security directive that effectively banned companies such as Huawei and ZTE from India's future 5G wireless networks.

Policymakers have also accelerated efforts to wean India from Chinese supply chains and investment. In the first three years of the Modi government, for example, Chinese investors such as Alibaba and Tencent Holdings pumped billions into India's tech sector. This funded a large tranche of India's unicorns. New constraints, however, were placed on the Automatic FDI Route, which had been established in 2015 to facilitate expeditious, free-flowing FDI into India. The action was aimed primarily at suppressing the influence of Chinese investment and an over-reliance on Chinese-made parts and components in India's nascent fabrication centres.

Regarding regional trade agreements, India's decision to stay out of the Regional Comprehensive Economic Partnership (RCEP) was based, in part on its contention that joining the free-trade agreement (FTA) would perpetuate the country's reliance on Chinese imports, particularly in the smartphone and other ESDM-related industries.

But, in general, India has signed very few FTAs, as both Modi's Bharatiya Janata Party (BJP) and Congress have shown an aversion to them. The agrarian sector in India, which generally opposes free trade agreements, also yields considerable influence.

INDIA'S DIGITAL LANDSCAPE

India has implemented the world's largest biometric ID system, known as 'Aadhaar', which is a testament to the country's technology prowess despite the challenges of dealing with a poor, mostly agrarian and highly diverse populace. Under the Aadhaar, the Unique Identification Authority of India (UIDAI) collected iris, fingerprint and facial data into a national database of 1.26 billion 12-digit individual identity numbers.

The Aadhaar ID number is used to dispense government services, including financial assistance and other direct benefit transfers across the country. As noted in *Rebooting India* by Nandan Nilekani, cofounder of Indian tech firm Infosys and former Chairman of the UIDAI, it is hoped that Aadhaar will revolutionise voting, digital medicine, banking and digital payments, tax collection, land, birth and marriage registry, small business management and more. India's government has leveraged Aadhaar's identity and authentication network via APIs with United Payment Interface to create the India Stack, a milestone in a country where people lack conventional documents or proof of identity.

As a member of the Global Partnership on Artificial Intelligence (GPAI), New Delhi has become central to discussions regarding technology standards and values. The Nation's External Affairs Ministry recently formulated the New and Emerging Strategic Technologies (NEST) division that aims to engage in techno-diplomacy to provide policy guidance on shaping international rules related to emerging technologies.

The Indian Supreme Court has ruled that no citizen should suffer for not participating in Aadhaar. That is, one cannot be denied access to critical services and benefits that the system was intended to facilitate, even if one chooses not to enrol. This presents a striking contrast to China's Sesame social credit-scoring system, which the NGO Freedom House has described as a tool of techno-authoritarianism.

All of this should factor into the attractiveness of India, as a democracy. In 2017, the Indian Supreme Court went a step further and issued a landmark ruling, which established that privacy was a fundamental right of Indian citizens.

As the world's largest and most complex democracy, then, India is an ideal testing ground for market-driven technologies that can protect a citizen's privacy needs and prevent unwanted surveillance. Consequently, with the right foreign investment, its innovation centres could be destined to produce the next generation of tech start-ups and corporate incubators focused on what I call the privacy economy.

Thus, India could be on the is on the verge of commencing possibly the world's largest fintech boom as millions of unbanked consumers come online. Financial inclusion and digitisation allow huge amounts of online transactions, and digital payments are already manifest in billions of daily mobile payments.

SOFTWARE AND ENGINEERING RESEARCH & DEVELOPMENT (ER&D)

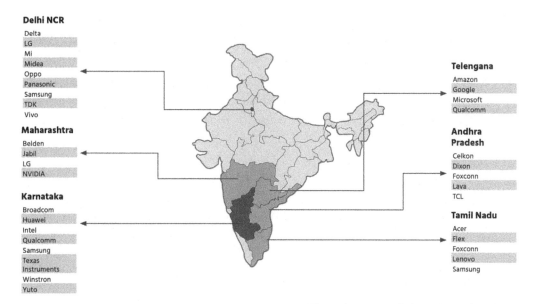

Delhi NCR
Delta
LG
Mi
Midea
Oppo
Panasonic
Samsung
TDK
Vivo

Maharashtra
Belden
Jabil
LG
NVIDIA

Karnataka
Broadcom
Huawei
Intel
Qualcomm
Samsung
Texas Instruments
Winstron
Yuto

Telengana
Amazon
Google
Microsoft
Qualcomm

Andhra Pradesh
Celkon
Dixon
Foxconn
Lava
TCL

Tamil Nadu
Acer
Flex
Foxconn
Lenovo
Samsung

*Electronics systems design and manufacturing

Source: https://www.investindia.gov.in/sector/electronic-systems

Figure 27.1   Map of India's Traditional Technology Hubs.

For decades, India has been known as an outsourcing centre for software development, where companies such as Infosys, Wipro, Mphasis and Tata Consultancy Services have become trusted service providers to the world's global firms. Beyond software development, however, there has been a steady rise in the number of Global In-house Centres (GICs). Multinational companies have been establishing GICs throughout India to test new ideas around digital transformation. Special emphasis has been on AI and machine learning, data sciences, the IoT and software as a service (SaaS).

A quarter of the world's Fortune 500 companies have set up shop in India, with some 1,750 GICs spread throughout the country's productivity hubs, including Bengaluru, Hyderabad, Chennai, Pune, Mumbai and Delhi NCR. By 2020, Goldman Sachs had approximately 10,000 analysts based in India, Microsoft had 75,000 and IBM had 100,000.

This trend will continue as wage arbitrage draws businesses to the low costs of Indian engineers. India's IT labour pool is massive: more than one million new graduates with engineering degrees enter the workforce each year.

No country, not even China, has more engineering-focused educational institutions than India. In 2020, the country boasted approximately 3,500 engineering colleges, 3,400 polytechnics, 4,000 management schools and an even larger number of vocational and training institutes. Getting such a large pool of talent to focus on innovation will require outside assistance.

India has invested heavily to create Innovation and Entrepreneurship hubs in higher education institutions that bring American universities to its campuses. Coordinated through the U.S.–India Knowledge Exchange programme, this could form a positive feedback loop involving the flow of top-notch Indian talent into American companies and institutions and the reciprocal flow of world-class academics and resources into India's universities.

Discerning economists, however, have questioned India's ability to transition from a low-cost outsourcing location for software to a legitimate manufacturing hub. According to McKinsey, manufacturing's share of India's GDP only grew by a couple of percentage points over two decades—from 15.3% in 2000 to 17.4% in 2020—despite years of industrial policies aimed at achieving higher outputs and exports. Other reports show an overall decrease in manufacturing as a percentage of real GDP. From 2022 through 2023, for example, India's manufacturing growth ended on an 18-month low.[8]

India continues to grapple with large trade imbalances in critical technology sectors. It continues to run deficits on imports of electronic components in chapters 84 and 85 of the Harmonised Tariff Schedule, which includes semiconductors, smartphones, laptops and other electronics.

THE PAIN-OF-DOING-BUSINESS IN INDIA

Previous export-focused policies in India have faltered because of the country's poor international ranking in ease of doing business (EoDB). Excessive regulations, taxes and a lack of coordination between central and state governments have prevented India from attracting and keeping investors.

From a governance perspective, businesses encounter problems arising from state governments' tendency to act as brokers between multinational enterprises (MNEs) and the central government. State-level politicians often engage in controversial land grabs, leading to legal challenges from local farmers (about 60% of land in India is agricultural). Paralysing litigation is not uncommon across India's business landscape.

Despite such problems, India's World Bank EoDB ranking jumped from 100th in the world to 63rd from 2017 to 2023—a substantial improvement in such a short time.

Labour laws have been revised from 140 different codes to just four codes. Industrial clusters can now be located anywhere inside the country and enjoy special economic zone (SEZ) status, which includes bonded warehouse manufacturing and tax-free importations for the manufacture of exports.

Corporate tax for newly established manufacturing entities was slashed from 25% to about 15% (excluding surcharge and cess). This is a good start, although cess, which is a state tax that is levied on top of national taxes, remains problematic for foreign firms.

On another positive note, Prime Minister Modi's BJP has managed to take control of the political apparatus within key manufacturing and innovation hubs, including Bengaluru in Karnataka, Delhi in the Capital Territory, Chennai in Tamil Nadu and Mumbai in Maharashtra.

These clusters hold the key to India's future and must be managed wisely.

Mr. Modi has also been successful in generating competition between India's states in a scheme like China's, where state officials are nominated or replaced based on key performance indicators around industrial policies.

Painstaking changes in political culture and the streamlining of regulatory and tax regimes are an improvement, but many stumbling blocks remain. Foreign companies, for example, are still subject to more regulation than domestic companies. India's customs adminis-tration is still one of the worst to deal with anywhere, with its intensive paperwork and slow and inefficient bureaucratic processes. At the time of this writing, the import of used tooling and manufacturing equipment to a manufacturing site (for maintenance or to operate existing equipment, for example) involve time consuming adminis-trative reviews and, in cases, may be denied entry.

Once a good is imported into India, the movement of these goods from one state to another within the country involves yet more admin-istrative and regulatory pain.

While some states, mentioned above, are drawing critical mass as technology hubs, others are sorely deficient, resulting in a very uneven investment environment. This is especially evident in the disparities in infrastructure, clean water and waste treatment around the country.

Thus, India's policymakers will need to keep working hard at improv-ing the overall investment, regulatory and infrastructure environment.

SMARTPHONES AND GEOPOLITICAL INFLUENCE

Smartphones have been at the heart of India's technology-manufacturing plan. Government policy calls for one billion smart-phones to be produced in India by 2025.

New Delhi has studied China's roadmap regarding the development, support, and promotion of technology ecosystems, especially when it comes to the importance of well-functioning Special Economic Zones (SEZ). That roadmap has helped China's low-cost handphone makers to penetrate India and other emerging markets in Africa and Asia in part by leveraging networks of Chinese state-backed firms such as Huawei, ZTE, Alibaba, Dahua and SenseTime.

Indian policymakers have come to appreciate the geopolitical advan-tages that this formula has conferred on Beijing. Smartphones are anchor products that reside at the centre of an ecosystem that also includes telecommunications infrastructure, AI and software systems. Combined, these elements form a powerful tool for the projection of economic and geopolitical power.

BUILDING WORLD-CLASS CLUSTERS WITH LOCAL MANUFACTURERS

There is great hope that world-class manufacturing clusters can finally emerge from India's technology landscape. Apple, for example, has set out to move at least a quarter, possibly up to 40% of all its global iPhone production out of China and into India's greater Chennai and Tamil Nadu region.[9] A fully functional ecosystem has now materialised: Apple's sub-contractors include Taiwan-based Foxconn, Pegatron, Wistron and Luxshare, all of which are producing and assembling key components for Apple in local facilities. Foxconn alone will invest US$1 billion in the move. Tata Electronics, a homegrown Indian company and iconic brand, is a key component manufacturer.

Samsung, the South Korean company, operates the largest handphone assembly site in the world in Noida, Uttar Pradesh. It runs a vertically integrated business model that relies on its own electronic manufacturing services (EMS), but a crop of locally grown Indian EMS players are slowly emerging in this space.

Micromax, Intex, Lava and Karbonn (the so-called 'MILK' EMS companies) have been growing India's local capacity to build electronic components. Dixon, another Indian EMS firm, has a market value of US$2.5.

Chinese low-cost handphone brands would seem the logical choice as partners for Indian firms. Under this scenario, firms such as Dixon are well positioned for technology and knowledge transfer from their Chinese counterparts. Partnerships would enable Indian firms to eventually break away as indigenous brands and compete directly with their former Chinese partners at home and abroad. This is, in fact, the techno-nationalist model that has served Beijing so well.

But Indian policymakers have doubled down on strategic decoupling. Despite short-term benefits, Indians have become increasingly wary of Chinese money.

In 2020, for example, when the People's Bank of China (PBOC) increased its shareholding position in India's Housing Development Finance Corporation (HDFC), the Indian political establishment reacted swiftly with new restrictions aimed primarily at Chinese investors. India overhauled its automatic FDI route, implemented in 2015, and mandated that all future FDI transactions require government approval.

How will India's unicorns fare without a pipeline to free-flowing Chinese money? Between 2015 and 2020, for example, Tencent, Alibaba, Didi Chuxing and other Chinese investors were instrumental in funding half of India's 30 unicorn companies, including Paytm (an electronic payment platform) and Flipkart (an e-commerce platform), which is now owned by Walmart.

With India's leadership eschewing Chinese dollar diplomacy, the search for the next round of investment and technology transfer has turned decidedly to the U.S., Taiwan, South Korea and Japan. Singapore and Israel also figure to play a larger role as investors.

PRINTED CIRCUIT BOARD ASSEMBLY AND SEMICONDUCTORS

All computing devices, including smartphones, require printed circuit board assemblies (PCBAs) to function. PCBAs are an integral part of global value chains because they drive upstream activities such as design and component assembly and downstream activities regarding the manufacturing of finished goods. One of the keys to expanding capacity as a tech hub, therefore, is to ramp up local production of PCBAs.

In 2020, China produced almost 50% of the world's PCBAs.

Now, as geopolitics compels firms to diversify their supply chains, India must work hard to capture these new value chains. The domestic and export markets for PCBAs in India are expected to grow rapidly.

PCBA manufacturing has already been shifting from China to Vietnam, Malaysia and Thailand, which hold real advantages. In the long term, if India is to offer manufacturing advantages over these Southeast Asian countries, its present leadership and its successors must continue to fix EoDB issues.

In addition to PCBAs, India must have access to a steady supply of semiconductors. Historically, India has imported all its semiconductors and has had no manufacturing capabilities of its own.

The Modi government has set its sights on a decadal plan to bring legacy semiconductor fabrication, assembly, testing and packaging to India. At the time of this writing, the Indian government had approved around US$15 billion in new projects.[10]

India's domestic chip market is estimated to be worth close to $30 billion in 2023.[11] At the same time, the need for more resilient, diversified global supply chains make India an attractive outsourcing location for the chip sector.

Under the so-called India Semiconductor Mission (ISM), India's National government offers financial assistance through production-linked incentive (PLI) schemes, covering around 50% of initial setup costs and provides additional incentives for production and export of chips. State governments also can kick up to another 20 % of costs.

In late 2023, Taiwan's Foxconn announced it was teaming up with STMicroelectronics, the Franco-Italian company, to bid on the building of a fab in Gujarat, to produce 40-nanometre legacy chips.[12] As we have discussed, this older generation technology is in high demand for automotive electronics, industrial automation, consumer electronics and connected devices, among other things.

Micron also put in a bid for funding, signing an MOU with the Gujarat government pledging to invest around US$2.75 billion in memory chips fab, while Advanced Micro Devices Inc. (AMD) and equipment maker Applied Materials Inc. pledged to spend US$400 million each on R&D and engineering centres in the southern tech hub of Bengaluru.[13]

All this activity prompted the Tata conglomerate, India's most iconic company and best-recognised brand, to announce it was investing in a semiconductor foray of its own in Gujarat. Thus, the country's first major fab will feature a US$11-billion joint venture between Tata Electronics and PSMC, and will produce older 28, 40, 55, and 110-nanometer chips, with a capacity of 50,000 wafers per month.[14]

The company also announced plans for an Outsourced Semiconductor Assembly and Testing (OSAT) plant in Assam. As we discussed in Chapter 8, this includes chip 'packaging,' which involves the increasingly advanced process of connecting and protecting a chip.

It should be noted that at the time of this writing, India's ISM initiative remains largely aspirational. Foxconn has virtually no core experience in semiconductors. Furthermore, Gujarat, the site much of the investment, is the home state of prime minister Modi, which some would view as an example of crony capitalism. The STMicroelectronics and Micron fabs, among others, apart from pledges and approvals, have yet to receive any money.

Meanwhile, India has already become a thriving research, chip design and equipment engineering centre, possessing some 20% of the world's chip design workforce (around 125,000 engineers).[15] One lesson that Delhi's technocrats have learned from China's decades' long attempts to develop an indigenous semiconductor ecosystem is that they must also get wafer-fab equipment (WFE) companies to invest in production facilities in India. Beijing failed to do this and, as we have seen, has been severely constrained as Washington and its allies weaponised supply chain choke points around WFE.

For now, geopolitics shines favourably on India in its efforts to attract semiconductor value chains. But New Delhi will have to go to great lengths to avoid repeat failures of industrial due to administrative red tape, corruption, over taxation. It will need to upskill middle-level portions of the workforce and improve infrastructure and logistics. Otherwise, other countries such as Malaysia, and Vietnam could end up taking away a big chunk of India's big chip opportunity.

There will be instances where Washington, in exchange for encouraging semiconductor investments from its allies, such as Japan, Taiwan and South Korea, will want concessions on India's dealing with Russia, for example, or to what extent it Delhi supports Beijing's efforts to pull the BRICS countries further into its geopolitical orbit—especially regarding its efforts to decouple from the U.S. dollar.

Chapter 28

Fragmented Finance

The same tectonic geopolitical and techno-nationalist forces that are fragmenting global supply chains are also affecting financial markets. Financial markets now face their own version of de-risking and decoupling scenarios, which are being accelerated by three distinct factors.

The first factor is the development of central bank digital currencies (CBDCs) and their attendant geopolitical side effects. The second involves increasingly demanding accounting standards and outbound investment restrictions, and the third factor involves export controls and sanctions, which put a large swath of the banking and fintech sectors under scrutiny—including sovereign wealth funds.

CENTRAL BANK-BACKED DIGITAL CURRENCIES

As part of its 14th five-year plan, China is said to investing heavily in R&D and new infrastructure for a digital currency. The e-CYN or 'e-yuan', figures to play a critical role in the Chinese Communist Party's domestic affairs and, further afield, in the pursuit of its geopolitical interests.[1]

Unlike a decentralised cryptocurrency issued by a private non-state actor, CBDCs are digital manifestations of a national currency and represent a store of value backed by a central bank.

There are opposing views on digital currencies. Privacy advocates argue that digital currencies give authoritarian governments the means to monitor and its populace and use the digital currency as a behaviour modification tool.

As for its more benign features, digitised currencies allow for the financial inclusion of people that are 'un-banked'—those that have no traditional bank account. As mobile smart devices proliferate in the world's poorest areas, CBDCs will empower the un-banked to participate in a burgeoning digital economy.[2]

Unlike private cryptocurrencies, CBDCs can reduce illicit transaction for money launderers, terrorists and tax evaders—although there will always be crypto currencies and the dark web for such activities.

By keeping monetary controls and transparency requirements in the hands of the state, CBDCs avoid the dangers of ceding too much power to private, non-state actors—such as the big tech companies like Amazon or Netflix whose own digital payment frameworks might be favoured over an official state-backed currency. This would create a situation where a central bank's mechanisms (buying or selling its currency to prevent wild swings in the currency's value) would be useless to prevent financial volatility.

This was one of the reasons the Ant Financial Group's Hong Kong IPO (an Alibaba company) was shut down by the Chinese government in 2020. Ant's payment platform was moving massive amounts of money, credit and even stock trading and risked destabilising the official economy.

According to analysis done by the Bank for International Settlements (BIS) already, by 2021, 86% of the world's central banks were experimenting with CBDCs and hoped to provide their citizens with increased retail-level commercial access via the use of CBDCs.

Digital currencies have been pulled into the geopolitical arena, and just as strategic supply chains are decoupling, CBDCs will fracture the global financial landscape into different blocs.

Two underlying issues make this a certainty.

First, Beijing is working to reduce its dependence on the U.S. dollar and diminish its exposure to U.S. sanctions and is doing everything in its power to internationalise the yuan, including its promotion along the Belt and Road Initiative (BRI) as the transactional currency of choice for credit and trade.[3]

China has been using its leadership role with the BRICS countries to push for the adoption of an alternate currency to the U.S. dollar, which would include the e-yuan in a weighted basket of CBDCs.

But the greenback remains the dominant global reserve and trading currency, which Washington continues to weaponise, which has long been the story.

During the Nixon administration, in 1971, at the Rome G10 meetings, the American Treasury Secretary John Connally famously said: 'The dollar is our currency, but it's your problem.'

More than fifty years later, most of the world's international transactions still rely on the US dollar and upon the Society for Worldwide Interbank Financial Telecommunications (SWIFT), a cross-border clearing system for banks. Any Chinese company, entity or individual, anywhere, placed under sanctions—or any third parties doing business with such a restricted entity, including banks—are effectively frozen out of the international banking system.

SWIFT is headquartered in Belgium, and Washington exerts inordinate control over the organisation, especially after the September 11, 2001, Al Qaeda attack on the World Trade Centre in New York. After the event, the U.S. and its allies increased their monitoring of SWIFT's daily transactions. The primary reason for this was to monitor possible transactions by terrorist organisations. American signals intelligence agencies have access to SWIFT transactions, and combined with the U.S. central bank's ability to trace U.S. dollars through the global financial system, Washington can exert incredible influence over SWIFT.

Geopolitics, therefore, have accelerated Beijing's efforts to build a parallel banking system and trading currency in place of SWIFT and the U.S. dollar. The Chinese understand that this is a long-term goal, which will require a well-funded and full-fledged fintech ecosystem.

Not surprisingly, Ant Group, Tencent Holdings and JD.com, all highly sophisticated Chinese tech giants, have been co-opted by the Chinese central government to work with the People's Bank of China (PBOC) and other state-owned banks as well as China's Digital Currency Research Institute to expedite the roll-out of the digital yuan. Huawei, meanwhile, has been developing mobile technologies that connect consumers' mobile devices to digital infrastructure at the PBOC and other state-backed banks.[4]

All of this presents a complicated risk landscape for foreign investors and multinational firms doing business with China. As the U.S.–China hybrid cold war drags on, Washington will likely adopt a guilt-by-association posture when assessing partnerships between foreign firms and Chinese entities linked to Beijing's CBDC ecosystem.

These scenarios make the long-term prospects for investors in China's fintech scene increasingly risky, as sanctions could come at any time, which will accelerate the need to de-risk and decouple. This will affect financial institutions and investors everywhere, from Singapore to Tel Aviv, from Copenhagen to Silicon Valley.

IDEOLOGY AND DIGITAL CURRENCY: A CLASH OF CIVILISATIONS

The second reason for financial decoupling is based on ideology. As digital currencies become ubiquitous, consumers will create an ever-expanding ocean of data. Here, CBDCs provide governments with a citizen's comprehensive digital footprint, which can be used for surveillance and leveraged to reward or punish behaviour.

The use of a CBDC to serve domestic and foreign agendas has put the e-yuan on a collision course with liberal democratic governments. As such, foreign firms embedded in China's fintech ecosystem could be seen as aiding and abetting Beijing's techno-authoritarian model and restricted from doing business with the likes of Tencent and Alibaba. This will galvanise both state and non-state actors to explore alternate CBDCs—or possibly even a trade-oriented cryptocurrency.

Navigating such murky waters will require sophisticated know-your-customer (KYC) capabilities. Large and small firms will need to achieve more transparency and traceability to determine, for example, if their business partners are linked to the Chinese state through Beijing's military–civil fusion initiative or whether they are part of a state-owned conglomerate.

Over the medium- to long-term, therefore, China's adoption of the e-yuan will intensify geopolitical rivalry and put in motion the fracturing of the global financial landscape.

DIGITAL DYSTOPIA

Together, digital money and techno-authoritarianism are the perfect recipe for a dystopic economy. Consider Alipay's so-called Sesame Credit programme. Sesame Credit is a Chinese social credit-scoring service developed by Ant Financial, part of the Alibaba family of companies that also includes Alipay, a third-party payment app with hundreds of millions of users. It was developed, largely by mandate, for the Chinese Communist Party (CCP).

This system goes beyond traditional credit scores by analysing five key data points: personal information, payment ability, credit history, social networks and user behaviours.

By combining these diverse data points, Sesame Credit assigns individuals a credit score. A high score unlocks benefits for users, such as access to loans with favourable terms, deposit-free services like, for example, rentals, travel and entertainment discounts and faster airport security checks. A high Sesame Credit score can enhance social interactions, as individuals with higher scores are perceived as more trustworthy and reliable.

The system offers a more comprehensive picture of an individual's creditworthiness and social standing, extending beyond the parameters of traditional credit scores.

While a high Sesame Credit score unlocks a world of convenience and benefits in China, the opposite holds true for those who earn a low score. These individuals face limitations and restrictions in different aspects of their lives.

Their access to essential financial services such as loans and credit cards is severely hampered, forcing them to accept unfavourable terms or simply be denied access altogether. Deposit-free rentals and other convenient services become inaccessible, adding further hurdles to daily life. Even online financial products and services offered by online service providers may become inaccessible.

Travelling becomes a burden for those with low Sesame Credit scores. Obtaining visas and securing travel-related services becomes considerably more difficult, coupled with limited access to travel discounts and benefits. Even airport security checks can become a source of inconvenience and delay.

Perhaps the most insidious impact of a low score is its social implications. Individuals may be ostracised or perceived as unreliable within their online and social circles. Online social groups become inaccessible. The stigma associated with a low score can permeate other aspects of life, creating a sense of exclusion and disadvantage— along with the possibility of being locked out of digital commerce.

This makes the Sesame Social credit scheme a powerful behaviour-altering tool for the CCP.[5] Theoretically, a social media post considered hostile or unflattering to the CCP could trigger the downgrading of an individual's score, and, because this negatively effects the scores of others that are socially linked to him, he is likely to be 'cancelled' by others in in his network. Such is the reality of digital money when it is the only option.

Speculation about the dystopic and Orwellian applications of the system are leading many to wonder what other data the system can capture, which almost certainly would include location tracking.

Liberal democracies, then, will look to impose export controls on outflows of technology seen to be aiding such techno-authoritarian practices, which will further bifurcate the financial sector.

This kind of technology–ideology linkage was previously seen when Washington blocked outflows of semiconductor technology to Chinese tech companies seen to be enabling Beijing's surveillance and internment of ethnic Uighurs in Xinjiang Province.

NEW ACCOUNTING STANDARDS AIMED AT CHINESE COMPANIES

In the U.S., new laws are being drafted with the intention of delisting Chinese companies from U.S. stock markets or making transparency requirements must more demanding. Legislation such as the Holding Foreign Companies Accountable Act (HFCAA), for example, was approved by Congress in December 2020 and requires Chinese companies to submit to third-party audits in line with Public Company Accounting Oversight Board (PCAOB) standards.[6]

The HFCAA was aimed at the financial statements of Chinese companies listed on U.S. stock exchanges, which have not been held to the higher standards of the PCAOB, going back to 2002 when it was instituted.

In April 2020, the discovery of accounting fraud involving more than US$300 million in the financial statements of U.S.-listed Chinese company Luckin Coffee led to a 75% drop in its share price and a backlash against corporate governance practices at Chinese companies.[7]

Despite the Luckin incident, however, the HFCAA was poorly received in the U.S. It was feared that Chinese companies would choose to delist rather than agree to invasive audits and the overhauling of opaque, questionable accounting practices. Presumably, companies such as Alibaba and Baidu would pack up and move to Hong Kong, which has less demanding accounting and reporting requirements.

The reality, however, was that the CCP tightened its grip on Hong Kong and on the tech sector, in general, and just two months after the HFCAA was approved by Congress, Beijing blocked the Hong Kong IPO of Alibaba's Ant Group—which wiped an estimated US$60 billion from the group's market capitalisation.

As Chinese companies have adopted PCAOB standards in the U.S., they have faced exposure in other ways, including questions regarding independence and true solvency, given the involvement and influence of the Chinese government in these companies.

Chinese companies, therefore, are stuck between Washington and Beijing in yet another example of the grey zone and how state interventionism is increasingly complicating the trade landscape.

The bottom line is that this will result in higher corporate governance costs as well as more fragmentation of financial markets.

THE U.S. OUTBOUND INVESTMENT TRANSPARENCY ACT

Since January 2021, U.S. investors have been prohibited from holding shares in Chinese companies believed to have links to the PLA.[8] Thus, banks and other American financial institutions were barred from investing in, for example, China Mobile and China Telecom, which have subsidiaries listed on U.S. stock exchanges.[9]

To increase controls around the flows of money into China's technology sectors, the U.S. Senate passed the Outbound Investment and Transparency Act in July 2023 by an overwhelming 91–6 bipartisan vote.

The Act demonstrates an escalation in U.S. outbound investment policy and how it seeks to exert more control over the activities of U.S. businesses abroad.

The law requires the U.S. Departments of the Treasury and Commerce to set up notification processes whereby businesses must alert the government 14 days prior to making an investment into 'countries of concern' such as China, Russia, Iran and North Korea.

The law singles out investment in AI, advanced semiconductors, quantum science, hypersonic technologies, satellite-based communications and laser technology.

Investors would be required to report acquisitions, debt obligations, the establishment of joint ventures and subsidiaries and other so-called 'know-how' transfers.

The legislation also seeks to coordinate with strategic partners and allies on a collaborative outbound screening process. This follows Washington's ongoing efforts of techno-diplomacy with its allies around resilient supply chains and export controls.

While the Outbound Investment Transparency Act is a scaled-back version of the Senate's earlier language in the National Defence

Authorisation Act, it adds significant obligations in an already fraught situation with tech investors and China.

For corporate governance, the ramifications of increased outbound investment restrictions in the financial sector will be enormous—if they are enforced. Given that China's 'military–civil fusion' philosophy has spilled over into all of its key technology sectors, most leading-edge companies, including financial and academic institutions in China, could be assumed to have ties to the Chinese military.

From a corporate governance perspective, due diligence, screening and vetting of Chinese companies regarding their ties to the People's Liberation Army (PLA) figures to become an expensive and compli-cated undertaking for American investors. This will impact large insti-tutional pension funds, investment banks, wealth funds and private investors.

Because of the opaque corporate governance practices that prevail in China, many investors will cut ties with Chinese investments if the U.S. government chooses to actively enforce the law. State activism will accelerate U.S.–China decoupling.

INTERNATIONAL BANKS CAUGHT BETWEEN BEIJING AND WASHINGTON

As the fallout of China–U.S. relations spills over into the world's finan-cial centres, international banks must adjust their corporate govern-ance to deal with Beijing and Washington's techno-nationalist agendas. Banks in Hong Kong, in particular, are at risk of being exposed to puni-tive and retaliatory measures from both governments.

One such bank, the Hong Kong and Shanghai Banking Corporation (HSBC), felt the full brunt of this reality on two separate occasions, and each instance was linked to geopolitics.

In 2020, HSBC—headquartered in the U.K., with its origins in British colonial Hong Kong—was the sixth largest bank in the world. HSBC had set aside US$100 billion in funds for loan applications associated with the IPO of Ant Financial. By the end of October 2020, HSBC had received about US$50 billion in applications.[10]

Prior to the doomed Ant Group IPO, HSBC had been dealing with the looming threat of U.S. sanctions and export controls because of another matter, and both Beijing and Washington were putting the bank under extreme pressure.

HSBC had been grappling with the consequences of working with Huawei, the Chinese telecoms equipment maker, and the bank's had alleged role in facilitating transactions with Skycom Tech Company Ltd.—which the Americans claimed was a front company that had been set up so Huawei could surreptitiously sell restricted U.S. technology in Iran, which was under U.S. sanctions.

Plenty was at stake: if HSBC had been complicit by association, the bank would be subject to punitive measures, including being banned from the U.S. banking system, and, more broadly, blocked from transacting with other banks in U.S. dollar denominated transactions.[11]

Dating back to 2012, HSBC provided financial services to Huawei in a series of transactions with Skycom. Later, when Huawei was under criminal investigation, HSBC conducted an internal probe of its own, in which it reported that Huawei had deliberately misled the bank by stating it had no ties with Skycom. This appeased Washington but infuriated Beijing.

CHINA PUNISHES HSBC

Even as HSBC was conducting crisis management regarding U.S. export controls, Chinese media accused it of having knowledge of Huawei's ties to Skycom and, consequently, colluding with U.S. authorities during its investigations in order to avoid U.S. sanctions. This chain of events ultimately led to the arrest of Meng Wanzhou, Huawei's CFO, in Canada at the request of Washington.

In retaliation, Beijing threatened to place HSBC on an 'unreliable entity list' for cooperating with the U.S. government in the Huawei investigation and, by extension, being complicit in Washington's global efforts to block Huawei's 5G expansion into overseas markets.[12]

Image 28.1   Photograph of Meng Wanzhou, the CFO of Huawei who was placed under house arrest in Canada, for three years, for the alleged involvement in U.S. Export Controls Violations.

Viewed in this light, Beijing used the blockage of the Ant Group IPO in Hong Kong not only to rein in an irreverent Chinese fintech giant but also to punish HSBC for earlier grievances.

When the CCP imposed its national security law in Hong Kong, HSBC, Standard Chartered and other international banks found themselves facing a dilemma.[13] Renouncement of the national security law would result in swift retribution from Beijing. But, bending to the CCP's will with the issuance of public statements that backed Beijing's law would expose HSBC to recriminations from Washington.

HSBC ultimately decided to issue a formal statement that read: 'HSBC . . . respects and supports all laws that stabilise Hong Kong's social order'.[14]

Although it is headquartered in London, most of HSBC's business is derived from Asia[15] and, specifically, China, where it works with a large base of customers, including state-owned entities such as the Ministry of Finance and the China Development Bank.[16,17]

When President Xi announced China's BRI, HSBC, as a leading financial institution, saw in it the potential to become a clearing house for currency exchange involving, BRI funding and capacity building.[18] It could ill afford to jeopardise all this by denouncing the national security law.

Washington's reaction to HSBC's China policies was predictable. In August 2020, the U.S. Senate passed the Hong Kong Autonomy Act, which stated that any institution engaging in or facilitating transactions with Chinese state-owned enterprises and named Communist Party officials would be seen as aiding and abetting Beijing's suppression of human rights in Hong Kong.[19]

Nevertheless, the U.S. Treasury's Office of Foreign Asset Control (OFAC) assured banks that they would first be contacted and questioned regarding their dealings with Chinese entities before it issued a new list of sanctioned entities.

TECHNO-NATIONALISM AND FINTECH DECOUPLING

From a corporate governance perspective, any bank doing business with Chinese entities, directly or indirectly, will have to expand the reach of their 'know your customer, (KYC) processes and increase traceability across all transactions. Negligently doing business with a restricted entity will spell catastrophe.

Many Hong Kong-based and even Singapore-based actors have been pulled into China's orbit as they participate in the design and roll-out of China's CBDC ecosystem in partnership with large Chinese tech companies. Many are working on digital payments and e-wallets, e-identity, blockchain and other forms of innovation required for China's techno-nationalist fintech landscape.

Hong Kong-based fintech firms (and others linked to them) find themselves directly and indirectly in collaboration with such champion tech firms as Tencent, Baidu, Alibaba, the Ant Group, SenseTime and Dahua, many of which are on U.S. restricted lists and are seen as quasi-government entities, given the key role they play in the CCP's techno-nationalist blueprint.

Alibaba, for example, is building cloud infrastructure, while Alipay is linking the government's Sesame Social credit rating system throughout. Tencent is building the blockchain and QR code technology, while SenseTime, Dahua and HikVision are providing ubiquitous AI and facial recognition tools and technology that comprise the bulwark of the CCP's techno-authoritarian apparatus.

Caught increasingly in the middle are foreign banks, venture capital firms and even individual angel investors, all of whom—from Washington's perspective—are susceptible to aiding and abetting, at least indirectly, of China's national security law in Hong Kong or further afield, Beijing's policies regarding the Uighur minorities in China's far West.

Thus, corporate governance must focus first and foremost on whether the gains of doing business with China's fintech sector outweigh the risks of sanctions and prohibitive compliance and risk management costs.

SOVEREIGN WEALTH FUNDS AND GEOPOLITICS

Sovereign Wealth Funds (SWF) are vast pools of nationally owned assets and investments. The portfolios of SWFs face increasing scrutiny due to their unavoidable involvement in markets that are affected by geopolitics and techno-nationalism.

Some of the wealthiest and most consequential SWFs include:

- China Investment Corporation (CIC) (US$1.35 trillion)
- Abu Dhabi Investment Authority (ADIA) (US$853 billion)
- Singapore's Temasek Holdings (US$380 billion)
- Saudi Arabian Public Investment Fund (US$776 billion)

SWFs investing in critical sectors like technology, infrastructure and resources can raise national security concerns, especially if the investor-nation has strained relations with the host country—or an affected third country. Fears of technology acquisition, data access and ownership of critical infrastructure drive calls for investment restrictions.

Escalating tensions between nations can spill over into the economic sphere, with SWFs becoming targets for sanctions, export controls and other restrictions. This happened with the Russia Sovereign Wealth Fund after the 2014 Crimea annexation, which highlights the vulnerability of these funds to broader political dynamics.

As SWFs seek diversification and higher returns, they may enter strategic partnerships or invest in industries that conflict with the economic interests of other nations. This can lead to trade disputes, protectionist measures and limitations on SWF activity.

Chapter 29

Techno-Diplomacy and the Road Ahead

Denmark became the first country to officially station its diplomats in Silicon Valley. While it may not be appropriate to say that Meta, Google, Apple and other tech giants qualify as de facto nations, in 2017, the government of Denmark saw the value of sending a tech ambassador to California—one Mr. Casper Klynge.[1]

This is one facet of the new techno-diplomacy. In this case, it was an example of government-to-business (G2B) relations, given the influence that technology companies now have on the security of nation-states. On Mr. Klynge's priority list: data privacy and data sovereignty issues, the proliferation of fake news and harmful content, AI ethics and rule-frameworks and R&D collaboration opportunities between Danish and American companies.

Regarding government-to-government (G2G) relations, adroit techno-diplomacy has now become a necessity for successful statecraft. More broadly, every self-respecting government should create a department of 'digital affairs' and staff it with people who speak the language of technology.

Traditional diplomats must receive back-to-school basic education in techno-nationalism and its impact on the affairs-of-state. Business leaders, meanwhile, need to understand about the paradigm shift that has changed the world and how their quarterly earnings statement may be affecting national security.

Techno-diplomacy, therefore, is the new realpolitik. It requires the use of enticements, partnerships, purpose-driven alliances and specialised agreements. It also involves coercion, if necessary, and the threat of punitive measures and negative outcomes. Should all these things fail, and should we become mired in yet another major war, its outcome will largely be decided by technology.

The paradigm shift in Washington has seen a focus on four distinct areas.

The first involves the creation of more resilient and secure supply chains. Assuming that the 'small-yard, high-fence' logic will continue to define the trade landscape, the world's strategic supply chains will continue to be reorganised. The great bifurcation of tech, and therefore, trading ecosystems will continue. Thus, the establishment of multilateral frameworks around the enforcement of export controls and sanctions is as vital as are re-shoring and near-shoring, which calls for G2G and G2B diplomacy.

Secondly, the U.S. and its allies are forming collaborative agreements for the setting of standards regarding, for example, generative AI, biotechnology and quantum computing. As we have discussed, these are potential enablers of authoritarian regimes as they seek to carry out mass surveillance, censorship and other forms of oppression. Thus, new rule-frameworks are coalescing around like-minded nations.

A third area involves the merging of security arrangement with technology transfer and supply chain resiliency agreements. Consider Pillar 2 of the AUKUS security pact involving Australia, the United Kingdom and the United States.

These trends are undermining mega free trade agreement (FTAs) and long-standing norms regarding big multilateral institutions, such as the World Trade Organization (WTO).

The result of all of this is a rapidly changing international landscape. The global economy is reorganising around U.S. and China spheres of influence, but also along north–south lines, as the BRICS countries look to exert more control over their destiny and as middle countries such as Saudi Arabia and Indonesia look to avoid having to choose sides. In short, a much more complex, multipolar world is emerging.

FROM FTAs TO MINI-LATERAL ARRANGEMENTS

The shift in international trade away from large multilateral FTAs is mostly attributable to geopolitics.

Consider the contrasts between the Comprehensive and Progressive Trans-Pacific Partnership (CPTPP), the so-called gold standard of FTAs, and the rise of a host of regional, sector-specific and bilateral agreements that are emerging as an alternative, which I will discuss below.

The CPTPP boasts progressive values around environmental sustainability, labour standards, transparency, government procurement and even gender diversity.

While these are all noble things to put into an FTA, they remain mostly aspirational. It is hugely challenging to verify and enforce such standards among such a diverse group of countries in such varied stages of economic development. When I began this writing, there were 11 member countries in the CPTPP: Canada, Mexico, Japan, Chile, Australia, New Zealand, Malaysia, Brunei, Singapore, Vietnam and Peru.[2] In July of 2023, the United Kingdom, became the twelfth country to join the FTA.

Thus, we have a conundrum: if gold standard provisions in a FTA are merely 'encouraged' but not enforced, there will be free riders that avail themselves of the FTA's benefits without meeting its benchmarks. But if its provisions go beyond aspirational and are in fact enforced, these free riders might be seriously challenged to achieve the desired standards.

Which is why nations have decided that smaller arrangement and forums between like-minded parties can work, and are more practical.

The WTO, meanwhile, has fallen into hard times as the global economy undergoes reorganisation—as I have pointed out, this is not 'deglobalisation'.

In 1995, the modern-day WTO became the designated multilateral institution charged with facilitating the rules around international trade. It has been the standard setter on customs valuation and rules of origin, for example, and has provided a dispute resolution mechanism for trade disagreements between countries. It has also been a forum for trade liberalisation and facilitation.

But as the paradigm shift in the West continued to gain sway, a pivotal question began to circulate in trade policy circles: Could a coalition of willing nations form a new global trade institution with *real* open market principles and democratic ideals? Such a forum would have to exclude China and other nations with 'non-market' economies.

This idea was proposed by Mogens Peter Carl, a former European Commission Director General for Trade and the Environment, and it began to gain currency around 2020.[3]

But nations had already begun to pursue their own arrangements, not through some alternative WTO-like organisation, but through mini-lateral groupings and pairings. Increasingly, non-binding 'forums' have become the engines of dialogue and collaboration.

Over a brief span of about four years, from 2019–2023, the number of regional, sector-specific and bilateral agreements grew rapidly. Consider this non-exhaustive list below. What is consistent with all these arrangements is that they reveal emerging blocks of nations that have coalesced around Washington and its key allies and strategic partners.

Regional Agreements
- Indo-Pacific Economic Framework (IPEF): Launched in 2022 by the U.S. with 14 member countries. IPEF promotes cooperation across different 'Pillars', including supply chain resilience.
- The E.U.–U.S. Trade and Technology Council (TTC): Addresses a range of technology issues, including supply chain challenges, and AI ethics standards.
- E.U.–Japan Economic Partnership Agreement (EPA): Includes provisions on cooperation on supply chain security and diversification.

Sector-Specific Agreements
- E.U. Chips Act (2023).
- U.S. CHIPS and Science Act (2022).
- Quad Semiconductor Partnership (2023) launched by the U.S., Japan, India and Australia regarding critical materials and equipment for semiconductor production.
- Critical Minerals Alliance (CMA) (2020) includes Australia, Canada, Finland, France, Germany, Japan, South Korea, Sweden, the U.K. and the E.U.

Bilateral Agreements
- U.S.–Japan Joint Statement on Semiconductor Cooperation: Announced in 2022, it strengthens collaboration on research, development and production of next-generation semiconductors.
- U.S.–E.U. Trade Action Plan: Agreed upon in 2020, it includes measures to address vulnerabilities in critical supply chains.
- E.U.–Korea FTA: Revised in 2021, the FTA promotes cooperation on supply chain security and transparency.

THE CHIP 4 ALLIANCE (FACT OR FICTION)

Perhaps the best barometer regarding the effectiveness, or lack thereof, of mini-lateral arrangements involves the so-called Chip 4 Alliance.

The Chip 4 alliance, formally known as the 'Fab 4' or 'Semiconductor Supply Chain Partnership', is a proposed collaboration between the U.S., Japan, South Korea and Taiwan. The U.S., as part of its overall China de-risking and decoupling efforts, is looking to onboard its historic allies in Asia, all of which have close security ties with the Washington and have growing economic ties via investments facilitated with CHIPS Act monies.

As we know, Washington aims to reduce dependence on Taiwan for advanced chips and China for older trailing-edge chips. The key is diversifying production and addressing potential supply chain choke points.

Goals of the Chip 4 alliance include the joint development of advanced chipmaking technologies by fostering R&D, the protection of intellectual property (IP) procedures and the establishment of unified standards and measures to safeguard sensitive chip technology.

In terms of chip production and trade, Washington wants Chip 4 to set norms and practices that encourage G2G and G2B protocols that can address supply and demand issues and maintain stable and open semiconductor markets.

But here is the problem: Chip 4 faces scepticism from Washington think tank analysts and other business observers who claim that the different parties, especially South Korea, Japan and Taiwan have different or even conflicting economic priorities and, therefore, will find it hard to work together.

For Washington's Chip 4 partners, there are real fears that Beijing might retaliate by closing off the Chinese market to their companies operating in China as punishment for their governments' cooperation with Washington. Critics also argue that the initiative lacks a formal agreement and timeline for concrete actions, and that, basically, nothing is really happening to move the alliance forward.

American techno-diplomacy regarding the Chip 4 alliance was on display in August 2023 during a Camp David summit between President Biden, Japanese Prime Minister Fumio Kishida and South Korean President Yoon Suk Yeol.

The three leaders released a joint statement reaffirming their commitment to 'building a more resilient, secure and diversified semiconductor supply chain' and they announced progress on 'early harvest initiatives', with concrete steps to be taken before a formal launch of Chip 4. This included mapping critical semiconductor materials and equipment, developing common standards for cybersecurity and working to establish public–private partnerships that can invest in critical infrastructure, such as chip foundries.

Also discussed was the strengthening of export controls and the promotion of transparency around such practices.

Here, sceptics would say that the Camp David meeting failed to produce a formal agreement with specific rules and nomenclatures for proper administration and management, such as those found, for example, in FTAs.

But keep in mind that FTAs take years to negotiate, and details must be hammered out by industry specialists, trade associations and affected businesses over many sessions. Informal arrangements like Chip 4 can come to fruition much more quickly than an FTA, and parties can address ongoing issues quickly and efficiently without getting bogged down in bureaucracy.

Thus, it is still too early to pass judgement against Chip 4. In the meantime, Japan, Taiwan and South Korea all fell in line with the enforcement of Washington's ratcheting up of export controls on semiconductor technology to China in October of 2023, in which they complied with the new restrictions of equipment and materials and also worked closely with Washington to get its consent on exceptions to the rules.

THE INDO-PACIFIC ECONOMIC FRAMEWORK

When the U.S. pulled out of the Trans-Pacific Partnership (TPP) after nine years of hard negotiations, like many others, I was disappointed in Washington's decision.

What followed were the Trump administration's tariff hikes, and the rest is history. But, as we have seen, the paradigm shift continued, much more methodically and on a larger scale with the incoming Biden administration, in 2020.

How, then, would 'Bidenomics' and a new team of China hawks in the White House address America's absence from Asia's reconstituted, somewhat watered-down Comprehensive and Progressive Trans-Pacific Partnership (CPTPP)?

The answer: The Indo-Pacific Economic Framework (IPEF).

Launched in May 2022, The IPEF is an ongoing initiative spearheaded by the Biden administration to strengthen economic ties and cooperation in the Indo-Pacific region. In 2023, it involved 14 member countries: Australia, Brunei, India, Indonesia, Japan, Korea, Malaysia, New Zealand, Philippines, Singapore, Thailand, Vietnam and the U.S.

The IPEF was built around core components, known as 'pillars' around trade flows, addressing custom procedures, digital trade and

448 Techno-Diplomacy and the Road Ahead

standards, supply chain resilience (reducing single-source dependencies), clean energy, decarbonisation, infrastructure and fair economies—tax and anti-corruption transparency measures.

IPEF differs from traditional FTAs in that it is not a binding agreement with predetermined obligations. Instead, it is a flexible framework where members work together to develop standards and best practices through working groups and joint initiatives. Participation is voluntary, and countries can choose which pillars they want to participate in.

The CPTPP, by contrast, is a traditional FTA with tariff reductions, market access guarantees and binding dispute settlement mechanisms. Unfortunately, from a traditional trade liberalisation perspective, Washington has not made market access the underlying motivation of the IPEF. Instead, it reinforces the administration's commitment to its techno-nationalist agenda while looking to promote economic interaction. Critics of the IPEF point to its lack of market access and claim that this is necessary to maintain interest of other members.

Keeping member countries engaged and moving forward without the binding force of a traditional agreement will be a challenge, as will balancing diverse economic priorities and goals of members.

Additionally, because China maintains significant economic ties with many IPEF countries, Beijing could potentially impact their level of engagement, especially if the U.S. is not providing tangible economic benefits beyond mere dialogue and promises of collaboration.

THE AUKUS TRILATERAL SECURITY AGREEMENT

Given the voluntary nature of the IPEF and the challenges that come with achieving alignment on issues among such a diverse group of nations, Washington will need to invest a great deal of effort for marginal gains.

But when techno-diplomacy is linked to transformative national security matters, and strategic partners are long-standing historic allies, the odds of success seem better.

AUKUS, short for 'Australia, the U.K. and U.S.' is a trilateral security partnership announced in September 2021. It aims to deepen intelligence sharing, technological cooperation and defence capabilities between the three nations, focusing on the Indo-Pacific region.

For Washington, AUKUS is a natural extension of the Australia, New Zealand and U.S. (ANZUS) Security Agreement that has been in place since 1951 and the Five Eyes intelligence-sharing network, going back to just after the Second World War, involving the U.S., the U.K., Australia, Canada and New Zealand.

AUKUS may well be the single most significant development in techno-diplomacy, dating as far back as the creation of the North Atlantic Treaty Organisation (NATO) in 1949—at least in terms of the magnitude of technologies that would be shared and brought to bear in a collective defence effort.

The technology pillar of AUKUS involves the transfer of nuclear-powered submarine propulsion systems and a host of other related technologies. In fact, the technology transfer associated with AUKUS covers virtually every twenty-first-century power multiplier technology on the list: robotics and autonomous undersea capabilities, quantum, AI, advanced cyber and electronic warfare, hypersonic and counter-hypersonic technologies and more.[4]

In a paper I co-wrote with Professor Robert Clark in September 2022 entitled 'Australia's Semiconductor National Moonshot', published by the Australian Strategic Policy Institute (ASPI), we argued that the AUKUS security pact would allow Australia to avail itself of key technology transfers through strategic public–private partnerships between defence, the private sector and academia.

Technology transfer strengthens secure supply chains, another core element of AUKUS. By developing domestic capabilities, AUKUS partners reduce reliance on potentially vulnerable external sources for critical technologies.

Secure supply chains, then, enable more robust national security partnerships, and stronger national security partnerships facilitate further technology transfer, creating a positive feedback loop that paves the way for even more innovation.

Japan has expressed a desire to join AUKUS. Such a move could enhance the strategic advantage of the existing tripartite agreement by adding yet more deterrence capability to the security pack. But it could also accelerate an arms race in the Indo-Pacific. Such a reality, however, is already playing out, regardless, thus the question is whether Japan could remain a trusted partner and ally over the long term.

The economic and technology-related benefits under Pillar 2 with Japan, however, could be substantial. This will be something worth watching closely.

THE QUADRILATERAL SECURITY DIALOGUE (QUAD)

The Quadrilateral Security Dialogue (Quad) is a loosely knit, informal grouping of four nations: Australia, India, Japan and the U.S. Unlike AUKUS, it is not a formal alliance or treaty but rather a mechanism for regular dialogue and cooperation on a range of issues, particularly the security in the Indo-Pacific region.

Quad members express a shared commitment to a 'free and open Indo-Pacific' based on respect for international law, sovereignty and territorial integrity. This includes countering China's perceived assertiveness in the region.

Key areas of dialogue include maritime domain awareness, freedom of navigation and disaster relief preparedness.

Regarding technology transfer, there is open-ended language about sharing best practices and promoting responsible development in areas such as cybersecurity, artificial intelligence (AI) and space exploration, as well as language that encourages joint efforts to address natural disasters and global health challenges. The Quad, for example, has supported vaccine production and distribution in Southeast Asia and Africa.

Like the IPEF, the Quad is an informal agreement that has similar limitations. While the Quad addresses broader security and economic issues, AUKUS primarily focuses on military technology and defence cooperation between three partners that are very closely intertwined through collective national security imperatives.

Like the IPEF, the Quad lacks a treaty or binding agreement, which may limit its effectiveness in tackling complex security challenges.

Members—although there are only four in the Quad as opposed to 14 in IPEF—have diverse priorities, potentially hindering consensus on specific initiatives. India's priorities as a BRICS country may not always align with those of the U.S., Japan and Australia, especially as New Delhi maintains strong ties with Russia.

On paper, at least, the Quad presents a united front against China's influence in the region, strengthening collective bargaining power. Some would argue that cooperation among the members on global issues strengthens member nations' reputations as responsible leaders on the world stage.

But full multilateral buy-in, on a regular basis, is essential if Washington's techno-diplomacy endgame is to succeed regarding the Quad.

BILATERAL TECHNO-DIPLOMACY

Given the paradigm shift away from big multilateral institutions and, essentially, non-binding forums such as IPEF and the QUAD, American diplomats have hedged their bets by pursuing a plethora of one-on-one dialogues, memorandums of understanding and joint statements with Japan, South Korea, Taiwan, India, Fiji, Singapore and other countries. Many of these overlap with other ongoing efforts already mentioned.

The areas of focus are all similar: semiconductors, critical minerals, AI and machine learning, undersea cables and low earth orbit communications satellites. There are now forums, brainstorming sessions, workshops and research-focused networks involving a wide range of stakeholders and subject matter experts, all of whom provide governments with input.

Defence-focused technology transfer under AUKUS and through ongoing NATO and DARPA initiatives—which are ring-fenced and classified—will remain within the realm of the defence establishment.

In general, however, techno-diplomacy will become increasingly pervasive, with overlapping and sometimes conflicting objectives.

In another area involving digital trade, diplomatic collaboration among concerned parties has been leaning towards 'digital only agreements' to lock in core values and ideologies specific to liberal democracies and market-oriented countries, such as data privacy guarantees, prohibitions against data localisation mandates and the mandatory turning over of corporate encryption and software code to government security agencies.

We see this development playing out in, for example, the Singapore-Australia Digital Economy Agreement (SADEA) and the UK-Singapore Digital Economy Agreement (UKSDEA). These agreements provide a template for other like-minded countries who want their standards and values reflected in their day-to-day trading relationships.

Typical differentiators between liberal democracies and authoritarian regimes like China include data localisation requirements, as well as data privacy matters, and requirements to protect IP and block governments from demanding foreign businesses to handover encryption keys and software code.

AI ETHICS AND THE PROMISE OF OPEN-SOURCED PLATFORMS

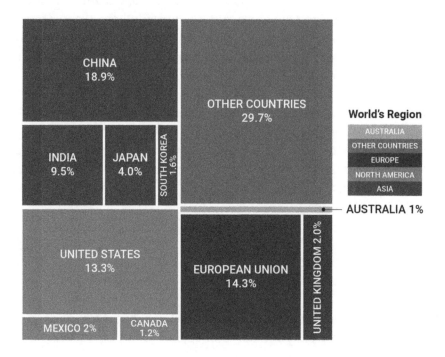

Figure 29.1   Digital Democracies Equal Approximately 50% of Global GDP (PPP Basis).

Even before the release of ChatGPT and other generative AI tools, governments had been grappling with the ideological linkages to AI, particularly in the context of U.S.–China rivalry.

In May 2020, the U.S. joined other G7 members, Canada, France, Germany, Italy, Japan and the U.K., in a technology-focused pact—the G7 AI initiative. Its purpose is to study and provide recommendations to encourage the creation of AI technologies that respect privacy and civil liberties.

Similar to the G7 AI initiative, the Global Partnership on Artificial Intelligence (GPAI) is an international initiative created by France and Canada along with Australia, the E.U., Germany, India, Italy, Japan, Mexico, New Zealand, the Republic of Korea, Singapore, Slovenia, the U.K. and the U.S.

The GPAI's mission is to guide responsible development and use of AI in a distinctly democratic way, and it seeks to instigate a series of well-funded public–private research partnerships that are focused not only on AI technical standards but also on privacy, free speech and surveillance.

As for the bifurcation of global supply chains and the dominance of a handful of state-backed tech companies, a possible countermeasure has emerged: the open sourcing of patents.

This option had been put forward by nations wishing to avoid choosing sides between China and the U.S.—and avoid the crushing effects of export controls and sanctions. The idea is to promote the open sourcing of patents. By pulling in more subject matter experts from a wider universe, this advances the state of the art while preventing monopolies and oligopolies (and nations) from controlling key technologies.

Not surprisingly, Chinese officials have called for the open sourcing of chips. The People's Liberation Army's (PLA) Academy of Military Sciences, for example, used an open-source standard known as RISC-V, to gain access to more programmers and engineers, which resulted in better-designed chips for cloud computing and smart cars, according to patent filings.[5]

American companies such as Intel and Advanced Micro Devices and Britain's Arm Holdings control the leading licensed platforms for chip design. Access to these is subject to payment, and the most advanced designs are off-limits due to export controls.

Recall that in Chapter 13, we discussed how a lot of China's big tech firms have, historically, designed their own platforms and AI using Western open-sourced architecture and software such as TensorFlow and Torch. As Washington ratchets up its export controls on chip design software and open architecture, this could close off these avenues. Thus, the PLA hopes to advance its own open-sourced innovation agenda.

The open-source argument goes back to Washington's war on Huawei and what became known as O-RAN (Open Radio Access Network) alliance.[6] The idea is that by establishing open standards and interfaces for wireless communication infrastructure, specifically for 5G, different vendors' hardware and software components can interoperate seamlessly, creating a more flexible and diverse ecosystem.

O-RAN or similar open platforms, theoretically, can help countries avoid choosing sides in the U.S.–China tech war.

Historically, 5G deployments have relied on specific vendors, often dominated by Huawei, Ericsson and Nokia. O-RAN, however, opens up the market to more vendors, including smaller players, reducing reliance on any single source. This diversifies the supply chain and reduces dependence on specific nations.

Reliance on just a few proprietary systems also raises security concerns, as vulnerabilities can be exploited by bad actors. O-RAN's open interfaces allow for greater scrutiny and collaboration on security, potentially making networks more resilient to cyberattacks regardless of their origin.

Open standards foster innovation as smaller players can contribute and compete. This creates a more dynamic environment where both U.S. and Chinese companies can participate on a level playing field, potentially leading to faster advancements in the field.

The O-RAN alliance has been dominated by AT&T from the U.S., Japan's NTT DOCOMO, Deutsche Telekom and Orange, of the Netherlands. China Mobile is a founding member, but even in a supposed open-sourced environment, the other telecoms have coalesced and have looked to promote Western technology.

THE GREAT REORGANISATION WILL GO ON

The BRICS countries (Brazil, Russia, India, China and South Africa), led by China, are agitating to break away from the influence of the U.S. and Europe and other G7 countries.

U.S. sanctions and the weaponisation of the U.S. dollar have sent the original five BRICS countries (along with another 22 countries that have applied for BRICS membership) seeking alternative currencies and trading opportunities.

Meanwhile, in certain instances, so-called 'middle countries'—such as Singapore, Vietnam, India, Mexico, or, for that matter, Germany or Sweden—will to have to make binary choices and choose sides when it comes to trade in dual-use strategic goods. In these instances, they must work towards an orderly decoupling scenario, which requires a realistic forward looking pragmatism.

As I write this, Olaf Scholz, Germany's Chancellor, has just returned home from a trip from China, where he assured Beijing of continued investment into China by Germany's big MNEs, even as other members of his government speak out about China's predatorial economic practices and neo-mercantilism.

There will be no way to have it both ways. Hard choices are coming for Germany and others. Again, we can strive for orderly decoupling where it is merited. But eventually, if China's rise reaches the next phase, where it becomes sufficiently muscular militarily, the paradox of ongoing trade with a formidable geopolitical rival may come back to haunt us all.

Graham Allison's Thucydides Trap is far from vanquished.

Meanwhile, in other areas, the U.S. will continue to press its allies for a new multilateral export controls regime, a cartel-like body that represents Washington and its trusted technology partners, such as the Semiconductor Group of Five. Other similar mini-lateral rules frameworks and forums will continue to emerge.

In other cases, the open sourcing of tech designs, code and other IP will allow third parties to avoid a binary choice.

For now, as the global economy reorganises and de-risks, there will be a lot of overlapping interests. Thus, in some cases, middle countries will be forced to choose sides in the U.S.–China tech competition; in other cases, they may find workarounds and loopholes. The dual-use grey zone will overshadow all trade, as will the threat of new sanctions and export controls. Cybersecurity threats will continue to grow.

Yet fragmentation of the global economy presents a myriad of new growth opportunities. Re-shoring, new strategic partnerships and new industries dealing with risk mitigation.

We can only hope that techno-nationalism results in deterrence and peace, rather than self-aggrandisement and aggression.

Notes

INTRODUCTION: MY CHINA LESSONS

1. UNCTAD. (2023). *World investment report 2023: Investing in sustainable energy for all.* https://unctad.org/publication/world-investment-report-2023

2. Horn, S., Reinhart, C. M., & Trebesch, C. (2019). *China's overseas lending* (Working Paper No. 26050). The National Bureau of Economic Research (NBER). https://www.nber.org/system/files/working_papers/w26050/w26050.pdf

3. Bian, L., Susan, Z., & David, T. (2005). *The Wal-Mart effect: An economic analysis of the impacts of Wal-Mart's growth in China.* The Brookings Institution.

4. Capri, A. (2020, January 17). *Semiconductors at the heart of the US-China tech war.* Hinrich Foundation. https://www.hinrichfoundation.com/research/wp/tech/semiconductors-at-the-heart-of-the-us-china-tech-war/

CHAPTER 1: TECHNO-NATIONALISM

1. Dimitropoulou, A. (2022, March 31). Economy rankings: Largest countries by GDP, 2022. *CEOWORLD magazine.* Retrieved from https://web.archive.org/web/20220331102746/https://ceoworld.biz/2022/03/31/economy-rankings-largest-countries-by-gdp-2022/

2. Myllyvirta, L., Qin, Q., Dai, J., Shen, X., & Qiu, C. (2024, January 25). *Analysis: Clean energy was top driver of China's economic growth in 2023.* CarbonBrief. https://www.carbonbrief.org/analysis-clean-energy-was-top-driver-of-chinas-economic-growth-in-2023/#:~:text=China's%20%24890bn%20investment%20in,%25%20year%2Don%2Dyear

3. Furukawa, Y., & Mochizuki, T. (2021, November 26). *Japan approves $6.8 billion boost for domestic chip industry*. Bloomberg. https://www.bloomberg.com/news/articles/2021-11-26/japan-approves-6-8-billion-boost-for-domestic-chip-industry?sref=jeNvC3eC

4. Badlam, J., Clark, S., Gajendragadkar, S., Kumar, A., O'Rourke, S. S., & Swartz, D. (2022, October 4). *The CHIPS and Science Act: Here's what's in it*. McKinsey & Company. https://www.mckinsey.com/industries/public-and-social-sector/our-insights/the-chips-and-science-act-heres-whats-in-it

5. Caballar, R. D. (2023, January 19). *5 Months after CHIPS Act, investment activity abounds in the chip industry*. Data Center Knowledge. https://www.datacenterknowledge.com/north-america/5-months-after-chips-act-investment-activity-abounds-chip-industry#close-modal

6. Ting-Fang, C. (2022, December 6). TSMC to triple U.S. chip investment to $40bn to serve Apple, others. *Nikkei Asia*. https://asia.nikkei.com/Business/Tech/Semiconductors/TSMC-to-triple-U.S.-chip-investment-to-40bn-to-serve-Apple-others

7. Peter G. Peterson Foundation. (2023, April 24). *The United States spends more on defense than the next 10 countries combined*. https://www.pgpf.org/blog/2023/04/the-united-states-spends-more-on-defense-than-the-next-10-countries-combined

8. Badlam, J., Clark, S., Gajendragadkar, S., Kumar, A., O'Rourke, S. S., & Swartz, D. (2022, October 4). *The CHIPS and Science Act: Here's what's in it*. McKinsey & Company. https://www.mckinsey.com/industries/public-and-social-sector/our-insights/the-chips-and-science-act-heres-whats-in-it

9. The White House. (2023, November 9). *Biden-Harris Administration celebrates historic progress in rebuilding America ahead of two-year anniversary of bipartisan infrastructure law* [Fact sheet]. https://www.whitehouse.gov/briefing-room/statements-releases/2023/11/09/fact-sheet-biden-harris-administration-celebrates-historic-progress-in-rebuilding-america-ahead-of-two-year-anniversary-of-bipartisan--infrastructure-law/?utm_source=link

10. Harvey, F., & Rankin, J. (2021, August 25). What is the European Green Deal and will it really cost €1tn? *The Guardian*. https://www.theguardian.com/world/2020/mar/09/what-is-the-european-green-deal-and-will-it-really-cost-1tn

11. Murtaugh, D. (2023, January 27). *Energy transition: China mulls solar export ban as trade tensions surge*. Australian Financial Review. https://www.afr.com/policy/energy-and-climate/china-mulls-solar-export-ban-as-trade-tensions-soar-20230127-p5cfy8#:~:text=Singapore%20%7C%20China%20is%20considering%20an,trying%20to%20strengthen%20their%20industries

12. Capri, A. (2021, April 8). *Commentary: How COVID-19 vaccines are being weaponised as countries jostle for influence*. CNA. https://www.channelnewsasia.com/commentary/covid-19-vaccines-weaponised-coronavirus-china-us-russia-199116

13. Capri, A. (2022, June 14). *After Ukraine: The new geopolitics of food secu-rity.* Hinrich Foundation. https://www.hinrichfoundation.com/research/wp/tech/ukraine-geopolitics-of-food-security/?utm_term=&utm_campaign=Search+%7C+Generic+%7C+Brand+Awareness&utm_source=adwords&utm_medium=ppc&hsa_acc=8724352572&hsa_cam=18241719097&hsa_grp=147625861160&hsa_ad=644521955253&hsa_src=g&hsa_tgt=aud-666254151587:dsa-2411127348472&hsa_kw=&hsa_mt=&hsa_net=adwords&hsa_ver=3&gad_source=1&gclid=CjwKCAjw5lmwBhBtEiwAFHDZx8JE87JmEWYN17lJSjgPpwAlYZVv_vUiq_JfY_VHJFusR0MqHlT-PxoCsKMQAvD_BwE

14. Wee, S. (2022, November 16). As G20 Summit ends, divisions persist on Russia sanctions. *The New York Times.* https://www.nytimes.com/2022/11/16/world/asia/g20-summit-sanctions-russia.html

15. The Business Times. (2021, June 20). *Wall Street banks struggle to cash in on China hiring binge.* https://www.businesstimes.com.sg/companies-markets/banking-finance/wall-street-banks-struggle-cash-china-hiring-binge

16. Huang, T., & Lardy, N. R. (2022, March 29). *Foreign corporates investing in China surged in 2021.* Peterson Institute for International Econom-ics.https://www.piie.com/blogs/realtime-economic-issues-watch/foreign-corporates-investing-china-surged-2021#:~:text=According%20to%20a%20survey%20of,increased%20investment%20compared%20with%202020

17. Donnan, S. (2022, December 3). *This could be a record year for US-China trade.* Bloomberg. https://www.bloomberg.com/news/newsletters/2022-12-03/a-record-year-for-us-china-trade-new-economy-saturday

18. Bade, G. (2023, January 27). *Key lawmaker: Biden mulling broad prohi-bitions on U.S. investments in Chinese tech.* Politico. https://www.politico.com/news/2023/01/27/biden-mulling-broad-prohibitions-investments-chinese-tech-00079995

CHAPTER 2: THE TECHNOLOGY FEEDBACK LOOP

1. Richard Arkwright. (2003, September 7). In *Wikipedia.* https://en.wikipedia.org/wiki/Richard_Arkwright

2. Founders Online. (n.d.). *Alexander Hamilton's final version of the report on the subject of manufactures, [5 December 1791].* National Archives. https://founders.archives.gov/documents/Hamilton/01-10-02-0001-0007

3. Founders Online. (n.d.). *From Alexander Hamilton to the directors of the Society for Establishing Useful Manufactures, [7 December 1791].* National Archives. https://founders.archives.gov/documents/Hamilton/01-10-02-0006

4. Welles, A. (1958, April). Father of our factory system. *American Herit-age, 9*(3). https://www.americanheritage.com/father-our-factory-system

5. Chernow, R. (2004). *Alexander Hamilton.* Penguin Books.

6. *Look Before You Leap.* (1796). [London] Printed for W. Row [etc.]. Retrieved from Internet Archive website: https://archive.org/details/lookbeforeyoulea00lond

7. Sutton, M. (2020, January 27). *Chemists at war.* Chemistry World. Retrieved February 1, 2023, from https://www.chemistryworld.com/features/chemists-at-war/7568.article

8. Sutton, M. (2020, January 27). *Chemists at war.* Chemistry World. Retrieved February 1, 2023, from https://www.chemistryworld.com/features/chemists-at-war/7568.article

9. Andrews, E. L. (1999, May 2). The business world; I.G. Farben: A lingering relic of the Nazi years. *The New York Times.* https://www.nytimes.com/1999/05/02/business/the-business-world-ig-farben-a-lingering-relic-of-the-nazi-years.html

10. Computer History Museum. (n.d.). *Revolution: The first 2000 years of computing.* https://www.computerhistory.org/revolution/

11. The National Museum of Computing (n.d.). *Colossus.* https://www.tnmoc.org/colossus

12. Baggot, J. (2009). *Atomic: The first war of physics and the secret history of the atomic bomb, 1939–49.* Icon.

13. Office of Legacy Management. (n.d.). *Manhattan project background information and preservation work.* U.S. Department of Energy. https://www.energy.gov/lm/manhattan-project-background-information-and-preservation-work

14. Baggot, J. (2009). *Atomic: The first war of physics and the secret history of the atomic bomb, 1939–49.* Icon.

15. Ambrose, S. E. (1993, June 1). [Review of the book *The Sputnik challenge: Eisenhower's response to the Soviet satellite* by Robert A. Divine]. *Foreign Affairs.* https://www.foreignaffairs.com/reviews/capsule-review

16. History, Art & Archives, United States House of Representatives. (1958). *National Defense Education Act.* https://history.house.gov/HouseRecord/Detail/15032436195

CHAPTER 3: PARADIGM SHIFT AND PARADOX

1. The White House. (2020, May). *United States strategic approach to the People's Republic of China.* National Archives. https://trumpwhitehouse.archives.gov/wp-content/uploads/2020/05/U.S.-Strategic-Approach-to-The-Peoples-Republic-of-China-Report-5.24v1.pdf

2. The White House. (2020, May). *United States strategic approach to the People's Republic of China.* National Archives. https://trumpwhitehouse.archives.gov/wp-content/uploads/2020/05/U.S.-Strategic-Approach-to-The-Peoples-Republic-of-China-Report-5.24v1.pdf

3. Sullivan, J. (2023, October 24). The sources of American power: A foreign policy for a changed world. *Foreign Affairs.* https://www.foreignaffairs.com/united-states/sources-american-power-biden-jake-sullivan

4. Kennan, G. F. (1947, July). The sources of Soviet conduct. *Foreign Affairs.* https://www.foreignaffairs.com/russian-federation/george-kennan-sources-soviet-conduct

5. Kimball, W., & Scott, R. E. (2014, December 11). *China trade, outsourcing and jobs.* Economic Policy Institute. https://www.epi.org/publication/china-trade-outsourcing

6. Stiglitz, J. E. (2003). *Globalization and its discontents.* W. W. Norton & Company.

7. GE Aerospace. (2011, January 23). *GE and AVIC sign agreement for integrated avionics joint venture.* https://www.geaerospace.com/news/press-releases/systems/ge-and-avic-sign-agreement-integrated-avionics-joint-venture

8. Air & Space Forces Magazine. (n.d.). *F-22 Raptor.* https://www.airandspaceforces.com/weapons-platforms/f-22/

9. Army Technology. (2024, March 1). *Patriot missile long-range air-defence system, USA.* https://www.army-technology.com/projects/patriot/

10. Angell, N. (1910). *The great illusion: A study of the relation of military power in nations to their economic and social advantage.*

CHAPTER 4: THE IN-CHINA-FOR-CHINA GREY ZONE

1. Allen, C. (2023, April 26). *Blog: Concerns about China's new anti-espionage law and recent cases targeting MNCs.* The US-China Business Council. https://www.uschina.org/blog-concerns-about-china%E2%80%99s-new-anti-espionage-law-and-recent-cases-targeting-mncs

2. Shepardson, D. (2024, March 14). *US House passes bill to force Byte Dance to divest TikTok or face ban.* Reuters. https://www.reuters.com/technology/us-house-vote-force-bytedance-divest-tiktok-or-face-ban-2024-03-13/

3. Bloomberg News. (2022, March 14). *China canceled H&M. Every other brand needs to understand why.* Bloomberg. https://www.bloomberg.com/graphics/2022-china-canceled-hm/#:~:text=H%26M's%20decision%20to%20stop%20using,Western%20companies%20taking%20similar%20action.

4. Capri, A. (2023, October 12). *The-in-China-for-China corporate gray zone.* The Hinrich Foundation. https://www.hinrichfoundation.com/research/wp/us-china/china-corporate-gray-zone/

5. Liao, R. (2023, June 15). *BYD is overtaking Tesla, but its EV dream skips the US for now.* TechCrunch. https://techcrunch.com/2023/06/15/byd-is-overtaking-tesla-but-its-ev-dream-skips-the-us-for-now/

6. Bradsher, K. (2023, April 14). China's car buyers have fallen out of love with foreign brands. *The New York Times.* https://www.nytimes.com/2023/04/14/business/china-shanghai-auto-show.html

7. Bradsher, K., & Forsythe, M. (2021, December 22). Why a Chinese company dominates electric car batteries. *The New York Times*. https://www.nytimes.com/2021/12/22/business/china-catl-electric-car-batteries.html

8. Statista Research Department. (2023, October 24). *EV lithium-ion battery production capacity shares worldwide 2021-2025, by country*. Statista. https://www.statista.com/statistics/1249871/share-of-the-global-lithium-ion-battery-manufacturing-capacity-by-country/#:~:text=EV%20lithium%2Dion%20battery%20production,worldwide%202021%2D2025%2C%20by%20country&text=China%20dominated%20the%20world's%20electric,that%20entered%20the%20global%20market.

9. Capri, A. (2023, October 12). *The-in-China-for-China corporate gray zone*. The Hinrich Foundation. https://www.hinrichfoundation.com/research/wp/us-china/china-corporate-gray-zone/

10. Pomfret, J., & Woo, A. (2023, May 2). *China's exit bans multiply as political control tightens under Xi*. Reuters. https://www.reuters.com/world/china/chinas-exit-bans-multiply-political-control-tightens-under-xi-2023-05-02/

CHAPTER 5: DE-RISKING AND DECOUPLING

1. Gross, A. (2023, April 18). Michael Dell says customers are demanding less reliance on China. *Financial Times*. https://www.ft.com/content/d6dc3fe2-f56c-4346-9a55-f1055967b1a5

2. Ting-Fang, C. (2023, January 5). Dell looks to phase out 'made in China' chips by 2024. *Nikkei Asia*. https://asia.nikkei.com/Spotlight/Supply-Chain/Dell-looks-to-phase-out-made-in-China-chips-by-2024

3. Li, L. (2023, January 24). Taiwan's Foxconn and others accelerate investment in Mexico. *Nikkei Asia*. https://asia.nikkei.com/Spotlight/Supply-Chain/Taiwan-s-Foxconn-and-others-accelerate-investment-in-Mexico

4. Statista Research Department. (2023, April 11). *Frozen assets of Bank of Russia due to the war in Ukraine 2022, by country*. Statista. https://www.statista.com/statistics/1298593/frozen-assets-of-bank-of-russia-by-country/

5. Blenkinsop, P. (2022, March 3). *EU bars 7 Russian banks from SWIFT, but spares those in energy*. Reuters. https://www.reuters.com/business/finance/eu-excludes-seven-russian-banks-swift-official-journal-2022-03-02/

6. Tomson, B. (2022, March 4). *Russian halt to fertilizer exports expected to boost prices, spur shortfalls*. Agri-Pulse. https://www.agri-pulse.com/articles/17312-russian-halt-to-fertilizer-exports-expected-to-boost-prices-spur-shortfalls

7. European Commission. (2022, September 7). *Statement by President von der Leyen on energy*. https://ec.europa.eu/commission/presscorner/

api/files/document/print/en/speech_22_5389/SPEECH_ 22_5389_EN.pdf

8. Elliott, S. (2022, August 10). *FEATURE: Europe's dash for new LNG import infrastructure picks up pace.* S&P Global. https://www.spglobal .com/commodityinsights/en/market-insights/latest-news/natural-gas/ 081022-feature-europes-dash-for-new-lng-import-infrastructure-picks-up-pace

9. Bloomberg News. (2022, March 17). *Canada's scrambling to fill a massive global fertilizer deficit.* MINING.com. https://www.mining.com/ web/canadas-scrambling-to-fill-a-massive-global-fertilizer-deficit/

10. Biden, J. (2021, February 24). *Executive order on America's supply chains.* The White House. https://www.whitehouse.gov/briefing-room/ presidential-actions/2021/02/24/executive-order-on-americas-supply-chains/

11. Yao, K. (2020, September 9). *What we know about China's 'dual circulation' economic strategy.* Reuters. https://www.reuters.com/article/idUSK BN2600B4/

12. Wei, L. (2019, March 5). Beijing drops contentious 'Made in China 2025' slogan, but policy remains. *The Wall Street Journal.* https://www.wsj .com/articles/china-drops-a-policy-the-u-s-dislikes-at-least-in-name-11551795370

CHAPTER 6: EXPORT CONTROLS

1. Capri, A. (2020, January 17). *Semiconductors at the heart of the US-China tech war.* Hinrich Foundation. https://research.hinrichfounda tion.com/hubfs/Capri%20Report%20-%20Jan%202020/Hinrich%20 Foundation%20report%20-%20US-China%20tech%20war%20and%20 semiconductors%20-%20January%2031%202020.pdf

2. Office of Foreign Assets Control. (n.d.). *Where is OFAC's Country List? What countries do I need to worry about in terms of U.S. sanctions?* U.S. Department of the Treasury. https://ofac.treasury.gov/sanctions-programs-and-country-information/where-is-ofacs-country-ntgp-what-countries-do-i-need-to-worry-about-in-terms-of-us-sanctions#:~:text=OFAC's% 20Specially%20Designated%20Nationals%20and,names%20 connected%20with%20sanctions%20targets.

3. Reuters. (2022, January 25). *Explainer: The U.S. export rule that hammered Huawei teed up to hit Russia.* https://www.reuters.com/business/ us-export-rule-that-hammered-huawei-teed-up-hit-russia-2022-01-24/

4. Made in China 2025. (2024, March 17). In *Wikipedia.* https://en.wikipedia .org/wiki/Made_in_China_2025#Strategic_initiatives

5. Kaur, D. (2023, March 7). *The US is still approving export licenses for blacklisted firms from China, including Huawei and SMIC.* Tech Wire Asia. https://techwireasia.com/03/2023/the-us-is-still-approving-export-licenses-for-blacklisted-firms-from-china-including-huawei-and-smic/

6. Butts, D. (2023, November 2). Qualcomm highlights China sales jump as it beats estimates, in latest signal of smartphone market rebound. *South China Morning Post*. https://www.scmp.com/tech/article/3240111/ qualcomm-highlights-china-sales-jump-it-beats-estimates-latest-signal-smartphone-market-rebound

7. Rai, S., & Lee, Y. (2023, November 10). *China AI startup stockpiled 18 months of Nvidia chips before ban*. Bloomberg. https://www .bloomberg.com/news/articles/2023-11-10/china-ai-startup-stockpiled-18-months-of-nvidia-chips-before-ban?sref=jeNvC3eC

8. Ghosh, K., & Nellis, S. (2023, August 10). *China's internet giants order $5 bln of Nvidia chips to power AI ambitions - FT*. Reuters. https://www .reuters.com/technology/chinas-internet-giants-order-5-bln-nvidia-chips-power-ai-ambitions-ft-2023-08-09/

9. Shilov, A. (2023, December 26). *China's chipmaking tool purchases increase 1,050% in November: Report*. Tom's Hardware. https://www .tomshardware.com/tech-industry/manufacturing/chinas-chipmaking-tool-purchases-increase-1050-in-november-report#:~:text=China's%20 chipmaking%20tool%20purchases%20increase%201%2C050%25% 20in%20November%3A%20Report,-News&text=More%20litho%20 tools%20for%20Chinese%20chipmakers.&text=The%20Nether-lands%20recently%20saw%20a,(via%20Yahoo!%20Finance).

10. Ye, J., Kirton, D., & Lin, C. (2023, June 21). *Focus: Inside China's underground market for high-end Nvidia AI chips*. Reuters. https://www .reuters.com/technology/inside-chinas-underground-market-high-end-nvidia-ai-chips-2023-06-19/

11. Olcott, E., & Liu, Q. (2023, March 9). Chinese AI groups use cloud services to evade US chip export controls. *Financial Times*. https://www .ft.com/content/9706c917-6440-4fa9-b588-b18fbc1503b9

12. Kerr, S., Al-Atrush, S., Liu, Q., & Murgia, M. (2023, October 9). Saudi-China collaboration raises concerns about access to AI chips. *Financial Times*. https://www.ft.com/content/2a636cee-b0d2-45c2-a815-11ca32371763

13. Choi, J. (2024, January 26). Massive operation smuggling semiconductors from US to China uncovered. *BusinessKorea*. https://www.businesskorea .co.kr/news/articleView.html?idxno=210248

14. Nardelli, A. (2024, January 25). *Most of Russia's war chips are made by US and European companies*. Bloomberg. https://www.bloomberg .com/news/articles/2024-01-25/russia-s-war-machine-powered-by-chips-from-intel-amd-infineon-stm?sref=jeNvC3eC

15. Reuters. (2024, February 29). *Applied materials receives new subpoenas on China shipments*. https://www.reuters.com/technology/applied-materials-receives-subpoena-sec-china-shipments-2024-02-27/ #:~:text=Applied%20Materials%2C%20the%20largest%20U.S., people%20said%20at%20the%20time.

CHAPTER 7: SEMICONDUCTOR GROUND ZERO

1. Morrison, S. (2023, May 15). *10 facts about the semiconductor industry.* Power & Beyond. https://www.power-and-beyond.com/10-facts-about-the-semiconductor-industry-a-c0e3bb177357fbf8e30b284877f88364/#:~:text=ASML%20estimated%20that%20in%202020,of%20the%20COVID%2D19%20coronavirus.
2. Rodgers, L., Clark, D., Joiner, S., Haslett, B., La torre Arenas, I. D., & Learner, S. (2024, February 28). Inside the miracle of modern chip manufacturing. *Financial Times.* https://ig.ft.com/microchips/
3. Ting-Fang, C., & Li, L. (2023, December 13). The great nanometer chip race. *Nikkei Asia.* https://asia.nikkei.com/Spotlight/The-Big-Story/The-great-nanometer-chip-race
4. Reuters. (2023, December 21). *ASML ships first "High NA" lithography system to Intel - statement.* https://www.reuters.com/technology/asml-ships-first-high-na-lithography-system-intel-statement-2023-12-21/
5. Semiconductor Industry Association. (2021, July 13). *Taking stock of China's semiconductor industry.* https://www.semiconductors.org/taking-stock-of-chinas-semiconductor-industry/

CHAPTER 8: CHINA'S SEMICONDUCTOR PROBLEM

1. Moriyasu, K. (2024, January 9). U.S. nervous about 'flood' of older-generation chips from China. *Nikkei Asia.* https://asia.nikkei.com/Business/Tech/Semiconductors/U.S.-nervous-about-flood-of-older-generation-chips-from-China
2. Global Insights. (2023, October 11). *Who's winning the US-China chip war?* Citi. https://www.citigroup.com/global/insights/global-insights/who-s-winning-the-us-china-chip-war-
3. Capri, A. (2020, January 17). *Semiconductors at the heart of the US-China tech war.* Hinrich Foundation. https://research.hinrichfoundation.com/hubfs/Capri%20Report%20-%20Jan%202020/Hinrich%20Foundation%20report%20-%20US-China%20tech%20war%20and%20semiconductors%20-%20January%2031%202020.pdf
4. Capri, A. (2020, January 17). *Semiconductors at the heart of the US-China tech war.* Hinrich Foundation. https://research.hinrichfoundation.com/hubfs/Capri%20Report%20-%20Jan%202020/Hinrich%20Foundation%20report%20-%20US-China%20tech%20war%20and%20semiconductors%20-%20January%2031%202020.pdf
5. Capri, A. (2020, January 17). *Semiconductors at the heart of the US-China tech war.* Hinrich Foundation. https://research.hinrichfoundation.com/hubfs/Capri%20Report%20-%20Jan%202020/Hinrich%20Foundation%20report%20-%20US-China%20tech%20war%20and%20semiconductors%20-%20January%2031%202020.pdf

6. Capri, A. (2020, January 17). *Semiconductors at the heart of the US-China tech war*. Hinrich Foundation. https://research.hinrichfoundation .com/hubfs/Capri%20Report%20-%20Jan%202020/Hinrich%20 Foundation%20report%20-%20US-China%20tech%20war%20and%20 semiconductors%20-%20January%2031%202020.pdf

7. Coughlin, T. (2020, October 20). Intel sells its NAND flash business to SK Hynix. *Forbes*. https://www.forbes.com/sites/tomcoughlin/2020/10/20/ intel-sells-its-nand-flash-business-to-sk-hynix/?sh

8. Pan, C. (2024, January 16). Tech war: Chinese chip-tool giant Naura fore-casts surge in 2023 sales on strong local demand amid US export con-trols. *South China Morning Post*. https://www.scmp.com/tech/tech-war/ article/3248610/tech-war-chinese-chip-tool-giant-naura-forecasts-surge-2023-sales-strong-local-demand-amid-us-export

9. Wildau, G. (2019, November 17). *China's industrial policies work. So copy them*. Bloomberg. https://www.bloomberg.com/view/articles/2019-11-17/ u-s-should-copy-rather-than-oppose-china-s-industrial-policy

10. VerWey, J. (2019, July). Chinese semiconductor industrial policy: Past and present. *Journal of International Commerce and Economics*. https:// www.usitc.gov/publications/332/journals/chinese_semiconductor_ industrial_policy_past_and_present_jice_july_2019.pdf

11. VerWey, J. (2019, July). Chinese semiconductor industrial policy: Past and present. *Journal of International Commerce and Economics*. https:// www.usitc.gov/publications/332/journals/chinese_semiconductor_ industrial_policy_past_and_present_jice_july_2019.pdf

12. VerWey, J. (2019, July). Chinese semiconductor industrial policy: Past and present. *Journal of International Commerce and Economics*. https:// www.usitc.gov/publications/332/journals/chinese_semiconductor_ industrial_policy_past_and_present_jice_july_2019.pdf

13. National Bureau of Statistics of China. (2023, September 18). *2022 National statistical bulletin on science and technology funding investment*. https:// www.stats.gov.cn/sj/zxfb/202309/t20230918_1942920.html

14. Lin, J. (2023, June 27). *China invested US$290.8 billion in semiconductor projects between 2021-2022*. DIGITIMES Asia. https://www.digitimes .com/news/a20230627VL205/china-ic-manufacturing-semiconductor-chips+components.html#:~:text=China%20invested%20US% 24290.8%20billion%20in%20semiconductor%20projects%20 between%202021%2D2022,-Judy%20Lin%2C%20DIGITIMES&text= Chinese%20semiconductor%20industry%20research%20firm, showed%20that%20more%20than%20CNY2

15. Bloomberg News. (2023, December 1). *China secretly transforms Huawei into most powerful chip war weapon*. Bloomberg. https://www .bloomberg.com/graphics/2023-china-huawei-semiconductor/ ?sref=jeNvC3eC

16. Ting-Fang, C., Lauly, L. (2021, May 5). US-China tech war: Beijing's secret chipmaking champions. *Nikkei Asia*. https://asia.nikkei.com/Spotlight/ The-Big-Story/US-China-tech-war

17. Ye, J. (2021, June 9). New Chinese semiconductor firms have tripled in 2021 as Beijing and Washington jockey over technological supremacy. *South China Morning Post*. https://www.scmp.com/tech/tech-war/article/3136660/new-chinese-semiconductor-firms-have-tripled-2021-beijing-and

CHAPTER 9: RE-SHORING CHIP MANUFACTURING TO AMERICA

1. Semiconductor Industry Association. (2023, July 13). *CHIPS for America Act & FABS Act*. https://www.semiconductors.org/chips/

2. CHIPS for America Act. H.R. 7178. 116th Cong. (2020). https://www.congress.gov/bill/116th-congress/house-bill/7178

3. CHIPS for America Act. H.R. 7178. 116th Cong. (2020). https://www.congress.gov/bill/116th-congress/house-bill/7178

4. Casanova, R. (2022, December 14). *The CHIPS Act has already sparked $300 billion in private investments for U.S. semiconductor production*. Semiconductor Industry Association. https://www.semiconductors.org/the-chips-act-has-already-sparked-200-billion-in-private-investments-for-u-s-semiconductor-production/

5. Nellis, S. (2021, May 14). *Exclusive TSMC looks to double down on U.S. chip factories as talks in Europe falter*. Reuters. https://www.reuters.com/technology/exclusive-tsmc-looks-double-down-us-chip-factories-talks-europe-falter-2021-05-14/#:~:text=TSMC%20is%20the%20world's%20most,a%20chip%20factory%20in%20Phoenix.

6. Kim, S. (2021, March 3). *Samsung details plans for $17 billion chip facility in U.S.* Bloomberg. https://www.bloomberg.com/news/articles/2021-03-03/samsung-details-plans-for-17-billion-chip-facility-in-u-s?utm_source=website&utm_medium=share&utm_campaign=copy

7. Leswing, K. (2021, March 24). *Intel is spending $20 billion to build two new chip plants in Arizona*. CNBC. https://www.cnbc.com/intel-is-spending-20-billion

8. Usui, Y. (2022, August 4). After CHIPS Act, Japanese supplier to triple U.S. semiconductor chemical output. *Nikkei Asia*. https://asia.nikkei.com/Business/Materials/After-CHIPS-Act-Japanese-supplier-to-triple-U.S.-semiconductor-chemical-output

9. Fortune Business Insights. (2024, June 10). *Semiconductor gases market size, share & industry analysis, by product (electronic special gas and electronic bulk gas), application (memory, logic, and others), and regional forecast, 2024-2032*. https://www.fortunebusinessinsights.com/semiconductor-gases-market-104121

10. Shepardson, D. (2024, January 4). *US plans $162 million award to microchip technology to boost production*. Reuters. https://www.reuters.com/technology/us-plans-162-million-award-microchip-technology-boost-production-2024-01-04/

11. Electronics Production. (2024, January 15) *US Department of Defense awards $190m contract to SkyWater.* Evertiq. https://evertiq.com/news/55050

12. Purdue University. (2024, April 3). *SK Hynix announces semiconductor advanced packaging investment in Purdue Research Park.* https://www.purdue.edu/newsroom/releases/2024/Q2/sk-hynix-announces-semiconductor-advanced-packaging-investment-in-purdue-research-park.html

13. GlobalFoundries. (2024, February 19). *GlobalFoundries and Biden-Harris administration announce CHIPS and Science Act funding for essential chip manufacturing* [Press release]. Semiconductor Industry Association. https://www.semiconductors.org/the-chips-act-has-already-sparked-200-billion-in-private-investments-for-u-s-semiconductor-production/

14. Varas, A., Varadarajan, R., Goodrich, J., & Yunug, F. (2021, April). *Strengthening the global semiconductor supply chain in an uncertain era.* BCG x Semiconductor Industry Association. https://www.semiconductors.org/wp-content/uploads/2021/05/BCG-x-SIA-Strengthening-the-Global-Semiconductor-Value-Chain-April-2021_1.pdf

15. Varas, A., Varadarajan, R., Goodrich, J., & Yinug, F. (2020). *Government incentives and US competitiveness in semiconductor manufacturing.* BCG x Semiconductor Industry Association. https://www.semiconductors.org/wp-content/uploads/2020/09/Government-Incentives-and-US-Competitiveness-in-Semiconductor-Manufacturing-Sep-2020.pdf

16. Matthews, D. (2022, March 17). *EU hails €80 billion Intel investment as first success for Chips Act.* Science | Business. https://sciencebusiness.net/news/eu-hails-eu80-billion-intel-investment-first-success-chips-act

17. Shilov, A. (2024, January 19). *Intel's German fab will be most advanced in the world and make 1.5nm chips, CEO says.* Tom's Hardware. https://www.tomshardware.com/tech-industry/manufacturing/intels-german-fab-will-be-most-advanced-in-the-world-and-make-15nm-chips-ceo-say

18. KBS World. (2021, May 17). *"K-Semiconductor Belt Strategy" to establish the world's largest supply network by 2030.* http://world.kbs.co.kr/service

19. Capri, A. (2022, December 23). *A semiconductor renaissance is under way. It will change the world.* Barron's. https://www.barrons.com/articles/semiconductors-geopolitics-taiwan-tsmc-globalization-51671746993

20. Capri, A. (2020, August 3). *Techno-nationalism and the US–China tech innovation race.* Hinrich Foundation. https://www.hinrichfoundation.com/research/wp/tech/us-china-tech-innovation-race

CHAPTER 10: THE WAR AGAINST HUAWEI

1. Xie, Y. (2024, March 8). *Huawei's EV is China's no. 1 among upstarts for second month.* Bloomberg. https://www.bloomberg.com/news/articles/2024-03-08/huawei-s-ev-is-china-s-no-1-among-upstarts-for-second-month?sref=jeNvC3eC

2. Huawei. (2024, February 17). In *Wikipedia*. https://en.wikipedia.org/wiki/Huawei

3. Udin, E. (2023, March 31). *Huawei is far ahead of the rest of the world in 5G network contribution*. GizChina. https://www.gizchina.com/2023/03/31/huawei-5g-network-contribution/

4. Robertson, J., & Riley, M. (2018, October 4). *The big hack: How China used a tiny chip to infiltrate U.S. companies*. Bloomberg. https://www.bloomberg.com/news/features/2018-10-04/the-big-hack-how-china-used-a-tiny-chip-to-infiltrate-america-s-top-companies?sref=jeNvC3eC

5. Robertson, J., & Riley, M. (2021, February 12). *The long hack: How China exploited a U.S. tech supplier*. Bloomberg. https://www.bloomberg.com/features/2021-supermicro/?sref=jeNvC3eC

6. Yap, C. (2019, December 25). State support helped fuel Huawei's global rise. *The Wall Street Journal*. https://www.wsj.com/articles/state-support-helped-fuel-huaweis-global-rise-11577280736

7. Yap, C. (2019, December 25). State support helped fuel Huawei's global rise. *The Wall Street Journal*. https://www.wsj.com/articles/state-support-helped-fuel-huaweis-global-rise-11577280736

8. Parkin, B. (2020, March 17). Anil Ambani vs Chinese banks: Court case exposes stunning decline. *Financial Times*. https://www.ft.com/content/af6efd52-645f-11ea-a6cd-df28cc3c6a68

9. Yap, C. (2019, December 25). State support helped fuel Huawei's global rise. *The Wall Street Journal*. https://www.wsj.com/articles/state-support-helped-fuel-huaweis-global-rise

10. Ellis, S. (2018, April 6). China's trillion-dollar plan to dominate global trade. *Vox*. https://www.vox.com/china-trade-belt-road-economy

11. U.S. Department of Commerce. (2019, October 7). *U.S. Department of Commerce adds 28 Chinese organizations to its entity list* [Press release]. https://2017-2021.commerce.gov/news/press-releases/2019/10/us-department-commerce-adds-28-chinese-organizations-its-entity-list.html

12. Capri, A. (2020, January 17). *Semiconductors at the heart of the US-China tech war*. Hinrich Foundation. https://www.hinrichfoundation.com/research/wp/tech/semiconductors-at-the-heart-of-the-us-china-tech-war/

13. U.S. Bureau of Economic Analysis. (n.d.). *International data*. https://apps.bea.gov/iTable/iTable.cfm?ReqID=62&step=1

14. Duckett, C. (2019, June 26). *Over $6b in IP royalties paid by Huawei, nearly 80% to US firms*. ZDNET. https://www.zdnet.com/over-6b-in-ip-royalties-paid-by-huawei

15. Bloomberg News. (2023, December 1). *China secretly transforms Huawei into most powerful chip war weapon*. Bloomberg. https://www.bloomberg.com/graphics/2023-china-huawei-semiconductor/

16. Bloomberg News. (2023, December 1). *China secretly transforms Huawei into most powerful chip war weapon*. Bloomberg. https://www.bloomberg.com/graphics/2023-china-huawei-semiconductor/

17. Bloomberg News. (2023, December 1). *China secretly transforms Huawei into most powerful chip war weapon*. Bloomberg. https://www.bloomberg.com/graphics/2023-china-huawei-semiconductor/

18. Robertson, J., & Riley, M. (2022, June 6). *Engineer who fled charges of stealing chip secrets now thrives in China (Repeat)*. Bloomberg. https://www.bloomberg.com/news/articles/2022-06-06/engineer-who-fled-us-charges-of-stealing-chip-technology-now-thrives-in-china?sref=jeNvC3eC

19. Robertson, J., & Riley, M. (2022, June 6). *Engineer who fled charges of stealing chip secrets now thrives in China (Repeat)*. Bloomberg. https://www.bloomberg.com/news/articles/2022-06-06/engineer-who-fled-us-charges-of-stealing-chip-technology-now-thrives-in-china?sref=jeNvC3eC

20. Reuters. (2019, November 12). *Huawei to give staff $286 million bonus for helping it ride out U.S. curbs*. https://www.reuters.com/article/idUSKBN1XM10Y/

21. Sing, C. K. (2021, December 21). *China's Huawei could be the surprise IPO of 2024*. Reuters. https://www.reuters.com/breakingviews/chinas-huawei-could-be-surprise-ipo-2024-2023-12-21/

CHAPTER 11: TRADECRAFT, STEALTH AND TECHNOLOGY

1. Reuters. (2011, August 15). *Pakistan let China see crashed U.S. "stealth" copter*. https://www.reuters.com/article/idUSTRE77D2BT/

2. Brook, C. (2011, June 30). *Byzantine Hades*. Threatpost. https://threatpost.com/byzantine-hades

3. The White House. (2021, August 31). *Remarks by President Biden on the end of the war in Afghanistan* [Speeches and remarks]. https://www.whitehouse.gov/briefing-room/speeches-remarks/2021/08/31/remarks-by-president-biden-on-the-end-of-the-war-in-afghanistan/#:~:text=My%20fellow%20Americans%2C%20the%20war,I've%20honored%20that%20commitment.

4. NBC News. (2004, April 23). *Al-Qaida timeline: Plots and attacks*. https://www.nbcnews.com/id/wbna4677978

5. Federal Bureau of Investigation. (n.d.). *USS Cole bombing*. https://www.fbi.gov/history/famous-cases/uss-cole-bombing

6. NBC News. (2004, April 23). *Al-Qaida timeline: Plots and attacks*. https://www.nbcnews.com/id/wbna4677978

7. Bergen, P. L. (2023, February 26). September 11 attacks. In *Encyclopedia Britannica*. https://www.britannica.com/event/September-11-attacks

8. The Washington Post. (2013, August 29). Raid that killed bin Laden guided by fleet of satellites, top-secret budget shows. *The Denver Post*. https://www.denverpost.com/raid-that-killed-bin-laden-guided-by-fleet-of-satellites-top-secret-budget-shows/

9. NPR. (2011, May 4). CIA used satellites to prep for Bin Laden raid. *All Things Considered* [Audio podcast]. https://www.npr.org/2011/05/04/135995089/cia-used-satellites-to-prep-for-bin-laden-raid

10. Peterson, A. (2013, August 29). The NSA has its own team of elite hackers. *The Washington Post.* https://www.washingtonpost.com/news/the-switch/wp/2013/08/29/the-nsa-has-its-own-team-of-elite-hackers/

11. U.S. Department of Justice. (2001). *The USA PATRIOT Act: Preserving life and liberty.* https://www.justice.gov/archive/ll/what_is_the_patriot_act.pdf

12. The Washington Post. (2013, August 29). Raid that killed bin Laden guided by fleet of satellites, top-secret budget shows. *The Denver Post.* https://www.denverpost.com/raid-that-killed-bin-laden-guided-by-fleet-of-satellites-top-secret-budget-shows/

13. NPR. (2011, May 4). CIA used satellites to prep for Bin Laden raid. *All Things Considered* [Audio podcast]. https://www.npr.org/2011/05/04/135995089/cia-used-satellites-to-prep-for-bin-laden-raid

14. Verger, R. (2021, May 3). *The stealth helicopters used in the 2011 raid on Osama bin Laden are still cloaked in mystery.* Popular Science. https://www.popsci.com/story/technology/osama-bin-laden-raid-anniversary-stealth-helicopters/

15. 9/11 Memorial & Museum. (n.d.). *Operation Neptune Spear.* https://www.911memorial.org/learn/resources/digital-exhibitions/digital-exhibition-revealed-hunt-bin-laden/operation-neptune-spear

16. Johnson, R. (2011, May 17). *Detailed account of the Bin Laden raid reveals how it nearly ended in disaster.* Business Insider. https://www.businessinsider.com/detailed-account-abbottabad-2011-5

17. Quade, A. (2020, March 17). *Exclusive: Legendary special operations aviator reveals Bin Laden mission details for the first time.* Military Times. https://www.militarytimes.com/news/your-military/2020/03/17/legendary-special-operations-aviator-reveals-bin-laden-mission-details-for-the-first-time/

18. Brown, A. (2012, September 10). *Bin Laden's death: How it happened.* BBC News. https://www.bbc.co.uk/news/world-south-asia-13257330

19. Reuters. (2011, August 15). *Pakistan let China see crashed U.S. "stealth" copter.* https://www.reuters.com/article/idUSTRE77D2BT/

20. Mazzetti, M. (2011, August 14). U.S. aides believe China examined stealth copter. *The New York Times.* https://www.nytimes.com/2011/08/15/world/asia/15copter.html

21. Rogin, J. (2011, May 9). Will Pakistan give the downed Navy SEALs helicopter to China? *Foreign Policy.* https://foreignpolicy.com/2011/05/09/will-pakistan-give-the-downed-navy-seals-helicopter-to-china/

22. The Week. (2021, June 1). *How Pakistan gave China military tech used by US in attacks on Bin Laden.* https://www.theweek.in/news/world/2021/06/01/how-pakistan-gave-china-military-tech-used-by-us-in-attacks-on-bin-laden.html

23. Information sharing in the era of Wikileaks: Balancing security and collaboration. 112th Cong. (2011). https://irp.fas.org/congress/2011_hr/infoshare.html

24. Gady, F. (2015, January 27). New Snowden documents reveal Chinese behind F-35 hack. *The Diplomat*. https://thediplomat.com/2015/01/new-snowden-documents-reveal-chinese-behind-f-35-hack/

25. Fuhrman, E. (2021, July 15). How China stole the designs for the F-35 stealth fighter. *19FortyFive*. Retrieved from https://web.archive.org/web/20210716023023/https://www.19fortyfive.com/2021/07/how-china-stole-the-designs-for-the-f-35-stealth-fighter/

26. Fuhrman, E. (2021, July 15). How China stole the designs for the F-35 stealth fighter. *19FortyFive*. Retrieved from https://web.archive.org/web/20210716023023/https://www.19fortyfive.com/2021/07/how-china-stole-the-designs-for-the-f-35-stealth-fighter/

27. Fuhrman, E. (2021, July 15). How China stole the designs for the F-35 stealth fighter. *19FortyFive*. Retrieved from https://web.archive.org/web/20210716023023/https://www.19fortyfive.com/2021/07/how-china-stole-the-designs-for-the-f-35-stealth-fighter/

28. Grow, B., & Hosenball, M. (2011, April 15). *China accused of stealing "terabytes" of US data*. iTnews. https://www.itnews.com.au/news/china-accused-of-stealing-terabytes-of-us-data-254647/page0

29. The Library of Congress. (n.d.). *Fascinating facts*. https://www.loc.gov/about/fascinating-facts/

30. Tirpak, J. (2023, January 3). $30 billion F-35 deal will see prices rise, deliveries dip. *Air & Space Forces Magazine*. https://www.airandspaceforces.com/30-billion-f-35-deal-will-see-prices-rise-deliveries-dip/

31. Thompson, L. (2019, May 13). The F-35 isn't just "stealthy": Here's how its electronic warfare system gives it an edge. *Forbes*. https://www.forbes.com/sites/lorenthompson/2019/05/13/how-a-super-agile-electronic-warfare-system-makes-f-35-the-most-invincible-combat-aircraft-ever

32. Thompson, L. (2019, May 13). The F-35 isn't just "stealthy": Here's how its electronic warfare system gives it an edge. *Forbes*. https://www.forbes.com/sites/lorenthompson/2019/05/13/how-a-super-agile-electronic-warfare-system-makes-f-35-the-most-invincible-combat-aircraft-ever

33. F-35 Lightning II. (n.d.). *Unrivaled capabilities*. https://www.f35.com/f35/about/5th-gen-capabilities.html

34. Ufimtsev, P. Y. (1971, September 7). *Method of edge waves in the physical theory of diffraction*. Defense Technical Information Center. https://apps.dtic.mil/sti/citations/AD0733203

35. U.S. Centennial of Flight Commission. (n.d.). *Stealth aircraft*. https://www.centennialofflight.net/essay/Air_Power/Stealth/AP46.htm

36. U.S. Centennial of Flight Commission. (n.d.). *Stealth aircraft*. https://www.centennialofflight.net/essay/Air_Power/Stealth/AP46.htm

37. U.S. Centennial of Flight Commission. (n.d.). *Stealth aircraft*. https://www.centennialofflight.net/essay/Air_Power/Stealth/AP46.htm

38. Capaccio, A. (2021, November 17). *Under-wraps B-21 bomber seen costing $203 billion into 2050s*. Bloomberg. https://www.bloomberg.com/news/articles/2021-11-17/under-wraps-b-21-bomber-is-seen-costing-203-billion-into-2050s

39. Crowley, M., Hassan, F., & Schmitt, E. (2020, July 9). U.S. strike in Iraq kills Qassim Suleimani, Commander of Iranian Forces. *The New York Times.* https://www.nytimes.com/2020/01/02/world/middleeast/qassem-soleimani-iraq-iran-attack.html

40. Outlook Web Desk. (2022, August 23). India plans to buy drones used in killing of Al-Qaeda leader Zawahiri amid tension with China. *Outlook.* https://www.outlookindia.com/national/india-plans-to-buy-drones-used-in-killing-of-al-qaeda-leader

41. Honrada, G. (2023, February 10). China's new stealth drone may revolutionize next-gen fighter. *Asia Times.* https://asiatimes.com/2023/02/chinas-new-stealth-drone-may-revolutionize-next-gen-fighter/

42. Bowman, B., Thompson, J., & Brobst, R. (2021, April 23). China's surprising drone sales in the Middle East. *Defense News.* https://www.defensenews.com/opinion/2021/04/23/chinas-surprising-drone-sales-in-the-middle-east/

CHAPTER 12: DATA, BIOTECH AND GEOPOLITICS

1. Sherman, A. (2020, August 24). *TikTok reveals detailed user numbers for the first time.* CNBC. https://www.cnbc.com/2020/08/24/tiktok-reveals-us-global-user-growth-numbers-for-first-time.html

2. Gibbs, M. (2015, January 30). *MIT researchers show you can be identified by a just few data points.* Network World. https://www.networkworld.com/article/2878394/mit-researchers-show-you-can-be-identified-by-a-just-few-data-points.html

3. Web Desk. (2020, August 12). *The information major tech companies (including Google, Apple, Facebook, TikTok) are collecting from their users.* Digital Information World. https://www.digitalinformationworld.com/2020/08/infographic-what-data-are-giant-tech-companies-collecting-from-you.html

4. CrowdStrike. (n.d.). *2020 global threat report.* https://www.crowdstrike.com/resources/reports/2020-crowdstrike-global-threat-report/

5. Tucker, E. (2020, September 17). *US charges 5 Chinese citizens in global hacking campaign.* Associated Press. https://apnews.com/article/technology-media-social-media-crime-china-abe63876eedc5a95c90a37ca88024809

6. O'Kane, S. (2018, December 21). *Chinese hackers charged with stealing data from NASA, IBM, and others.* The Verge. https://www.theverge.com/2018/12/20/18150275/chinese-hackers-stealing-data-nasa-ibm-charged

7. Taylor, P. (2023, November 16). *Amount of data created, consumed, and stored 2010-2020, with forecasts to 2025.* Statista. https://www.statista.com/statistics/871513/worldwide-data-created/

8. Needham, K. (2020, August 5). *Special report: COVID opens new doors for China's gene giant.* Reuters. https://www.reuters.com/article/us-health-coronavirus-bgi-specialreport-idINKCN2511CE

9. Needham, K. (2020, August 5). *Special report: COVID opens new doors for China's gene giant.* Reuters. https://www.reuters.com/article/us-health-coronavirus-bgi-specialreport-idINKCN2511CE

10. National Genomics Data Center. (n.d.). https://ngdc.cncb.ac.cn/

11. Needham, K., & Baldwin, C. (2021, July 7). *China's gene giant harvests data from millions of pregnant women.* Reuters. https://www.reuters.com/investigates/special-report/health-china-bgi-dna/

12. Needham, K., & Baldwin, C. (2021, July 7). *China's gene giant harvests data from millions of pregnant women.* Reuters. https://www.reuters.com/investigates/special-report/health-china-bgi-dna/

13. Berger, M. (2015, September 11). *What are nanobots?* Nanowerk. https://www.nanowerk.com/what-are-nanobots.php

14. NSCAI. (2021, May 5). *Commissioners.* https://www.nscai.gov/commissioners/

15. The NSCAI has 15 'commissioners', 12 of which are appointed by Congress and two who are appointed by the Secretary of Defence and one by the Secretary of Commerce. NSCAI has commissioners representing Oracle, Microsoft, Google and NASA's Jet Propulsion Lab. NSCAI represents the importance of public–private partnerships that stress the link between AI and data when it comes to geopolitics. The official NSCAO mission: '*to foster greater emphasis and investments in basic and advanced research to stimulate private, public, academic and combined initiatives in artificial intelligence, machine learning, and other associated technologies, to the extent that such efforts have application materially related to national security and defense*'.

16. Monegain, B. (2018, July 25). *23andMe lands $300 million investment from GlaxoSmithKline.* Healthcare IT News. https://www.healthcareitnews.com/news/23andme-lands-300-million-investment-glaxosmithkline

17. Paul, K. (2021, February 9). Fears over DNA privacy as 23andMe plans to go public in deal with Richard Branson. *The Guardian.* https://www.theguardian.com/technology/2021/feb/09/23andme-dna-privacy-richard-branson-genetics

18. GDPR. (2019, February 19). *General Data Protection Regulation (GDPR) Compliance Guidelines.* https://gdpr.eu/

19. Hollings, A. (2020, October 15). Here's why the Pentagon says you shouldn't use 23andMe or Ancestry DNA. *Sandboxx.* https://www.sandboxx.us/blog/heres-why-the-pentagon-says-you-shouldnt-use-23andme-or-ancestry-dna/

20. Dorling, P. (2013, August 2). X-Keyscore spy program tracks "nearly all" web use. *The Sydney Morning Herald.* https://www.smh.com.au/technology/xkeyscore-spy-program-tracks-nearly-all-web-use-20130802-hv17w.html

21. Dorling, P. (2013, August 2). X-Keyscore spy program tracks "nearly all" web use. *The Sydney Morning Herald.* https://www.smh.com.au/technology/xkeyscore-spy-program-tracks-nearly-all-web-use-20130802-hv17w.html

22. Chai, W. (2020, April 6). *Five eyes alliance.* TechTarget. https://www
    .techtarget.com/whatis/definition/Five-Eyes-Alliance

23. Electrospaces.net. (2021, May 18) *What the NSA provides to its foreign
    partners, and vice versa.* https://www.electrospaces.net/2021/05/what-
    nsa-provides-to-its-foreign.html

24. Privacy Bee News Team. (2021, August 30). *These are the largest data
    brokers in America.* Privacy Bee. https://privacybee.com/blog/these-
    are-the-largest-data-brokers-in-america/

25. Privacy Bee News Team. (2021, August 30). *These are the largest data
    brokers in America.* Privacy Bee. https://privacybee.com/blog/these-
    are-the-largest-data-brokers-in-america/

26. McMillan, A. F. (2021, July 5). *China blocks Didi, two other U.S. IPOs
    from signing new customers.* TheStreet. https://realmoney.thestreet
    .com/investing/china-blocks-didi-two-other-u-s-ipos-from-signing-
    new-customers-15702543

27. The Guardian. (n.d.). *The Cambridge Analytica files.* https://www
    .theguardian.com/news/series/cambridge-analytica-files

28. Ma, A. (2018, March 19). *Everyone is talking about Cambridge Analytica,
    the Trump-linked data firm that harvested 50 million Facebook profiles—
    here's what's going on.* Business Insider Nederland. https://www
    .businessinsider.nl/cambridge-analytica-a-guide-to-the-trump-linked-
    data-firm

29. BBC News. (2018, March 22). *Cambridge Analytica: The data firm's
    global influence.* https://www.bbc.com/news/world-43476762

30. Hern, A. (2018, May 6). Cambridge Analytica: How did it turn clicks into
    votes? *The Guardian.* https://www.theguardian.com/news/2018/may/
    06/cambridge-analytica-how-turn-clicks-into-votes-christopher-wylie

31. Greenberg, A. (2019, February 27). *US hackers' strike on Russian trolls
    sends a message—but what kind?* WIRED. https://www.wired.com/
    story/cyber-command-ira-strike-sends-signal/

32. Barnes, J., & Sanger, D. (2020, July 28). Russian intelligence agencies
    push disinformation on pandemic. *The New York Times.* https://www
    .nytimes.com/2020/07/28/us/politics/russia-disinformation-
    coronavirus.html

33. Barnes, J., & Sanger, D. (2020, July 28). Russian intelligence agencies
    push disinformation on pandemic. *The New York Times.* https://www
    .nytimes.com/2020/07/28/us/politics/russia-disinformation-
    coronavirus.html

34. O'sullivan, D. (2022, September 27). *Meta shuts down covert influence
    campaigns it says were run from China and Russia.* CNN. https://edition
    .cnn.com/2022/09/27/tech/meta-china-russia-influence-campaigns/
    index.html

35. Gan, N. (2021, March 26). *Chinese celebrities rush to defend Beijing's
    Xinjiang policy by cutting ties with international brands.* CNN. https://
    edition.cnn.com/style/article/chinese-celebrities-xj-cotton-intl-hnk/
    index.html

36. Gan, N. (2021, March 26). *Chinese celebrities rush to defend Beijing's Xinjiang policy by cutting ties with international brands.* CNN. https://edition.cnn.com/style/article/chinese-celebrities-xj-cotton-intl-hnk/index.html

37. Romero, A. (2022, August 4). *Chinese netizen cancels JJ Lin, Michelle Yeoh, Jet Li, Dee Hsu and other celebs for failing to support 'One China' after Pelosi's visit to Taiwan.* The Independent Singapore. https://theindependent.sg/chinese-netizen-cancels-jj-lin-michelle-yeoh-jet-li-dee-hsu-and-other-celebs-for-failing-to-support-one-china-after-pelosis-visit-to-taiwan/

38. Moss, S. (2022, April 29). NSA re-awards $10bn WildandStormy cloud computing contract to AWS. *Data Center Dynamics.* https://www.datacenterdynamics.com/en/news/nsa-re-awards-10bn-wildandstormy-cloud-computing-contract-to-aws/

39. Mellor, C. (2021, October 26). *Sovereignty? We've heard of it. UK government gives contract to store MI5, MI6 and GCHQ's data to AWS.* The Register. https://www.theregister.com/2021/10/26/uk_security_services_aws/

40. Mellor, C. (2021, October 26). *Sovereignty? We've heard of it. UK government gives contract to store MI5, MI6 and GCHQ's data to AWS.* The Register. https://www.theregister.com/2021/10/26/uk_security_services_aws/

41. Kaiser, J. (2019, November 7). A judge said police can search the DNA of 1 million Americans without their consent. *Science.* https://www.science.org/content/article/judge-said-police-can-search-dna-millions-americans-without-their-consent-what-s-next

CHAPTER 13: THE AI ARMS RACE

1. Ivanenkov, Y. A., Polykovskiy, D., Bezrukov, D., Zagribelnyy, B., Aladinskiy, V., Kamya, P., Aliper, A., Ren, F., & Zhavoronkov, A. (2023). Chemistry42: An AI-driven platform for molecular design and optimization. *Journal of Chemical Information and Modeling, 63*(3), 695–701. https://doi.org/10.1021/acs.jcim.2c01191

2. Thormundsson, B. (2024, February 21). *Artificial intelligence (AI) market size/revenue comparisons 2018-2030.* Statista. https://www.statista.com/statistics/941835/artificial-intelligence-market-size-revenue-comparisons/.

3. Statista. (2023, April). *Artificial intelligence: In-depth market analysis.* https://www.statista.com/study/50485/in-depth-report-artificial-intelligence/.

4. U.S. Department of Defense. (2022, November 22). *2022 military and security developments involving the Peoples Republic of China.* https://www.defense.gov/News/Releases/Release/Article/3230516/2022-report-on-military-and-security-developments-involving-the-peoples-republi/

5. Fortune Business Insights. (2023, April 19). *Global cyber security market size [2023-2030] to reach USD 424.97 billion and exhibit a CAGR of 13.8%.* GlobeNewswire News Room. https://www.globenewswire.com/

news-release/2023/04/19/2649842/0/en/Global-Cyber-Security-Market-Size-2023-2030-to-Reach-USD-424-97-Billion-and-Exhibit-a-CAGR-of-13-8.html

6. Mouriquand, D. (2023, March 23). *How AI is putting President Macron at the heart of the French pension protests.* Euronews. https://www .euronews.com/culture/2023/03/23/how-ai-is-putting-president-macron-at-the-heart-of-the-french-pension-protests

7. Duarte, F. (2023, November 30). *Number of ChatGPT users (Dec 2023).* Exploding Topics. Retrieved from https://web.archive.org/web/202311 30143912/https://explodingtopics.com/blog/chatgpt-users

8. Nellis, S., & Lee, J. (2023, March 22). *Nvidia tweaks flagship H100 chip for export to China as H800.* Reuters. https://www.reuters.com/ technology/nvidia-tweaks-flagship-h100-chip-export-china-h800-2023-03-21/#:~:text=Transfer%20speed%20is%20important%20 when,rate%20of%20the%20flagship%20H100.

9. Ladha, V. (2022, May 29). *NVIDIA's revenue breakdown by region (bill to location).* Business Quant. https://businessquant.com/nvidia-revenue-by-region-bill-to-location

10. Kaur, D. (2023, July 14). *Intel joins Nvidia in tackling the US ban with an AI chip for China.* Tech Wire Asia. https://techwireasia.com/07/2023/ intel-joins-nvidia-in-tackling-the-us-ban-with-an-ai-chip-for-china/

CHAPTER 14: QUANTUM TECHNOLOGIES

1. Gibney, E. (2019, October 23). Hello quantum world! Google publishes landmark quantum supremacy claim. *Nature.* https://www.nature.com/ articles/d41586-019-03213-z

2. Ball, P. (2020, December 3). Physicists in China challenge Google's 'quantum advantage.' *Nature.* https://www.nature.com/articles/d41586-020-03434-7#ref-CR1

3. Medina, A. (2020, July 22). *Classical binary computation.* ARA MEDINA. https://definitelynotavampire.com/blog/2020/7/21/classical-binary-computation

4. Gerbert, P., & Ruess, F. (2018, November 15). *The next decade in quantum computing—and how to play.* BCG Global. https://www.bcg.com/ publications/2018/next-decade-quantum-computing-how-play

5. Gerbert, P., & Ruess, F. (2018, November 15). *The next decade in quantum computing—and how to play.* BCG Global. https://www.bcg.com/ publications/2018/next-decade-quantum-computing-how-play

6. Inside Quantum Technology. (2019, August 15). New *report forecasts $780 million quantum computing market in 2025 and profiles 42 leading quantum computing organizations.* GlobeNewswire News Room. https://www.globenewswire.com/news-release/2019/08/15/1902730/0/ en/New-Report-Forecasts-780-Million-Quantum-Computing-Market-in-2025-and-Profiles-42-Leading-Quantum-Computing-Organizations .html

7. Weinstein, E. (2021, February 5). Don't underestimate China's military-civil fusion efforts. *Foreign Policy*. https://foreignpolicy.com/2021/02/05/dont-underestimate-chinas-military-civil-fusion-efforts/

8. IISS. (2019). Quantum computing and defence. In *The Military Balance 2019* (pp. 18–20). https://www.iiss.org/publications/the-military-balance/the-military-balance-2019/quantum-computing-and-defence

9. Rej, A. (2021, April 6). United States' DARPA announces new 'Quantum Benchmarking' program. *The Diplomat*. https://thediplomat.com/2021/04/united-states-darpa-announces-new-quantum-benchmarking-program/

10. Chu, J. (2016, March 3). *The beginning of the end for encryption schemes?* MIT News. https://news.mit.edu/2016/quantum-computer-end-encryption-schemes-0303

11. Sanger, D. E., & Perlroth, N. (2021, July 19). More hacking attacks found, officials warn of risk to U.S. Government. *The New York Times*. https://www.nytimes.com/2020/12/17/us/politics/russia-cyber-hack-trump.html

12. Turton, W., & Robertson, J. (2021, March 7). *Microsoft attack blamed on china morphs into global crisis*. Bloomberg. https://www.bloomberg.com/news/articles/2021-03-07/hackers-breach-thousands-of-microsoft-customers-around-the-world?sref=jeNvC3eC

13. Santacreu, A. M., & Zhu, H. (2018). What does China's rise in patents mean? A look at quality vs. quantity. *Economic Synopses*. https://doi.org/10.20955/es.2018.14

14. Oikawa, A., Okoshi, Y., Misumi, Y. (2021, March 14). China emerges as quantum tech leader while Biden vows to catch up. *Nikkei Asia*. https://asia.nikkei.com/Spotlight/Datawatch/China-emerges-as-quantum-tech-leader-while-Biden-vows-to-catch-up

15. Chen, Y.A., Zhang, Q., Chen, T., Cai, W., Liao, S., Zhang, J., Chen, K., Yin, J., Ren, J., Chen, Z., Han, S., Yu, Q., Liang, K., Zhou, F., Yuan, X., Zhao, M., Wang, T., Jiang, X., Zhang, L., Liu, W., Li, Y., Shen, Q., Cao, Y., Lu, C., Shu, R., Wang, J., Li, L., Liu, N., Xu, F., Wang, X., Peng, C., & Pan, J. (2021, January 6). An integrated space-to-ground quantum communication. *Nature*, 589, 214–219. https://www.nature.com/articles/s41586-020-03093-8

16. Chen, Y.A., Zhang, Q., Chen, T., Cai, W., Liao, S., Zhang, J., Chen, K., Yin, J., Ren, J., Chen, Z., Han, S., Yu, Q., Liang, K., Zhou, F., Yuan, X., Zhao, M., Wang, T., Jiang, X., Zhang, L., Liu, W., Li, Y., Shen, Q., Cao, Y., Lu, C., Shu, R., Wang, J., Li, L., Liu, N., Xu, F., Wang, X., Peng, C., & Pan, J. (2021, January 6). An integrated space-to-ground quantum communication. *Nature*, 589, 214–219. https://www.nature.com/articles/s41586-020-03093-8

17. Swayne, M. (2020, June 19). *Honeywell claims the world's highest performing quantum computer is here*. The Quantum Insider. https://thequantumdaily.com/2020/06/19/honeywell-claims-the-worlds-highest-performing-quantum-computer-is-here/

18. Bureau of Industry and Security. (n.d.). *License Exception ENC*. U.S. Department of Commerce. https://www.bis.doc.gov/index.php/component/content/article/223-new-encryption/1234-740-17b2?Itemid=1050

19. Defense Advanced Research Projects Agency. (2021, February 4). *Quantifying utility of quantum computers.* https://www.darpa.mil/news-events/2021-04-02

20. Mancuso, M. P. C. (2020, January 28). *Anticipating a turning point in U.S. export controls for tech.* Kirkland & Ellis LLP. https://www.kirkland.com/publications/article/2020/01/anticipating-turning-point-us-export-controls-tech

21. van Amerongen, M. (2021, June 3). Quantum technologies in defence & security. *NATO Review.* https://www.nato.int/docu/review/articles/2021/06/03/quantum-technologies-in-defence-security/index.html

22. Dannen. (1945, July 17). *A petition to the President of the United States.* http://www.dannen.com/decision/45-07-17.html

CHAPTER 15: HYPERSONIC SPEED

1. U.S. Department of Defense. (2021). *2021 military and security developments involving the Peoples Republic of China.* https://media.defense.gov/2021/Nov/03/2002885874/-1/-1/0/2021-CMPR-FINAL.PDF

2. Rogin, J. (2023, April 13). The most shocking Intel leak reveals new Chinese military advances. *The Washington Post.* https://www.washingtonpost.com/opinions/2023/04/13/china-hypersonic-missile-intelligence-leak/

3. Lee, L. (2022, October 5). *The Navy just deployed its $13 billion aircraft carrier, which was both commissioned and panned by Trump, who ranted, "it just doesn't look right."* Business Insider. https://www.businessinsider.in/defense/news/the-navy-just-deployed-its-13-billion-aircraft-carrier-which-was-both-commissioned

4. Tingley, B. (2023, February 1). *DARPA's hypersonic HAWC completes final flight test at over Mach 5.* Space. https://www.space.com/darpa-hypersonic-air-breathing-weapon-final-flight-test

CHAPTER 16: THE GREAT UNDERSEA CABLE DECOUPLING

1. The Economist. (2023, December 20). *Big tech and geopolitics are reshaping the internet's plumbing.* https://www.economist.com/business/2023/12/20/big-tech-and-geopolitics-are-reshaping-the-internets-plumbing

2. TeleGeography. (n.d.). *Submarine cable: Frequently asked questions.* https://www2.telegeography.com/submarine-cable-faqs-frequently-asked-questions

3. Siebold, S. (2023, May 3). *NATO says Moscow may sabotage undersea cables as part of war on Ukraine.* Reuters. https://www.reuters.com/

world/moscow-may-sabotage-undersea-cables-part-its-war-ukraine-nato-2023-05-03/

4. Hengtong Group. (n.d.). *Submarine system.* http://www.hengtonggroup .com/en/home/products/index/categoryId/3.html

5. HMN Technologies Co. Ltd. (2020, November 3). *Huawei Marine Networks rebrands as HMN Technologies* [Press release]. HMNTech. https:// www.hmntech.com/enPressReleases/37764.jhtml#:~:text=In%20 the%20first%20half%20of,New%20Saxon%202019%20Ltd.

6. Brock, J. (2023, March 24). *U.S. and China wage war beneath the waves – over internet cables.* Reuters. https://www.reuters.com/investigates/ special-report/us-china-tech-cables/

7. Reuters. (2023). *HMN Tech's global cable network.* https://www.reuters .com/graphics/US-CHINA-TECH/CABLES/zjvqjnndapx/

8. TeleGeography. (2023). *Submarine cable map 2023.* https://submarine-cable-map-2023.telegeography.com/

9. Brock, J. (2023, March 24). *U.S. and China wage war beneath the waves – over internet cables.* Reuters. https://www.reuters.com/investigates/ special-report/us-china-tech-cables/

10. Office of Public Affairs. (2020, June 17). *Team Telecom recommends that the FCC deny Pacific Light Cable Network System's Hong Kong Undersea Cable Connection to the United States* [Press release]. U.S. Department of Justice. https://www.justice.gov/opa/pr/team-telecom-recommends-fcc-deny-pacific-light-cable-network-system-s-hong-kong-undersea#:~:text=Team%20Telecom%20today%20recommended%20 to,United%20States%20and%20Hong%20Kong.

11. Packham, C. (2019, August 28). *Ousting Huawei, Australia finishes laying undersea internet cable for Pacific allies.* Reuters. https://www.reuters .com/article/idUSKCN1VI08H/

12. SEA-ME-WE 6. (2024, February 24). In *Wikipedia.* https://en.wikipedia .org/wiki/SEA-ME-WE_6#:~:text=Bangladesh%2C%20Singapore% 2C%20Malaysia%2C%20Indonesia,ME%2DWE%2D6%20 Consortium.

13. Brock, J. (2023, March 24). *U.S. and China wage war beneath the waves – over internet cables.* Reuters. https://www.reuters.com/investigates/ special-report/us-china-tech-cables/

14. Brock, J. (2023, March 24). *U.S. and China wage war beneath the waves – over internet cables.* Reuters. https://www.reuters.com/investigates/ special-report/us-china-tech-cables/

15. Clark, R. (2020, January 24). *Hengtong set to shape the global subsea market.* Submarine Telecoms Forum. https://subtelforum.com/hengtong-set-to-shape-the-global-subsea-market/

16. The Economist. (2023, December 20). *Big tech and geopolitics are reshaping the internet's plumbing.* https://www.economist.com/business/ 2023/12/20/big-tech-and-geopolitics-are-reshaping-the-internets-plumbing

17. The Economist. (2023, December 20). *Big tech and geopolitics are reshaping the internet's plumbing.* https://www.economist.com/business/2023/12/20/big-tech-and-geopolitics-are-reshaping-the-internets-plumbing

18. Wu, H., & Lai, J. (2023, April 18). *Taiwan suspects Chinese ships cut islands' internet cables.* Associated Press. https://apnews.com/article/matsu-taiwan-internet-cables-cut-china-65f10f5f73a346fa788436366d7a7c70

19. Tegler, E. (2023, November 28). Investigating the Chinese ship that 'accidentally' hit undersea lines. *Forbes.* https://www.forbes.com/sites/erictegler/2023/11/28/investigating-the-chinese-ship-that-accidentally-hit-undersea-lines/?sh=55e4238f40bf

20. Tegler, E. (2023, November 28). Investigating the Chinese ship that 'accidentally' hit undersea lines. *Forbes.* https://www.forbes.com/sites/erictegler/2023/11/28/investigating-the-chinese-ship-that-accidentally-hit-undersea-lines/?sh=55e4238f40bf

21. Siebold, S. (2023, May 3). *NATO says Moscow may sabotage undersea cables as part of war on Ukraine.* Reuters. https://www.reuters.com/world/moscow-may-sabotage-undersea-cables-part-its-war-ukraine-nato-2023-05-03/

22. Operation Ivy Bells. (2024, February 24). In *Wikipedia.* https://en.wikipedia.org/wiki/Operation_Ivy_Bells

CHAPTER 17: SPACE-BASED INTERNET

1. The European Space Agency. (n.d.). *ESA – Eduspace EN – Home – Satellite orbits.* https://www.esa.int/SPECIALS/Eduspace

2. Weishaupt, J. (2023, January 26). How much does a satellite cost? The surprising answer! *Optics Mag.* https://opticsmag.com/how-much-does-a-satellite-cost

3. Sheetz, M. (2023, February 28). *SpaceX begins launching second-generation Starlink satellites with four times the network capacity.* CNBC. https://www.cnbc.com/2023/02/28/spacex-launches-v2-mini-starlink-satellites.html

4. Marquina, C. (2022, February 18) *How low-earth orbit satellite technology can connect the unconnected.* World Economic Forum. https://www.weforum.org/agenda/2022/02/explainer-how-low-earth-orbit-satellite-technology-can-connect-the-unconnected/

5. Machi, V. (2021, June). *US military places a bet on LEO for space security.* SDA. https://www.sda.mil/us-military-places-a-bet-on-leo-for-space-security/

6. Daehnick, C., Klinghoffer, I., Maritz, B., & Wiseman, B. (2020, May 4). *Large LEO satellite constellations: Will it be different this time?* McKinsey & Company. https://www.mckinsey.com/industries/aerospace-

and-defense/our-insights/large-leo-satellite-constellations-will-it-be-different-this-time

7. Machi, V. (2021, June). *US military places a bet on LEO for space security.* SDA. https://www.sda.mil/us-military-places-a-bet-on-leo-for-space-security/

8. Machi, V. (2021, June). *US military places a bet on LEO for space security.* SDA. https://www.sda.mil/us-military-places-a-bet-on-leo-for-space-security/

9. Flyvbjerg, B. (2022, June 14). *SpaceX vs. NASA: Cost.* Geek Culture. https://medium.com/geekculture/spacex-vs-nasa-cost

10. Arevalo, E. J. (2022, March 18). *SpaceX Falcon 9 will be reused a record-breaking 12th time during upcoming Starlink mission – Watch it live!* Tesmanian. https://www.tesmanian.com/blogs/tesmanian-blog/march-star

11. Wall, M. (2023, February 4). *SpaceX's 200th Falcon 9 rocket launch looks absolutely gorgeous in these photos.* Space. https://www.space.com/spacex-falcon-9-200th-launch-photos

12. United States Space Force. (n.d.). *About the Space Force.* https://www.spaceforce.mil/About-Us/About-Space-Force/

13. Crilly, R. (2023, March 15). *China has launched hundreds of satellites to target US: Space Force chief says Beijing is developing anti-satellite missiles, electronic jammers, lasers and technology that can move rival orbiting platforms.* Mail Online. https://www.dailymail.co.uk/news/article-11864231/Space-Force-chief-says-China-developing-anti-satellite-missiles-electronic-jammers-lasers.html

14. Zissis, C. (2007, February 22). *China's anti-satellite test.* Council on Foreign Relations. https://www.cfr.org/backgrounder/chinas-anti-satellite-test

15. Machi, V. (2021, June). *US military places a bet on LEO for space security.* SDA. https://www.sda.mil/us-military-places-a-bet-on-leo-for-space-security/

16. Strout, N. (2019, July 25). What will the Space Development Agency really do? *C4ISRNet.* https://www.c4isrnet.com/battlefield-tech/space/2019/07/24/what-will-the-space-development-agency-really-do/

17. Albon, C. (2023, April 2). SpaceX rocket launches Space Development Agency's first satellites. *C4ISRNet.* https://www.c4isrnet.com/battlefield-tech/space/2023/04/02/spacex-rocket-launches-space-development-agencys-first-satellites/

18. Chen, S. (2023, February 24). China aims to launch nearly 13,000 satellites to 'suppress' Elon Musk's Starlink, researchers say. *South China Morning Post.* https://www.scmp.com/news/china/article/3211438/china-aims-launch-nearly-13000-satellites-suppress-elon-musks-starlink-researchers-say

19. Reuters. (2023, March 2). *China gears up to compete with SpaceX's Starlink this year.* https://www.reuters.com/business/aerospace-defense/china-gears-up-compete-with-spacexs-starlink-this-year-2023-03-02/

20. Reuters. (2020, June 8). *Denmark wants 5G suppliers from closely allied countries, says defence minister.* https://www.reuters.com/article/idUSK BN23F1IH/

21. Blinken, A. J. (2023, January 19). *Significant new U.S. Military assistance to Ukraine* [Press statement]. U.S. Department of State. https://www .state.gov/significant-new-u-s-military-assistance-to-ukraine/

22. Pultarova, T., Howell, E., Dobrijevic, D., & Mann, A. (2022, November 23). *Starlink satellites: Everything you need to know about the controversial internet megaconstellation.* Space. https://www.space.com/ spacex-starlink-satellites.html

23. Jayanti, A. (2023, March 9). *Starlink and the Russia-Ukraine War: A case of commercial technology and public purpose?* Belfer Center. https:// www.belfercenter.org/publication/starlink-and-russia-ukraine-war-case-commercial-technology-and-public-purpose

24. Fidler, S. (2023, February 15). Russia likely lost more than half of its tanks in Ukraine, estimates show. *The Wall Street Journal.* https://www.wsj .com/articles/russia-likely-lost-more-than-half-of-its-tanks-in-ukraine-estimates-show-c23dabc2

25. Edwards, J. (2022, December 27). *US to Provide Lithuania with AeroVironment-made Switchblade 600 drones.* ExecutiveBiz. https:// blog.executivebiz.com/2022/12/us-to-provide-lithuania-with-aerovironment-made-switchblade-600-drones/

26. Hille, K. (2023, January 6). Taiwan plans domestic satellite champion to resist any China attack. *Financial Times.* https://www.ft.com/content/ 07c6e48b-5068-4231-8dcf-fe15cb3d0478

27. Rabie, P. (2022, May 27). *Chinese researchers publish strategy to destroy Elon Musk's Starlink.* Gizmodo. https://gizmodo.com/spacex-starlink-china-military-1848982845

28. European Data Portal. (n.d.). *DigitalGlobe – Open data platform.* https:// data.europa.eu/sites/default/files/use-cases/usa_-_digitalglobe.pdf

29. Pitrelli, M. (2022, July 28). *Hacktivist group Anonymous is using six top techniques to "embarrass" Russia.* CNBC. https://www.cnbc.com/2022/ 07/28/how-is-anonymous-attacking-russia-the-top-six-ways-ranked- .html

30. Pitrelli, M. (2022, July 28). *Hacktivist group Anonymous is using six top techniques to "embarrass" Russia.* CNBC. https://www.cnbc.com/2022/ 07/28/how-is-anonymous-attacking-russia-the-top-six-ways-ranked- .html

31. Marquardt, A. (2022, October 14). *Exclusive: Musk's SpaceX says it can no longer pay for critical satellite services in Ukraine, asks Pentagon to pick up the tab.* CNN. https://edition.cnn.com/2022/10/13/politics/ elon-musk-spacex-starlink-ukraine/index.html

32. Reuters. (2022, October 18). *Pentagon considers funding Musk's Starlink network for Ukraine – Politico.* https://www.reuters.com/world/ pentagon-considers-funding-starlink-ukraine-politico-2022-10-17/

33. Marquina, C. (2022, February 18) *How low-earth orbit satellite technology can connect the unconnected.* World Economic Forum. https://www.weforum.org/agenda/2022/02/explainer-how-low-earth-orbit-satellite-technology-can-connect-the-unconnected/

34. United States Government Accountability Office. (2022). *Large constellations of satellites.* In *GAO (GAO-22-105166).* https://www.gao.gov/assets/gao-22-105166.pdf

CHAPTER 18: THE TWENTY-FIRST-CENTURY SPACE RACE

1. Spaceflight Now. (2023, September 3). *SpaceX Falcon 9 rocket launches record-breaking 62nd mission of the year.* https://spaceflightnow.com/2023/09/03/live-coverage-falcon-9-rocket-counting-down-to-spacexs-record-breaking-62nd-launch-of-the-year/

CHAPTER 19: DRONES, ROBOTS AND AUTONOMOUS WEAPONS

1. The Times and The Sunday Times. (2024, March 5). *Ukrainian drones destroy Russian ship near Crimea* [Video]. YouTube. https://www.youtube.com/watch?v=fd6WhIC2lTI

2. MAGURA V5. (2024, March 16). In *Wikipedia.* https://en.wikipedia.org/wiki/MAGURA_V5

3. Sutton, H. I. (2024, January 24). *Exclusive: New Ukrainian underwater drone project to dominate the Black Sea.* Naval News. https://www.navalnews.com/naval-news/2024/01/exclusive-new-ukrainian-underwater-drone-project-to-dominate-the-black-sea/#:~:text=Now%20a%20Ukrainian%20project%20seeks,underwater%20drones%20to%20the%20fight.&text=Imagine%20a%20future%20where%20Ukrainian,daring%20to%20do%20just%20that%20.

4. Fernholz, T. (2022, March 2). *A cheap drone is giving Ukraine's military an edge against Russia.* Quartz. https://qz.com/2135820/the-cheap-tb2-drone-gives-ukraine-an-edge-against-russia

5. Fernholz, T. (2022, March 2). *A cheap drone is giving Ukraine's military an edge against Russia.* Quartz. https://qz.com/2135820/the-cheap-tb2-drone-gives-ukraine-an-edge-against-russia

6. Knights, M., & Almeida, A. (2022, November 10). *What Iran's drones in Ukraine mean for the future of war.* The Washington Institute for Near East Policy. https://www.washingtoninstitute.org/policy-analysis/what-irans-drones-ukraine-mean-future-war

7. Manuel, R. (2022, July 25). US sending 580 Phoenix Ghost kamikaze drones to Ukraine. *The Defense Post.* https://www.thedefensepost.com/2022/07/25/us-phoenix-drones-ukraine/

8. Jerusalem Post Staff (2022, July 25). What is the Phoenix Ghost Drone that is set to be used in Ukraine? *The Jerusalem Post*. https://www.jpost .com/international/article-712976

9. Adamowski, J. (2022, December 24). Lithuania buys Switchblade 600 drones. *Defense News*. https://www.defensenews.com/unmanned/2022/ 12/23/lithuania-buys-switchblade-600-drones/

10. Eurasian Times Desk (2020, November 13). *After shooting-down over 250 Russian aircraft, US to replace its most dangerous man portable missiles.* The EurAsian Times. https://www.eurasiantimes.com/us-to-retire-its-most-dangerous-missiles-that-shot-down-atleast-269-russian-aircraft/

CHAPTER 20: CLIMATE CHANGE AND GEOPOLITICS

1. International Energy Agency (IEA). (2021). *Net zero by 2050.* https:// www.iea.org/reports/net-zero-by-2050

2. International Energy Agency (IEA). (2021). *Net zero by 2050.* https:// www.iea.org/reports/net-zero-by-2050

3. Quartz Creative. (2019). *The Belt and Road's decarbonization dilemma.* Quartz. https://qz.com/1760615/china-quits-coal-at-home-but-promotes-the-fossil-fuel-in-developing-countries/

4. Global Carbon Atlas. (n.d.). *Global carbon atlas.* https://globalcarbonatlas .org/

5. Reve. (2021, March 13). *China takes up 7 spots among the world's top 10 wind turbine manufacturers for wind power.* https://www.evwind .es/2021/03/13/china-takes-up-7-spots-among-the-worlds-top-10-wind-turbine-manufacturers-for-wind-power/79787

6. BNEF. (2019, August 20). *BloombergNEF New Energy Outlook 2019.* Global Infrastructure Hub. https://www.gihub.org/resources/publications/ bnef-new-energy-outlook-2019/

7. Dlouhy, J. A. (2021, October 22). *Rich nations hatch plan for $100 billion climate aid.* Bloomberg. https://www.bloomberg.com/news/articles/ 2021-10-22/deal-struck-on-100-billion-climate-aid-plan-for-poor-nations

8. Ruinan, Z. (2021, July 31). BRI wind farm bringing green energy to Ethiopia. *China Daily.* https://global.chinadaily.com.cn/a/202107/31/WS6104cdc7a 310efa1bd665b55.html

9. Deboutte, G. (2020, December 15). First unit of 250 MW floating PV project comes online in Ghana. *pv magazine International.* https://www .pv-magazine.com/2020/12/15/first-unit-of-250-mw-floating-pv-project-comes-online-in-ghana/

10. Russel, D., & Locklear, S. (2020, October 22). China is weaponizing the Belt and Road. What can the US do about it? *The Diplomat.* https://

thediplomat.com/2020/10/china-is-weaponizing-the-belt-and-road-what-can-the-us-do-about-it/

11. The Korea Times. (2021, October 11). China's African infrastructure deals face growing concern that locals don't feel the benefits. *The Korea Times.* https://www.koreatimes.co.kr/www/world/2021/10/672_316805.html#

12. ClientEarth Communications. (2020, December 22). *What is a carbon sink?* ClientEarth. https://www.clientearth.org/latest/news/what-is-a-carbon-sink/

13. BirdLife International. (2021, February 3). *Major manufacturing companies oppose mining in Atewa Forest, Ghana.* https://www.birdlife.org/news/2021/02/03/major-manufacturing-companies-oppose-mining-in-atewa-forest-ghana/

14. Hillman, J., & Tippett, A. (2021, July 6). *Who built that? Labor and the Belt and Road Initiative.* Council on Foreign Relations. https://www.cfr.org/blog/who-built-labor-and-belt-and-road-initiative

15. Mureithi, C. (2021, August 18). *China's business operations in Africa may have a human rights problem.* Quartz. https://qz.com/africa/2049284/do-chinas-operations-in-africa-have-a-human-rights-problem

16. Egbunike, N. (2021, September 22). *Chinese firms in Nigeria face widespread labour abuse allegations, tainting bilateral relationship.* Global Voices. https://globalvoices.org/2021/09/22/chinese-firms-in-nigeria-face-widespread-labour-abuse-allegations-tainting-bilateral-relationship/

17. Berman, J. (2018, October 26). *How the US will transform its investment role in Africa with a new $60 billion agency.* Quartz. https://qz.com/africa/1439026/us-africa-investments-will-transform-take-on-china-with-idfc

18. Raaymakers, S. (2020, September 11). *China expands its island-building strategy into the Pacific.* The Strategist. https://www.aspistrategist.org.au/china-expands-its-island-building-strategy-into-the-pacific/

19. Fang, A. (2020, August 27). US blacklists Belt and Road builder for role in South China Sea. *Nikkei Asia.* https://asia.nikkei.com/Politics/International-relations/US-China-tensions/US-blacklists-Belt-and-Road-builder-for-role-in-South-China-Sea

20. U.S. Department of Commerce. (2020, August 26). *Commerce Department adds 24 Chinese companies to the entity list for helping build military islands in the South China Sea* [Press release]. https://2017-2021.commerce.gov/news/press-releases/2020/08/commerce-department-adds-24-chinese-companies-entity-ntgp-helping-build.html

21. GCR Staff. (2021, May 7). *China plans to modernise 2km airstrip in centre of Pacific Ocean.* Global Construction Review. https://www.globalconstructionreview.com/china-plans-modernise-2km-airstrip-centre-pacific/

22. Westerman, A. (2019, November 23). *Some Pacific Island nations are turning to China. Climate change is a factor.* NPR. https://choice.npr.org/index.html?origin=https://www.npr.org/2019/11/23/775986892/some-pacific-island-nations-are-turning-to-china-climate-change-is-a-factor

CHAPTER 21: THE GEOPOLITICS OF ELECTRIC VEHICLES

1. Reuters. (2023, August 11). *BYD calls on China automakers to unite, 'demolish the old' in global push.* https://www.reuters.com/business/autos-transportation/byd-calls-china-automakers-unite-demolish-old-global-push-2023-08-11/
2. Valdes-Dapena, P., & Sherman, I. (2019, October 10). *Electric cars have been around since before the US Civil War.* CNN. https://edition.cnn.com/interactive/2019/07/business/electric-car-timeline/index.html
3. Conzade, J., Cornet, A., Hertzke, P., Hensley, R., Heuss, R., Möller, T., Schaufuss, P., Schenk, S., Tschiesner, A., & Laufenberg, K. V. (2021, September 7). *Why the automotive future is electric.* McKinsey & Company. https://www.mckinsey.com/industries/automotive-and-assembly/our-insights/why-the-automotive-future-is-electric
4. White, A. (2021, June 10). Here's what it will take for EVs to take over the car market. *Car and Driver.* https://www.caranddriver.com/news/a36676835/ev-report-net-zero-2050/
5. *Exclusive look inside a new electric vehicle battery mega-factory* [Video]. (2021, April 20). NBC News. https://www.nbcnews.com/business/autos/mercedes-benz-go-all-electric-2030-n1274708
6. Leggett, T. (2021, February 15). *Jaguar car brand to be all-electric by 2025.* BBC News. https://www.bbc.com/news/business-56072019
7. Tucker, S. (2021, June 21). *Report: Audi will go all electric by 2026.* Kelley Blue Book. https://www.kbb.com/archive/report-audi-will-go-all-electric-by-2026/
8. TechXplore. (2021, October 4). *Volvo Cars announces IPO to raise nearly $2.9 billion.* https://techxplore.com/news/2021-10-volvo-cars-ipo-billion.html
9. Szymkowski, S. (2021, June 28). *Volkswagen will go all-electric in Europe by 2035, US to follow shortly after.* CNET. https://www.cnet.com/roadshow/news/volkswagen-all-electric-ev-europe-us/
10. Woods, B. (2021, June 14). *GM, Ford are all-in on EVs. Here's how their dealers feel about it.* CNBC. https://www.cnbc.com/2021/06/13/gm-ford-are-all-in-on-evs-heres-how-dealers-feel-about-it-.html
11. Ford Motor Company. (n.d.). *2023 Ford F-150® Lightning.* https://www.ford.com/trucks/f150/f150-lightning/
12. GMC (n.d.). *Hummer EV Pickup and Hummer EV SUV.* https://www.gmc.com/electric/hummer-ev/pickup-trucks-suvs
13. Toohey, R. (2021, February 8). *Put it all on green: Nissan's going all-electric in 2030s, CO2-neutral by 2050.* MotorBiscuit. https://www.motorbiscuit.com/put-it-all-on-green-nissans-going-all-electric-in-2030s-CO2-neutral-by-2050/

14. Bloomberg. (2021, June 23). *Honda goes all in on EVs in contrast to rival Toyota.* Automotive News Europe. https://europe.autonews.com/automakers/honda-goes-all-evs-contrast-rival-toyota

15. National Geographic. (2021, October). *The revolution is here.* https://www.nationalgeographic.com/magazine/issue/october-2021

16. Merchant, N. (2021, May 3). *5 innovators making the electric vehicle battery more sustainable.* World Economic Forum. https://www.weforum.org/agenda/2021/05/electric-vehicle-battery-recycling-circular-economy/

17. Stevis-Gridneff, M., Novak, B., & Pronczuk, M. (2021, July 20). E.U. reaches deal on major budget and stimulus package. *The New York Times.* https://www.nytimes.com/2020/12/10/world/europe/eu-deal-poland-hungary.html

18. Abnett, K. (2020, December 4). *EU to target 30 million electric cars by 2030 - draft.* Reuters. https://www.reuters.com/article/idUSKBN28E2KL/

19. Miller, J., & Campbell, P. (2021, October 4). Electric vehicles: The revolution is finally here. *Financial Times.* https://www.ft.com/content/fb4d1d64-5d90-4e27-b77f-6e221bc02696

20. Stauffer, N. W. (2020, November 25). *China's transition to electric vehicles.* MIT Energy Initiative. https://energy.mit.edu/news/chinas-transition-to-electric-vehicles/

21. The White House. (2021, August 5). *President Biden announces steps to drive American leadership forward on clean cars and trucks.* [Fact sheet]. https://www.whitehouse.gov/briefing-room/statements-releases/2021/08/05/fact-sheet-president-biden-announces-steps-to-drive-american-leadership-forward-on-clean-cars-and-trucks/

22. Drive Electric. (n.d.). *What is an EV?* https://driveelectric.org.nz/consumer/what-is-an-ev/

23. Brar, A. (2023, December 28). Chinese electric car maker livestreams 600-mile drive on single charge. *Newsweek.* https://www.newsweek.com/china-electric-vehicles-nio-et7-600-miles-single-charge-1856099

24. Gielen, D., & Lyons, M. (2022). *Critical materials for the energy transition: Rare earth elements.* International Renewable Energy Agency. https://www.irena.org/-/media/Irena/Files/Technical-papers/IRENA_Rare_Earth_Elements_2022.pdf?rev=6b1d592393f245f193b08eeed6512abc

25. Dal, B. (2024, March 5). *China's grip on rare earth elements loosens.* Carbon Credits. https://carboncredits.com/chinas-grip-on-rare-earth-elements-loosens/

26. Capri, A. (2020, October 8). How to break China's monopoly on rare earths. *ThinkChina.* https://www.thinkchina.sg/how-break-chinas-monopoly-rare-earths

27. Bradsher, K. (2010, September 22). Amid tension, China blocks vital exports to Japan. *The New York Times.* https://www.nytimes.com/2010/09/23/business/global/23rare.html

28. Vella, H. (2020, January 16). *Australia and the US: A rare, rare-earth partnership*. Mining Technology. https://www.mining-technology.com/features/australia-and-the-us-a-rare-rare-earth-partnership/

29. Vella, H. (2020, January 16). *Australia and the US: A rare, rare-earth partnership*. Mining Technology. https://www.mining-technology.com/features/australia-and-the-us-a-rare-rare-earth-partnership/

30. Scheyder, E. (2020, July 16). *U.S. rare earths miner MP Materials to go public in $1.47 billion deal*. Reuters. https://www.reuters.com/article/us-mp-materials-ipo/u-s-rare-earths-miner-mp-materials-to-go-public-in-1-47-billion-deal-idUSKCN24G1WT/

31. Capri, A. (2020, October 8). How to break China's monopoly on rare earths. *ThinkChina*. https://www.thinkchina.sg/how-break-chinas-monopoly-rare-earths

32. SAFE. (n.d.). *Supply Chain Initiatives - SAFE*. https://secureenergy.org/commandingheights/

33. Democratic Republic of Congo, DRC is the world's largest supplier of cobalt.

34. Democratic Republic of Congo, DRC is the world's largest supplier of cobalt.

35. Dezenski, E., Austin, J. C. (2021, June 8). *Rebuilding America's economy and foreign policy with 'ally-shoring'*. Brookings. https://www.brookings.edu/articles/rebuilding-americas-economy-and-foreign-policy-with-ally-shoring/

36. LeVine, S. (2021, February 5). *Who will win the age of battery nationalism?* The Mobilist. https://themobilist.medium.com/who-will-win-the-age-of-battery-nationalism-89fd6a3f8d5a

37. The Economist. (2021, July 17). *China's 'dreamchild' is stealthily winning the battery race*. https://www.economist.com/business/2021/07/17/chinas-dreamchild-is-stealthily-winning-the-battery-race

38. Bloomberg News. (2020, May 21). *China's got a new plan to overtake the U.S. in tech*. Bloomberg. https://www.bloomberg.com/news/articles/2020-05-20/china-has-a-new-1-4-trillion-plan-to-overtake-the-u-s-in-tech?leadSource=uverify%20wall&sref=jeNvC3eC

39. Siddiqui, F. (2021, September 15). The government helped Tesla conquer electric cars. Now it's helping Detroit, and Elon Musk isn't happy. *The Washington Post*. https://www.washingtonpost.com/technology/2021/09/15/tesla-biden-administration/

40. Hawkins, A. J. (2021, January 26). *Biden wants to replace government fleet with electric vehicles*. The Verge. https://www.theverge.com/2021/1/25/22249237/biden-electric-vehicle-government-fleet-ev

41. Lewis, M. (2021, May 25). *EGEB: Korean companies to spend nearly $40 billion to build EV tech in the US*. Electrek. https://electrek.co/2021/05/25/egeb-korean-companies-to-spend-nearly-40-billion-to-build-ev-tech-in-the-us/

42. Korosec, K. (2021, September 28). *Ford, SK to spend $11.4B to build two US manufacturing campuses dedicated to EVs and batteries.* TechCrunch. https://techcrunch.com/2021/09/27/ford-sk-to-spend-11-4b-to-build-two-us-manufacturing-campuses-dedicated-to-evs-and-batteries/

43. Wayland, M. (2021, April 20). *GM and LG to spend $2.3 billion on second EV battery plant in U.S.* CNBC. https://www.cnbc.com/2021/04/16/gm-and-lg-to-spend-2point3-billion-on-second-ev-battery-plant-in-us.html

44. Westwater Resources. (n.d.). *Graphite projects overview.* https://westwaterresources.net/projects/graphite/

CHAPTER 22: SEMICONDUCTORS AND ELECTRIC VEHICLE WARS

1. Lawrence, A. & VerWey, J. (2019, May). *The automotive semiconductor market – Key determinants of U.S. firm competitiveness.* U.S. International Trade Commission (USITC). https://www.usitc.gov/publications/332/executive_briefings/ebot_amanda_lawrence_john_verwey_the_automotive_semiconductor_market_pdf.pdf

2. Wayland, M. (2021, September 23). *Chip shortage expected to cost auto industry $210 billion in revenue in 2021.* CNBC. https://www.cnbc.com/2021/09/23/chip-shortage-expected-to-cost-auto-industry-210-billion-in-2021.html

3. Bloomberg News. (2024, March 15). *China urges EV makers to buy local chips as US clash deepens.* Bloomberg. https://www.bloomberg.com/news/articles/2024-03-15/china-urges-byd-ev-makers-to-buy-chinese-chips-as-tensions-with-us-escalate?sref=jeNvC3eC

4. GlobalFoundries. (2021, July 19). *GlobalFoundries plans to build new fab in Upstate New York in private-public partnership to support U.S. semiconductormanufacturing* [Press release]. https://gf.com/dresden-press-release/globalfoundries-plans-build-new-fab-upstate-new-york-private-public-partnership/

5. Fitch, A. (2021, September 12). Chip shortage drives tech companies and car makers closer. *The Wall Street Journal.* https://www.wsj.com/articles/chip-shortage-drives-tech-companies-and-car-makers-closer-11631455202

6. Hodgson, J. (2021). *Qualcomm kicks automotive ambitions up a gear with a US$4.6 billion Veoneer offer.* ABIresearch. https://www.abiresearch.com/market-research/insight/7779779-qualcomm-kicks-automotive-ambitions-up-a-g/

7. Hawkins, A. J. (2021, September 7). *Intel's Mobileye will launch a robot-taxi service in Germany in 2022.* The Verge. https://www.theverge.com/2021/9/7/22659366/intel-mobileye-robotaxi-germany-sixt-moovit

8. Ting-Fang, C., Li, L. (2021, July 29). Huawei drops 5G for new P50 phones as US sanctions grip. *Nikkei Asia.* https://asia.nikkei.com/Spotlight/

Huawei-crackdown/Huawei-drops-5G-for-new-P50-phones-as-US-sanctions-grip

9. Korosec, K. (2020, April 29). *EV startup Nio secures $1 billion investment from China entities*. TechCrunch. https://techcrunch.com/2020/04/29/ev-startup-nio-secures-1-billion-investment-from-china-entities/

10. Goswami, R. (2024, January 4). *Mobileye shares plunge after chipmaker warns of order pullback*. CNBC. https://www.cnbc.com/2024/01/04/mobileye-shares-plunge-after-chipmaker-warns-of-order-pullback.html#:~:text=Intel%20first%20announced%20it%20would,88%25%20stake%20in%20the%20company.

11. Liao, R. (2021, May 6). *Tesla supplier Delta Electronics invests $7M in AI chip startup Kneron*. TechCrunch. https://techcrunch.com/2021/05/05/delta-electronics-kneron/

12. Liao, R. (2021, May 6). *Tesla supplier Delta Electronics invests $7M in AI chip startup Kneron*. TechCrunch. https://techcrunch.com/2021/05/05/delta-electronics-kneron/

13. King, I., Coppola, G., & Bloomberg. (2021, October 3). Silicon Valley's answer to EV question calls for less silicon. *The Taipei Times*, p. 16. https://www.taipeitimes.com/News/biz/archives/2021/10/03/2003765405

14. King, I., Coppola, G., & Bloomberg. (2021, October 3). Silicon Valley's answer to EV question calls for less silicon. *The Taipei Times*, p. 16. https://www.taipeitimes.com/News/biz/archives/2021/10/03/2003765405

15. Toh, M. (2021, May 26). *Tesla sets up China data center amid spying concerns*. CNN Business. https://edition.cnn.com/2021/05/26/business/tesla-china-data-center-intl-hnk/index.html

16. Bloomberg News. (2020, May 21). *China's got a new plan to overtake the U.S. in tech*. Bloomberg. https://www.bloomberg.com/news/articles/2020-05-20/china-has-a-new-1-4-trillion-plan-to-overtake-the-u-s-in-tech?leadSource=uverify%20wall&sref=jeNvC3eC

CHAPTER 23: FOOD SECURITY AND TECHNO-NATIONALISM

1. Statista Research Department. (2022, April 6). *Russia's and Ukraine's share of global trade in selected agricultural products 2020*. Statista. https://www.statista.com/statistics/1300876/russia-s-and-ukraine-s-share-of-global-trade-in-agricultural-products/

2. Statista Research Department. (2023, April 11). *Commodity price increase due to the Russia-Ukraine war 2022*. Statista. https://www.statista.com/statistics/1298241/commodity-price-growth-due-to-russia-ukraine-war/

3. Chazan, G. (2022, May 14). G7 warns of global hunger crisis unless Russia lifts Ukraine blockade. *Financial Times*. https://www.ft.com/content/2d76bbe5-1163-473b-82cf-c327f3672134

4. Statista Research Department. (2023, October 6). *Russian and Ukrainian wheat dependence in African and least developed countries 2022*. Statista. https://www.statista.com/statistics/1302810/russian-and-ukrainian-wheat-dependence-african-and-least-developed-countries/

5. Malpass, D. (2022, April 8). *A new global food crisis is building.* World Bank Blogs. https://blogs.worldbank.org/voices/new-global-food-crisis-building?sfw=pass1652822410

6. Domm, P. (2022, April 6). *A fertilizer shortage, worsened by war in Ukraine, is driving up global food prices and scarcity.* CNBC. https://www.cnbc.com/2022/04/06/a-fertilizer-shortage-worsened-by-war-in-ukraine-is-driving-up-global-food-prices-and-scarcity.html

7. Myers, S. (2021, December 13). *Too many to count: Factors driving fertilizer prices higher and higher.* American Farm Bureau Federation. https://www.fb.org/market-intel/too-many-to-count-factors-driving-fertilizer-prices-higher-and-higher

8. Nicas, J., & Spigariol, A. (2022, May 8). Brazil replenishes stockpiles of Russian fertilizer. *The New York Times.* https://www.nytimes.com/2022/05/08/world/americas/brazil-russian-fertilizer-sanctions.html

9. Bloomberg News. (2022, March 17). *Canada's scrambling to fill a massive global fertilizer deficit.* MINING.com. https://www.mining.com/web/canadas-scrambling-to-fill-a-massive-global-fertilizer-deficit/

10. Watts, J. (2019, February 6). Met Office: Global warming could exceed 1.5C within five years. *The Guardian.* https://www.theguardian.com/environment/2019/feb/06/met-office-global-warming-could-exceed-1-point-5-c-in-five-years

11. Rajan, Y. (2021, May). *World's top 10 agrochemical companies redefining agriculture by using latest technology.* Verified Market Research. https://www.verifiedmarketresearch.com/blog/worlds-top-agrochemical-companies/

12. Bayer. (2021, March 12). *Bayer's unmatched R&D investment powers industry-leading Crop Science portfolio.* https://media.bayer.com/baynews/baynews.nsf/id/Bayers-unmatched-RD-investment-powers-industry-leading-Crop-Science-portfolio

13. Rajan, Y. (2021, May). *World's top 10 agrochemical companies redefining agriculture by using latest technology.* Verified Market Research. https://www.verifiedmarketresearch.com/blog/worlds-top-agrochemical-companies/

14. Federal Trade Commission. (2017, October 4). *File No. 161 0093, Docket No. C-4610.* The Federal Register. https://www.federalregister.gov/documents/2017/04/10/2017-07069/china-national-chemical-corporation-a-corporation-adama-agricultural-solutions-ltd-a-corporation-and

15. Tsang, A. (2017, April 5). China moves a step closer in its quest for food security. *The New York Times.* https://www.nytimes.com/2017/04/05/business/syngenta-chemchina-takeover.html

16. Sharma, A., Sharma, A., Tselykh, A., Bozhenyuk, A., Choudhury, T., Alomar, M. & Sánchez-Chero, M. (2023). Artificial intelligence and

internet of things oriented sustainable precision farming: Towards modern agriculture. *Open Life Sciences, 18*(1). https://doi.org/10.1515/biol-2022-0713

17. Capri, A. (2020, August). *Techno-nationalism: The US-China tech innovation race.* Hinrich Foundation. https://s3.iois.me/Hinrich-Foundation-Techno-nationalism-and-the-US-China-tech-innovation-race-August-2020.pdf

18. McKinnon, J. D. (2021, June 8). Senate approves $250 billion bill to boost tech research. *The Wall Street Journal.* https://www.wsj.com/articles/senate-approves-250-billion-bill-to-boost-tech-research-11623192584

19. The Fish Site. (2022, February 23). *INSEACT opens Singapore's largest insect protein facility.* https://thefishsite.com/articles/inseact-opens-singapores-largest-insect-protein-facility

20. Klein-Hessling, H., & Zimmermann-Loessl, C. (2021, March 11). *A little history on the most recent evolution of vertical, urban farming in Singapore.* Association for Vertical Farming. https://vertical-farming.net/blog/2021/03/11/a-little-history-on-the-most-recent-evolution-of-vertical-urban-farming-in-singapore/

21. Klein-Hessling, H., & Zimmermann-Loessl, C. (2021, March 11). *A little history on the most recent evolution of vertical, urban farming in Singapore.* Association for Vertical Farming. https://vertical-farming.net/blog/2021/03/11/a-little-history-on-the-most-recent-evolution-of-vertical-urban-farming-in-singapore/

22. Morgan, R. (2018, March 23). *Bill Gates and Richard Branson are betting lab-grown meat might be the food of the future.* CNBC. https://www.cnbc.com/2018/03/23/bill-gates-and-richard-branson-bet-on-lab-grown-meat-startup.html

23. The Futures Centre. (2018, May 16). *Meat giant Tyson invests to make lab-grown meat mainstream.* https://www.thefuturescentre.org/signal/meat-giant-tyson-invests-to-make-lab-grown-meat-mainstream/

24. Origin Agritech. (2021, March 25). *Origin Agritech and Beijing Dabeinong Technology Group ink collaboration agreement* [News release]. https://originagritech.com/investor-relations/news-releases/?qmodStoryID=5655332736346493

25. Office of Public Affairs. (2018, April 4). *Chinese scientist sentenced to prison in theft of engineered rice* [Press release]. The U.S. Department of Justice. https://www.justice.gov/opa/pr/chinese-scientist-sentenced-prison-theft-engineered-rice

26. Office of Public Affairs. (2018, April 4). *Chinese scientist sentenced to prison in theft of engineered rice* [Press release]. The U.S. Department of Justice. https://www.justice.gov/opa/pr/chinese-scientist-sentenced-prison-theft-engineered-rice

27. Office of Public Affairs. (2019, November 21). *Chinese national who worked at Monsanto indicted on economic espionage charges* [Press release]. The U.S. Department of Justice. https://www.justice.gov/opa/

pr/chinese-national-who-worked-monsanto-indicted-economic-espionage-charges

28. Agricultural Intelligence Measures Act of 2021, S. 1242, 117th Cong. (2021). https://www.cotton.senate.gov/imo/media/doc/aim_act.pdf

29. Boretti, A., & Rosa, L. (2019, July 31). Reassessing the projections of the World Water Development Report. *Nature*. https://www.nature.com/articles/s41545-019-0039-9

30. Salas, E. B. (2023, April 17). *Selected water and wastewater treatment companies globally 2021, by revenue.* Statista. https://www.statista.com/statistics/1302810/russian-and-ukrainian-wheat-dependence-african-and-least-developed-countries/

31. Astute Analytica (2022, January 18). *Wastewater treatment market size is estimated to reach US$ 462.49 billion by 2030, CAGR 7.41%.* PR Newswire. https://www.prnewswire.com/news-releases/wastewater-treatment-market-size-is-estimated-to-reach-us-462-49-bn-by-2030--cagr-7-41-astute-analytica-301462434.html

32. Stevis-Gridneff, M., & Kingsley, P. (2020, February 28). Turkey pressing E.U. for help in Syria, threatens to open border to refugees. *The New York Times*. https://www.nytimes.com/2020/02/28/world/europe/turkey-refugees-Geece-erdogan.html

33. Eyler, B., Kwan, R., & Weatherby, C. (2020, April 13). *How China turned off the tap on the Mekong River.* Stimson. https://www.stimson.org/2020/new-evidence-how-china-turned-off-the-mekong-tap/

34. Roney, T. (2021, July 1). *What are the impacts of dams on the Mekong River?* The Third Pole. https://www.thethirdpole.net/en/energy/what-are-the-impacts-of-dams-on-the-mekong-river/

CHAPTER 24: TECHNO-NATIONALISM ON CAMPUS

1. Raymond, N. (2020, June 16). *Harvard professor pleads not guilty in U.S. to lying about China ties.* Reuters. https://www.reuters.com/article/us-usa-china-crime/harvard-professor-pleads-not-guilty-in-u-s-to-lying-about-china-ties-idUSKBN23N2PK

2. Service, R. F. (2020, February 4). Why did a Chinese university hire Charles Lieber to do battery research? *Science*. https://www.sciencemag.org/news/2020/02/why-did-chinese-university-hire-charles-lieber-do-battery-research

3. Ciu, L., Ting-Fang, C., & Li, L. (2020, June 17). US blacklists 'China's MIT' as tech war enters new phase. *Nikkei Asia*. https://asia.nikkei.com/Business/Technology/US-blacklists-China-s-MIT-as-tech-war-enters-new-phase

4. National Foundation for American Policy. (2017, October). *The importance of international students to American science and engineering.*

The Immigrant Learning Center. https://www.immigrationresearch.org/node/2617

5. Institute of International Education. (2019, November 18). *Number of international students in the United States hits all-time high.* https://www.iie.org/Why-IIE/Announcements/2019/11/Number-of-International-Students-in-the-United-States-Hits-All-Time-High

6. R&D World. (2020). *2020 R&D Global funding forecast: Special August 2020 mid-year update* (p. 12). https://www.rdworldonline.com/2020-rd-global-funding-forecast-preview/

7. Thousand Talents Plan. (2024, February 24). In *Wikipedia.* https://en.wikipedia.org/wiki/Thousand_Talents_Plan

8. JASON. (2019, December 11). *Fundamental research security.* Mitre. https://www.mitre.org/sites/default/files/publications/JASON-Fundamental-Research-Security-12-19.pdf

9. Croteau, S. J. (2020, January 28). Chinese People's Liberation Army lieutenant, Yanqing Ye, assessed US military websites, researched professors while studying at Boston University, federal authorities say. MassLive. https://www.masslive.com/boston/2020/01/chinese-peoples-liberation-army-lieutenant-yanqing-ye-assessed-us-military-websites-researched-professors-while-studying-at-boston-university-federal-authorities-say.html

10. Euractiv Network. (2019, October 19). *China funded 'propaganda' course at Czech University.* Euractiv. https://www.euractiv.com/section/politics/news/china-funded-propaganda-course-at-czech-university/

11. Manyika, J., McRaven, W. H., & Segal, A. (2019). *Innovation and national security: Keeping our edge* (Independent Task Force Report No. 77), p. 46. Council on Foreign Relations. https://www.cfr.org/report/keeping-our-edge/pdf/TFR_Innovation_Strategy.pdf

CHAPTER 25: CHIP SCHOOLS

1. Purdue University. (2022, June 28). *Purdue university partners with leading global chipmaker on semiconductor design center.* https://www.purdue.edu/newsroom/releases/2022/Q2/purdue-university-partners-with-leading-global-chipmaker-on-midwests-first-semiconductor-design-center.html

2. Ira A. Fulton Schools of Engineering. (2023). *Enrolment and degrees granted.* Arizona State University. https://engineering.asu.edu/enrollment/#:~:text=Fall%202022%20total%20enrollment%3A%2030%2C297

3. Arizona State University. (n.d.). *Powering the revival of American microelectronics.* https://microelectronics.asu.edu/

4. Munro, B., Capri, A., Clark, R. (2023, November 2). *Australia's semiconductor manufacturing moonshot: Securing semiconductor talent.* Australian Strategic Policy Institute (ASPI). https://www.aspi.org.au/report/australias-semiconductor-manufacturing-moonshot-securing-semiconductor-talent

5. The New Economy Initiative. (2023). *Leading for the future: Driving solutions*. Arizona Board of Regents. https://www.azregents.edu/sites/default/files/public/new-economy-initiative/NEI_Jan_2023-onepager.pdf

6. Munro, B., Capri, A., Clark, R. (2023, November 2). *Australia's semiconductor manufacturing moonshot: Securing semiconductor talent*. Australian Strategic Policy Institute (ASPI). https://www.aspi.org.au/report/australias-semiconductor-manufacturing-moonshot-securing-semiconductor-talent

7. Munro, B., Capri, A., Clark, R. (2023, November 2). *Australia's semiconductor manufacturing moonshot: Securing semiconductor talent*. Australian Strategic Policy Institute (ASPI). https://www.aspi.org.au/report/australias-semiconductor-manufacturing-moonshot-securing-semiconductor-talent

8. Micron. (2023, May 20). *Micron launches U.S.-Japan University Partnership for Workforce Advancement and Research & Development in Semiconductors (UPWARDS) for the Future* [Press release]. Micron Technology. https://investors.micron.com/news-releases/news-release-details/micron-launches-us-japan-university-partnership-workforce

9. Micron. (2023, May 20). *Micron launches U.S.-Japan University Partnership for Workforce Advancement and Research & Development in Semiconductors (UPWARDS) for the Future* [Press release]. Micron Technology. https://investors.micron.com/news-releases/news-release-details/micron-launches-us-japan-university-partnership-workforce

10. Micron. (2023, May 20). *Micron launches U.S.-Japan University Partnership for Workforce Advancement and Research & Development in Semiconductors (UPWARDS) for the Future* [Press release]. Micron Technology. https://investors.micron.com/news-releases/news-release-details/micron-launches-us-japan-university-partnership-workforce

11. Huchel, B. (2023, May 10). *Purdue and India establish milestone semiconductor alliance; sign partnership in the presence of Minister Ashwini Vaishnaw*. Purdue University. https://www.purdue.edu/newsroom/releases/2023/Q2/purdue-establishes-milestone-semiconductor-alliance-with-india-agreement-provides-foundation-to-advance-workforce-development-joint-research-and-innovation-and-global-industry-collaborations.html

12. Munro, B., Capri, A., Clark, R. (2023, November 2). *Australia's semiconductor manufacturing moonshot: Securing semiconductor talent*. Australian Strategic Policy Institute (ASPI). https://www.aspi.org.au/report/australias-semiconductor-manufacturing-moonshot-securing-semiconductor-talent

13. Munro, B., Capri, A., Clark, R. (2023, November 2). *Australia's semiconductor manufacturing moonshot: Securing semiconductor talent*. Australian Strategic Policy Institute (ASPI). https://www.aspi.org.au/report/australias-semiconductor-manufacturing-moonshot-securing-semiconductor-talent

14. Park, K. (2023, May 18). *Micron to invest 3.6B in Japan for next-gen memory chips.* TechCrunch. https://techcrunch.com/2023/05/18/micron-to-invest-3-6b-in-japan-for-next-gen-memory-chips/

15. U.S. Department of State. (2023, May 20). *Memorandum of cooperation in education signed between the United States and Japan.* https://www.state.gov/memorandum-of-cooperation-in-education-signed-between-the-united-states-and-japan/

16. U.S. Department of State. (2023, May 20). *Memorandum of cooperation in education signed between the United States and Japan.* https://www.state.gov/memorandum-of-cooperation-in-education-signed-between-the-united-states-and-japan/

17. Sharma, Y. (2021, October 22). *Asian universities step up semiconductor programmes.* University World News. https://www.universityworldnews.com/post.php?story=20211021144726611#:~:text=Four%20new%20semiconductor%20research%20centres,it%20had%20also%20approved%20new

18. National Taiwan University. (n.d.). *Taiwan Semiconductor Scholarship Program for Visiting Students.* https://tscsp.ntu.edu.tw/?openExternalBrowser=1

19. Sharma, Y. (2021, October 22). *Asian universities step up semiconductor programmes.* University World News. https://www.universityworldnews.com/post.php?story=20211021144726611#:~:text=Four%20new%20semiconductor%20research%20centres,it%20had%20also%20approved%20new

20. Munro, B., Capri, A., Clark, R. (2023, November 2). *Australia's semiconductor manufacturing moonshot: Securing semiconductor talent.* Australian Strategic Policy Institute (ASPI). https://www.aspi.org.au/report/australias-semiconductor-manufacturing-moonshot-securing-semiconductor-talent

21. Tech Xplore. (2022, May 20). *Taiwan tightens laws against China economic espionage.* https://techxplore.com/news/2022-05-taiwan-tightens-laws-china-economic.html

22. Tech Xplore. (2022, May 20). *Taiwan tightens laws against China economic espionage.* https://techxplore.com/news/2022-05-taiwan-tightens-laws-china-economic.html

23. Weisz, K., Lewis, T., Kulik, B., & Stewart, D. (2022). *The global semiconductor talent shortage.* Deloitte. https://www2.deloitte.com/content/dam/Deloitte/us/Documents/technology-media-telecommunications/us-tmt-global-semiconductor-shortage-pov-v3.pdf

24. Hsu, C. (2022, August 16). Semiconductor hiring slows amid labor shortage. *Taipei Times.* https://www.taipeitimes.com/News/biz/archives/2022/08/16/2003783578

25. Alam, S., Garand, D., Hadley, C., Hardin, S., & Alsheik, S.(2022). *The competitive etch: Addressing the talent gap in the semiconductor industry.* Accenture. https://www.accenture.com/content/dam/accenture/final/

industry/high-tech/document/Accenture-The-Competitive-Etch-Addressing-the-Talent-Gap-Final.pdf

26. Valero de Urquia, B. (2022, June 28). *Skills shortage threatens Japan's semiconductor industry*. Engineering and Technology. https://eandt.theiet.org/2022/06/28/skills-shortage-threatens-japans-semiconductor-industry#:~:text=From%20Toshiba%20to%20Sony%2C%20Japan's,by%20a%20shortage%20of%20engineers

27. Choe, M., Jeong, J., & Choi, Y. (2022, June 10). Why Korean Chipmakers Struggle with Talent Shortages. *The Korea Economic Daily*. https://www.kedglobal.com/the-deep-dive/newsView/ked202206100004#:~:text=Over%20the%20next%2010%20years,year%2C%20according%20to%20the%20association

28. Zhu, J. (2022, December 14). *Exclusive: China readying $143 billion package for its chip firms in face of U.S. curbs*. Reuters. https://www.reuters.com/technology/china-plans-over-143-bln-push-boost-domestic-chips-compete-with-us-sources-2022-12-13/#:~:text=HONG%20KONG%2C%20Dec%2013%20(Reuters,at%20slowing%20its%20technological%20advances.

29. Pan, C. (2022, June 10). China chip makers scramble for semiconductor talent, showering fresh graduates with offers as peers in other fields face dim prospects. *South China Morning Post*. https://www.scmp.com/tech/big-tech/article/3181209/china-chip-makers-scramble-semiconductor-talent-showering-fresh

CHAPTER 26: THE INNOVATION HORSE RACE

1. Schmidt, E. (2020, February 27). Eric Schmidt: I used to run Google. Silicon Valley could lose to China. *The New York Times*. https://www.nytimes.com/2020/02/27/opinion/eric-schmidt-ai-china.html

2. Bianchi, T. (2024, January 31). Alphabet: Research and development expenditure 2013–2023. Statista. https://www.statista.com/statistics/507858/alphabet-google-rd-costs/

3. X. (n.d.). *X, the moonshot factory*. https://x.company/

4. Hall, L. (2019, July 15). *Going to the moon was hard — but the benefits were huge, for all of us*. NASA. https://www.nasa.gov/directorates/spacetech/feature/Going_to_the_Moon_Was_Hard_But_the_Benefits_Were_Huge

5. NASA spin-off technologies. (2024, February 7). In *Wikipedia*. https://en.wikipedia.org/wiki/NASA_spinoff_technologies#cite_note-6

6. Atkinson, R. D. (2023, March 9). *How 'national developmentalism' built America*. Information Technology & Innovation Foundation. https://itif.org/publications/2023/03/09/how-national-developmentalism-built-america/

7. Hao, K. (2022, November 18). China's Xi stacks government with science and tech expert amid rivalry with U.S. *The Wall Street Journal*. https://

www.wsj.com/articles/chinas-xi-stacks-government-with-science-and-tech-experts-amid-rivalry-with-u-s-11668772682

8. China SCIO. (2023, January 30). *China's R&D spending hits 3 trillion yuan in 2022.* The State Council Information of the People's Republic of China. http://english.scio.gov.cn/pressroom/2023-01/30/content_85080177 .htm#:~:text=China's%20total%20expenditure%20on%20research, Bureau%20of%20Statistics%20announced%20recently.

9. Dyvik, E. H. (2023, September 20). Leading countries by R&D spending as share of GDP globally 2022. Statista. https://www.statista.com/ statistics/732269/worldwide-research-and-development-share-of-gdp-top-countries/

10. Korhonen, V. (2023, June 2). U.S. gross expenditure on R&D 2020–2022. Statista. https://www.statista.com/statistics/1345767/gross-research-development-expenditure-us/

11. Australian Strategic Policy Institute (ASPI). (n.d.). *Who is leading the critical technology race?* https://techtracker.aspi.org.au/

12. Fukuoka, K., Tabeta, S., & Oikawa, A. (2023, January 16). China trounces U.S. in AI research output and quality. *Nikkei Asia.* https://asia.nikkei .com/Business/China-tech/China-trounces-US-in-AI-research-output-and-quality#:~:text=TOKYO%2FBEIJING%20%2D%2D%20China%20 is,in%20both%20quantity%20and%20quality

13. Fickling, D. (2019, February 6). Alstom and Siemens show how not to deal with China. Bloomberg. https://www.bloomberg.com/view/ articles/2019-02-06/alstom-and-siemens-show-how-not-to-deal-with-china-and-vestager?sref=jeNvC3eC

14. Nikkei Staff Writers. (2023, September 29). Japan allocates $1.2bn subsidy for Micron's Hiroshima chip plant. *Nikkei Asia.* https://asia.nikkei .com/Business/Tech/Semiconductors/Japan-allocates-1.2bn-subsidy-for-Micron-s-Hiroshima-chip-plant

15. Mann, T. (2023, September 1). *Rapidus ramps as construction begins on 2nm wafer fab.* The Register. https://www.theregister.com/2023/09/01/ rapidus_hiring_fab/

16. U.S. Department of State. (2019, December 19). *Tokyo statement on quantum cooperation.* https://www.state.gov/tokyo-statement-on-quantum-cooperation/

17. Anselmo, J. (2023, December 6). *Siemens, Intel partner on semiconductor manufacturing.* Manufacturing Dive. https://www.manufacturingdive .com/news/siemens-intel-partner-to-boost-semiconductor-manufacturing/701611/#:~:text=The%20partnership%20between%20 the%20two,consumption%2C%20according%20to%20the%20release.

18. Shilov, A. (2024, January 19). *Intel's German fab will be most advanced in the world and make 1.5nm chips, CEO says.* Tom's Hardware. https:// www.tomshardware.com/tech-industry/manufacturing/intels-german-fab-will-be-most-advanced-in-the-world-and-make-15nm-chips-ceo-say

19. Research in Germany. (n.d.). *R&D policy framework.* Federal Ministry of Education and Research. https://www.research-in-germany.org/en/ research-landscape/why-germany/r-d-policy-framework.html#: ~:text=Germany%20has%20set%20itself%20the,the%20money%20 will%20be%20invested.

20. Casassus, B. (2023, December 8). Massive shake-up of French science system is biggest in decades. *Nature*. https://www.nature.com/articles/d41586-023-03957-9

21. Kim, S. (2024, January 15). *South Korea lays out $470 billion plan to build chipmaking hub*. Bloomberg. https://www.bloomberg.com/news/articles/2024-01-15/south-korea-lays-out-470-billion-plan-to-build-chipmaking-hub?sref=jeNvC3eC

22. Normile, D. (2023, September 19). South Korea, a science spending champion, proposes cutbacks. *Science*. https://www.science.org/content/article/south-korea-science-spending-champion-proposes-cutbacks

23. SEMATECH. (2023, October 12). In *Wikipedia*. https://en.wikipedia.org/wiki/SEMATECH

24. Capri, A. (2020, January 17). *Semiconductors at the heart of the US-China tech war*. Hinrich Foundation. https://www.hinrichfoundation.com/research/wp/tech/semiconductors-at-the-heart-of-the-us-china-tech-war/

CHAPTER 27: INDIA RISING?

1. The White House. (2023, January 31). *United States and India elevate strategic partnership with the initiative on Critical and Emerging Technology (iCET)* [Fact sheet]. https://www.whitehouse.gov/briefing-room/statements-releases/2023/01/31/fact-sheet-united-states-and-india-elevate-strategic-partnership-with-the-initiative-on-critical-and-emerging-technology-icet/#:~:text=President%20Biden%20and%20Prime%20Minister,institutions%20of%20our%20two%20countries.

2. U.S. Department of Defense. (2024, February 21). *India-U.S. Defense Acceleration Ecosystem (INDUS-X)* [Fact sheet]. https://www.defense.gov/News/Releases/Release/Article/3682879/fact-sheet-india-us-defense-acceleration-ecosystem-indus-x/

3. Markey, D., & Youssef, H. (2022, July 28). *What you need to know about the I2U2*. United States Institute of Peace. https://www.usip.org/publications/2022/07/what-you-need-know-about-i2u2

4. PTI. (2024, February 5). India's crude oil imports from Russia hit 12-month low but long-term appetite remains intact. *The Economic Times*. https://economictimes.indiatimes.com/industry/energy/oil-gas/indias-crude-oil-imports-from-russia-hit-12-month-low-but-long-term-appetite-remains-intact/articleshow/107417941.cms?from=mdr

5. Statista. (2023, July). *Market size of e-commerce industry across India from 2014 to 2018, with forecasts until 2030*. https://www.statista.com/statistics/792047/india-e-commerce-market-size/

6. PTI. (2023, October 4). E-commerce to grow to $300 bn by 2030, shipments by third-party logistics firms to 17 billion: Redseer report. *The Economic Times*. https://economictimes.indiatimes.com/industry/services/

retail/e-commerce-to-grow-to-300-bn-by-2030-shipments-by-third-party-logistics-firms-to-17-billion-redseer-report/articleshow/104167749.cms?from=mdr

7. Capri, A. (2021, March 30). *India: A 21st century technology hub?* Hinrich Foundation. https://www.hinrichfoundation.com/research/wp/tech/india-21st-centry-tech-hub/

8. Chandak, A. (2024, January 3). *India's factory growth ends 2023 at 18-month low on weaker new orders, output.* Reuters. https://www.reuters.com/world/india/indias-factory-growth-ends-2023-18-month-low-weaker-new-orders-output-2024-01-03/

9. Roy, R. (2023, December 8). Apple aims to make a quarter of the world's iPhones in India. *The Wall Street Journal.* https://www.wsj.com/tech/apple-aims-to-make-a-quarter-of-the-worlds-iphones-in-india-ab7f6342

10. Moore, S. K. (2024, March 6). *India injects $15 billion into semiconductors.* IEEE Spectrum. https://spectrum.ieee.org/indian-semiconductor-manufacturing

11. Market Research Store. (n.d.). *India semiconductor market size, share, report, forecast, PDF 2032.* Custom Market Insights. https://aws.amazon.com/marketplace/pp/prodview-v7kuxdpxzcmvk#offers

12. India Today Business Desk. (2023, September 7). *Foxconn teams up with STMicro for semiconductor plant in India: Report.* India Today. https://www.indiatoday.in/business/story/foxconn-stmicroelectronics-partnership-semiconductor-chip-factory-in-india-2432444-2023-09-07

13. Bloomberg. (2023, September 7). *Foxconn seeks to work with STMicro to build India chip plant after parting ways with Vedanta.* Livemint. https://www.livemint.com/companies/news/foxconn-seeks-to-work-with-stmicro-to-build-india-chip-plant-after-parting-ways-with-vedanta-11694088082442.html

14. Moore, S. K. (2024, March 6). *India injects $15 billion into semiconductors.* IEEE Spectrum. https://spectrum.ieee.org/indian-semiconductor-manufacturing

15. Ezell, S. (2024, February 14). *Assessing India's readiness to assume a greater role in global semiconductor value chains.* Information Technology and Innovation Foundation. https://itif.org/publications/2024/02/14/india-semiconductor-readiness/

CHAPTER 28: FRAGMENTED FINANCE

1. Capri, A. (2021, April 29). How China's digital currency could fracture global finance. *Forbes.* https://www.forbes.com/sites/alexcapri/2021/04/29/how-chinas-digital-currency-could-fracture-global-finance/?sh=3339fa2956da

2. Capri, A. (2021, April 29). How China's digital currency could fracture global finance. *Forbes.* https://www.forbes.com/sites/alexcapri/2021/04/29/how-chinas-digital-currency-could-fracture-global-finance/?sh=3339fa2956da

3. Capri, A. (2021, April 29). How China's digital currency could fracture global finance. *Forbes*. https://www.forbes.com/sites/alexcapri/2021/04/29/how-chinas-digital-currency-could-fracture-global-finance/?sh=3339fa2956da

4. Capri, A. (2021, April 29). How China's digital currency could fracture global finance. *Forbes*. https://www.forbes.com/sites/alexcapri/2021/04/29/how-chinas-digital-currency-could-fracture-global-finance/?sh=3339fa2956da

5. Campbell, C. (2019). How China is using "social credit scores" to reward and punish its citizens. *Time*. https://time.com/collection/davos-2019/5502592/china-social-credit-score/

6. Reuters. (2020, December 3). *Bill forcing Chinese firms to meet U.S. accounting standards passes Congress*. CNBC. https://www.cnbc.com/2020/12/02/bill-forcing-chinese-firms-to-meet-us-accounting-standards-passes-congress-.html?__source=sharebar%7Cemail&par=sharebar

7. Garcia, T. (2020, April 3). *Luckin Coffee shares plummet 75% after financial misconduct investigation launched*. MarketWatch. https://www.marketwatch.com/story/luckin-coffee-shares-plummet-72-after-financial-misconduct-investigation-launched-2020-04-02?mod=article_inline

8. The White House. (2021, June 3). *Executive order on addressing the threat from securities investments that finance certain companies of the People's Republic of China*. https://www.whitehouse.gov/briefing-room/presidential-actions/2021/06/03/executive-order-on-addressing-the-threat-from-securities-investments-that-finance-certain-companies-of-the-peoples-republic-of-china/

9. Sevastopulo, D. (2020, November 13). US investors barred from shares in China military-linked companies. *Financial Times*. https://www.ft.com/content/c3c034cd-15bb-415d-89d7-203b1681523e

10. http://www.aastocks.com/en/stocks/news/aafn-con/NOW.1051686/popular-news

11. Freifeld, K., & Stecklow, S. (2019, February 27). *Exclusive: HSBC probe helped lead to U.S. charges against Huawei CFO*. Reuters. https://www.reuters.com/article/us-huawei-hsbc-exclusive-idUSKCN1QF1IA

12. Yeung, K. (2020, September 22). China's ambiguous Unreliable Entity List gives Beijing 'leeway' to take punitive actions against foreign firms. *South China Morning Post*. https://www.scmp.com/economy/china-economy/article/3102520/chinas-unreliable-entity-ntgp-gives-beijing-leeway-take

13. Makortoff, K. (2020, September 30). How HSBC got caught in a geopolitical storm over Hong Kong security law. *The Guardian*. https://www.theguardian.com/world/2020/sep/30/how-hsbc-got-caught-in-a-geopolitical-storm-over-hong-kong-security-law

14. Chatterjee, S., & White, L. (2020, June 3). *HSBC and StanChart back China security law for Hong Kong*. Reuters. https://www.reuters.com/article/us-hongkong-protests-hsbc-hldg-idUSKBN23A1ZO

15. HSBC. (2020, February 18). *Annual report and accounts 2019.* https://www.hsbc.com/-/files/hsbc/investors/hsbc-results/2019/annual/pdfs/hsbc-holdings-plc/200218-annual-report-and-accounts-2019.pdf

16. Bray, C. (2020, November 18). HSBC is in from the cold as China's finance ministry adds bank in latest €4 billion bond sale after previous exclusion. *South China Morning Post.* https://www.scmp.com/business/banking-finance/article/3110317/chinas-ministry-finance-includes-hsbc-latest-eu4-billion;

17. China Development Bank Corporation. (2010, October 15). *Prospectus.* https://www.ebanking.hsbc.com.hk/1/content/hongkong/pdf/investments/bonds_rmb_101019e.pdf

18. Rapoza, K. (2017, May 17). Why HSBC loves China's Silk Road. *Forbes.* https://www.forbes.com/sites/kenrapoza/2017/05/17/why-hsbc-loves-chinas-silk-road/?sh=6f627aea697e

19. The US, EU and other countries are increasingly linking sanctions to China's public record on human rights.

CHAPTER 29: TECHNO-DIPLOMACY AND THE ROAD AHEAD

1. Foremski, T. (2019, February 1). *The first ambassador to Silicon Valley struggles with 'TechPlomacy'.* ZDNET. https://www.zdnet.com/article/danish-ambassador-to-silicon-valley-struggles-with-techplomacy/

2. Government of Canada. (n.d.). *CPTPP explained.* https://www.international.gc.ca/trade-commerce/trade-agreements-accords-commerciaux/agr-acc/cptpp-ptgp/cptpp_explained-ptpgp_apercu.aspx?lang=eng

3. Stewart, T. (2020, July 25). *A new WTO without China? The July 20, 2020 Les Echos opinion piece by Mogens Peter Carl, a former EC Director General for Trade and then Environment.* Washington International Trade Association. https://www.wita.org/blogs/a-new-wto-without-china/

4. Department of the Prime Minister and Cabinet. (2022). *Implementation of the Australia – United Kingdom – United States partnership (AUKUS)* [Factsheet]. https://pmtranscripts.pmc.gov.au/sites/default/files/AUKUS-factsheet.pdf

5. Baptista, E. (2024, February 5*). China bets on open-source chips as US export controls mount.* Reuters. https://www.reuters.com/technology/china-bets-open-source-chips-us-export-controls-mount-2024-02-05/#:~:text=BEIJING%2C%20Feb%205%20(Reuters),market%20and%20withstand%20U.S.%20sanctions.

6. O-RAN Alliance. (n.d.). *Transforming radio access networks towards open, intelligent, virtualized and fully interoperable RAN.* https://www.o-ran.org/

Acknowledgements

Researching and writing this book was a most extraordinary journey. What I thought would take one year turned into four years, and during that time, I interviewed, engaged in public discourse and maintained ongoing correspondence with hundreds of subject matter experts.

My journey began with early writings on various media platforms and gained momentum through my academic lectures and ongoing executive education workshops. This work allowed me to interact with a wide range of people in private industry and government, at universities and think tanks and in the news media.

Readers may recognise some portions of my research from a series of publications on techno-nationalism that I authored as a research fellow at the Hinrich Foundation in Singapore. For that opportunity, I am grateful to Merle Hinrich and also to Kathryn Dioth, who encouraged me to pursue my topic of techno-nationalism after I initially defined it in a white paper on semiconductors, published in January of 2020. Regarding the Hinrich Foundation's other outstanding people, I am grateful to Berenice Voets, Andrew Staples, Dini Sari Djalal and Chuin Wei Yap for their editorial acumen.

I must also extend my thanks to Robert Olsen at Forbes for his excellent and enthusiastic editorial support of my early writings at the magazine, which eventually became the launchpad for many of the themes in this book.

The National University of Singapore (NUS) served as an accelerant for my research, both at the Lee Kuan Yew School of Public Policy (LKYSPP) and at the NUS Business School.

A special thanks to Associate Professor Razeen Sally for allowing me to co-teach his course on trade policy and global value chains over the span of 6 years. My humble thanks also go to Professor Danny Quah, Dean of the LKYSPP, and to Professor Francesco Mancini for including me in the school's outstanding executive education programmes in public policy and international relations.

At the NUS Business School, I am indebted to many colleagues and mentors, including, among many others, Dr Andrew Delios, Dr Mabel Chou, Dr Kulwant Singh, Dr Chung Piaw Teo, Dr Jussi Keppo, Dr Joel Goh, Dr Andrew Rose and Keith Carter.

Special thanks also go to Jai Arya, Bridget Tee and Aaron Goh at the NUS Business School's Executive Education department, as well as to Ye-Her Wu at the School of Continuing and Lifelong Education (SCALE) for allowing me to discuss and explore the book's many themes over the years with executives from scores of the world's top companies.

I have been fortunate to have participated in collaborative research projects that directly influenced the content of this book. I am grateful to Wolfgang Lehmacher during his time at the World Economic Forum (WEF) and our work on global supply chains. At the Australian Strategic Policy Institute (ASPI), I am grateful to Professor Robert Clark, Fergus Hanson, Justin Bassi, Bronte Munro and Dr Alexandra Caples. I also wish to acknowledge and thank James Carouso, former U.S. Ambassador to Australia, now at the Center for Strategic and International Studies (CSIS) in Washington, D.C. and April Palmerlee, CEO of AmCham Australia.

On the topic of semiconductors, I am grateful to Jimmy Goodrich at the Semiconductor Industry Association (SIA) for making time for my queries. Thank you also to Ang Wee Seng at the Singapore Semiconductor Industry Association (SSIA), where, in partnership with Singapore's Human Capital Leadership Institute (HCLI), I conducted a series of lectures over the course of three years on technonationalism and, in the process, learned a great deal about the chip sector from SSIA's participants.

I owe a debt of gratitude to many others with working knowledge of the semiconductor industry, all of whom generously agreed to interviews, supported my research or simply provided encouragement. Special thanks go to Karmi Leiman, Karen Murphy, Paul Triolo, Chris Miller, Eric Vennekens, Mung Chiang and Mark Lundstrum.

A wide range of other subject matter experts, intellectuals and consultants also provided insights, support and inspiration. Thanks especially to Matt Bell, Kevin Wolf, Noah Barkin, James Crabtree, Aki Ranin, Deborah Elms, Jeffrey Bean, Bilahari Kausikan, Stephen Olsen, Frank Debets, George Zaharatos, Frank Lavin, Taimur Baig, James Andrade, Neal Horowitz, Hans Vriens, Ernie Bower, Ulf Änggårdh and Risto Penttilä.

I wish to also highlight those who embraced me as a public speaker and, in the process, introduced me to global thought leaders, policymakers, journalists and industry champions. Special thanks, then, to Anne Godlasky of the National Press Foundation and Radu Palamariu at Alcott Global.

I am particularly grateful to Colley Hwang, Ethan Su and Judy Lin at DigiTimes for opening the door to Taiwan's technology landscape and for providing access to their incredible research and data—not to mention introducing me to executive leadership at some of the most accomplished tech companies on the planet.

For many others who wished not to be publicly identified, I extend a warm thank you for imparting their unique wisdom and support.

Finally, I owe a massive debt of gratitude to Robert Shackleton, retired Senior Analyst at the U.S. Congressional Budget Office, who graciously and painstakingly edited the book and assisted with key research. Thanks also to Sanjana Kumar and Gitanjali Bindu for assisting with editing and citations.

I will end by humbly thanking my publisher, Wiley.

I am especially grateful to Gladys (Syd) Ganaden and Stacey Rivera, who never lost faith in me and showed incredible patience while I completed this work.

Index

5 Eyes intelligence network, inclusion, 100
5G wireless equipment, Huawei supply, 149
23andMe, GlaxoSmithKline (GSK) deal, 192

A

Academia
espionage, 377–379
funding sources, screening, 380–382
landscape, changes, 373–374
military, relationship, 382–384
oversight, forms, 379
ring-fencing, 374–375
rule frameworks/research security,
379–380
Academic cross-border friend-
shoring, 391–393
Acemoglu, Daron, 28
Active flow control (AFC), usage, 180
Acxiom, consumer data accumulation, 195
Advanced Micro Devices (AMD),
376, 407, 425
advanced chips, Russia illicit
collection, 98–99
China ban, 65
Advanced Research Projects Agency,
establishment, 48
Agent-based modeling (ABM)
techniques, 243
Agriculture Intelligence Measures (AIM)
Act, 365–366
Agritech
impact, 29
industrial espionage, impact, 364–366
Airborne warning and control system
(AWACS) plane, Air Force usage, 170
AI Superpowers (Lee), 212
Alibaba, 195, 417, 422
Alibaba Cloud, data storage engineering, 203

Allende, Salvador (CIA destabilisation), 153
Alliance for American Manufacturing
(AAM), 399
Alliance of Small Island States, 326
Alphabet, R&D, 398
Al Qaeda, impact, 167
Ambani, Anil, 156
Analogue chips, usage, 120
Angelakis, Dimitris, 233
Angell, Norman, 62
Anonymous (hacktivist group), 270
Anti-Access/Area Denial (A2/AD)
strategy, 242–243
Anti-Espionage Law (China), impact, 71
Anti-Espionage laws (2023), passage, 23
Anti-satellite (ASAT) weapons, 292
Apple
capitalisation, 37–38
chips, stacking, 108f
Applied Materials (AMAT)
CVD specialisation, 115
subpoenas, 100
Tokyo Electron competition, 116
Arizona State University (ASU), chip
manufacturing, 389–391
Arkwright, Richard, 31
spinning frame, 35f
Artemis programme, 277, 287, 290, 295
Artificial general intelligence (AGI),
206–207, 211, 221
Artificial Intelligence (AI), 205–208
advancement, 181
arms race, 205
capacity, country ranking, 212f
chip wars, relationship, 216–218
cyberwarfare, relationship, 210–214
duality, 207
dual-use nature, 209

Artificial Intelligence (*Continued*)
impact, 178–179
involvement, 121
memory chip fab (SK hynix), 140
misinformation, 215–216
race, China competition, 115
role, 242–243
war weapons, relationship, 208–210
weaponization, 211
Artificial intelligence platform (AIP)
sales, 209–210
Art of War, The (Sun Tzu), 28, 61, 166–167
Asia, arms, 26
ASML
breakthroughs, 128
domestic export control, impact, 92
DUV/EUV photolithography machine, 113f
high-numerical aperture (NA) EUV
machines, impact, 114–115
Assembly, Testing, and Packaging (ATP), 107
Asteroid Mining Corporation, 281
Atkinson, Rob, 401
Atomic bomb (Manhattan Project), 44f
Atomic bombs, impact, 44–45
AT&T, CIA/NSA/FBI exploitation (accusa-
tions), 152–154
AUKUS defense/security pacts, 21, 55
AUKUS trilateral security agreement, 448–450
Australia, New Zealand and U.S. (ANZUS)
Security Agreement, 449
*Australia's Semiconductor Moonshot:
Securing semiconductor talent*, 391
'Australia's Semiconductor National
Moonshot' (Clark), 449
Automotive industry, electrification, 331–332
Autonomous guidance, navigation, and
control (AGNC), 285
Autonomous systems, ethical
dilemma, 311–312
Autonomous weapons, 301, 307–311
Aviation Industry Corporation of China
(AVIC), GE partnership, 61
Azure Top Secret data hosting technology
(Microsoft), 202

B

B-2 Stealth bomber information, Chinese
hacker theft, 173
B-21 aircraft, creation, 177–178
Backdoor spyware, insertion, 150–151
Baldwin, Richard, 49
Ballistic missile defence (BMD), 293
Baltic Sea, undersea cables (cutting/
disabling), 251
Bard, usage, 213, 375

Barriers-to-entry, creation, 110
Belt and Road Initiative (BRI), 150, 157, 158,
254, 316–317, 381, 429, 438
green infrastructure projects, China
expenditure, 319–320
Bernstein, Willian J., 40
Bezos, Jeff, 288
BGI Group, 184–187
Bharatiya Janata Party (India), Cambridge
Analytica (impact), 198
Biden, Joe, 53, 134–135, 343–344, 413
Bidenomics policies, 58, 83
Bifurcated global value chains, 266–267
Bilateral agreements, 445
Bilateral techno-diplomacy, 451–452
Bilateral trade, increase, 23–24
Binge-buying, 95–97
Bin Laden, Osama
discovery, technology (usage), 168–170
murder, 165, 170–171
Biomimetic shapes, usage, 209
Biosecurity-genome technology feedback
loop, 187–188
Biotechnology, 181
Bi-Partisan Infrastructure bill, 16
Bipartisan Infrastructure Investment and Jobs
Act (Biden), 54
Birck Nanotechnology Center, funding, 388
Birkeland-Eyde process, 42
Blacklisted entities, 90–91
Black markets, 97–99
Bletchley Park, 45
Blue Dot Initiative (BDI), 316
Blue Dot Network (BDN), 322–326
Blue Origin, 276, 287–288
Blue-sky experimentation, government
activism (importance), 399–400
Boost-glide missiles, launch, 244
Boot, Max, 28
Borderless World, The (Ohmae), 8
Bosch/BASF, government funding, 42
Boston Consulting Group (BCG),
research, 140
Brain drain/brain gain, 403
Brazil, Russia, India, China, and South Africa
(BRICS), 20, 267, 429, 443
Brexit, 18, 197–198
BRI Group, DNA data harvesting, 192
British export controls, 33–34
Brynjolfsson, Erik, 45
Build-back campaign, 54
Bureau of Industry and Security (BIS)
Chinese companies, ban, 216
criticism, 95–97
ECCN usage, 88–89

Entity list, 90, 92, 148, 250
    export control, 88, 183
    semiconductor technology export
        controls, 79
Byzantine Hades (operation), 172–174

C

C2E Cloud contact, 202
Cambridge Analytica, impact, 184, 196–198
Carbon fibre-reinforced polymers (CRFPs)/
        ceramic matrix composites (CMCs)
        combination, 239
Carl, Mogens Peter, 444
Carrier killer missiles, 26, 61, 237–242, 240f
Cartwright, Edmund, 33
Central Bank Digital Currencies (CBDCs),
        impact, 427–431, 438
'Century of Humiliation,' 6, 41
Chan, Eason, 201
Changdu, Wang, 213
Chang, Morris, 141
ChatGPT, 206, 209, 212–213
    social media traffic, 216
    usage, 191, 453
Chemical vapour deposition (CVD) tools,
        AMAT specialisation, 115
Chemistry42, data analysis, 207–208
Chengdu J-20 (mighty dragon), stealth
        capabilities, 178
Chief executive officers (CEOs),
        techno-nationalists (contrast), 56–59
China
    academic espionage, 377–379
    companies, accounting stand-
        ards, 433–434
    decoupling, acceleration, 416–417
    global satellite system, construction, 404
    self-sufficiency, achievement, 5
    techno-nationalism, milestones, 404–405
    Thousand Talent Programme, 377–379
China (Beijing)
    4IR feedback loop, 49
    anti-espionage laws, 70–73
    catastrophes, 6
    Civil-Military Fusion initiatives, 25, 99, 295
    consulting firms, interaction, 4
    Cybersecurity Law, 182
    de-Americanisation long-game, 84, 136
    decoupling, 17, 59, 82–83
    de-risking, 82–83
    Digital Belt and Road Initiative, 157–158
    domestic semiconductor capabilities
        advance, thwarting (BIS attempts),
        87
    drones, effectiveness/reliability, 180

Dual Circulation policy, articulation,
        83, 84, 94
dynamic random access memory (DRAM)
        production, 130
economic-techno-nationalism, 154–156
electric vehicle (EV), shift/market, 66, 148
electron-beam lithography (EBL) (e-beam)
        exploration, 128–129
false-positive chip test, 127–129
Five Year Plan (1981–1985), 130
forced technology-transfer practices, US
        cost (USTR estimate), 3
foreign corporate personnel, detention, 72
foreign MNEs, punishment (risk), 64–65
foreign office government raids, 72
foundries, focus, 122
global consultancy expenditures, 4
helicopter stealth technology, 171–172
'hide and bide' period, 60
H&M boycotts/store closures, 65
hypersonic technology, 238–240
industrial espionage, 334
infrastructure-for-resources deals, 320–321
island-building diplomacy, 326–328
lessons, 5–9
MNE middle ground, location, 66
National Bureau of Statistics
        report, 123, 130
National Security Law (2020), 90
National Security Laws, 182
nonmarket economy, incongruities, 5
One China policy, 201
opening, 130
paradoxes/contradictions, 21–22
QKD, 230–231
questions, 27–29
re-education camps, 158
self-reliance, 6–7
semiconductors, shortage/prob-
        lems, 69, 121
South China Sea reclamation activities, 61
space race, 8
state-backed hackers, infiltrations,
        172–173
state-centric economic system, 3
state-owned enterprises (SOEs), 317, 320,
        322–323, 336, 367
technology, 25, 67–70, 94–95
techno-nationalist counteroffensive, 93
tradecraft, 171–172, 176–178
trade practices, USTR investigation, 52
TV manufacturing plants, closure, 69
whole nation approach, 136
China Aerospace Science and Industry Corp
        (CASIC), 266

China ATL (CATL), 341–343, 345
China-free supply chain initiatives, mobilisation, 23
Chinese Communist Party (CCP)
  brain trust, 60
  content, promotion, 381
  Five-Year Plan (2021–2025), 83
  information flow, 214
  loyalty pledges, 378
  modernisation goals, 3, 402
  opponents, labelling, 167
  proxy, 250–251
Chip 4 Alliance, 55, 138, 445–447
Chips
  challenges/scepticism/assumptions, 140–144
  chip-centric geopolitics, 104–105
  chip-manufacturing choke points, 111–117
  companies, R&D expenditures, 125
  fabrication, 112, 134–136
  manufacturing, 112f, 128, 133
  schools, 385
  self-sufficiency, Huawei quest, 160–164
  supply chain expansion, potential, 143
  trailing-edge revolution, 138–140
  wars, 104, 216–218
CHIPS American Act, success, 387
CHIPS and Science Act (2022), 54, 59, 124, 134–138, 382, 385, 411
  budgeting, 15–16
  goals, 141, 296–297
  programmes, 142
  promise, 144, 388
Chip War (Miller), 29
Chokepoints, 121, 128
CH Rainbow drones, 179
Church Committee (Senate Select Committee to Study Governmental Operations with Respect to Intelligence Activities), 152–154
Cisco, state grants/subsidies/tax breaks, 155
Civil-Military Fusion initiatives (China), 25, 99, 295
Clausewitz, Carl von, 28
Cleantech, Chinese dominance, 316, 318
Cleantech, impact, 29
Clean technology, 15–16
Climate change, 29, 315
Cloud access, 97–99
Cloud services, 158, 227
Coating, processes, 125
Cold War, 7, 12, 21, 48, 151, 154, 253, 270
  cessation, 101
  doctrine of Containment, 53

export control regime, evolution, 86–87
  spread/unpleasantness, 292, 374
Colossus, WWII role, 45, 224
Commerce Control List (CCL), 88
Commercial Crew Program (CCP), NASA establishment, 276
Commercial Orbiter Transportation Services (COTS) programme, 282–283
Committee on Foreign Investment in the United States (CFIUS), 183, 352, 362
Company activities, misclassification/mischaracterisation, 132
Completely built-up (CBU) product, placement, 67
Comprehensive and Progressive Trans-Pacific Partnership (CPTPP), FTA gold standard, 443–445, 447
Computers, impact, 44–45
Conference of the Parties (COP26), 318–319
Contemporary Ameprex Technology Co. Ltd. (CATL) (Chinese battery maker, impact), 68
Controlled unclassified information (CUI), security implications, 372
Coordinating Committee for Multilateral Export Controls (COCOM), 100–101
Copilot (Microsoft), 206
Coral Sea Cable project, 253–254
Corneliszoon van Titgeest, Cornelis, 39
Cornerstone, photoresist development, 162
COVID-19, 17–19
  lessons, 69
  restrictions, 24, 71
  SARs-CoV-2 virus, impact, 109
  social media claim, 200
  supply chain disruptions, 75
Creative destruction, 20
Crony capitalism, 156
Cross-border data flows, disruption, 19
Cross-border microchip innovation, 350–351
Cyber Command (US), attack, 199–200
Cyber espionage/sabotage, risks, 151
Cyber-insecurity, 61–62
Cyber-intrusion campaign (PLA), 176
Cybersecurity, 61–62
  standards, development, 446
Cybersecurity Law (China), 182
Cyberspace Administration of China (CAC), Micron Semiconductor computer memory/storage chips ban, 64–65
Cyberthreat, 211
Cyberwarfare, 26, 226, 293
  AI, relationship, 210–214
Cyber weapons, usage, 195

D

Data
   access, government demands, 203–204
   analytics, usage, 197–198
   brokers, 194
   capitalism, 190, 192–193, 195
   Chemistry42 analysis, 207
   commoditisation, 195
   defining, 185
   DNA data harvesting, 192
   filtration, free-market mechanisms
         (usage), 184
   geopolitics, 183–184, 196
   importance, 185
   intermediaries, 194–195
   theft, 195
   value, 181
Datasphere, 184
De-Americanisation (China long-game), 84
Decoupling, 22–24, 55, 75, 77, 93, 247
   acceleration, 416–417
Deepfakes, 215–216
Deep-learning AI frameworks, offering, 213
Deep ultraviolet (DUC) processes, usage, 114
Defence articles exports, USML control, 89
Defence Innovation Unit (DUI), DoD
         creation, 291
Defense Advanced Research Projects
         Agency (DARPA), 48, 99, 208–209,
         227, 233, 372, 382
   hypersonic technology, response, 244–245
   impact, 294–295, 411
   initiatives, 451
   Molecular Machines and Biomolecular
         (MOMAD) programme, 383
   Starlink, connection, 265
Dell, supply chain diversification/de-risking
         measures, 75–76
Deng Xiaoping, 60, 130
De-risking, 12, 17, 55, 75, 77, 79–81
de Saint-Exupery, Antoine, 11
Diamond, Jared, 28
Die-cutting, 118
Digital Belt and Road Initiative
         (China), 157–158
Digital commons, data capitalism, 190
Digital currency, 430–431
Digital democracies, global GDP
         (relationship), 452f
Digital dystopia, 431–432
Digital global commons, open-sourced
         war, 269–270
DigitalGlobe Open Data Programme, 270
Digital infrastructure, 157–158, 324–326

Digital scene matching (DSM), usage, 239
Discrete semiconductors, impact, 106
DJI Technology Company (DJI), 25, 271
Domestic semiconductor capabilities
         advance, thwarting (BIS attempts), 87
Dong Feng missiles (DF-27), 61,
         240–242, 240f, 403
Doshi, Rosh, 5
Drones, 179–180, 269, 301–303, 308f
Dual Circulation policy, articulation, 83
Dual-use category, 59
Dual-use concept, 88
Dual-use dilemma, 14
Dual-use goods, trade shutdown, 78
Dual-Use List and Military Lists,
         publication, 101
Dual-use technologies, usage, 78
Dutch financial system, innovation
         (success), 40
Dutch technology feedback loop (Golden
         Age), 37–40
Dynamic random access memory (DRAM),
         China domestic production, 130

E

Ease of doing business (EoDB),
         ranking, 420–421
E-commerce services, 158
Economic co-dependencies, 22
Economic-techno-nationalism
         (China), 154–156
Edge computing, usage, 352
Electric car/lithium batteries, 339f
Electric motors, simplicity, 334
Electric vehicles (EVs)
   battery techno-nationalism, 341–342
   Chinese companies, geopolitical
         competition (shift), 66
   Chinese suppliers, forced
         reliance, 342–343
   Chinese techno-nationalism, 335–336
   components/minerals, 340
   connections/national security
         risks, 354–355
   dual-use EV technologies,
         challenges, 349–350
   ecosystem/composition, 333–334
   geopolitics, 329
   grey zone, complications, 70
   regulations/funding, 332–333
   semiconductors, wars/subsidies,
         347, 355–356
   software/hardware open
         platform, 352–353

Electric vehicles (*Continued*)
  technonationalism, 330
    US/Europe subsidies/initiatives/
      techno-nationalism, 343
    US techno-diplomacy, 343–344
Electric vehicles (EVs)fragmentation/
    clusters, 344–345
Electron-beam lithography (EBL) (e-beam),
    China exploration/Group of Five
    advantage, 128–129
Electronic design automation (EDA),
    chokepoint, 121
Electronics Resurgence Initiative, 382
Electronics systems design and manufacturing
    (ESDM) capabilities, 416
Emerging markets, climate competition,
    318–320
Emerging markets, state-backed cheap
    credit, 156–157
End-to-end 5G incumbent contract provider
    (Huawei), 149
Energy infrastructure, geopolitics,
    317–318
Engelardt, Dorothy, 310f
ENIAC, 44f, 45, 224
Error-free quantum computing,
    applications, 226f
European Union (EU)
  de-risking/decoupling actions, 81
  Green Deal, 355–356
Export Administration Regulations (EAR),
    Commerce Control List (CCL), 88
Export Control Classification Number
    (ECCN), 88–89
Export controls, 85–89, 266–267
Export-Import Bank, surveillance technology
    purchase, 156–157
Extraterritoriality, 91–94
Extreme ultraviolet (EUV) processes,
    impact, 114

F

F-22 Raptor, 173, 175
F-35 Lightning, 174f, 175
F-117 Nighthawk stealth bomber,
    creation, 177
Fabless chip designers, company
    representation, 111
Fabless companies, R&D focus/microchip
    designs, 107, 118
Fairchild Semiconductor
    Corporation, sale, 12
False-positive chip test (China),
    127–129
Fear of missing out (FOMO), 29

Ferguson, Niall, 18
Fifth-generation fighter jets, 173–176
Finance
  fragmentation, 427
  ideology, 430–431
Financial services, QC (usage), 227
Fintech decoupling, techno-nationalism
    (relationship), 438–439
First Industrial Revolution, technology
    sharing, 86
First Technical Reconnaissance Bureau (TRB)
    (PLA), 173
First World War, government support, 48
Five Eyes intelligence cooperative, 193–194
Floating solar farm, 319f
Food. *See* Agritech
  laboratory-grown protein, 364
  protectionism, increase, 358–359
  supply chains, friend-shoring, 359–360
Food security
  technology, areas, 361
  technology, impact, 360–362
  techno-nationalism, relationship, 357
Foreign corporate personnel, China
    detention, 72
Foreign currency convertible bonds (FCCBs),
    repayment reliance, 156
Foreign direct investment (FDI)
Foreign Direct Product Rule (FDPR),
    91–92, 148, 160
Foreign-held technologies, reverse
    engineering, 131
Foreign Intelligence Service (SVR), InfoRus/
    OneWorldPress (link), 200
Foreign MNEs, punishment/uncertainty/
    danger, 64–65, 70
Foreign offices, China government raids,
    72
Foreign venture capital (geopolitical
    context), 351–352
Forward-operating base (FOB), 170
Foundational technologies, 13f
Foundries, impact, 107–108
Fourth Industrial Revolution (4IR), 8, 14,
    45, 276, 397
  China 4IR, 49
  game-changing technologies, 178
  technologies, 18, 86
Foxconn, 76
Free-trade agreement (FTA), 417,
    443, 445–448
Free trade, death, 142–143
Friend-shoring, 12, 55, 119, 135, 359–360
Fuchs, Klaus, 47
Full electric vehicles (FEVs), 333–334

G

Gallagher, Mark, 63
Gallium arsenide (GaAs), usage, 106
Gallium nitrogen chips, usage, 353–354
Gates, function, 109–110
GCHQ, electrical/radio communications eavesdropping, 202
Gelsinger, Pat, 129
General Data Protection Regulations, 192
Generation Z, nationalism, 6
Generative AI, 207–208, 213, 216
Genetic data, 186–187
Genomic-wide association studies (GWAS), DNA sequence search, 186
Geopolitical landscape, data analytics (usage), 197–198
Geopolitics, 181, 183–184, 196, 248–251, 315
Geosynchronous orbits (GSO), 260–261
Germany, industrial policy, 408–410
Gilsinger, Pat, 349
GlobalFoundries, trailing-edge IC manufacture, 140
Global In-house Centres (GICs), increase, 419
Globalisation, 57–58, 142–143
Globalization and Its Discontents (Stiglitz), 58
Global navigation satellite systems (GNSS), usage, 239
Global Partnership on Artificial Intelligence (GPAI), 418
Global Science Research, 197
Golden Age (Dutch technology feedback loop), 37–40
Government-to-business (G2B) relations, 441–442
Government-to-government (G2G) relations, 441–442
Grace periods, 95–97
Great Bifurcation, 19–21
Great Convergence, The (Baldwin), 49
Great Divergence, The, 49
Great Illusion, The (Angell), 62
Great Reorganisation, 17–19
Green Deal, impact, 17
Grey zone, 24–27, 63–66, 204, 265–266
  states/firms involvement/contract, 255–256, 270–271
Group of 7 (G7), 14–15, 323–324, 387
  Brazil, Russia, India, China, and South Africa (BRICS), rift, 20
  economies, production activities (shutdown), 57
  multinational firms, China anchor, 21
Group of Five (Group of 5), 101, 123, 126, 129
  allies, 141

chip supply chain expansion, potential, 143
Groves, Leslie, 47
Gunpowder, invention, 85
Guns, Germs, and Steel (Diamond), 28
GuoWang LEO constellation, 266

H

Haitao Xiang, arrest, 365
Haley, Usha, 155
Hall, Theodore, 47
Hamilton, Alexander, 31–32, 35f, 36f, 37, 39
Hangzhou Jinqu Science and Technology Co., backdoor spyware insertion, 150
Harari, Yuval Noah, 28
HAVE Blue programme, 177
'Hide and bide' period, 60
High approval rates, 95–97
High mobility artillery rocket system (HIMARS), usage, 268
High purity chemicals (HPC), requirement, 116
High-throughput e-beam production, 129
HiSilicon, semiconductor/chip design, 93, 160
Holding Foreign Companies Accountable Act (HFCAA), 433
Home Deus (Harari), 28
Hong Kong and Shanghai Banking Corporation (HSBC), 435
  Chinese punishment, 436–438
House Select Committee on the Chinese Communist Party (CCP), 122, 124
Huanta ETCH, dry etching equipment manufacture, 116
Huawei Marine Networks (HMN), 147, 250–252, 255
Huawei Rule, 92
Huawei Technologies Company Ltd
  advantage of scale, 163
  ban, 149
  blacklist, 160
  chip self-sufficiency, quest, 160–164
  data storage engineering, 203
  Entity List (BIS placement), 92
  export control defiance, 126
  export licence applications, US government approval, 95–96
  future, 163–164
  hard drives, Seagate sales (US fine), 100
  in-person dealings, 148–149
  Kirin 9000 7-nanometre chip, 161f
  Mate 60 Smartphone, 161f, 162, 405
  neoliberal model, problems, 159–160
  partnerships, 93

Huawei Technologies Company Ltd
(*Continued*)
reference points, 150
sanctions, 436
state assistance, 155
third-party IP licence payment, 159
TSMC chip supply, cessation, 92
U.S.-China hybrid cold war, 148
US export controls effectiveness (test), 90
war, 147
Hu Jintao, 49
Human capital development, 135
Human genome, data capitalism
(relationship), 192–193
Hybrid cold war, 12
Hybrid electric vehicles (HEVs), 334, 347
Hyper-globalisation, 17–18
Hypersonic Air-breathing Weapons Concept
(HAWC), 244
Hypersonic speed, 237
Hypersonic technology (China), 238–240

I

IBM Blue Gene Supercomputer, 214f
iFlyTec, BIS Entity List entry/restriction, 97
I.G. Farben, government funding, 42–43
Illicit transfers, prevention, 101
Imperial Chemical Industries (ICI),
creation, 43
In-China-for-China, 27, 96, 122–123
grey zone, 63
model, 67
India
Bharatiya Janata Party (BHP), 198, 417, 421
digital landscape, 417–418
economy/technology, 415–416
growth, 413
Housing Development Finance
Corporation (HDFC), China
shareolding increase, 423
pain-of-doing-business, 420–422
technology hubs, 419f
India Semiconductor Mission (ISM), 425
India-U.S. Defense Acceleration Ecosystem
(INDUS-X), 414
Indo-Pacific arms race, 26
Indo-Pacific economic framework,
447–448
Indo-Pacific Economic Framework (IPEF), 55,
447–448, 450–451
Industrial espionage, importance, 163
Industrial policy, 20, 405–406
Industrial Revolution, 31–34
Inertial guidance systems (IGS), usage, 239
Inertial navigation systems (INS), usage, 239

Infineon Technologies AG, advanced
chips, 99, 348
Inflation Reduction Act (IRA), 16–17, 54
Information
flow, 214
wars, 196, 199–200
Information and communication technology
(ICT), 159, 226
InfoRus, GRU/SVR (link), 200
initiative on Critical and Emerging Technol-
ogy (iCET), 413–414
Innovation, 30, 86, 110, 397
competition, 55, 93
mercantilism, 20
Integrated circuits (ICs), semiconductors,
106
Integrated device manufacturers
(IDMs), 107, 139
Intel, 110–111
advanced chips, Russia importation,
98–99
ASML NA EUV sales, 115
China ban, 65
foundries/R&D facilities investment
announcement, 143
Gaudi 2 chip, usage, 217
Intellectual property (IP), 372, 446
Intelligence agencies, private company
reliance, 202–203
Intercompany data transfers, impeding, 71
International banks, problems, 435
International Development Finance
Corporation (IDFC), 323
International Space Station (ISS),
275–277, 289
International talent wars, 32–33
International Traffic in Arms Regulations
(ITAR), 89, 260, 414
Internet, balkanisation, 19
Internet-of-Things (IoT), 182
Internet Research Agency (IRA)
(Russia), 199–200
'Invisible hand,' impact, 56
Iranian Shahed/Arash-2 drones, 306f
Italy (Resurgent Party), Cambridge Analytica
(impact), 198
ITT, CIA/NSA/FBI exploitation
(accusations), 152–154
Ivy Bells, 257

J

James Webb Space Telescope (JWST), 299
Japan
industrial policy, 406–407
lost decades, 7

Jiangsu Changjiang Electronics Technology Co. (JCET), package technology development, 118
JSR, photoresist market share, 116
JW Consulting, semiconductor report, 131

K

Källenius, Ola, 79
Kennan, George, 53
Kennedy, Pal, 28
Kenya, Cambridge Analytica (impact), 198
King Abdullah University of Science and Technology (KAUST), AceGPT research/training, 98, 375
Kirin 9000 chips, 120, 160, 161f
KLA, defect inspection/metrology equipment, 115
Klynge, Casper, 441
Know your customer (KYC) processes, 438
Krupp, government funding, 42–43

L

Laissez-faire capitalism, 155
Lam, Carrie (US sanctions), 90–91
Lam Research, 115, 116
Large language models (LLMs), 191, 213, 375
    open source, 206
    weaponisation, 215
Leading-edge chips, 106, 119–121, 125–126, 136
Leading-edge technology, 14, 67, 174
Lee, Kai-Fu, 212, 214
Legacy DUV, Chinese imports, 122
Legacy pure play fab, 139
Legacy technologies, sharing/selling, 67
Lehman Brothers, collapse, 6
Lethal autonomous weapons (LAWS), usage, 307–311
Lieber, Charles (arrest), 371–372, 378–379
Lightspeed (Telesat), 265–266
Lithium-ion batteries, 371
    Chinese dominance, 339
    production, geographic ring-fencing, 340–341
Liwei, Lang, 8
Local manufacturers, world-class clusters (building), 423–424
Logic chips, usage, 106, 120
Low earth orbit (LEO) satellites, 259–263, 261f, 272, 277, 288, 294
Lowell, Francis Cabot, 33, 34

M

Machines, impact, 302–303
Macron, Emmanuel, 215, 409
Made in China 2025 (MIC 2025), 82–83, 83f
Magnetic compass, invention, 85–86
Malicious worm, categorization, 211
Managed trade, 20
Manhattan Project, 44f, 46-48, 235
Market efficiencies, 119
Matsu Islands, cables (cutting), 256–257
Mature-node fabs, online operation, 124
Mavic 3 drone, usage, 304
McAfee, Andrew, 45
McCaul, Michael, 95
McRaven, William ('holy shit' moment), 237
Meiji Restoration, 41
Memory chips, usage, 106
Meng Wangzhou, 437f
Meng Wanzhou (SDN list presence), 90
Merkel, Angela, 409
Meta, Amazon, Microsoft, Apple and Alphabet (MAMAA) companies, power, 272
Metadata, description/trends, 185, 190
MI6, external UK intelligence, 202
Microchips, fabrication/ advancement, 105, 109
Microchip Technologies, DOC award, 1390
Microelectronics Commons Hubs, 388
Micron Semiconductor Manufacturing Company, 64–65, 426
Microsoft, China ban, 65
Middle country strategic partners, 100
Middle-country universities, issues, 375–376
Midjourney Inc., 215
Military aircraft design/production, Chinese prototypes, 175
Military-Civil Fusion (MCF) system, 254–255
Millennial generation, nationalism, 6
Miller, Chris, 29, 104
Mini-lateral agreement/dialogue, 55
Mini-lateral arrangements, 443–445
Missile navigation/tracking systems, information, Chinese hacker theft, 173
Mitsubishi Gas Chemicals, supplier inflow, 137
Mitsubishi Motors Corp., China manufacturing operations closure, 67, 69
Mi, Yang, 200–201
Mo Hailong, arrest, 364
Moonshot Factory, 398

Moore, Gordon, 109
Moore's Law, 47, 104–105, 108–111
Multilateral export control regime, 99–100
Multilateral Export Controls Regime (MECR), proposal, 234
Multilateral infrastructure alliances, 322–324
Multinational enterprises (MNEs), 421
  de-risking strategies, 79
  difficulties, 63–64
  foreign MNEs, punishment (risk), 64–65
  geopolitical agnosticism, 23
  global operational efficiencies/economies-of-scale, decrease, 64
  governments, struggle/conflict, 22, 26
  in-China-for-China strategy, 96
  information collection, knowledge (difficulty), 71
  intra-company sales/technology transfers, tax management problems, 71
  legal standards/treatment, contrasts, 72
  middle ground, location, 66
  public statements, control, 65
  revenue, receiving, 159
Musk, Elon, 259–260, 271, 282–283, 287

N

Nana, Ouyang, 201
NAND flash fab (Dailan), 124
Narrative wars, 215–216
National Aeronautics and Space Administration (NASA), 151, 183, 202, 244–245, 275–276
National chip hubs, increase, 388–389
National Defense Education Act (1958), 48
National Integrated Circuit Industry Investment Fund (CICF), funding source, 131
National Laboratory for Quantum Information Sciences, establishment, 227
National Reconnaissance Office (NRO), impact, 168–169
National security, 186–187
National Security Act (NSA), 394
National Security Agency (NSA) (1952), 48, 168–169, 193
National Security Commission of Artificial Intelligence (NSCAI), competition/innovation, 189
National Security Laws (China), 182
National Security Presidents Memorandum 33 (NSPM 33), 380
National Semiconductor Technology Center (NSTC), creation, 142
Near-shoring, 12

Neoliberal argument, 143
Neoliberal logic, 160
Neoliberal model, 57–58, 159–160
Neoliberals, techno-nationalists (contrast), 288–290
Next-generation 2-nanometre chips, TSMC construction, 136–137
Nigeria, Cambridge Analytica (impact), 198
Nilekani, Nandan, 417–418
Nixon, Richard, 153
Non-binding bilateral agreement/dialogue, 55
Non-invasive prenatal tests (NIPTs), genetic information access, 186
North Atlantic Treaty Organisation (NATO), 406, 449, 451
Northrop Grumman, Scramjet Hypersonic Engine, 244f
Nvidia, chips, 97, 98, 217
NXP Semiconductors NV (NXP), advanced chips (Russia illicit collection), 98–99
Nye, Joseph, 21–22

O

Obama, Barack, 169–170
Office of Foreign Assets Control (OFAC), 89, 438
Offshoring fabrication, 58
Ohmae, Kenichi, 8
OneWeb, LEO operation, 288–289
OneWorldPress, 200
On War (Clausewitz), 28
Open Radio Access Network (O-RAN), 454
Open-sourced war, 269–270
Operation Byzantine Hades, 172–174
Operation Ivy Bells, 257
Operation Neptune Spear, 165–166
Opium Wars, impact, 6
Oppenheimer, Robert, 46
Optoelectronics, 106
Orange Revolution (Ukraine), Cambridge Analytica (impact), 198
Orca XLUUV Test nAsset System, christening, 310f
Original data suppliers (ODS), 190–195, 203
Original design manufacturer (ODM), microchip delivery, 108
Original equipment manufacturer (OEM), 108, 118–119, 139, 191, 295, 416
Outbound Investment Transparency Act, 25
Outsourced, Assembly and Testing (OSAT), 107
Oxidation, processes, 125

P

Pacific Light Cable Network (PLCN), licence denial, 253
Packaging, 117–118
Palantir Technologies, artificial intelligence platform (AIP) sales, 209–210
Pan Jiawen, 233
Paradigm shift, 51–56
Paris Agreement, 315
Partnership for Global Infrastructure and Investment (PGII), 316, 323, 325
Patent Act, role, 32–33
Patent filings, benchmark, 230
Pax Britannica, enforcement, 41
Paxlovid, Pfizer development, 189
PEACE cable, 255
Pelosi, Nancy (Taiwan visit), 201
People's Liberation Army (PLA)
    A2/AD strategies, 242–243
    Academy of Military Sciences, RISC-V standard usage, 453
    BGI, interaction, 187
    Chinese companies, U.S. investor ban, 434
    Civil-Military Fusion initiatives, 25
    cyber-intrusion campaign, 176
    DF 26B missile, design, 240–242
    Dong Feng missiles (DF-27), 61, 240–242, 240f
    hacking activity, 173
    HIT, relationship, 375
    hypersonic carrier killer missiles development, 26, 237–239
    invasion, possibility, 63, 269
    Military-Civil Fusion (MCF) system, 254–255
    military confrontation, 78
    stolen data usage/R&D efforts, 179
    Third Department hackers, 173
Perón, Isabel, 154
Pharmaceuticals/chemistry/healthcare, QC (usage), 227–228
Pharmacogenomics, 188–189
Phoenix Ghost drones, usage, 307
Photolithography process, 113–114
Pinochet, Augusto, 153
Planarisation, 118
Plant DNA, editing, 360f
Platform diplomacy, 201–202
Pomeranz, Kenneth, 49
Power
    multipliers, 29, 41–42, 178, 269
    multiplying effects, impact, 14
    soft power, 196
Practical quantum, achievement, 220
Precision agriculture/farming, 362

Printed circuit board assembly (PCBA), 424–426
Production-linked incentive (PLI) schemes, 425
Project 908 (China), 130
Project Blackjack, 265
Project Fury, 302, 310
Project Kuiper (Amazon), 265–266, 288
Public Company Accounting Oversight Board (PCAOB) standards, 433
Public key cryptography, reinvention, 229–231
Public-private partnerships (PPPs), 15, 32, 259, 278, 289, 372, 382, 391, 400–401, 410
    establishment, 446
Purdue Polytechnic Institute, programs, 385–388

Q

Qingyun L540 notebook, 5-nm chip (usage), 127
QR codes, usage, 212, 438–439
Quadrilateral Security Dialogue (QUAD), 55, 413, 450–451
Quantum advantage, 220
Quantum, areas, 220
Quantum computing (QC), 220–222, 222f, 223f, 226, 231–232
Quantum countermeasures, usage, 229
Quantum Daily (media platform), 231
Quantum Economic Development Consortium, 234
Quantum ethics/standards/rules, 234–235
Quantum Key Distribution (QKD), 220, 225, 230–231
Quantum Sensing (quantum-sensing), 220, 221
Quantum speedup, 222
Quantum supremacy/limitations, 223–225
Quantum technologies, 219, 225–226, 232–234
Qubits, usage, 222–224

R

Raimondo, Gina, 58–59, 122
Rare earth materials
    Chinese dominance, 336–337
    re-shoring/ring-fencing, 338–339
    supply chains, decoupling (acceleration), 337
Rationalisation (supply chain), 118–120
Reaper drones, usage, 179
Rebooting India (Nilekani), 417–418

Re-education camps, 158
Regional agreements, 444
Regional Comprehensive Economic
    Partnership (RCEP), 417
Regulatory landscapes, 195–196
Reich, Robert, 12
Reliance Communications, Chinese bank
    loan/bankruptcy, 156
Report of Manufacturers Presented to the
    U.S. House of Representatives
    (Hamilton), 35f
'Report on Manufactures' (Hamilton), 32
'Republic of the Seven United Netherlands',
    money flow, 38
Research and development (R&D)
    bifurcation, 20
    government activism, impor-
        tance, 399–400
    paradigm shift, 402–403
Re-shoring, 12, 55, 93, 119, 297–298, 338–339
Resurgent Party (Italy), Cambridge Analytica
    (impact), 198
'Return-to-greatness narrative,' 6–7
Reusable rockets, 283–286
Ricardo, David, 56
Ringfencing (ring-fencing), 93, 119, 232,
    338–339, 374–375
RISC-V open-source standard, PLA
    usage, 453
Rise and Fall of Great Powers, The
    (Kennedy), 28
Robinson, James, 28
Robots, 301
Rohrabacher, Dana, 172
Rome G10 meetings, 429
Roosevelt, Franklin D., 46
Roscosmos, 270, 276, 289
Russia, India (relationship), 414
Russian Central Bank, databases, 270
Russia, problems, 80–82
    China backing, 126
    restricted semiconductors, illicit
        collection, 98–99
    social media influence, 198–200
Russia-Ukraine war, 267–269, 302–304,
    357–358

S
Sally, Razeen, 9–10
Samsung
    capital expenditures, 110–111
    fabrication factory, groundbreaking, 137
Satellite technology, trends, 260–261
Schmidt, Eric, 189, 398
Schools, techno-nationalism, 371

Schumpeter, Joseph, 20
Science-technology data hegemony, 193–194
Science, technology, engineering, and math
    (STEM), 45, 48, 233–234, 386, 389
    talent pool, fostering, 391
Scramjet Hypersonic Engine, 244f
Seagate Technology Holdings PLC, US
    fines, 100
Search engine optimisation (SEO) technique,
    usage, 199
Second Industrial Revolution, technology
    sharing, 86
Second island chain (archipelagos), 241
Sector-specific agreements, 445
Semiconductor Industry Association (SIA)
    study, 133
Semiconductor Manufacturing International
    Corporation (SMIC), 25, 93,
    96–97, 126
Semiconductor Manufacturing Technology
    (SEMATECH), chip production,
    144, 410–411
Semiconductors, 103, 105–106,
    286–288, 424–426
    equipment companies, impact, 108
    foundational technology, 112
    global value chains, 107–111
    industrial policy, 119
    packaging, 117–118
    problems (China), 121
    production, national pride, 127
    R&D, allocations, 142
    technology, export controls (BIS
        expansion), 79
'Semiconductors at the Heart of the
    U.S.-China Tech War' (Capri), 10
Semiconductors in America Coalition (SIAC),
    formation, 135
SEMI non-governmental
    organisation, 123–124
Senegal Digital Infrastructure Backbone
    (SDIB), 325
Sensational interests, evaluation, 197
SenseTime, 438
    data storage engineering, 203
    Washington blacklist, 25, 97
Sesame Credit, 431–432
Shanghai Micro Electronics Equipment
    (SMEE), 127–129
Shanghai Stock Exchange, 164
Shanghai Zhangjiang Group, state
    ownership, 127
Shenlong 'Divine Dragon' (China), 293
Shenzhen Major Industry Investment Fund,
    funding source, 131

Showa Denko, high purity gas
    production, 137
SiCarrier, founding, 162
Silicon carbide (SiC), usage, 106, 353–354
Silicon Crossroads, growth, 139–140
Singapore-Australia Digital Economy
    Agreement (SADEA), 452
Single-digit nanometre chips,
    multi-patterning techniques, 114
Single nucleotide polymorphisms (SNPs),
    mapping, 186–187
Sino-American great power competition,
    62
Sino-Japanese Wars, ravages, 6
SK Group, high purity gas production, 137
SK hynix, AI memory chip fab (building),
    140
Skunkworks, 176–178
Skywater Technologies, legacy pure
    play fab, 139
Slater, Samuel, 33, 34, 36f
Small Business Innovation Research (SBIR)/
    Small Business Technology Transfer
    (STTR) programmes, 291
Smallsat technology/manufacturing,
    revolution, 262–263
Small-yard-high-fence strategy, 55
Smartphones, geopolitical influence, 422
Smith, Adam, 56
Snowden, Edward, 193
Social media, impact, 198–201
Society for Establishing Useful
    Manufacturers, The, 32
Society for Worldwide Interbank Financial
    Telecommunication (SWIFT),
    80, 429–430
Soft power, 196
Sogou (Tencent Holdings acquisition), 214
Solemani, Qasem (killing), 179
'Sources of American Policy, The (Sullivan),
    53
South China Sea (SCS), China reclamation
    activities/control, 61, 241–242,
    326–328
Southeast Asia-Middle East-Western Europe
    6 (SEA-ME-WE-6), 251, 254–255
Sovereign Wealth Funds (SWF), geopolitics
    (relationship), 439–440
Space
    blocs, 298–299
    capitalism, 287
    commercialisation, 277–278
    geopolitics, 260–261
    militarisation, 292–294
    monopolies, increase, 272

multilateral rules framework, 272–273
    race, impact, 44–45, 275, 286–288
    research, bifurcation, 294–295
    robots, 281
Space-based Internet, 259, 264–265
Space-based laser technology, information,
    Chinese hacker theft, 173
Space Development Agency (SDA),
    264–265
SpacePharma, bioreactor development/
    operation, 280
SpaceX, 202, 259–264, 266, 271–272
    Falcon 9, 263–264, 275–278, 282f, 285f, 289
    Falcon Heavy, 263, 281, 293
    impact/problems, 282–286
    Psyche 16 Asteroid Mining Mission,
        280–281, 283
    rocket stages, 284f
Special Economic Zone (SEZ), 421, 422
Specially Designated Nationals (SDN) List,
    application (OFAC control), 89
Spektr-UV Space Telescope (Russia),
    299
Spinning frame (Arkwright), 35f
Spy agencies, investigations/surveillance
    satellite usage, 152–154, 167–168
Spyware, usage, 151, 210
Starlink Internet, 260–261, 267–269,
    285f, 301, 401
State-funded innovation, 12
State, power, 14–17
States, firms (competition), 79
Stealth, 165, 171–172, 178–179
Stiglitz, Joseph, 58
ST Microelectronics NV, advanced chips
    (Russia illicit collection), 99
Strategic decoupling, 12, 77
Strategic ecosystems, export controls/
    ring-fencing, 233–234
Strategic partnerships, 12
Strategic public-private-partnerships,
    innovation (occurrence), 110
Strategic technologies, 13f
Stratified global value chains, 77–78
Student nationalities, impact, 376–377
Stuxnet, introduction, 211
SubCom, selection, 253–255
Sullivan, Jake, 53–55, 58
Sun Tzu, 28, 61, 166–167
Supermicro, 150–151
Supply chains
    COVID-19 disruption, 75
    de-Americanisation, 125
    diversification, 76
    rationalisation, 118–120
    weaponisation, 12, 55, 93

Surveillance
  capitalism, 185–186
  technology , Export-Import Bank
      purchase, 156–157
Swtichblade drones, usage, 306–307
System in Package (SiP), electronic
      components integration, 117
System on a chip (SoC), energy
      efficiency, 351

T

Tai, Katherine, 122
Tailored Access Operations, 168–169
Taiwan
  China aggression, 126
  Chip 4 Alliance, 55, 138
  global talent development strategy, 393–394
  industrial policy, 407–408
  Japan (colonial rule), 41
  offshoring fabrication, 58
  PLA invasion, possibility, 63, 269
Taiwan Semiconductor Manufacturing
      Company (TSMC)
  capital expenditures, 110–111
  chips, 92, 94, 110, 134, 296, 349
  Japan collaboration, 143
  mega-fabs (Arizona), 142
  next-generation 2-nanometre chips,
      construction, 137
  private money, 16
  pure play contract manufacturer, 107–108
  semiconductor industrial policy, 119
Taiwan Straits, tensions, 64, 251
Talent
  shortage, 394–395
  wars, 12
TASA, 269
TCL Technology/Panasonic, manufacturing
      joint venture, 69
Technical data, USML control, 89
Techno-authoritarianism, 185–186
Techno-diplomacy, 376, 441
  quantum technology, relationship, 234
  undersea cables, relationship, 253–254
Technology
  alliances, 12
  competitors, 252–253
  feedback loop, 31, 34–40, 105, 166,
      187–188, 209
  tech-diplomacy, 12
  techno-diplomacy, 93
Technology and War (Van Creveld), 28
Techno-nationalism, 9–12, 29, 41–42, 225–226
  international alliances, requirements, 135
  pharmacogenomics, relationship, 188–189

  quantum technologies, relationship, 232–233
Techno-nationalist agenda, 60
Techno-nationalist competition, 14, 55
Techno-nationalist feedback loop, 37f
  F-35, relationship, 175
Techno-nationalists
  chief executive officers (CEOs),
      contrast, 56–59
  choke points, 104
  neoliberals, contrast, 288–290
  priorities, 126
Telecoms-espionage monopoly, 151–152
Telecoms infrastructure, building, 151–152
Tencent, data/co-optation, 195, 203, 430
Terrain reference navigation (TRN),
      usage, 239
Tesla Inc., China competition (impact), 68
Third Department hackers (China), 173
Third Industrial Revolution (3IR), 45, 47–49,
      86
Third-party backdoors, 97–99
Third-party data supply services, information
      purchase, 190
Three-dimensional (3D) packaging, 117
Thucydides Trap, 21, 26
ThyssenKrupp, government funding, 43
TikTok (ByteDance)
  ban, attempt, 65
  divestment, 182
  mistrust, 183
  private data, accumulation, 72
Tokyo Electron, AMAT/Lam Research
      competition, 116
Tokyo Ohka Kogyo Co. (TOK) photoresist
      market share, 116
Trade Act (1974), Section 301, 52–53
Tradecraft (trade-craft), 12, 34, 93,
      165, 171–172
Trade liberalisation, benefits, 76
Trade/logistics/transportation, QC
      (usage), 228
Trailing-edge chips, 107, 123–125, 136–140
Trailing-edge IC manufacture, 140
Trailing-edge technologies, sharing/
      selling, 67
Tranche 0, launch, 266
Trans-Pacific Partnership (TPP), 447–448
TrendForce, market analysis, 124
Trojan horses, impact, 210
Trump, Donald, 9–10, 18, 52, 197–198, 380
Truth economy, fostering, 215
Turing, Alan, 45
Turing NLG, usage, 213
Turkish Aerospace Industries Anka-3 Combat
      Drone, 305f
Turkish/Iranian drones, usage, 304–306

U

U-2 spy plane programme (CIA), 176
Ukraine (Orange Revolution), Cambridge
    Analytica (impact), 198
Ukraine War, de-risking/decoupling
    issues, 80–81
UK-Singapore Digital Economy Agreement
    (UKSDA), 452
Undercurrents, 29
Undersea cables, 248–251
    decoupling, 247
    networks, 249f
    sabotage/attacks, 251
Underwater Prototype Development
    Programme (UPD), 382–383
Underwater, unmanned underwater vehicles
    (UUAVs), usage, 242
Unique Identification Authority of India
    (UIDAI), national database, 417–418
United Launch Alliance (ULA), 284
United Microelectronics Corporation (UMC)
    foundry, deposition/etch tools
    development, 116
United States (America)
    Airforce F-35 Stealth fighter, frontal
        view, 174f
    Airforce MQ-9 Reaper Killer Drone,
        309f
    AT&T/ITT, win-win relationships, 157
    Beijing retaliation, 65
    China hybrid cold war, 148
    chip manufacturing, re-shoring, 133
    chip policies, 410–412
    companies, American Chamber of
        Commerce survey, 23
    embassies, truck bombings, 167–168
    investment banks, bailout, 58
    Military Bell Invictus helicopter, 171f
    Navy, weapons systems, 62
    Outbound Investment Transparency
        Act, 25
    questions, 27–29
    technology transfer, DOC restriction, 25
    unipolar moment, 7, 397–398
    War on Terror, distractions, 166–168
United States Munitions List (USML),
    controls, 89
University Partnership for Workforce
    Advancement and Research &
    Development in Semiconductors
    (UPWARDS), 392
Unmanned aerial vehicles (UAVs), 168, 176,
    208, 242, 306
Unmanned surface vehicles (USVs),
    usage, 301–302

Unmanned underwater vehicles (UUVs),
    usage, 302, 310–311, 383
U.S.-China strategic supply, bifurcation, 136
US Cloud services, preventions, 97
User-generated content, 190–191
U.S. Outbound Investment Transparency
    Act, 434–435
USS *Gerald R. Ford,* abilities, 241
U.S. Telecoms, Senate investiga-
    tions, 152–154

V

Values-driven infrastructure projects, 321–322
Van Creveld, Martin, 28
Vereenigde Oost-Indische Compagnie
    (VOC), 37–38, 40
Vertical farming, 363–364
Volkswagen AG China, SAIC Motor
    ownership, 68
von der Leyen, Ursula, 55

W

Wang Huiwen, 213
Wang Xiaochuan, 213–214
War Made New (Boot), 28
Warring States period, 60–61
Washington Consensus, impact, 51
Washingtonparadigm shift, 134, 442
Wassenaar 2.0, 101
Wassenaar Arrangement on Export Controls
    for Conventional Arms and Dual-Use
    Goods and Technologies,
    establishment, 101
Water scarcity/technology, 366
    geopolitics, 366–367
Web browsers, usage, 191
WeChat, ban (discussions), 72
Weijiang Zhang, charge/sentencing, 365
Western laissez-faire capitalism, incon-
    gruities, 5
'West *versus* the Rest,' term (usage), 18
'Where to Invest When China Pulls Back from
    COVID-Zero' (Morgan Stanley), 24
Whittaker, Red, 281
Why Nations Fail (Acemoglu/Robinson), 28
Wicked paradox, 59–62
Wind-powered sawmill (Corneliszoon), 39f
Workarounds/loopholes/backdoors, 94–95
World Trade Center (WTC), Al Qaeda bomb
    attempt, 167, 169, 429
World Trade Organization (WTO), 442, 444
    China accession, 4, 18
    derailment, 58
Worms, impact, 210–211
Wuxi Factory No. 742 (Huajing Group),
    establishment, 129–130

X

X-10 Graphite Reactor, invention, 46
X37-B Autonomous Robotic Orbital Space
    Plane, 292–293, 292f
Xi Jinping, 24, 49, 66, 317, 326, 337, 402
    Made in China 2025, importance, 82
XKeyscore (NSA), 193
Xuntian Space Telescope (China), 299

Y

Y-12, invention, 12
Yangtze Memory Technologies Company
    Ltd. (YMTC)
    Tsinghua Unigroup, impact, 124
    Washington blacklist, 25
Yanqing Ye, arrest, 378–379

Yellen, Janet, 58–59
Yew, Lee Kuan, 9–10
York Space Systems, 266

Z

Zarya Control Module/Zvezda Service
    Module, 298
Zeetop Technologies, optical component
    construction, 162
Zhong Xing Telecommunications Equipment
    Company (ZTE), Washington
    blacklist, 25
Zhou Bowen, 213
Zongchang Yu, 163
ZTE, 149, 156–158, 254–255, 422
Zuboff, Shoshana, 190
Zyklon B, production, 43